KEEPING BETTER COMPANY

Keeping Better Company
Corporate Governance Ten Years On

JONATHAN P. CHARKHAM

WITH HÉLÈNE PLOIX

OXFORD

UNIVERSITY PRESS

OXFORD

UNIVERSITY PRESS

Great Clarendon Street, Oxford OX2 6DP

Oxford University Press is a department of the University of Oxford.
It furthers the University's objective of excellence in research, scholarship,
and education by publishing worldwide in

Oxford New York

Auckland Cape Town Dar es Salaam Hong Kong Karachi
Kuala Lumpur Madrid Melbourne Mexico City Nairobi
New Delhi Shanghai Taipei Toronto

With offices in

Argentina Austria Brazil Chile Czech Republic France Greece
Guatemala Hungary Italy Japan Poland Portugal Singapore
South Korea Switzerland Thailand Turkey Ukraine Vietnam

Oxford is a registered trade mark of Oxford University Press
in the UK and in certain other countries

Published in the United States
by Oxford University Press Inc., New York

© Jonathan Charkham 2005

British Library Cataloguing in Publication Data

Data available

Library of Congress Cataloging in Publication Data

Data available

Typeset by SPI Publisher Services, Pondicherry, India
Printed in Great Britain on acid-free paper by
Antony Rowe Ltd., Chippenham, Wiltshire

ISBN 0-19-924318-2 978-019-924318-1
3 5 7 9 10 8 6 4 2

To Lydia

FOREWORD

It is a privilege and a pleasure to be invited to write a preface to *Keeping Better Company*. There is now a wealth of literature on corporate governance, but Jonathan Charkham's book undoubtedly fills an important gap. It fills it through the breadth and depth of its analysis of the governance framework within which companies, primarily publicly quoted ones, carry on their activities in Germany, Japan, France, the United States, and Britain. It builds on the author's previous book *Keeping Good Company*, which was the first comparative study of its kind to be published. The book makes sense of current governance practices in the five countries and highlights both how they are currently changing and where those changes may be leading.

Where the book stands alone is in the author's ability to take us beyond a textbook description of governance structures and systems, which are all too often not quite what they may seem, and to shed light on the way in which they work in practice. This understanding of the practical realities of governance derives from Jonathan Charkham's wealth of experience in the governance field. He has advised the Bank of England, helped to draw up codes of best practice for boards in Britain and internationally, and established himself as an authoritative writer and lecturer on the subject of corporate governance. His singular advantage as an author lies in his practical experience as a director of both family and public companies, and of what it actually means to be a board member in this country and abroad. It is his knowledge of governance in theory and in action which illuminates his analysis of the governance scene around the world.

The book begins with a succinct introduction to the subject of corporate governance and explains why and how it has levitated in a remarkably short space of time from the arcane vocabulary of accountancy and law to heading the agenda of world summit meetings. It ends, appropriately, with unfinished business, with those governance issues which remain to be resolved and should, therefore, be on the agenda of all those concerned with their outcome.

The country chapters follow a common format which facilitates comparisons between them. They start with the legal position of companies in each jurisdiction. This is a key aspect of governance, because of the importance of the form of the legal framework itself and because of the influence it has on the pattern of non-statutory regulation. The nature of governance structures, of shareholdings, and of markets follow naturally on, country by country. It is in these areas that the experience of a practitioner is invaluable. To understand, for example, the system of governance in a country, the starting point is the manner in which their boards are formally structured. Beyond the formal structure, however, there is always an informal one which provides the dynamic within the system, and is the means by which form is turned into substance. To understand even the workings of the informal structure, it is necessary to appreciate the role of the key players within it. As the author says, corporate governance is about enterprise, transparency, and accountability. It is, therefore, about power, and to understand how companies are in reality governed in different countries we need to know who holds the levers of power within the corporate structure and how accountable they are for its use.

The book analyses how much the governance frameworks in the countries it covers have in common and where they differ. This points to the degree to which there is likely to be convergence between them and the form which it might take. The drivers for convergence are the international institutional investors, in whose hands publicly traded shares are becoming increasingly concentrated, and world capital markets. Both investors and lenders are looking for common standards of board effectiveness and of disclosure from those they fund. The worldwide interest in corporate governance follows on from the growth of cross-border investment. Capital will flow to countries and companies which inspire trust. Trust is in turn based on comparative standards of corporate governance. As the author explains, there is no direct way of proving that good governance leads to good corporate performance. The fact, however, that the majority of investors take account of corporate governance in making their investment decisions confirms that the market regards good governance as the best available proxy for good performance.

In that context, the author introduces a useful yardstick for comparing governance systems and structures—how good are they at dealing with ineffective management? The book's analysis helps in making that kind of judgement, because it clarifies the differences in practice and in operation between similar-sounding governance structures. American boards, for example, differ from British boards in their composition, in the way their members are selected and in their ability to insulate themselves from shareholder pressure. Apparently similar appellations can conceal significant operational differences. The whole debate over the ability of shareholders to influence boards has been driven by the growing power of the investing institutions and their increasing activism. Active engagement by investors with companies raises its own questions. What are the issues over which investors can most constructively engage and how accountable are they in doing so to those whose money they are investing?

Shareholder activism comes under the heading of unfinished business, as do the rule of law, accounting and auditing, transparency, the oppression of minorities, the governance of banks and corporate social responsibility. These are complex and interrelated issues on all of which Jonathan Charkham provides wise and timely guidance. They are evidence that the governance debate is set to continue and anyone with an interest in the present state of corporate governance worldwide and in its likely future development will benefit from reading *Keeping Better Company*. It has the significant plus of being admirably written. The essential facts and the informed analyses are all there, but leavened by the author's turn of phrase. He sums up, for example, the central issue of succession planning for family firms, as follows:

Being succeeded by one's offspring gratifies an understandable human desire to defy mortality, but appears only too often to hasten the mortality of the business.

Keeping Better Company is today's corporate governance vade mecum.

Adrian Cadbury

ACKNOWLEDGEMENTS

The five studies on which the first edition, *Keeping Good Company*, were based were made between 1986 and 1990 and were updated in the second half of 1992. During the intervening period I have maintained a continuous interest in corporate governance and have supplemented studies by serving on several boards of companies of various sizes invariably serving on the audit committee—often as chairman. I have also participated in conferences around the world and produced a booklet of guidance for bank directors for the World Bank.

The first edition is now out of date in many particulars, although I believe its general thrust has proved sound. So during 2003 and 2004 I revisited the countries previously covered to bring the text up to date and chart the various changes, many of which are significant and not necessarily obvious. These visits involved many discussions and I list below some of the organizations and people that provided help, data, and guidance. I owe a particular debt to the accounting profession, some of whose leading firms arrange seminars on an extremely wide range of relevant topics which afford an opportunity to consider subjects in the round with practitioners.

The new edition differs in one important way: one chapter, France, was not drafted by me but by Mme Hélène Ploix, whose career has afforded her the opportunity of becoming an expert on an international scale. She sits on the boards of major companies in both France and the UK and has headed up a major French savings institution. I am deeply indebted to her for undertaking this work and for her guidance on many other aspects of the book. She in turn wishes to acknowledge with grateful thanks the advice and help she received from Madame Charvenat.

I would also like to thank Sheeja Sivaprasad of Cass Business School, who helped me with my researches.

General

I would like to acknowledge gratefully the general guidance given at various times and on various subjects by:

Mr N. Oya, Chief Executive Officer and Managing Director, Mizuho International London, without whose support and encouragement the work could never have been completed.
Sir Adrian Cadbury
Mrs Anne Simpson (World Bank and ICGN)
Mr David Musson, Oxford University Press
Sir David Walker, Morgan Stanley
Arthur Levi, SFI

Germany

My especial thanks go to Ms Jella Susanne Benner-Heinacher, Geschäftsführerin of DSW Düsseldorf, the largest shareholders organization, whose biennial conferences bring together a wide range of German industrialists, professionals, and officials domestic and international. Many of the tables are a product of their research.

The German Embassy in London: Martin Wieland (Bundesbank Representative)
Cromme Standing Commission: Dr Gerhard Cromme
University of Frankfurt: Dr Theodore Baums
Technische Universität Berlin: Prof. Axel Von Werder
Universität fur International Recht München: Prof. Dr Claus Hopt
Proshare (UK)
Daimler-Chrysler AG: Dr Michael Mühlbayer
Johannes Gutenberg Universität: Prof. Dr Uwe H. Schneider
C.E. Computer Equipment, Bielefield, Milan Stahl
ComputerLinks AG, Munich: Stephen Link, Vorstandsvorsitzender
ICGN: André Baladi

Japan

Especial thanks go to my colleagues in Mizuho who helped arrange my programme and also provided current data and examined my drafts: Mr Takaya Seki and Ms Ryoko Ueda, of J-Iris Research; and to Mr Ariyoshi Okumura of ICGN & Lotus Corporate Advisory, whose wise counsel I have long valued. I am very grateful too for the help I received from the British Embassy:

HM Ambassador to Japan Sir Stephen Gomersall
HM Ambassador to Japan (after July 2004) Mr Graham Fry
Mr Peter Green, Financial Counsellor

It would be difficult to list all the people who were ready to discuss the various elements of Japanese governance; they include:

Mizuho Securities: Mr Yoshio Osawa, President
Mizuho Holdings: Mr Terunobu Maeda, President
Mizuho Corporate Bank: Mr Hiroshi Saito, President
Canon: Mr Toshizo Tanaka, Senior Manager Director
Sony corporation: Mr Teruo Masaki, Corporate Senior Executive
ORIX: Mr Yoshihiko Miyauchi, Chairman
Nissan Motors: M. Thierry Moulonguet, Executive Vice-President
Omron: Mr Nobuo Tateishi, Chairman
Fuji Xerox: Mr Yotaro Kobayashi, Chairman,
Mercian: Mr Tadao Suzuki, President,
Kikkoman: Mr Kenzaburo Mogi, Deputy President
Teijin: Mr Shosaku Yasui, Chairman
Merrill Lynch Japan Securities: Mr Yoshiyuki Fujisawa, Chairman
Hitachi: Mr Kazuo Kumagai, Executive Vice-President
IBM Japan: Mr Katutaro Kitashiro, President
Pension Fund Association: Mr Tomomi Yano, Senior Managing Director
DIAM: Mr Hiroki Yamada, Vice-President
Government Pension Investment Fund: Mr Haruo Maruyama, Director
The Dai-Ichi Mutual Life Insurance: Mr Koichi Iki, Managing Director
Tokyo Stock Exchange: Mr Masaaki Tsuchida, President and Mr Eisuke
    Nagatomo, Executive Officer
Bank of Japan: Mr Masaaki Shirakawa, Executive Director
Japan Investor Relations Association: Mr Yoichi Yazawa, Executive Director
Tokyo University: Prof. Tak Wakasugi
Asahi Shimbun: Mr Horoshi Ogino, Editorial writer
Hitotsubashi University: Professor Christina Ahmadjin
Shojihomu: Mr Takuo Takeuchi, Editor
JCAA: Mr Hiroyuki Takahashi, Executive Managing Director
Tokyo University: Prof. Hideki Kanda
Pension Fund Association for Local Government Officials: Mr Katsuya
    Kamiseki, Secretary-General
Central Glass: Mr Sadayoshi Nakamura, President

USA

My especial thanks go to Weil Gotshall & Manges, LLP: Ira Millstein, Holly Gregory, and Gabriel Matus, who provided me with much of the background data and material as well as sound advice. And also to John Corrigan,

Attorney of Adler Pollock and Sheehan LLP, who read my draft and made many sound and helpful suggestions—in which he was assisted by John S. D'Alimonte and Rose Di Martino of Wilkie Farr & Gallagher. Martin Lipton of Lipton Washtell has informed and guided me over the years—especially in the whole area of takeovers. I also had the benefit of considerable help from:

Conference Board, New York: Ronald Berenbeim
Securities & Exchange Commission: Harvey Goldshmid
World Bank: Teresa Barger, Alyssa Machold
PCAOB: Kayla Gillan
Council of Institutional Investors: Ann Yerger
The Corporate Library: Bob Monks, Nell Minow
Institute for International Finance: John Price
National Association of Corporate Directors: Peter Gleason
TIAA CRFF: Peter Clapman

UK

Lawrence Graham, Victoria Younghusband
Institute of Directors: Patricia Peter and Anna Burmajster
Bank of England: Alistair Clark, Mike Young, Sue Milton, Mario Bleiber
Investment Management Association
London Stock Exchange
Mrs Anne Simpson: World Bank & ICGN
Pension Investment Research Consultants: Alan MacDougall and Janice Hayward
UKSA: David Blundell and Toby Keynes
Korn/Ferry International
Institutional Shareholders Committee
KPMG
PriceWaterhouseCoopers
Financial Services Authority
Hermes: Tim Bush and Alastair Ross Goobey; David Pitt-Watson
Association of British Insurers: Peter Montagnon
Herriot-Watt University: Prof. Claire Marston
Board Performance Ltd.: Prof. Bob Garratt
CIMA: Charles Tilley
Cass Business School, City University: Professor Selim, Henrietta Royle
Proshare: Dr Agbenyega,

Friends Ivory and Sime
Aurum Fund: Alison Fleming
MMO2
James Cook, Edinburgh
The Work Foundation: Will Hutton,
The Smith Institute: Wilf Stevenson

CONTENTS

FIGURES

TABLES

ABBREVIATIONS

ABI	Association of British Insurers
ACI	Audit Committee Institute
ADAM	Association pour le Défence des Actionnaires Minoritaires
ADR	American Depositary Receipts
AFEP	Association des Entreprises Privées
AG	Aktiengesellschaft
AGM	annual general meeting
AIM	Alternative Investment Market
AMF	Autorité des Marchés Financiers
ASB	Accounting Standards Board
BDA	Bundesvereinigung der Deutschen Arbeitsgeberverbände
BDI	Federation of German Industries
BJSPP	Bank of Japan share purchase programme
BNP	Banque National de Paris
BRT	business round table
BSPP	Banks Shareholding Purchase Programme
CAC	Compagnie des Agents de Change
CB	Conference Board
CBI	Confederation of British Industries
CC	Commercial Code
CCCG	Combined Code of Corporate Governance
CEO	Chief Executive Officer
CFO	Chief Finance Director
CMF	Conseil des Marchés Financiers
CNPF	Conseil National du Patronat Français
COB	Commission des Opérations de Bourse
COO	Chief Operating Officer
COSO	Committee of Sponsoring Organizations
CSR	corporate social responsibility
D&O	directors and officers
DAX	Deutscher Aktienindex
DM	Deutsche Mark
DRRR	Directors' Remuneration Report Regulations
DSVR	deposited share voting rights
DSW	Deutsche Schutzvereinigung für Wertpapierbesitz

DTI	Department of Trade and Industry
EGM	extraordinary general meeting
ERISA	Employment Retirement Income Security Act
FSA	Financial Services Authority
FTSE	Financial Times Stock Exchange
GAAP	generally accepted accounting practices
GCGC	German Corporate Governance Code
GEM	Global Entrepreneurship Monitor
GmbH	Gesellschaft mit beschränkter Haftung
IAS	International Accounting Standards
ICGN	International Corporate Governance Network
IFRS	International Financial Reporting Standards
IPO	initial public offering
IRCJ	Industrial Revitalization Corporation of Japan
ISC	Institutional Shareholders' Committee
ISS	Institutional Shareholders Services
JCAA	Japan Corporate Auditors' Association
KGaA	Kommanditgesellschaft auf Aktien
KPI	key performance indicators
LBO	leveraged buy-out
LSF	Loi de Sécurité Financière
LTIP	long-term incentive programme
M&A	mergers and acquisitions
MBO	management buy-out
MD&A	management description and analysis
MEDEF	Mouvement des Entreprises de France
METI	Ministry of Economy, Trade, and Industry
MITI	Ministry of International Trade and Industry
NACD	National Association of Corporate Directors
NASDAQ	National Association of Securities Dealers Automated Quotations
NED	non-executive director
NRE	Nouvelles Regulations Économiques
NYSE	New York Stock Exchange
OECD	Organization for Economic Cooperation and Development
OFR	operating and financial review
P&L	profit and loss (accounts)
PCAOB	Public Company Accounting Oversight Board
PDG	Président Directeur Général.
PFA	Pension Fund Association
PIRC	Pensions Investment Research Consultants

PLC	public limited company
PSAG	private sector advising group
PTP	public to private
S&P	Standard & Poor's
SA	Société Anonyme
SAR	stock appreciation rights
SARL	Société à Responsabilité Limitée
SAS	Société par Actions Simplifiée
SEC	Securities and Exchange Commission
SID	senior independent director
SME	small and medium enterprises
SOX	Sarbanes–Oxley Act
SRI	socially responsible investment
TOP	Takeover Panel
TSE	Tokyo Stock Exchange
WWF	World Wildlife Fund

1

The Essence of Governance

Introduction

This book is about the way companies are directed and controlled, and relate to their sources of finance—what has come to be called *corporate governance*. The term 'company' is better than 'corporation' as it reflects the human dimension; companies are collections of people, not just inanimate structures.

There are separate chapters describing corporate governance in five leading economies—Germany, Japan, France, the USA, and the UK. Each chapter is descriptive, not normative. The aim is to make sense of current practice and to shed light on the main changes and probable developments bearing in mind what has already taken place since *Keeping Good Company* was written in 1991. Had this book been written in 2025 not 2003–4, it would have contained chapters on the three economies which by then may have surpassed in size all except the USA—China, India, and Russia. The main focus is on *quoted* companies, but the principles of good governance apply to companies of almost any size, though their application may vary according to circumstances; unquoted companies will be considered because of their significance and the special problems they pose.

Now as in 1991 we need to stress the importance of individual companies to every country's economy since prosperity so largely hinges on the way they are run. They provide employment and are therefore an important element in social cohesion. They produce taxes and therefore the sinews of civilization—law and order, defence, and welfare of many kinds. Above all they produce the goods and services people want or need. There are those who still see them simply as engines for maximizing returns on capital and consider that is their sole purpose. The extreme view was discredited in the nineteenth century when the UK Parliament passed legislation to stop children working in coal mines, although the owners protested they would be ruined. In some jurisdictions companies are seen primarily as social instruments with shareholders as helpless also-rans. This clash of cultures, which is very important and is considered further, can be reconciled if we are ready to accept that 'The purpose of the company is to provide *ethically and profitably* the goods and services people need or want'.

The origins of the limited liability company in the UK

Companies are not the only way of organizing business activity. Partnerships of various kinds have their place—as well as their limitations. This book willingly acknowledges their use but does not cover them. Its scope is confined to what is sometimes called a 'joint stock company'—which has a pleasant historical ring to it, but I prefer the term 'limited liability company'—as it better reflects probably the most important feature of the modern company world. Many countries developed upon similar lines (and this is covered in subsequent chapters). I use the UK as an example and because it was early in the field.

In the UK this world starts in the mid-nineteenth century. There are companies in many parts of the world including Great Britain older than that, but the Act of 1855 provides the first successful introduction of a law which makes incorporation easy and limits the liability of those who risk their savings in an enterprise to the money they have invested. Eleven years earlier in 1844, the UK Parliament had passed a law which made incorporation easy but left shareholders with the residual liability if the business failed. It did not work—investors were not prepared to risk their entire fortunes for a few shares.

The UK law of 1855 provided four things:

- a means of collecting savings from a wide range of subscribers, which now became possible thanks to limited liability;
- the possibility of corporate immortality (unlike partnerships);
- a means of providing leadership to the enterprise;
- a process for holding the leadership accountable for its stewardship of the company's business.

It is no accident that the 1855 Act was enacted in the UK. The rapid expansion in the number of large-scale enterprises in the Industrial Revolution meant that it was far too costly and cumbersome to go to Parliament for a special law to incorporate an individual enterprise. Smaller family businesses also found the company framework more convenient for managing their affairs than partnerships had been.

The Act implicitly recognized that in a free market economy competition imposes a sort of de facto discipline and this drives and constrains managers. The 1855 Act hugely facilitated it. Competition acts as a spur to competence;

for a market-based system it is a necessary precondition. Governments go to great lengths by various anti-monopoly laws to encourage competition. They face a dilemma since the logical end to competition is monopoly, even if the subsequent abuse of economic power encourages new entrants *eventually*. Competition is necessary for market economies, but insufficient for their optimal functioning. Even the most cursory look at the history of great companies illustrates the need for good governance as one instrument of competitive advantage. The *Stock Exchange Year Book* for 1962 for instance now reads like a corporate Valhalla—it is so full of corporate corpses. There is therefore no substitute for accountability precisely because one of the main things for which managers are held accountable is their success in coping with the competition. The role of the state in the developing and conducting of industrial enterprises has varied from country to country as we shall see, but the accountability of management remains a constant and that implies transparency.

The structure of the companies prescribed in the Act fitted the type of major enterprises which were the backbone of the Industrial Revolution—capital intensive. Much of the world economy is still in the hands of such businesses—oil, gas, power, aviation, and pharmaceuticals to mention only a few. In most companies, however good the management, there are always successors to hand. Although there are exceptions many of the new companies of the world of information technology and the like are not capital intensive; their success depends on a relative handful of individuals. So if they leave they may be irreplaceable. Many of these companies exist to start with 'on the smell of an oil rag' and those who participate are often rewarded mainly by options. In many ways they are akin to partnerships. Governance always matters but it will look and feel different in fledgling companies. When they have grown to a certain size, and capital has been increased (and is widely distributed) normal practices apply. It is no coincidence that Bill Gates's Microsoft has now stopped issuing share options.

The law

Companies are not creatures of nature. They come about because the law provides a facility which cannot be conveniently organized within the framework of other existing laws—the law of contract for example. They only exist if special laws are introduced and this means that it is logical to start any description of any country's system with a brief account of the relevant law. As we look at each of the five in turn, we will discover many similarities in the formal legal frameworks but also many differences in practice which reflect national attitudes. Sometimes, as in the case of Germany, there is apparently a major distinction—their two-tier board contrasted with the UK's and USA's 'unitary' board. We will look at this in detail later; things are not always what they seem.

The rule of law

The five countries studied have one thing in common—a long experience of the rule of law, whether based on Roman Dutch Law, the Code Napoléon, or the English Common Law. The way the law is used varies greatly, as the contrast between Japan and the USA shows. Even so there is a common element of a proper legal framework, sound legal process, and uncorrupt courts. This means that investors can risk their money knowing that they could get redress if it were justified (though not necessarily cheaply, as the law is seldom inexpensive). Furthermore, this does not simply apply to civil actions for damages, but also to crime. Those who defraud or steal can, if caught and convicted, expect to be punished.

All this is so obvious it hardly needed stating before. Now that corporate governance has spread its wings it cannot be stated too loudly. The constructive work of the World Bank in the developing world highlights the problems where the rule of law does not exist or where the system of justice creaks.

All countries know that theft of a company's assets with apparent impunity will undermine confidence. Words are not enough. I assisted in the drafting of a governance code for the Russian oil company SIBNEFT in 1999 which they published. I was heavily criticized by those who asserted that its exemplary terms were not matched by the way the company was actually run. Words are fine, but they should be a reflection of integrity, not a cloak for dishonesty. The Russians understand all this very clearly and have gained much respect and many investors because of the progress they have made in beginning to make the rule of law a reality to serve the population and foreigners alike swiftly and fairly.

There are sadly many developing countries where little of this is true and where corruption is rife. If the courts don't work, systems of governance in individual companies will lack proper means of enforcement. Corporate governance is generally a grandchild of sound governance: in an ineffective or corrupt regime it is bound to be a sickly infant. Multinational companies operating in such countries can set an example (partly because malefactors can be sued or prosecuted in their home country). Any reader with decent feelings will recoil at photographs of undernourished and sick children, and will wish either to contribute personally to the alleviation of their suffering or influence aid bodies to that end. What they will not wish is for the funds provided to end up in the offshore accounts of corrupt officials. With countries or with companies it is no use pouring funds down leaky hose-pipes. Investors who use their own money may run such risks: they are free to waste it any way they choose. But institutions that manage funds for others are in a fiduciary position and are duty bound to make sure they have the possibility of redress if things go wrong because of theft or pillage. The implications for international aid organizations are clear but unpalatable. And in the context of corporate governance, it means recognizing its limitations until the rule of law is established, and integrity is no longer an orphan.

The development of corporate governance

There is a copious quantity of literature on almost every aspect of management, going back into the nineteenth century, but oddly enough, precious little about directors and boards. In the UK this might reflect the legal position. Under the great 1948 Companies Act any company could be run by two directors; boards are not mentioned! The situation was not much changed by the 1985 Act. The UK is now revising its primary legislation and it will doubtless reflect current usage better. But I think it is deeper than that. Corporate governance is about enterprise, transparency, and accountability—which immediately affect the exercise of power and patronage. One interferes with either at one's peril! The USA has never had a Federal equivalent of the Companies Acts; this is left to individual states. When we consider the USA later we shall encounter the formidable Round Table of company chairmen/CEOs—as powerful a group as ever wielded economic influence in a democracy. We therefore find that Federal interest in corporate governance tends to be confined to reactions to particular scandals and notorious frauds such as led to the setting up of the Treadway Commission (USA 1978), the Enron debacle (which resulted in the Sarbanes-Oxley Act USA 2002). Even in the UK it took unexpected collapses to stimulate the appointment of the Cadbury committee in 1992, at which point the modern governance movement started.

The problem with governmental reaction is that it tends to be excessive and ill-considered. Sometimes the political imperative for a rapid response means that laws are drafted without the care a complex subject demands. One must sympathize with politicians' difficulties in striking a sensible balance between competing pressure groups. Only when they can no longer avoid acting do they like to show that they care about the general interest. The Cadbury committee (on which I served) had less pressure and was able to consult widely on the draft report and Code. The report did not cover everything—our terms of reference precluded that—but its publication sparked an acceleration of interest in many countries around the world, and it contained a remarkably clear statement of general principles.

There have been special reasons since for the increase in general interest in corporate governance. The first was the liberalization of capital flows and the increased opportunities for cross-border investment. Eventually investors everywhere woke up to the fact that this meant that governance was recognized as an important medium- and longer-term issue; in the short term anything might go, but sustainability was in this sphere as in many others becoming an important element, because the wastage caused by failures that can be attributed to bad governance is costly. It is economically advantageous, politically stabilizing, and ethically desirable to secure improvements in governance and the rule of law. It is worth a sustained effort, if only because the poorer the country the less it can bear the cost of either being inadequate. The increased possibilities for cross-border investment accentuated the importance of transparency and the trustworthiness of accounts. This in turn highlighted a range of issues in relation to accounting and auditing standards, some of which are gradually being resolved.

The second development was the still incomplete shift to market economies which introduced in its train the whole concept of corporate governance—with its different relationships from those which obtain in a command economy. The technical aspects of such a change can be studied and taught, but harnessing the support of the people is far harder. There are many who spent a lifetime learning how to 'work the system' in the old regimes: how to manipulate targets, obtain supplies, achieve norms. Sometimes they attained outstanding excellence—the first man in space was a Russian. China today is at a sort of halfway house between the two systems. Of course, some people will find it difficult to change and adapt—learning new skills will not come easily. One isn't born understanding costings, for example.

There have been many teething troubles. Some smart operators soon spotted how to take advantage of the opportunities to enrich themselves outrageously, not necessarily by fair means. In 'frontier' economies people tend to test the boundaries of the law—till it catches up with them. With the passage of time collective amnesia descends on the origins of wealth as it has over our memories of the US tycoons and industrial pirates of the last quarter of the nineteenth century. Many atoned by philanthropy in old age; and absolution of a sort is granted because we care more for what their money can do than the way it was acquired.

The third factor was globalization, a term which can mean many things, from the increased propensity of major companies to trade right round the world, to a better understanding of the widespread effects of latter-day economic power. At one time major companies transferred manufacturing plants abroad to capture the benefits of well-trained and low-cost workforces (and they still do), but now services can be based offshore too—UK call centres based in India for example.

International organizations

It is such thinking that lies behind the admirable initiatives inspired and funded by the World Bank and IFC. These and others are covered in the Annex at the end of Chapter 7.

Codes galore: cacophony or convergence?

Meanwhile in the aftermath of Cadbury many countries produced their own reports, sometimes with codes. On closer examination the striking thing about them is not their differences but their similarities, despite all the variations in the law, in traditions, and in general approach. Perhaps this is due to that fact that there is a growing perception that the problems companies face are truly universal in nature and the cures for them are likely to contain similar ingredients. The work of the international organizations has tended to secure a higher degree of convergence as the precepts they adumbrated became more centred on principles than detail and rendered them adaptable to a country's particular circumstances.

When researching *Keeping Good Company* the question I always asked was how good the system was at dealing with the decline in the ability of its executive management to run the business effectively. Assuming this is not a matter for governments, there are only so many possible answers—boards, shareholders, takeovers. Each has its place, and that is why codes tend to be similar, though the emphasis may be different—as indeed may be their status. Here is a list of some of the reports, many of which have codes attached:

France: Viénot I and II, Bouton
Germany: Cromme Commission Code
Japan: Governance Forum Principles
UK: the combined Code
USA: BRT Principles, the NACD Report
Republic of South Africa: King I and II

It would be boring for readers to wade through all these and not very profitable since so much is changing so quickly. A book can only produce a series of 'stills' whereas we are looking at a movie. The list demonstrates how true this is, so a careful study of any country in which a reader happens to be interested will pay dividends.

The Basic Principles

Enterprise

We are now approaching the heart of good governance. It is not, as is sometimes supposed, to turn some directors into 'policemen'. Every company needs an 'engine', that is to say managers and directors who can drive it forward against competition by producing profitably (and ethically) the range of goods or services in which it specializes. This is the most important element of good governance. It may be the vision of one man that starts it all off, or of partners, or of a team. If we seek to judge or value any company, therefore, the first question we should ask is about transparency (without which we have no basis for a judgement). The second is about the entrepreneurial dynamic. To put it in other terms: executive management must be free, and indeed encouraged, to drive the business forward. When we come to consider governance in any country, we must ask ourselves about the limitations in force there—including the propensity of the government to intervene.

That fits neatly with the way the law is structured, and it makes little difference whether there is a separate supervisory tier; dispersed owners have neither the right nor the ability to run the company on a day-to-day basis. They have to appoint people to run it and let them get on with it. Only if the managers—in practice, the CEO—show they are not up to the job does the board take action. It is probably the most important thing it ever does.

Even a rapid *tour d'horizon* will tell us that managerial freedom is circumscribed in every country, but much more in some than others. Indian entrepreneurs for instance may still bemoan the cost and delays of dealing with their ubiquitous bureaucracy (the least helpful part of the British legacy). The USA has an increasing and very expensive burden in being the ideological home of the 'blame culture' and a hungry legal profession. I witnessed an exercise at Tulane University some years ago—a case study on the appropriate sequence of events when a factory chimney started to make noxious emissions. In Britain the management would have sent an engineer—in the USA the right course was to send for the lawyer to limit liability. It must be said, however, that despite the worst the lawyers can do in that paradise for litigators, the USA remains one of the most productive and innovative economies in the world.

Before the UK becomes complacent however, it should consider the expanding reach of the Financial Services Authority, whose activities increasingly penetrate into what had once been managerial preserves. This may be justifiable, but that it curtails managerial freedom is beyond doubt and this affects the entire financial sector.

Caveat emptor—let the buyer beware—was an admirable rule when buyers of normal wit could judge what was going on if they paid attention. This has long ceased to be so, and the UK's Sale of Goods Act 1893, a great consolidating statute, imported implied conditions to help them. Many other countries have long had similar measures, and very necessary they are in our increasingly technical and scientific world. That is not the point. The fact remains that all such conditions and restrictions may impose limitations on entrepreneurial freedom. In the modern world managers are bound to face constraints; not having unnecessary ones confers competitive advantage.

Accountability

Accountability requires flows of sound information—the Cadbury committee's terms of reference were more concerned with this than decision making. All the shareholders in companies of any size, quoted or not, have a right to know; there can be no excuse for withholding information from them about the company's progress, position, profits, prospects, and people, especially the directors. We do not need to prove that *transparency* is right: it is self-evident. Viewed another way, it may be the premium the company should pay for keeping shareholders' noses out of its market operations; and the board's first job is to see it is paid whatever the effects on the share price and their own remuneration. In many cases involving false or misleading information via specious accounts, the drivers of the malpractices were the desire to sustain the share price till options or incentive plans matured.

It follows that the shareholders need to have confidence that the information is correct. True, they have the auditors' fiat, but experience shows that there are many areas of judgement and that there are strong temptations to paint rosy pictures (or gloomy ones if it suits the directors). However good the auditors are, their task is far more difficult if the executives are wilfully misleading them. For this reason it is desirable—as the Cadbury report pointed out—that there be effective checks and balances in the processing of information so that it is clear and reliable. Transparency between managers and directors is vital; cases like Enron and Equitable illustrate what happens when it fails. There are problems with maintaining the auditors' independence (see Chapter 7).

There are those who oppose the corporate governance movement, arguing that it is bound to deflect managers and directors from their main priority—enterprise, that is to say straining every muscle to drive the business forward. Such arguments must be taken with a grain of salt, for in truth no one *likes* to be accountable. Some indeed fear it precisely because they have much they wish to hide. Nevertheless, whilst the evidence seems to suggest it really matters, it is equally clear that in business it is not all that matters. There is, however, no respectable argument against the absolute requirement to produce reliable information.

From the beginning, it was understood that the shareholders were entitled to be told 'the bottom line'—i.e. the financial result for the period concerned. Some boards said as little as possible beyond this, on the principle that if the numbers were good they spoke for themselves, and that if they were not the less said the better. In private companies this doctrine often still prevails. In public companies, however, management has gone far beyond the basic imperative to report in readily comprehensible language material facts and developments. Indeed, some companies now produce a report the size of a New York telephone directory (but far less interesting) to choke the cat with cream. Nor does the volume of paper stop their hiding important financial data in an obscure footnote without a mention in the narrative.

For understandable reasons much of the emphasis in the governance movement has been on accountability but it is only too easy for the balance to tilt in that direction—which could well prove more harmful than an over-revving engine.

The historical background

Before we turn to modern accountability, it is instructive to consider how this aspect was viewed by the original legislators in the nineteenth century, as this sheds light on the whole subject. As noted above, governance in any country may be heavily affected by its history—social, political, and economic. The UK Parliamentary debates on the Companies Act show—as does the law—that one of the main concerns of members of the UK Parliament at the time was that investors might be fleeced by unscrupulous *promoters* as many had been a century earlier in the wild greed that surrounded spurious enterprises in the era of the South Sea Bubble affair.

On the issue of the board's accountability, however, Parliament seemed less concerned. This too has historical causes. It is seldom noticed, but there was a long policy tradition in Britain of not interfering with the way business was conducted. Occasionally Parliament panicked and did interfere but this was generally after some grave crisis, like the Black Death, when it sought to contain wages and prices. Generally, the state saw itself in an enabling role (and a sound legal system was part of this). It was disinclined to get into prescriptive mode. This stance conferred many advantages. A populace at work would be less likely to get into mischief. As Dr Johnson put it 250 years ago: 'Sir, there are few ways in which a man can be more innocently employed than in getting money.' Some business practices were not so innocent. In the nineteenth century fear of revolution coupled with a more sensitive conscience eventually caused governments to intervene in what had been regarded as private matters like sending children down coal mines or up chimneys or indeed slavery itself. The debates of the time show vividly how such interference was resented.

Basic attitudes to corporate governance do, as we have already remarked, reflect a country's history and preferences. The exercise of economic power and the requirement for transparency and accountability are likely to reflect ideas about the exercise of political power, and accountability for that. It is not a coincidence that the governance debate has been so vigorous in democratic countries. It is not just 'Anglo-Saxon'; as we shall see, there are substantial differences between the USA and the UK.

Accountability in practice: the directors at work

It is this principle—accountability for the use of power—that was welded into the basic UK company laws from the beginning. It has now come to the fore because it is the weakest part of the governance system. No one disputes it as a principle but it does not always work well; sometimes it does not work at all. Companies from the smallest to the largest have their share of dominating directors; domination itself may not matter, but abuse of power does, and the one often leads to the other.

The original structure and process were based on the assumption that even if the directors were agents of the shareholders (in the economists' sense) it would be in their own interests as well as that of the shareholders for it to succeed and that therefore they would need to ensure that management was competent. They would not only want the rewards which would accrue if the company were successful, but would also benefit personally from having a reputation in which they were associated with success.

In practice this has worked well much of the time. Many companies are doomed to decline and fail, for instance by being overwhelmed by new technology—others disappear by being absorbed by another. The weakness of the system is that it is difficult to organize effective action if the directors are not up to the job. The failure may be due to greed—the directors skimming all the cream for themselves—or it may be incompetence, either of a dramatic kind associated with particular bad decisions like a disastrous acquisition or, less obviously, a failure to keep up with the market over time, leading to decline (which can take years). Sometimes directors betray their trust and act fraudulently. A wholly executive team might well conspire to perpetrate such a fraud and it was examples of this kind that led to the first governmental reaction in the USA in the form of the appointment of the

Treadway Commission in 1978. This mandated the use of outside directors on quoted company boards. It was left to the exchanges to enforce and the New York Stock Exchange took the lead, followed by the others some time later. Thereafter it was a condition of quotation there.

Accountability in practice: the shareholders' role and increasing 'activism'

The shareholders were left by the law with what amounts to a reserve power—to get the board into shape if it proved incompetent or dishonest and failed to act. They seldom did. It was easier to take one's losses and sell in the market. As Berle and Means pointed out in the early 1930s, the fragmentation of shareholdings made effective concerted action virtually impossible. This was indeed true of US quoted companies but not of many quoted companies in countries like Germany and France which have a big block of shares in the hands of a single holder (or a family group). It ought in theory to be less true where there is a separate supervisory tier representing shareholders. This used to be the case in Germany before the co-determination Acts brought employees' representatives on to the supervisory tier.

Meanwhile a major shift in the pattern of shareholdings had occurred in many countries. Collective savings—occupational pensions, mutual funds, and life insurance policies—had increased dramatically, and direct holdings by individuals had declined. At the same time the institutions that managed these funds switched a substantial proportion of their portfolios from bonds into equities despite the technically greater risk, in order to seek better protection from the rise in levels of inflation in the 1950s, 1960s, and 1970s.

Here are the figures (as percentages) for some countries for equity shares:

UK (end 2002)[1]

Institutions	49.4
Individual holdings	14.3
Foreign holders	32.1
Banks	2.1

Japan (end 2000)[2]

Financial institutions	35
Individual holdings	20
Foreign holders	19
Non-financial corporation	22

[1] Office of National Statistics, 18 July 2003.
[2] These are approximate figures based on the Stock Exchange's survey of share ownership.

By the mid-1980s substantially more than half of US equities were in the hands of the institutions; in the UK it was around two-thirds. Theoretically the Berle-Means analysis was no longer valid, since it would have been feasible had they chosen to do so for the institutions to gang together to put pressure on poorly performing company leadership. Institutions come in all shapes and sizes and the smaller ones could still use the 'Wall Street walk' to get rid of shares where they had lost confidence in management, i.e. they could walk away. This was far more difficult for the big institutions as their sales might move the market against them—and as the purchaser would probably be another institution they would merely be passing on the problem, not solving it. Even so, concerted action was extremely rare in the USA; encouraged by the Bank of England there were occasional examples in the UK but these died away—despite being successful.

It gradually became apparent that managing funds actively was expensive and rarely rewarding whether it was done in-house or farmed out to fund managers; most would have done better in most years simply to have 'bought the Index', i.e. to buy a quantity of shares in all the companies that comprised an index in proportion to their weighting in the index. Such a policy had two results. First, the cost of managing the portfolio dropped dramatically. Second, the fund manager could no longer sell the shares in a company perceived to be underperforming because it was in the index. It therefore became clear that if they could not sell, they must care. They had an incentive to monitor actively, and could use the savings in costs realized by abandoning active management.

'Shareholder activism', as it came to be called, took many forms. At the very minimum it emphasized the obligation to vote. In the USA it was recognized that private pension funds should regard the right to vote as part of the plan assets (under a pronouncement about the working of the ERISA rules). Some of the big US retirement funds, like CalPERS and TIAA-CREF, started to follow a policy of always exercising their votes and also of engaging with company management; sometimes they would express disappointment with performance publicly, more often behind closed doors. On occasions 'black-lists' of companies deemed to be underperforming were made public. Management often resisted; who were outsiders to tell them how to run the company? There were cases of outsiders being nominated for election to the board on a reform and reconstruction programme, only to find the board fending them off and then later adopting the policies they advocated.

The simple solution—for institutions to get together to share the costs of action—was seldom adopted. There were many reasons for this, a reluctance to share analyses, a dislike of hassle, cost, and 'free riders', conflicts of interest, and lack of confidence. Company managers are closer to the action than fund managers and it takes confidence to face them out if they resist. Besides, the institutions are concerned about political repercussions if they stand to be accused of 'bully-boy' tactics, whatever their rights are.

The last decade has, however, seen a shift in attitude among many institutions towards more active dialogue with and monitoring of the companies in which they have significant investments. What happens varies from country to country and will be described in its place.

There has been an interesting development in recent years designed to make money for shareholders by rectifying governance shortcomings. Certain investors have set up funds with this express purpose. An early example was the Lens fund set up in the USA by R. A. G. Monks, a veteran corporate governance guru and experienced investor. Later he joined up with the UK's Hermes Fund to do a similar operation. Fidelity's Special Situations Fund has similarities. The free rider issue is less important if one has a big enough stake oneself. Whatever real effect such stakes may have on a company, the news that it has been targeted is likely to be positive for the share price—at least in the short term.

The latest twist to the story of developing accountability is that the institutions themselves should be accountable to the people on whose behalf they invest for the policies they pursue and the actions they take. At last there is a governance answer to the great philosophical question 'Who, then, will guard the guardians?'—*Quis ipsos custodies custodiet?* It is the beneficiaries.

Accountability in practice: the role of the banks

In the UK and the USA banks played little part in governance matters as they saw themselves mainly as providers of short-term money. In some other countries, notably post-war Germany and Japan, a company's main bank (*Hausbank*) would keep a watchful eye on the way it was governed and discreetly take the necessary action. Its leverage came not from its legal powers, but from its powerful position as lender (and supplier of other services and sometimes with a seat on a supervisory board). This role has diminished; the banks have too many problems of their own. It used to have advantages especially in the period after the Second World War when the economies were recovering, but it was always full of contradictions and conflicts of interest.

Escaping accountability

From this narrative it becomes clear that accountability—or lack of it—is not just an 'Anglo-Saxon' problem nor confined to quoted companies. The idea that those who exercise power should be accountable for the way they do so is of universal application and in all spheres. In business as in politics, the greater the power, the greater the danger. Unconstrained power in a small business may have limited consequences—though good governance practices help small companies as well as large ones. Major companies in small economies may have such a commanding position that they are almost above authority—especially if they have co-opted politicians. Even in the USA with its huge economy some have come close to that. It gets worse. Some companies whose lack of accountability has been jealously preserved by managers who hate it may even so be such an important part of the economy that their government feels constrained to support them if they are endangered.

There are signs that a perceived overdose of accountability may be more than the patient's constitution (or its temperament) can stand. To some, the less searching accountability when a company is not publicly quoted has stimulated some boards to seek to take their company private. To put it bluntly, managers find accountability invasive and much prefer to have less of it. So it is that the role of 'private equity' is growing. If they contrive to buy the assets below their real value they can enjoy a less stressful life whilst they build up the company, and if they succeed and have a mind to do so they can make a real killing by returning to the market. Where control of a business rests with the board of an unquoted company, minority shareholders beware. They are poorly protected.

The second set of reasons why accountability is limited or non-existent relates to the shape of shareholdings and also perhaps voting rights as well. In some countries the usual pattern is for shareholdings to be dispersed and as we saw this gave rise to the era of managerial control, described by Berle and Means in 1933. But in some countries the pattern had always been different. Most companies will have a controlling shareholder (control being defined as 20%+). An OECD report of November 2003 contains the following details from various countries around the world (*Experiences from the Regional Corporate Governance Roundtables*, table 3, p. 16). These percentages refer to quoted companies:

Korea	Widely held 43.2	Family controlled	48.4
Malaysia	Widely held 10.3	Family controlled	67.2
Thailand	Widely held 6.6	Family controlled	61.6

Closer to home, it appears that in only 2.4% of UK quoted companies is there a holder with majority control, compared with 64.2% in Germany and 56.15 in Italy. France too has a high proportion of companies with concentrated ownership (Barca and Becht 2001).

A variation on this theme mentioned in the same OECD report (p. 17) is the control pyramid. A controlling shareholder owns all the stock of the company at the top of the pyramid, which in turn owns half the shares in company B. B owns say 60% of C and 40% of D. The report gives an example from Hong Kong. The dangers both to the economy and to the state are obvious.

These cases reveal the curious combination of managerial freedom from effective accountability and the unspoken liability of the state to pick up the pieces in times of disaster.

Making accountability real

We can compare accountability to a telephone call—or in these days an e-mail. If there is no one at the other end to listen to what is being said or to read what has been written, the exercise becomes of less practical use than prayer—whereby a true believer's soul is nourished whatever the outcome.

If shareholders disregard the signals they have only themselves to blame. Many are mesmerized by the share price. If it is headed north anything goes, and a great many losses have been incurred as a result of complacency and oversimplification resulting from apparent success.

On the other hand careful attention to the signal does not mean overreacting. It is and always was the case that managers should be given as much freedom as possible to get on with the job; they are not to be harried and worried at every turn. They are entitled to make some mistakes. It is a case of watching to see how they make out in all the circumstances and how they are doing relative to competitors. Having said this, managers would be less than human were they not to put the best possible face on their achievements or lack of them, and shareholders must aim for this. Rational shareholders do not therefore jump up and down in anguish at each passing mishap; their concern is twofold—medium- and longer-term trends and the process within the company itself which should improve the quality of decisions and at the same time ensure an accurate flow of information, even if from time to time it proves disappointing, which is inevitable. All this assumes that the institutional shareholders regard themselves as owners—in the hedge fund jargon 'long only'. It is difficult to see how investors in a long/short fund can do so. It is a different type of activity. Even 'long only' investors do not necessarily share a similar view with management, who may have a different time scale in mind. There are pressures on all the parties; better communications and understanding may relieve them but may not abolish them.

Accountability: process

The most interesting development over the last ten years has been concern about the way the board works and reports. This takes us away from the worlds of law and economics into the behavioural sciences. As anyone knows who has sat on a board or committee the interaction of those present is hugely complex and very difficult to reduce to formulas. Chairmanship is of the greatest importance and boards can be transformed by a change at the top. The concentration on structure in all its aspects—having a separate chairman, independent directors, a nominated senior independent director, committees—all these are actually a proxy for process. The skill of the leaders is still paramount—as has been said, better to have good people in a bad structure than bad ones in a good structure. 'Structuralists' would argue that the right structure facilitates excellence—true perhaps, but it does not ensure it. As we know from the sporting world, good teams do not automatically result from having well-qualified individuals on them. The modern fashion of laying special emphasis on the board's containing sufficient 'independent' directors is based on the assumption that a better process will automatically result for maintaining honesty and competence. There are several causes of failure in the cases of Enron, Worldcom, and Marconi, but somewhere along the line it may well be that the process was not good enough, even if there was no *mens rea* (deliberate intent) in the criminal law sense. If there was dishonesty it makes good process impossible, since it is deliberately designed to nullify it. Structure alone is not enough, hence the growing interest in board assessment and in the training of directors.

I saw an interesting example of deteriorating process in the case of a group which once enjoyed much success under the leadership of a triumvirate. (Outside directors played little if any part.) Two of the three retired, but the charismatic man who was left in sole command soon ran into trouble and the company declined. Although the triumvirate would not have satisfied modern governance criteria, there seems little doubt that the process which involved three able people who were roughly equal and respected each other did provide the checks and balances which are so essential. And as a general point, I have often observed that where a company has enjoyed some success, has a weak board and a dominating leader it is almost certainly heading for trouble if he is also the darling of the media. Accountability is unlikely to exist in any meaningful way. The heady attentions of the press impair judgement; and the press are merciless to the fallen.

Accountability: does the message get through?

Even in quoted companies shareholders do not always receive automatically the information to which they are entitled— for instance where for reasons of convenience or economy they are held in nominee accounts—'street names'. There may be provisions to ensure that the shareholder can get the information, but these may be expensive, cumbersome, or slow. Secondly where shares are held in a company registered abroad, the distribution of information across borders, including voting papers, is likewise often snail-like if it exists at all. In many cases the shares are or may have to be held in nominee or depositories' names. If accountability is to be taken seriously in our increasingly international world, there need to be conventions covering the timing of documents relating to governance. At the moment it may be difficult to vote. This is wrong. It is not enough for voting papers to reach shareholders in time for them to respond; they are entitled to have seen the relevant report and accounts and to have studied them, so as to be able to make a considered judgement upon them. These principles should apply whether shares are held in registered or bearer form and whether or not it is obligatory to use a depository.

Finally there is the broader question of institutional investors and the beneficiaries on whose behalf they hold shares. This raises questions of their accountability to the beneficiaries so that the latter know about the holdings and their institution's view of the way in which it conceives and discharges its obligation.

Having said all that, it is clear that over the last decade communication between major companies and their institutional shareholders has improved by sustained efforts by both parties. Some technical impediments described above can be eased if they have a mind to it. But institutions come in many shapes and sizes and the smaller ones lack the resources for wide coverage and sustained efforts to improve communications that the larger ones now make. Smaller companies (outside the 'go-go' industries) find shareholder relations uphill work because maintaining interest in a relatively small holding looks like a poor use of resources to the institution concerned. The consequences are not always benign.

The Ethical Dimension

General

Protests against capitalism, globalization, and big business seldom nowadays reflect a strongly held alternative coherent policy; Marxism used to fill this role but it had its chance, was shown to work badly, and is discredited. Concerns about the workings of big business may still be genuine even though they may be contradictory and muddled. Perhaps because of an increasing awareness of the power of the modern company and its outreach into so many corners of society, the last decade has seen the rapid growth of concerns about this under the titles of 'stakeholders' and 'corporate social responsibility'.

There are no easy answers to some of the questions. There is for instance an outcry about the importation of cheap goods made in very substandard conditions in some of the world's poorest communities. But what does it do to those communities if they cannot sell their products at all?

Attitudes are not necessarily consistent. American technology may be admired and in some cases seem indispensable. Big Macs may seem a cultural threat or alternatively regarded as the acceptable face of US ingenuity. And both views can be held simultaneously!

Employees in a big multinational company can find themselves un-employed by an apparently random decision made in an obscure office thousands of miles away. A system that appeared satisfactory within a state's borders may not be wholly suited to the conduct of operations abroad—as the Germans have found after the Mercedes-Chrysler merger. In short, big companies may seem to be insufficiently accountable; they are quite capable of snubbing the state one moment and begging for favours the next. No one in this modern world wants state supervision (though it already exists for the financial sector and is getting tighter). But effective accountability is absolutely essential and in the absence of the state the duty falls to theshareholders. And as accountability requires transparency, a good dose of both might take the sting out of the fear of the abuse of power that underlies many protests. Words are bandied about without considering their precise meaning—like 'legitimacy'. We can dismiss them as muddled or misguided, but it would be unwise to ignore the basic feelings that underlie peoples' concerns.

Socially responsible investment

Socially responsible investment (SRI) is sometimes called ethical investing and is concerned with what a company does and how it does it from the point of view of the potential investor. It is an old notion; there have been funds for many years that would not buy shares in companies that produced alcohol, or tobacco, or armaments, for instance. One modern variation is to avoid companies that knowingly buy products made by exploited labour. Another is to avoid companies operating under a politically oppressive regime. A company that focuses on corporate social responsibility may even so seem objectionable to some investors by virtue of what it produces. The English judge Megarry pointed out years ago that trustees must put the interests of the beneficiaries first and that they were not free to allow their own delicate sentiments full play.

'Stakeholders'

'Stakeholders' is a convenient portmanteau expression into which many different items can be packed. At its simplest it means that there are many groups of people who are affected by a company's activities and who therefore have an interest in the way they are conducted. They include customers (without whom nothing moves at all), employees, suppliers, bankers and bondholders, and local communities. To say that any well-run company will 'take account of' these interests is true. To extrapolate from this to a proposition that a company's management is 'accountable to' any or all of these groups is false. The directors are accountable only to the shareholders—but this means they are accountable for the way they serve stakeholders' interests too. Many of the relationships are in any case covered by law—contract and employment law being prime examples. (The law may not be effective, as many small suppliers have found when they are being squeezed or held up for payment by a large customer.) Boards are often faced with real difficulties as far as so-called stakeholders are concerned. Take suppliers as an example. If a supplier commits a large proportion of his capacity to a single customer he may fairly be said to have a stake in its success. But he must recognize that his customer is accountable too—to his shareholders and must sometimes make unpleasant decisions. Marks & Spencer in the UK had long-term enlightened contractual relations with some suppliers—partnership sourcing—but some wilted under pressure from foreign competition.

Of all the stakeholders, employees have the greatest interest in the business; indeed, in some countries the shareholders' interests have been subordinated to them. Now that employees have interests in pension funds they need companies to prosper and pay dividends too. In fact there is an increasing tendency to entitle employees to participate in their governance process through consultation involving works councils and the like. The OECD report (op. cit., paras. 237 et seq.) records that 'In 18 of 32 Round Table jurisdictions for which data are available workers have the right to choose some members of the board, appoint works councils, and or some constitutional right to participate in the decision making process of the company.' The cynical spirit which underlies the old adage 'Honesty is the best policy' is alive and well, both in regard to 'stakeholders' and to 'corporate social responsibility' (CSR). We could feel more comfortable if there were greater emphasis on personal integrity. Notions based on 'rights' or 'obligations' can change but integrity is indivisible.

In the current discussions about stakeholders, the term is used to contrast them with shareholders, to assert in other words that shareholders must not believe they are the only ones connected with a company who matter. There is, however, the uncomfortable fact that minority shareholders are themselves often abused. In some countries sometimes quoted companies are controlled by an individual, family, or grouping who can and do manipulate events in such a way as to disadvantage the minority. There are organizations in some countries to defend minority holders. In France for instance there is the Association pour le Défence des Actionnaires Minoritaires—ADAM. This is an issue worthy of attention even though the minority shareholders in a quoted company can always sell, it may be impossible to get a fair deal.

Corporate social responsibility

There is an overlap between the stakeholder thesis and CSR. A convenient way to separate them is to regard the latter as being concerned mainly with the external world to which the company is not bound by contract but which may be affected by its operations—especially the environment. At one level, for instance, is the myriad of fast food outlets whose customers dump their unwanted packaging in adjacent streets; at another are the great extractive industries whose operations affect both land and sea. A section on CSR in company reports is more and more required—with numbers where appropriate. Some companies go to great lengths to support the local communities where they operate. They regard this as not only right in itself but part of their 'licence to operate'.

As with much else, CSR is a matter of balance, but economics are an iron vice. To force a company to retain unneeded staff, for instance, may appear ethical—but ruin it. There is no joy for any of the parties, or the community, in a company's being ethical but broke. If a company cannot be run ethically, arguably it should not be run at all, but this begs the question of the ethical standards to be applied—and these vary hugely. There is a real danger with CSR of competing, contradictory, and incompatible objectives. When we examine Japan this will be on the agenda. Meanwhile, responsible and forward looking organizations like the Work Foundation have explored the relationship between dedication to CSR and better performance.[3]

To keep a proper sense of perspective on CSR we might revert to our formulation of the purpose of the company: 'To provide *ethically and profitably* the goods and services people want or need'. The concern for profitability will stick less harshly in the throats of those who resent it when they consider whose capital is being used nowadays—mainly pensioners and other savers; they will be less concerned if there is an ethical dimension to the company's operations—in addition to all the other benefits it provides like

---

[3] 'Achieving high performance: CSR at the heart of the business', March 2004.

employment, a sense of community, social cohesion, and the products and services themselves.

Finally, big salaries have become contentious in some countries. The 'Anglo-Saxon' solution has been to concentrate on improving the process of salary determination—with appropriate structures to make this easier— like a remuneration committee. This thorny subject exemplifies the contrasting views of those who on the one hand see the issue in stark economic terms (even if it means institutionalizing greed) and those who consider that unrestrained greed is a breach of corporate social responsibility—society is a fabric and it cannot be stretched indefinitely.

Takeovers

Takeovers as a substitute for effective governance

Mergers have long been a part of the economic scene in all developed economies. Most are 'friendly'—a deal between two willing parties for any of a number of reasons, including economies of scale, the entry into new markets, and succession problems. The last forty years has seen the growth of takeovers, many of which are classed as 'hostile' because they are launched by a bidder against an unwilling 'target'. Some had a respectable rationale like strategic development. Others were frankly opportunistic. A bidder realized that the share price was so low that the company could be dismembered at a profit. Slater Walker in the UK were experts at this in the sixties. The pickings were so easy that many company managements did become more aware of their vulnerability if they sat on underperforming assets. To this extent pressure from the stock market acted as a sharp spur. Opponents of this process argued that it was bound to promote 'short-termism' because management would become obsessed with the share price and would not risk the market's undervaluing projects and products where the road to full profitability was inevitably long. As we shall see various countries slowed or stopped 'hostile' bids by all sorts of methods from cross-holdings in Japan to 'poison pills' in the USA.

From the shareholders' viewpoint the strategic logic behind many such takeovers was dubious; if management needed refreshing by one or two changes it seemed an extraordinarily expensive route to change total ownership at the same time—and it often produced an inferior structure. The evidence suggests that although these bids usually brought an immediate gain to shareholders in the target company (provided they sold) the ensuing structure was likely to show that the value of the new entity was less than that of the sum of the pre-merger parts. There are indeed good reasons for takeovers, but changing a manager or two is not among them. The expected synergies so often prayed in aid of a takeover are notoriously difficult to realize; indeed it is said that the only place to find 'synergy' is in the dictionary. And of course unquoted companies were not so threatened anyway.

The better a company's governance is then the less likely it is that it will be threatened by opportunistic hostile takeovers. But that leads on to a more general question—whether it makes a difference generally.

Does Sound Governance Make a Difference?

Does all the work on governance serve any useful purpose? Companies, like other organisms grow, fade, and die. On the Darwinian principle, there would not be enough room for them in the world if they did not do so. It might be thought that there was clear proof positive of a direct connection between good governance and economic prosperity. When the Bank of England's interest in governance was aroused in the 1970s and 1980s it was because of the simple observation that in the companies with which they were concerned, management lacked grip and that the board was too weak to take the necessary steps. The effect of good governance may be asymmetric. It may be better at inhibiting bad decisions and preventing false and misleading accounting than it is at securing successful enterprise (even though it includes replacing executive management where necessary). It is very difficult to be sure that the sequence of cause and effect has been correctly identified. Was the Marconi debacle a result of poor governance or poor judgement? In that case fraud was not an issue, but in cases where it is, or where there have been serious accounting irregularities, it is not always certain that better governance would have done the trick if executive management were intent on concealing the facts. In other words, if governance is not based on a foundation of executive integrity it may not be able to work.

It is difficult to tell from the outside how well a company's governance system is actually working. There are clues in terms of the governance 'architecture' and it is these on which many judgements and assessments are made—which may have the effect of enhancing the share price, even though they are far from conclusive. Structure is one thing, dynamics another. Does the proportion of 'independent' directors on a board ensure greater profitability or larger profitable growth? Again, it is asymmetric; such boards may be better at inhibiting commercial folly than they are at inculcating wisdom. Is it yet possible to ask of Corporate Governance 'If A...then B?' The answer is 'No'. Corporate governance is not and never will be a panacea. But those of us who have experienced bad governance are convinced that it is an unnecessary hazard on the road to commercial success.

There have been numerous attempts to research the 'If A then B' proposition. UK fund managers Hermes (about whom more is said in the UK section) did a *tour d'horizon* for their 2003 conference. They quoted a 2002 McKinsey report that 80% of the 200 institutional investors in their survey would pay a premium for well-governed companies. This conclusion is supported by other studies; investors, it seems, do better by selecting well-governed companies. Research based on a single feature such as the correlation of board independence with commercial success have proved inconclusive.

In the USA some major institutional shareholders, especially CalPERS and TIAA-CREF have graded company governance systems. Those with more highly graded systems seemed to produce better returns than their peers. In some scandalous cases, malpractice and sloppy governance may be obvious—*ex post*. I have seen evidence that good governance can produce a brilliant performance—by getting better managers in place. But more work needs to be done on cause and effect in this sphere.

Even the best governance systems may not be proof against a corrupt and ruthless management, organizing a conspiracy with great skill, bribing or threatening its way to secure silence. Even keen honest auditors can be fooled. That this is so does not provide an excuse for auditors and NEDs not to be vigilant and use their 'sense of smell'. The better the 'architecture' and process, the greater their chance of getting at the truth, but there is no guarantee that they will.[4]

Unquoted companies

Unquoted companies are far more numerous than quoted companies everywhere and tomorrow's great companies are among them. So, unfortunately are most of tomorrow's bankruptcies. In the Darwinian jungle in which they all operate some of this is inevitable. There are dozens of reasons for failure. Even so these businesses constitute an important chunk of economies everywhere. The laws under which they operate differ in all five countries from those for quoted companies. In some cases there is a halfway house—a company comes under a different law when it reaches a certain size whether quoted or not.

---

[4] The question was explored at length in relation to the USA by veteran US lawyer Ira M. Millstein and leading US academic Paul W. MacAvoy in Millstein and MacAvoy 2003: 32–94.

Small companies may seem to have little in common with the giants in respect of the principles of governance, but on closer inspection this boils down to one major factor—it is meaningless to talk about accountability if the same people are managers, directors, and owners. As companies develop— indeed as soon as they employ managers—there is a degree of formal accountability, internally. No bell rings when governance becomes meaningful and indeed many unquoted companies are well governed; like M. Jourdain, they are speaking prose without recognizing it. For the proprietor of a firm on a cold, dark, winter's morning standing in the Billingsgate fish market the notion of 'corporate governance' may seem unreal. The fact remains that if his firm is soundly governed its prospects for survival and prosperity are improved. They are not guaranteed of course—that depends above all on its enterprise skills. But as they grow all companies need to focus on the adequacy of the resources they will need, their medium- and longer-term aims and objectives, succession, and internal financial disciplines. To do these things well means setting time aside—no easy matter in businesses where all the leading people are deeply immersed in the problems of the day; it probably means creating some kind of special meeting and it may mean bringing in help in one form or another to supplement the skills the business already possesses and to introduce an element of objectivity. Such arrangements need not be either complicated or expensive, and they are at the very heart of good governance.

If we were to define the moment where accountability becomes significant it would be the point at which there are shareholders who are not on the board. This often arises when one of the original directors dies and bequeaths his shares. The troubling questions are whether such shareholders are entitled to receive the report and accounts, whether they actually do so, and what their remedies are if they are oppressed, including 'exit'. In some cases there is no real accountability and no practical remedy.

Professionals taking stakes in unquoted companies usually do so with protective provisions like 'put' options—they can require the majority to buy them out on reasonable terms. But I have had to stand by and watch the majority shareholders of a UK company, most of whom were actively engaged in their business, milk it dry to the disadvantage of the minority. In another case it was not enough to make the business pay for the chairman's wife's car—it paid for the vicar's too! The fact is that many proprietors of family businesses treat the company's assets as if they were their own private property. This is wrong, but understandable when they own 100% of the shares. But their attitude may not change when it has grown large and even when there are outside shareholders.

There are therefore two separate reasons for not excluding unquoted companies from discussions on corporate governance. The first is that as they develop, good governance is ever more desirable operationally. The second is that more light needs to be shed on the awkward subject of the oppression of minorities.

Summary

The descriptions of each of the five countries will therefore cover:

- The general background
- The main laws and 'soft' law
- The sources of finance (banks and stock market)
- The way shares are held and by whom (private, institutional, foreign)
- Directors and boards
- Reporting to the shareholders
- Shareholders' rights and activism
- Stakeholders and corporate social responsibility
- Litigation

Changes over the last decade will be highlighted in the narrative and at the end we have included an agenda of 'unfinished business' covering some of the issues touched upon above and some others.

Market Changes in the Five Countries

I have included Table 1.1 for general interest if only to show that markets as a whole do not march in step. Will better governance all round make a difference to this?

Table 1.1. Market changes in the five countries

	US (S&P500)	UK (FTSE)	France (CAC)	Germany (DAX)	Japan (Nikkei)
1988	12.4	6.5	57.4	31.1	39.9
1989	27.3	30.0	27.1	35.8	29.0
1990	−6.6	−14.3	−24.8	−19.9	−38.7
1991	26.3	15.1	17.3	5.7	−3.6
1992	4.5	14.8	5.2	−6.6	−26.4
1993	7.1	23.3	22.1	43.2	2.9
1994	−1.5	−9.5	−17.1	−7.2	13.2
1995	34.1	18.5	−0.5	4.2	0.7
1996	20.3	11.7	23.7	23.3	−2.6
1997	31.0	19.7	329.5	41.0	−21.2
1998	26.7	10.9	31.5	14.6	−9.3
1999	19.5	21.2	51.1	33.6	3.7
2000	−10.1	−8.0	−0.5	−7.5	−27.2
2001	−13.0	−15.4	−22.0	−19.7	−23.5
2002	−23.4	−25.0	−33.7	−43.5	−18.6
2003	26.4	16.6	16.1	34.8	24.5

2

Germany

Introduction

To understand the system by which companies are directed and controlled in Germany—corporate governance—as in any country means studying both its structure and its dynamics, that is to say, not just the legal framework and institutions but also personal relationships. Looking at the formal framework tells only a fraction of the story: the attitudes people have and their patterns of behaviour are just as important. To attempt to describe these, however, means leaving behind the comfortable clarity of the law and making an excursion into the misty world of immeasurable generalizations. The people of Germany are as varied and diverse in character as those of any other nation, so any generalization is bound to be more true of some than others. The reason why it is worth risking generalizations at all is to show that the transplanting of formal structures will not necessarily produce identical patterns of behaviour. German institutions work the way they do because their composition itself reflects a certain mode of thought, which is also reflected in the way people work within them. Generalized observations are by definition imprecise, but they may nevertheless be true enough to matter. They are often made (which does not of course justify their content), and not just by British authors. Yoshimiti Yamashita, for instance, in writing about Japanese management in 1992, said, among other interesting remarks: 'The Japanese executive approaches management intuitively rather than rationally, while the Western executive is too rational' (*Directors and Boards*, 17/1 (Fall 1992), 25). He was president of Arthur D. Little, Inc.

Background

Conflict and cooperation

If there were a spectrum with 'confrontation' at one end and 'cooperation' at the other, we would confidently place German attitudes and behaviour far closer to the 'cooperation' end than, say, those of the British or Americans. In the economic sphere the Germans have never been obsessed by the idea that their economy will work best if unrestricted competition is studiously enforced: cartels existed in the nineteenth century. There is competition between companies, of course, but very often cooperation between them at the same time (not in price fixing but in, say, jointly producing certain common components). The adversarial approach does not commend itself as the best way of reaching conclusions even though Germans are doughty fighters. A more cooperative approach facilitates taking a long perspective in thinking about things and people and it lowers concern about potential conflicts of interest by trusting people to use sensitive information in an appropriate way and not improperly. If one cherishes a relationship one does not betray it.

It is worth considering for a moment why there should be so marked an emphasis on cooperation and long-term thinking. Does it reflect in some way Germany's geographical position? The land mass of central Europe occupied for centuries by German speaking people has no clearly defined natural boundaries in the west and east other than rivers, and the consequential restlessness goes back beyond and through Roman times up to our own day. We have only to think of the unrest that followed the dismemberment of the Austro-Hungarian Empire from 1919 to the present day. This political restlessness with its varying inward and outward pressures and the contrasting tendencies of centralization and fragmentation means that in everyone's mind there are echoes of changing political boundaries and war. There are those who used to believe that Louis XIV's seizure of Strasbourg and devastation of the Palatinate left scars as yet unhealed—though the catastrophic wars of the twentieth century have effaced many older memories.

Was it a reaction to this history of central Europe so punctuated by invasion and destruction that caused the Germans to attach much importance to cooperation and to good order? Certain attitudes have clear historical causes. Hyperinflation so disrupted order in every aspect of life that the fear of it was a dominant feature of the German consensus after 1945 and it probably still lurks below the surface. It gave the Bundesbank, which enjoys a high degree of independence from the state by virtue of its constitutional position, a firm base of moral unity in pursuing a consistent anti-inflationary policy. It is not too much to suggest that the general perception that the European Central Bank has inherited this stance is one of the foundations of its authority.

Much of the modern German economic and social framework has clearly discernible historical origins. Compulsory schooling had been introduced in Prussia by Frederick the Great. Welfare legislation, which others developed, started in Bismarck's day and contained a streak of idealism which some might

label 'Socialist' except that it owes nothing to Marxist economics. The importance of the banking system as a source of finance for industry relative to the
stock market reflects the later development of a centralized German state and
accounted for the close relationship between banks and companies. The two-
tier system was introduced in the General Commercial Code of 1861 and made
mandatory in 1870 when it no longer became necessary to have a governmental
representative on the board. The present system dates back to 1937. It has
sometimes been called the 'social market economy model' (*soziale Markt-
wirtschaft*), which is a direct descendant of those early days. Another title
might be 'cooperative managerial capitalism'. Whatever the name, it is certainly
a special type of market economy, although it does appear that over the last
decade the system has drawn closer to the US model in ways we shall discuss.

   It would be interesting to know how much attitudes and behaviour are
affected by having a written constitution and legal code. I found the law
frequently mentioned, not in the context of recourse to litigation in contract
and tort, however, but rather as applications to the courts in administrative
matters. To take an example: employees can take an employer to court for
breaches of the laws which cover works councils. Many, perhaps most, civil
servants are trained as lawyers; lawyers often switch into industry. Recourse
to the courts or other kinds of administrative tribunal appears to be increasing in industrial and administrative contexts. What I did find—and it
surfaced at a German Governance Conference in late 2004—was deference
to authority—the state and its laws—that would feel unusual in countries
like the UK and USA where people are suspicious of authority in general and
the state in particular.

Social obligation

The sense of cooperation is also evident in the social sphere. Although
individual Germans or their organizations are as adept at pursuing self-
interest as anyone else, this pursuit may be constrained by a genuine sense
of obligation to the community. The assumption behind cooperation, for
example, is that it will produce a general benefit for the community as a
whole. The grounds on which a commercial decision is taken may not relate
narrowly to the company's immediate interests: there was, for instance, a case
where the board would not permit management to use the insurance money
from a burnt-down plant to enhance production elsewhere. They argued
successfully that economic criteria came second to social duty and the company was obligated to the community in which the factory had stood. Again,
firms often train too many people not simply to cover potential wastage but as
a conscious attempt to produce more well-trained people for the country.

This sense of cooperation and social obligation sits well with an approach both to planning and education which seems generally geared to the longer term. German industrial managers, members of management boards and of the supervisory tier, are alike in this respect. Bankers also seem to think long-term and not to expect too much too soon. The limited influence the capital markets have on German industrial behaviour may have many causes, not least of which is that so few firms use them: certainly an emphasis on 'shareholder value' is suspect if it appears to emphasize the short term far too much. Even annual reports and accounts are as much concerned with the narrative as the figures: as the interest is in the longer term, figures (which are only a snapshot of the past) are by themselves an inadequate indication of the future. The relative unimportance of the capital market may have quite separate economic causes, but the attitude of the banks, through which a high proportion of savings was and is channelled, does directly reflect the prevailing ethos: companies think likewise but perhaps their shareholders are refocusing.

Education

This emphasis on social obligation and a long time scale is also consistent with the Germans setting great store by education and devoting much time to it (and starting working careers later). Formal qualifications are much valued as marks of earned distinction by which people can be classified. They have helped to take much of the importance away from the class system by strengthening the meritocracy—a process assisted by Germany only having a single school system. Germans do not feel that this investment of time and money in acquiring a sound education and first-rate professional and technical knowledge automatically implies a career in banking or the civil service; on the contrary, many of the most talented go into commerce and industry. German industry enjoys the benefit of large numbers of well-trained recruits at various levels and spends heavily on improving, completing, and updating their training. The Federal Statistics Office and the Statistical Offices of the Länder (24 February 2004) report that the number of young people obtaining an education as an apprentice was 1,622,441 in 2002. This combination of on-the-job training and theoretical instruction at school lasts about three years, thus producing skilled workers for trade and industry.

The German educational system works closely with industry and has never undervalued—much less despised—it. In this it reflects the prevalent attitude of esteem towards industry. It is socially not just acceptable but really well considered: the children of successful entrepreneurs are often proud to follow their fathers and keep the business in the family.

The purpose of companies

The social aspect of business is underlined in Article 14(2) of the German constitution, which states, 'Property imposes duties. Its use should also serve the public weal.' This should not be read as an echo of socialism but as a background to the legislation, serving much the same purpose as the pre- amble to a British statute. Against such a background it is not surprising to find a consensus in Germany that the purpose of companies is to deliver to the community the goods and services it needs on a continuing basis. This is significant in two ways. First, that there is no divergence between sectors of society about the purpose of companies, and second, that profit, whilst important, is not the be all and end all. It does however seem to be the case that the focus on shareholder value has become sharper over the last decade, and some commentators see this as leading towards convergence with the priorities of the US/UK model. This may well be so especially as the UK has moved in the opposite direction and has become more concerned with corporate social responsibility, which is embedded in the German consti- tution as noted above. It has always been the case, however, that consistently poor profits and a depressed share price have reflected on the competence of management. Traditionally German management thinks of its customers and employees first, but there is now ample evidence of a change of emphasis for instance in moving manufacturing facilities abroad. Shareholders are one set of stakeholders among several.

The late Ellen Schneider-Lenne, then a member of the management board of Deutsche Bank, made the point as follows in an article in the *Oxford Review of Economic Policy* in Autumn 1992: 'The objectives of German companies however do not stop at maximisation of the return on investment. Their philosophy is based on "The concept of the interest of the company as a whole", a key concept of German corporate culture.' She enlarged on this theme in her 1992 Stockton Lecture, quoting Hermann Joseph Abs, whom she described as 'the grand old man of Deutsche Bank': 'Profit is as necessary as the air we breathe but it would be terrible if we worked only to make a profit, just as it would be terrible if we lived only to breathe.'

Were she still alive, she might have noted that the return on investment has moved up the agenda, not least because one of the effects of globalization is that the proportion of shares in the hands of foreigners has increased. Not only that, but the German public has been shifting its financial assets away from bank deposits towards insurance and securities (O'Sullivan 2003: 45). Shares and mutual funds accounted for 23.1% at the end of 1999 compared with 10.6% in 1991. Competition from German savings institutions fuels the move towards better returns.

The law and 'soft' law

The main features of German Company law are described in a Foreword to the 2003 Corporate Governance Code which emphasizes the clear definition of the top structure, viz:

The Management Board (the Vorstand) is responsible for managing the enterprise. Its members are jointly accountable. The Chairman of the Management Board co-ordinates its work. The Supervisory Board (Aufsichtsrat) appoints, supervises, and advises the members of the Management Board and is directly involved in decisions of vital importance to the enterprise. The Chairman coordinates its work.

Both these organs are described in detail below.

There have been significant developments over the last seven years, starting with the Control and Transparency Law of May 1998 (KonTraG), some of whose main features were as follows:

- AG company boards had to ensure there were adequate risk management arrangements.
- The reporting obligations on planning (by the Vorstand to the Aufsichtsrat) were increased.
- The number of permitted seats on Aufsichtsrate was reduced.
- More information had to be given on the background and commitments of new candidates for membership of an Aufsichtsrat.
- More meetings—and a report to shareholders on how many—and how many committee meetings.
- The banks' voting rights as depositories were modified to bring sharehold-ers more into the picture and give them a greater say. There is also a limitation—to 5%—on their voting their own holdings.
- Plural voting rights were curtailed and have now ended—so have artificial caps. Note however that Volkswagen has an Act of its own which preserves a curious structure to protect the interests of the Länder of lower Saxony where the headquarters are situated.
- There are provisions designed to enhance auditors' independence. The limits on their liability have been increased both for AG and GmbH companies.

This was followed by a code of best practice developed by the Frankfurt Commission in February 2000, which covered mainly the relationship of management to the supervisory board and to the auditors. That same summer the government set up a commission (under Professor Theodor Baums), the Baums Commission, which presented a 320-page report in July 2001 including about 150 recommendations. This was closely followed by the Cromme Commission (under Dr Gerhard Cromme, the chairman of Thyssen Krupp). The latest version, including amendments in May 2003, is covered in the narrative below with appropriate references as GCGC (it is otherwise known as the Kodex). Dr Cromme leads a standing commission (unlike most such bodies) which will have the duty to revise the way the code works and, from time to time, to suggest amendments. The Kodex is reprinted in full in the Annex to this chapter, and is reproduced in a 'convenience translation' by kind permission of the commission.

The GCGC distinguishes between three different types of command. 'Must' is unequivocal and refers to provisions German firms are compelled to observe under German law. 'Shall' provisions come under a 'conform or explain' regime and the company must report on its compliance. This regime has the force of law via Article 161 of the Stock Corporation Act (AktG) which came into force on 26 July 2002. As to the rest—'should' or 'can' suggestions—the company need not comment on what it has or has not done.

The GCGC is aimed at listed companies but advises others 'to respect' it. To keep a sense of perspective it is worth noting that only 15% of the German labour force work in large quoted companies.

The intention is to review it annually. Certainly levels of consciousness about corporate governance have been raised, even if only 9% of the companies responding to the Korn/Ferry International study (2003: 13) had a formal committee to review its corporate governance processes or written guidelines. And only 1% of directors are regularly evaluated. On the other hand some companies do now include a corporate governance statement, as does the Deutsche Borse itself (pp. 102–3).

A study by Werder, Talaulicar, and Kolat of the Technical University of Berlin in late 2003 covered all 864 corporations listed on the Frankfurt Stock Exchange. The analysis is based on the responses from 30 companies in the DAX index, 69 in the MDAX index, 40 in the NEMAX index, and 49 in SDAX index. It is open to a company to reject the Code and say so, but none does. In fact 20 companies in the sample (4.9%) assert that they fully comply and others have signified their intention to do so (12.8%). Thus the majority are betwixt and between; broadly speaking, the bigger they are the more of the code they apply; among the less observed provisions are those applying to more personal issues like the personal liability of board members, full disclosure of remuneration, age limits for board members, and, among small companies, committees of the board. They simply don't feel they would add to efficiency. If we add it all up, it is clear that the Code generally commands wide respect.

A refinement of the analysis for DAX companies takes in 'Neuralgic' recommendations (those that do not fall into the 'shall' or 'must' categories). It seems that nearly all supervisory boards already discuss the structure of the Vorstand's compensation system, but that only 28.6% of them reveal individuals' figures (likely to rise marginally). Few companies impose age limits on members of the Vorstand. In most companies (61% and rising) the chairman of the Aufsichtsrat does not chair the audit committee.

Meanwhile a new takeover law came into effect on 1 January 2002 which superseded the takeover Code. Among its provisions are:

- If a bid is launched management may take defensive action against unsolicited bids—and search for 'white knights' but only with the supervisory board's approval. If that is forthcoming, management can seek the approval of a General Meeting for defensive measures without having to specify them in detail.
- The Act prohibits bidders offering generous terms to existing directors to stand down.
- Bidders must inform the target company's shareholders and employees in detail about its effects. (This statement must be in German.)
- A requirement to make an offer to remaining shareholders if 30%+ of a company's voting shares are to be acquired.
- An obligation to make a cash offer if the bidder has acquired more than 5% of the target company's shares or voting rights within the last three months before bidding and has paid cash for more than 1% of the company's voting rights during the takeover procedure.
- There is for the first time a squeeze-out provision if a purchaser gets 95% of the equity and the shareholders so resolve. (Thus amending the Stock Corporation Act.)

It is beyond the scope of this book to look at the oppression of minorities in unquoted companies—a worldwide problem. In quoted companies minority shareholders always have the right to exit via the stock market. Even though they have an equal entitlement to dividend streams, there are two sets of problems to face. The first is where the managers are helping themselves to such an extent as to leave little for the shareholders; the second is where management is incompetent but entrenched— in the sense that neither board nor shareholders are inclined to take the appropriate action. Good systems of governance address both issues. Takeovers in Germany do not appear to have solved this question. Indeed Jenkinson and Ljungqvist (1997) state that their analysis of seventeen cases of hostile takeovers suggests that minority Shareholders suffered rather than benefited.

UMAG

On the stocks there is a law for 'The integrity of companies and the modernization of the law for shareholder claims', scheduled for 2005, which appears to facilitate shareholder suits against the board on behalf of the company, provisions to make proxy voting easier, and new rules for general meetings.

Accounting standards

Historically the German approach to accounting differed from the UK convention that accounts should show a 'true and fair view'; in Germany the auditors' philosophy is the principle of commercial prudence and this is authorized in legislation. Heinrich Weiss, then president of the Federation of German Industries (BDI), speaking in London on 23 June 1992 to the Royal Society of Arts, said, 'This means that whenever you see a risk you have a right to make a reserve in the balance sheet or make a deduction on the assets side, creating some reserve for risks, which of course means that at the time you reduce your profits but you get a reserve in case you have some problems with the company.' German companies do in fact tuck substantial reserves away, and their employees through their membership of works councils and Aufsichtsrat know perfectly well what is going on and approve, as it strengthens the company's power to survive and enhances their own prospect of continuity of employment. Paul Rutterman of accountants Ernst & Young, speaking in Oxford in September 1992, said that one analysis suggested that, by using the accounting treatment appropriate to each country, the same figures would produce profits of: 88 in Spain, 89 in Germany, 94 in Holland, 100 in France, 117 in Italy, and 129 in the UK. Underlying this view of best accounting practice is the German evaluation of the importance of stakeholders, particularly employees, customers, and community, relative to shareholders. It is the continuity of the business that has top priority, so prudence takes precedence over profits. And although this is not tax driven it doubtless has tax advantages too.

German companies used to have the right to choose between a standard and advanced model when producing their accounts. Most DAX companies chose the latter as it is felt the market pays a premium for the extra information. Smaller, more tightly held companies were less concerned about the market and unworried about the prospect of takeover, so they were prepared to suffer the discount that goes with relative opacity. The European Commission decision in February 2001 has changed all that. From 2005 German companies, as in the rest of the EEC countries, will report on the basis of International Accounting Standards (IAS). This change is neither insignificant nor cosmetic. Its aim is to harmonize standards. The differences are well set out in the Deutsche Bundesbank's comparison of accounting standards (Monthly Report June 2002). There was a belated consensus on IAS 39 which covers hedge accounting. Meanwhile German companies which seek a Wall Street quotation must comply with US GAAP.

Reconciling US GAAP and IAS is a labour of Hercules. And from July 2002 there are the provisions of the Sarbanes-Oxley Act (SOX) which will apply to German companies with quotations on US exchanges. Details of these are listed in Chapter 5.

The Bundesbank article describes the differences succinctly:

In contrast to the German commercial balance sheet, a financial statement drawn up according to IAS or US GAAP does not serve to measure distributable profit, let alone to measure distributable profit prudently. The tried and tested system of German GAAP based on the Commercial Code prevents income from being reported before gains have actually been realized or the risk of loss has been permanently averted. Financial statements drawn up according to international accounting standards are geared solely towards providing information considered relevant for investors' decisions, in particular, and are designed to give a true and fair view of a company's assets, financial situation and profitability.

We have noted below some of the problems that emerged in the Daimler-Chrysler merger which reflected the systemic differences The differences came under the spotlight in 1993 in the course of the DaimlerChrysler merger, because Daimler wanted a quotation on the NYSE and were required to conform to US GAAP; this meant presenting the figures both ways. The German shareholders were not best pleased to discover Daimler had hidden reserves of $2.4 billion—some of which might well have been distributed to them. The point is that German shareholders do know every year what proportion of income is being retained in reserves, but have no idea what happens to it afterwards. A spate of actions ensued. A settlement was proposed in which shareholders would receive $300 million from the company.

Two other laws are the Reform on Company Act (Bilanzrechts Reform Gesetz), which will deal with the scope of services like tax advice, IAS, and the disclosure of auditors' fees; and one dealing with the oversight of the audit profession (Abschlusspruferaufsichts Gesetz) which will introduce a new independent body (APAK) to cover the quality control system and public oversight.

A third law is in the pipeline (possibly in July 2005—for a Financial Reporting Enforcement Panel, Lian Kontroll Gesetz). It will be dealing with the review of financial statements but its precise provisions have yet to be finalized.

Industrial relations

Although good industrial relations are essential for the long-term well-being of a company and of all the employees in it, paragraphs on this subject are not prominent in works on corporate governance systems in most countries, or at best are regarded as peripheral. In Germany, however, good industrial relations are much nearer centre stage and it is appropriate to start with them, taking in sequence unions, works councils, and company boards.

Unions

Germany has a simple union structure, introduced by the UK after the war and based on industry not craft. The consultative arrangements operate harmoniously, though some unions, notably metalworkers and printers, are more militant than others. At one time some unionists were inspired by political rather than economic motives, but the collapse of Communism has discredited the overt pursuit of political objectives by industrial means.

Works councils

Works councils have existed in Germany since the enactment of the Betrieb-statutungsgesetz of 1920. After the Nazis, a new law was passed in 1952, the Betriebsverfassungsgesetz—the Works Councils Act. Amended in a new law in January 1972, and amended again in 2001 to take account of alteration in the methods of work and in technology, this lays down the rights of the body representing workers' interests at plant level in private (i.e. non-state) companies. The definition of 'worker' has been extended to include trainees, external workers, and employees using telephonic means of communication. In practice the Act covers virtually all German businesses except the miniscule. In the case of bigger businesses there will be a main works council to which the others are joined. The size of a council is relative to the size of the establishment. Its members are chosen, for a period of four years, by election from the workforce, whether an individual worker belongs to a union or not. The council has to meet quarterly at least; its members continue receiving pay for the time they spend on their duties, and woe betide any management that tries to bully them or discriminate against them.

The business of the councils is, broadly speaking, all matters appertaining to conditions of employment: hours, flexible working, overtime, payment, leave, safety at work, incentives, suggestion schemes. Councils negotiate agreements with their employers, and there is a conciliation procedure if they fail—a committee with a neutral chairman which can make a binding settlement. The works council also has rights of co-determination in the case of dismissals, in the field of employees' vocational training, and in the case of grievances.

In bigger companies (those with more than 100 employees), there must also be a small economic committee. This does not have rights of co-determination but rights to information—and these are extensive, including information on:

> the economic and financial situation of the company;
> the production and sales situation;
> the investment programme;
> rationalization projects and closures;
> organizational changes, including mergers;
> proposed changes in method.

The idea behind the works councils is that co-determination, that is the right to participate in decisions (about matters that affect them, plus getting crucial background information about the enterprise), should promote trust, cooperation, and harmony. What actually seems to happen is that this helps improve the whole network of relationships between employer and employee, because the mere existence of a formal right to be consulted ensures that informal discussions occur. And the supply of information forms the background for participation at board level.

It must not be imagined that employers regard works councils as superfluous structures, inflicted on them by a socialistic state. They are an embodiment of the attitude of cooperation rather than confrontation. Employers believe that informed and trusted employees are more likely to have the welfare of the business at heart, to be sympathetic to its aims and understanding of its problems—and it would seem they are. The price employers pay is that action is slowed and any promised change can be turned into a bargaining counter: 'If you want A, we demand B.' Cooperation comes at a price.

The relationship of works councils to trade unions is particularly interesting. The unions have sole bargaining rights on basic pay and conditions, backed by a right to strike; agreements are on a regional basis (roughly but not precisely corresponding to the Länder boundaries). Works councils do not have the right to strike and must deal with disagreements through the conciliation procedures and ultimately, if necessary, through the labour courts. The councils do not formally have bargaining rights, but in practice enjoy them for all matters outside the unions' domain. They will negotiate, for instance, on terms and conditions, above those agreed nationally. The more heavily unionized a firm is, the more likely it is that union officials will be elected as members of the works councils. There may even be tension between unions and works councils, with the former worrying that the latter are muscling in on their territory; if union members see councils negotiating deals above the nationally agreed minimums, for instance, the unions may find themselves being criticized. Some unionists as a consequence would prefer a shop steward system, which would keep the power more firmly in their hands. If, however, a firm is not unionized, management is in a better position to impose its will on a works council unless the employee representatives have strong characters.

Employees on the board

We shall examine the German board system in detail later. Suffice it to say here that all big companies have a supervisory tier (Aufsichtsrat), as well as a management board (Vorstand). As far back as 1920/2 legislation provided for two members of the works council to sit on the Aufsichtsrat, but the Nazis abolished this provision in January 1934. In March 1947, the British military government accepted the German trade unions' request for seats on the Aufsichtsrat and the employers agreed for fear of getting something worse. There were intense discussions in the following years and threatened strikes. A series of laws followed, the last one of which was the Co-determination Act of May 1976. The law not only sets out the proportions of employee and shareholder representatives but also requires that one of the directors on the management board shall have special responsibility for labour matters.

At one time the unions and management struggled about the limits of employees' rights and in particular about the casting vote of a shareholder chairman of the supervisory tier. The present arrangements are frequently a matter of discussion as they are (like most systems!) flawed. There has been a suggestion for instance that rather than having employees on the Aufsichtsrat, there should be a consultative board for them which would have the right to information but no decision-making powers. I did not gain the impression that a change on these lines was imminent.

For the most part shareholders and employee representatives on the Aufsichtsrat share management's concern about the prosperity of the enterprise and would much rather proceed by cooperation than confrontation. They therefore respond best when treated well and trusted, but can get spiky when they are not. The existence of a formal obligation to inform and consult often means that there are extensive prior consultations to run over the ground, for example, on complex accounts (which as members of the supervisory board the employee representatives must approve). The employees take a long-term view of the business and are relatively unconcerned about dividends; their general view is quite close to that of the banks (though of course they have their particular interests like pay and conditions to pursue). They would, for instance, be wholly supportive of a company being prudent in its accounting by tucking 'profits' away for a rainy day. Nowadays they participate in committees of the board which give them additional insights. These are discussed below.

Although employees routinely see confidential information, there is no recorded case of their having released it (though others, such as directors' wives and disaffected secretaries, have).

Trade unions value the system highly, even though it can cause awkward conflicts of interest for their members. There is common ground that it results in employees' representatives being better informed and in their taking a more rational approach to problems: and it is seen to have a political benefit. As one industrialist put it to me, 'No employee has ever walked off an Aufsichtsrat even though there was a strike on and near rioting in the streets.' Lufthansa is an interesting case of the strengths and weaknesses of the system. In 1992 it faced several problems and these were discussed jointly by employees, unions, Vorstand, and Aufsichtsrat, although all parties knew that painless solutions were impossible. In the event it involved job losses and a pay freeze as well as a concession by management on the proposed structure. More recently it was an employee member of the Aufsichtsrat who was also a Trade Unionist, who called a damaging strike. This pointed up his conflict of interest and loyalty. Which should prevail, the company or his members' immediate interests?

My interlocutors felt that the principle of co-determination would be unworkable on a unitary board. It follows that they preferred a two-tier system. Besides, they liked the clarity of having a defined division of function.

For as long as I can remember employees have had reservations about employees being on the Aufsichtsrat. *Les Échos* in Paris on the weekend of 12/ 13 September 2004 commented that employee organizations BDA and BDI had gone on record against the system, quoting M. Rogowski the BDI president as saying co-determination was an 'error of history' and a 'waste of time'. Perhaps, but there is, it seems plenty of life in it yet.

Types of company

General

German law provides for various types of framework for business ranging from partnerships to PLCs, but most of German industry is carried out by two types of incorporated company, namely:

1. GmbH (Gesellschaft mit beschränkter Haftung; i.e. a company with limited liability);
2. AG (Aktiengesellschaft; i.e. a 'share company'); 75 of the top 100 companies were in this form in 2002.

There are some significant German companies which do not fall into either of these categorizes, and are hybrids. The background to these is often that the family has retained and wishes to maintain control. An example is the KGaA company (Kommanditgesellschaft auf Aktien), in which one group of shareholders have limited liability and the other group, who run the business, are personally liable with all of their assets.

The Monopolkommission report 'Netzwetterbewerb durch Regulierung' of 2002 provides some interesting data about the shape of German industry and commerce. At the end of 2001 there were about 3.31 million companies domiciled in Germany. Of these about 1.35 million were subsidiaries, of which more than 900,000 were controlled by a majority shareholder, i.e. an ultimate owner. More than half of these—500,000—were in a group with two or more other companies. Around 21,000 German subsidiaries were controlled by a foreign owner. Altogether there are nearly 137,000 groups of companies in Germany of which around 27,000 are ultimate owners which as German companies themselves belong to the group. (The other owners are not companies—they are natural persons, foundations, or territorial authorities, or they are domiciled abroad.)

Groups differ sharply. The average is three or four companies but the ten biggest groups, each with more than 500, average 1,000. The biggest, with 2,683, was the federal agency related to Reunification (BvS). E.ON AG had 1,086. The service sector accounts for about 60% of these companies, 20% are in the 'producing sector', and 20% in trade, hotels, and catering.

Such data do not tell us much about individual companies but the report goes on to mention 'value added' as a measure of size and it seems that the biggest companies are drawing away from the rest. The average increase in value added was 4.19% over the preceding period (1996–8) but the hundred biggest companies had increased by 11.58% (to about 274 billion euros).

Unlimited partnerships

One structure to be found among even major German companies is the unlimited partnership. (The Monopolkommission in 1984/5 noted that ten of the top 100 companies were not joint stock companies (p. 446), and were therefore presumably partnerships.) The partners between them own the business and if it failed would be personally liable for its debts. The partnership as such does not pay tax but each partner does, depending on his or her emoluments and personal tax position. Such a partnership may have a limited liability company (GmbH or AG) as a subsidiary. The laws governing works councils apply to the partnership, but not the laws about boards. There is formally no supervisory tier, so there are no employee representatives, though the partners may if they choose appoint an advisory committee. If they do there is nothing to prevent someone serving on both management and advisory committees. The advantages of such a structure are its total freedom from market pressure and the threat of takeover; its disadvantages include the impossibility of tapping the capital markets and, of course, personal liability. It works best when partners are content to see profits ploughed back (the main source of new money), and are not in a hurry to realize their investment. Some big businesses have run like this for years; the history of Merck is illuminating.

Merck of Darmstadt is more than 200 years old, and its turnover amounted to nearly DM 3.8 billion in 1991 (DM 4.6 billion if the Lipha group is included), and it then employed over 25,000 people in 42 countries. The partners' equity in 1991 stood at DM 1,344.9 million. It finally went public in 1995 as a KGaA, though the family still holds 73.8% of the capital. 168 companies in 56 countries are fully consolidated in the financial statements. They employ over 34,000 people with sales of 7,202 million euros.

Nationalized industries

In one way or another the Western German state found itself owning or having interest in an extraordinarily wide range of commercial and industrial operations—not just heavy industry and utilities like the railways, the water industry, and telecoms but also enterprises such as travel agencies, hotels, and even the Bonn Press Club. There were almost 400 enterprises involved. It has been government policy for some time to extricate itself from enterprises it did not need to run: Deutsche Telekom and Lufthansa are cases in point. Even so Germany still has a number of nationalized industries, and they have the AG structure. The main difference is in the composition of the Aufsichtsrat, to which the state, as controlling shareholder, makes the nominations. It frequently chooses officials and junior ministers. If a left-wing minister is appointed he may vote with the employee representatives and thus give them a majority. Denationalization of the railways would require an amendment to the Federal constitution and therefore a two-thirds majority in Parliament. Apart from these points there is no particular aspect that impinges on governance.

The integration of East Germany after reunification was facilitated by the Treuhandanstalf, which set about privatization with a vengeance. But the fixing of the exchange rate on the basis of 1 : 1 meant in the opinion of one commentator that the wages of new Länder reached the level of the USA while productivity of the whole of East Germany was only that of Mexico.

Number of companies

Considering the size of the economy, few German companies are quoted—only 774 out of the 2,806 AGs in Germany at the end of 2001. A large proportion of industry is in the hands of unquoted AGs and GmbHs: small businesses (with less than 500 employees or a turnover of less than DM 100 million), usually family owned, account for two-thirds of the workforce, take 86 per cent of the apprentices, and produce nearly half of the GNP. There are about 433,731 private limited liability companies. On the other hand some of the quoted AGs, such as Siemens, Daimler-Benz, and Volkswagen, are big by any standards. (In 1990 their turnovers would have put them above all UK companies except BP and Shell.)

Board Structure

The two-tier principle

From the early days of German industrialization small or medium businesses were managed by their owners. As time went on and shareholdings split and many shareholders were no longer in the business, the general meetings of such companies became too big and the idea was developed of putting control, or at least supervision, into the hands of a committee of the shareholders; joint stock companies were supervised by the state. State supervision was abolished in 1870. Since the last century Germany has had a governance system for all companies with more than 500 employees, based on the premiss that the function of supervising management, which is implied in some other systems, should be made explicit and should be separated. The line between 'direction' and 'management' is always difficult to draw with absolute clarity, and the German system does not attempt it. It simply identifies one particular function (supervision), sets bounds to it, and places it in the hands of a separate body of people (the Aufsichtsrat). One of the reasons underlying this division is that the stronger management is (and arguably needs to be) the less safe it is to assume that its interests coincide with those of the owners of the business. Thus all the functions of direction and management are placed in the hands of the management board—the Vorstand—except appointment to the Vorstand itself, which is the responsibility of the supervisory tier—the Aufsichtsrat. All AGs must have a Vorstand; GmbH companies have a managing director (Geschäftsführer).

In small GmbH companies—those with fewer than 500 employees—the structure is simple. The business is run by the Geschäftsführer, who is appointed by a resolution of the shareholders, or if permitted by the Articles of Association (Satzung) by a committee of shareholders or the advisory board if they have one—the Beirat. There is no requirement to have a board, but the Satzung may permit more than one managing director. If there is no supervisory organ the managing director is accountable directly to the shareholders.

In the bigger GmbH companies the principle of co-determination applies and they must have a supervisory tier—and this is true even where the shares are in one man's hands. The determining factor is the number of employees: the structure therefore consists of the management board (the Vorstand) and the Aufsichtsrat on which shareholders have two-thirds of the seats; and employees/unions one-third.

The same arrangements and proportions apply to AG companies with fewer than 2,000 employees.

The AG companies with more than 2,000 employees have a similar structure, but the composition of the Aufsichtsrat is different. The total number of seats relates to the number of employees in the company, but the proportion is 50 : 50. In a company with 2,000–10,000 employees, for instance, the board is twelve strong. Typically two of the six employee representatives will be external trade unionists. Note, however, that this only applies to employees working in Germany, and not to those working elsewhere in the company or group. We consider below how this was resolved in the DaimlerChrysler merger.

But there are more subtleties. Of the employee representatives one must come from the salaried and one from the executive staff. The chairman is always drawn from the shareholders' representatives. If a vote is deadlocked a second vote is taken and he has two votes, a right he cannot delegate. Coal, iron, and steel companies form a separate category, in that the chairman is not drawn from the shareholders, but is neutral (under the Montan Co-determination Act).

The Vorstand

The German system has a different starting point from most others in that the law confers power on the Vorstand as an organ. It is the board, with a massive concentration of power. It is envisaged as an entity and is expected to operate collegiately. The GCGC puts it thus: 'The Vorstand is responsible for independently managing the enterprise. In doing so, it is obliged to act in the enterprise's best interests and undertakes to increase the sustainable value of the enterprise' (4.1.1). The remainder of the section emphasizes its role in developing strategy, implementing it, ensuring sound risk management and control, and complying with the law throughout the group. This description has a different flavour to the 1937 version—'The Vorstand is on its own responsibility to manage the corporation for the good of the enterprise, for the common weal of the people [volk] and the demands of the State [Reich].' This version touches on the role of the company in society, which still matters. GCGC emphasizes the need for transparency (sect. 6) and singles out the holding or disposal of a substantial stake in (6.2). It emphasizes the need to treat all shareholders equally (6.3).

What the Vorstand actually does depends on the size and structure of the business. In a very large company, for instance, the main subsidiaries may have Vorstands (and Aufsichtsrate) of their own and the main board will in effect be a holding company: the Vorstand may be running the German subsidiary of a great multinational like Ford or IBM. But whatever the size, the fundamental fact remains—it is by law the engine of management and no one may instruct it (for reasons which may appear valid in a wider context) to act in a way that is injurious to the business. If, for instance, a foreign owner wished to instruct its German subsidiary to market products that failed in some way to meet German standards, the members of the German Vorstand would have to refuse under threat of personal liability. Again the members of a German Vorstand must satisfy themselves that if they depend on a parent company for finance it will be forthcoming, or they may risk personal liability.

Of course all groups tend to want good leaders and the Vorstand is no different. What the leader is called, and how his role is conceived depend formally on the Aufsichtsrat. The GCGC instructs Vorstands to have a chairman or Sprecher (spokesman) (4.2.1) and in some companies the leadership varies with the role. In law no specific powers are ascribed to the leader. The term Sprecher is commonly found in German companies, the idea being to give the clear impression that the leader of the Vorstand is a *primus inter pares*. In many companies, however, the Sprecher looks more and more like his American counterpart—a CEO. So much depends on the personalities. In some cases the leader of the Vorstand is indeed called 'chairman', which may indicate a more powerful role. The members of the Vorstand generally feel more accountable to the body as a whole than to the Sprecher or chairman alone. One exception to the general rule is where the founder (or a powerful member of the founding family) remains head of the Vorstand. In such cases there may be no doubt who is 'boss' and this casts a quite different light on the collegiality of the board.

As the Sprecher or chairman's role varies so much in accordance with his personality or power, the relative power of his fellow members on the Vorstand must vary also. They often have clearly defined spheres of executive responsibility within the business, but even so, are expected to think and act collegiately rather than as a series of warring barons each trying to defend his own patch. This is also reflected in law. Members of the Vorstand have, to a certain extent, to have an eye on what is going on in their colleagues' departments and can be held liable if they fail to do so. The consensual approach is emphasized. On the Vorstand, when it comes to the crunch—which it seldom does—it is 'one person one vote'. Lack of consensus on the Vorstand *never* implies reference to the Aufsichtsrat. The Vorstand usually meets once a week. Meetings are far from perfunctory and may well last all day.

Commentators on the comparative merits of the supervisory system have been inclined to overlook the important issue of patronage. The power of appointment to the Vorstand lies formally with the supervisory board and requires a two-thirds majority. If a decision is not reached in the first round of voting a simple majority will suffice. This means the employees' representatives can register their feelings but not prevent a nomination going through. The source of nominations is usually the Vorstand itself and the Aufsichtsrat. There have been cases when the Aufsichtsrat has nominated candidates from outside; this is rare, not least because it implies a far higher degree of responsibility for the person's performance than if they had agreed on the internal nominee. And if the Aufsichtsrat does decide to appoint its own nominee the Vorstand has no right of veto. The idea that the Aufsichtsrat is a mere rubber stamp in patronage matters is not borne out by reports especially in difficult times. The position of the Vorstand (in the nominating process) in the big firms, like Volkswagen, is completely different from that in smaller firms (subsidiaries; family-owned AGs).

Indeed, the shareholding structure may affect profoundly the way the process works. If the founding family or a major shareholder is represented on the Aufsichtsrat (or sometimes even if they are not), they are nevertheless in a position to exert influence, and the balance of power may shift substantially away from the Vorstand.

Members of the Vorstand enjoy reasonable security—a deliberate stratagem to prevent boards being 'packed' or over-dominated even after a takeover. They are usually appointed by the Aufsichtsrat for five years (the maximum permitted by law), and can only be dismissed for very good reasons such as gross breach of duty, inability to exercise proper management, or after the passing of a vote of no confidence by the general meeting, provided this is not done arbitrarily. Even in this case the Aufsichtsrat is free to decide whether to dismiss the respective member of the Vorstand or not. A contract may be renewed, but not more than six months before it is due to expire. A Geschäftsführer may however be dismissed at any time regardless of the contractual rights (unless the articles say otherwise), though he remains entitled to his contractual payments.

The Vorstand itself monitors the individual competence of its own members. If a member's performance declines, the treatment he gets will depend on his age and the gravity of the situation. Whenever possible he will be allowed to serve out his contract, though his position may be made clear to all by the appointment of a deputy. If he is asked to retire early it will be done discreetly and generously: the Aufsichtsrat alone has the power to compel a member of a Vorstand to stand down. Neither the Vorstand itself nor the shareholders in general meetings can do so.

According to the Korn/Ferry International study (2003: 12), 40% of German companies have a management succession committee or process.

Remuneration

The remuneration of top executives is under the spotlight in a way that would have been unthinkable a decade ago, but is still modest by international standards. The largest shareholders' organization, Deutsche Schutz-vereinigung für Wertpapierbesitz (DSW), published a survey on directors' pay in 2003 putting it in the context of foreign wrangles such as those affecting GlaxoSmithKline and Richard Grasso of the New York Stock Exchange.

DSW divided the thirty companies at the top of the DAX index into two groups—those who disclosed top executive salaries, bonuses, and share options in line with the German corporate governance code (updated on 21 May 2003) and those that did not. Only six did so. The code requires individual disclosure but twenty-three firms presented figures for the Vorstand as a whole. DSW did get a generally helpful response to its supplementary enquiry but felt that transparency still left much to be desired and fell short of the new requirement to disclose the main pillars of pay components and the changes that have taken place.

As to numbers, the average pay of executives in the top thirty DAX companies was 1.16 million euros in 2001, 1,279 million euros in 2002, and 1,420 million euros in 2003, up 11%; the average profit of DAX 30 companies rose 30% during the same period. The pattern is inconsistent.

Twelve companies' earnings decreased; executive pay did not—indeed in five cases it rose and in three of these the company made a loss! The company that paid the most paid roughly 3.4 million euros more than number 30 on the list. The CEO or Sprecher received on average 1.75 times the amount paid to colleagues. DSW likes remuneration to reflect performance by way of bonus which it feels should be linked to earnings. It also complains about a dearth of information about pensions. (Tables 2.1 and 2.2 cover the DAX 30. Table 2.1 shows the breakdown into fixed and variable; Table 2.2 shows the relationship with earnings per share.) The revision to the GCGC in July 2003 was in the direction of greater disclosure.

The process by which the remuneration of members of the Vorstand is determined was changed by a revision of the GCGC on 4 July 2003. Thereafter a plenary session of the Aufsichtsrat, not just a committee (praesidial or remuneration), was required to discuss the structure of remuneration and review it regularly. The revision also mandated demanding reference standards for stock options etc. and gave instructions about publicizing them (website; annual report). The revision also recommends the publication of details of each member of the Vorstand, not just as a group.

There has been much more activity in regard to top executive pay than there used to be—witness the wrath of activists in regard to the pay of the CEO of Deutsche Bank, Josef Ackermann (mentioned in the *Financial News*, 15–21 March 2004). More examples are given below of institutional shareholder activity.

Although companies are not required by the Kodex to have remuneration committees, it has plenty to say about composition and composition. GCGC 5.4 stresses the need for independence, appropriate skills, and the need to avoid conflicts of interest. Not more than two ex-members of the Vorstand may sit on the Aufsichtsrat. And the principles of remuneration are laid down in 5.4–5—fixed and performance related, the latter embracing long-term elements.

German companies have been most reluctant to reveal the remuneration of individual directors, a fact that has caused public indignation and political criticism (from Hans Eichel, the Finance Minister, and Horst Köhler, the Federal President, among others). There is indeed a threat to legislate on the subject unless a significant number of companies have produced the figures by the summer of 2005. A draft European Commission recommendation goes even further.

The French newspaper *Les Échos*, quoting a DSW report, listed twenty people (28–29 November 2004) (Table 2.3).

Table 2.1. DSW survey on directors' pay of the DAX 30 companies 2003 (€)

Rank	Company	Average remuneration per director in 2002	Average remuneration per director in 2001	Percentage change 2001–2002	Proportion fix/var.* 2002		Proportion fix/var.* 2001	
23	Adidas-Salomon[a]	959,181	928,693	3.28	49.2	50.8	53.4	46.6
12	Allianz[ac]	1,386,869	1,439,691	−3.67	45.6	54.4	42.02	57.98
13	Altana[ab]	1,212,446	1,466,667	−17.33	27.36	72.64	20	80
10	BASF[a]	1,497,797	1,062,857	40.92	32.35	67.65	—	—
24	Bayer[bc]	848,898	948,886	−10.54	47.5	52.5	49.3	50.7
8	BMW[a]	1,551,499	1,531,429	1.31	18.49	81.51	19.4	80.6
14	Commerzbank	1,189,389	1,237,454	−3.88	—	44.16	—	55.5
20	Continental[a]	967,742	495,356	95.36	50	50	—	—
1	DaimlerChrysler[a]	3,694,545	1,600,000	130.91	26.38	73.62	—	—
2	Deutsche Bank[abc]	2,063,500	2,936,925	−29.74	32.49	67.51	13.02	86.98
27	Deutsche Börse[b]	621,404	552,200	12.53	52.69	47.31	—	—
22	Deutsche Post[a]	964,798	682,353	41.39	51.35	48.65	—	—
5	Deutsche Telekom[a]	1,677,731	1,581,714	6.07	60	40	50	50
9	E.ON[a]	1,507,692	1,353,846	11.36	46.94	53.06	45.45	54.55
29	Fresenius Medical Care[a]	521,095	662,645	−21.36	100	0	100	0
17	Henkel	1,053,947	1,100,606	−4.24	41.99	48.01	42.61	57.39
18	Hypo-Vereinsbank	1,043,841	1,944,210	−46.31	60	40	56.52	43.48
30	Infineon Technologies[a]	278,261	202,435	37.46	100	—	100	—
15	Linde[a]	1,107,386	950,000	16.57	40.21	59.79	37.57	62.43
25	Deutsche Lufthansa[a]	787,234	531,915	48.00	53	47	72	28
28	MAN[a]	535,238	530,000	0.99	70.53	29.47	69.24	30.76

6	Metro[a]	1,663,158	1,621,053	2.60	50.63	49.37	—	—
19	Münchener Rück	982,609	638,298	53.94	54.87	45.13	57.33	42.67
11	RWE	1,429,688	1,403,238	1.88	44.53	55.47	—	—
21	SAP[ab]	966,115	1,217,620	−20.66	46.9	53.1	37.65	62.35
4	Schering[d]	1,713,211	1,609,507	6.44	24.9	75.1	27.2	72.8
7	Siemens[a]	1,588,946	984,456	61.40	50	50	30.44	69.56
26	ThyssenKrupp[ab]	775,400	784,314	−1.14	59.41	40.59	62.5	—
16	TUI[a]	1,098,222	971,111	13.09	55.32	44.68	57.59	42.41
3	Volkswagen[a]	1,821,884	1,940,050	−6.09	—	71.37	—	—

[a] DSW calculation.

[b] Individualized disclosure in 2002.

[c] Figures 2002 based on directors being active as of 31 Dec. 2002.

[d] Individualized disclosure of CEO remuneration.

Table 2.2. DSW survey on directors' pay of the Dax 30 companies 2004 (€)

Rank	Company	Average remuneration per director in 2003	Average remuneration per director in 2002	Percentage change	CEO remuneration 2003	Earnings per share 2003	Earnings per share 2002	Change in earnings per share
1	Deutsche Bank[ad]	3.726 m.	2.064 m.	80.57	7.7 m.	2.44	0.64	↑
2	DaimlerChrysler	2.985 m.	3.695 m.	−19.22	5.2 m.	0.44	4.68	↓
3	E.ON	2.800 m.	1.600 m.	75.00	4.9 m.	7.11	4.26	↑
4	SAP[1]	2.182 m.	0.885 m.	146.61	3.4 m.	3.48	1.63	↑
5	Siemens[h]	2.051 m.	1.598 m.	28.38	3.6 m.	2.75	1.87	↑
6	Schering[c]	1.876 m.	1.702 m.	10.22	2.2 m.	2.28	2.35	→
7	RWE[bd]	1.670 m.	1.430 m.	16.81	2.5 m.	1.69	2.40	↓
8	Metro	1.621 m.	1.663 m.	−2.53	2.8 m.	1.52	1.36	↑
9	Deutsche Telekom[bf]	1.609 m.	1.670 m.	−3.66	2.6 m.	0.30	−5.86	↑
10	Allianz	1.594 m.	1.387 m.	14.93	2.8 m.	4.77	−4.44	↑
11	BMW	1.585 m.	1.552 m.	2.71	2.8 m.	2.89	3.00	↓
12	VW	1.534 m.	1.822 m.	−15.81	2.7 m.	2.84	6.72	↑
13	Henkel[e]	1.401 m.	1.257 m.	11.46	2.2 m.	3.44	3.06	↑
14	BASF[f]	1.258 m.	1.498 m.	−16.01	2.2 m.	1.62	2.60	↓
15	Linde	1.155 m.	1.198 m.	−3.57	max. 2.3 m.	0.91	2.01	→
16	Deutsche Börse[af]	1.155 m.	0.724 m.	59.55	2.2 m.	2.20	2.18	→
17	Münchener Rück	1.100 m.	0.983 m.	11.95	1.9 m.	−2.25	1.54	↓
18	Deutsche Post[b]	1.098 m.	0.871 m.	26.06	1.7 m.	1.18	0.59	↑
19	TUI	1.089 m.	1.098 m.	−0.81	1.9 m.	1.54	0.18	↑
20	Infineon	1.078 m.	0.835 m.	29.17	1.9 m.	−0.60	−1.47	↑
21	Altana[a]	0.994 m.	1.214 m.	−18.06	1.7 m.	2.53	2.37	↑

22	Continental	0.973 m.	0.49	1.7 m.	2.37	1.75	↑
23	Adidas-Salomon	0.943 m.	4.23	1.65 m.	5.72	5.04	↑
24	Commerzbank[c]	0.915 m.	−23.07	1.42 m.	−4.26	−0.56	→
25	Bayer[ad]	0.911 m.	2.22	1.6 m.	−1.86	1.45	→
26	Hypo-Vereinsbank	0.900 m.	−13.82	1.4 m.	−4.92	−1.51	→
27	ThyssenKrupp[af]	0.887 m.	12.21	1.4 m.	1.01	0.42	↑
28	MAN	0.630 m.	17.73	0.9 m.	1.54	0.92	↑
29	FMC[g]	0.448 m.	−14.03	0.8 m.	3.42	3.00	↑
30	Lufthansa[f]	0.433 m.	−45.04	0.8 m.	−2.58	1.88	→
	Average peak	1.420 m.	11.02	2.43 m.			
	Average peak (excl. Deutsche Bank and DaimlerChrysler)	**1.282 m.**	10.04	2.14 m.			

[a] Individual disclosure since 2002.
[b] Individual disclosure since 2003.
[c] CEO payment disclosed individually.
[d] Figures based on directors being active as of the end of the financial year.
[e] Earnings per preference share.
[f] Average remuneration includes remuneration for the deputy CEO.
[g] Earnings per share in USD.
[h] Earnings per share 2002 adjusted to exceptional capital profit.

Table 2.3. The best-paid top men

Name	Company	Remuneration(€)
Josef Ackermann	Deutsche Bank	7,700,000
Jürgen E. Schrempp	DaimlerChrysler	5,200,000
Wulf H. Bernotat	E.ON	4,900,000
Heinrich von Pierer	Siemens	3,600,000
Henning Kagermann	SAP	3,400,000
Hans-Joachim Körber	Metro	2,800,000
Michael Diekmann	Allianz	2,800,000
Helmut Panke	BMW	2,800,000
Bernd Pischetsrieder	Volkswagen	2,700,000
Kai-Uwe Ricke	Deutsche Telekom	2,600,000
Harry Roels	RWE	2,500,000
Wolfgang Reitzle	Linde	2,300,000
Hubertus Erlen	Schering	2,200,000
Ulrich Lehner	Henkel	2,200,000
Jürgen Hambrecht	BASF	2,200,000
Werner G. Seifert	Deutsche Börse	2,200,000
Hans-Jürgen Schinzler	Münich Ré	1,900,000
Michael Frenzel	TUI	1,900,000
Ulrich Schumacher	Infineon	1,900,000
Klaus Zumwinkel	Deutsche Post	1,700,000

Source: DSW survey quoted in *Les Échos*, 28–29 November 2004.

The Aufsichtsrat

Functions

The area of the Aufsichtsrat's authority is prescribed by law and covers:

- the company's accounts for a specified period (usually quarterly);
- major capital expenditure and strategic acquisitions; closures;
- appointments to the Vorstand;
- approving the dividend;
- management compensation (Cromme Commission 2003).

This list is often extended by a company's articles, but even so the function of the Aufsichtsrat used to be limited to approval or disapproval. The GCGC (5.1) says: 'The task of the Aufsichstrat is to advise regularly and supervise the Vorstand in the management of the enterprise. It must be involved in decisions of fundamental importance to the enterprise.' Even so we can say that the Vorstand proposes, the Aufsichtsrat disposes. Properly speaking, therefore, Germany does not have two-tier boards and much misunderstanding flows from so describing them.

The primary function of the Aufsichtsrat is to ensure the competence of the Vorstand, whose members it has the power to appoint and dismiss. It should ensure there is adequate succession planning (5.1.2). To act effectively it needs to be able to operate collegiately itself—which imposes a considerable burden of leadership upon the chairman, who has to build a consensus. The chairman needs to know what is happening. GCGC 5.2 is specific about his maintaining contact with the Sprecher of the Vorstand and that he must summon the Aufsichtsrat if the facts demand it. A second important function is the approval of the annual profit-and-loss statement and balance sheet prepared by the Vorstand. Both are audited by independent public accountants who report to the Aufsichtsrat and can be questioned by it. The Aufsichtsrat must also approve the dividend. According to the GCGC, 'The Aufsichtsrat shall regularly evaluate its efficiency.' It is unclear how many do so and by what means, as reports of such activity are sparse.

The formal time commitment of members of an Aufsichtsrat is considerably less than that of a non-executive director in the UK, reflecting the smaller number of meetings—three or four a year. There will, however, be other informal meetings, and preparatory work. Bankers are particularly well placed to cope because of the support they get, or they could not assume the loads they bear. Ornamental directors and 'Frühstück' directors (so called because of their partiality for late lunches) are going out of fashion. It seems that as the role of the Aufsichtsrat is taken ever more seriously the queue of candidates for them has shrunk. The new technology companies pose problems. The judgements to be made on propositions put by the Vorstand require a technical understanding that few members of an average Aufsichtsrat would normally possess, though they may set up special committees to deal with particular problems. The Aufsichtsrat may, moreover, appoint inspectors on matters of concern to it, who will have to report back direct, not through the Vorstand.

The importance of the presence of employee representatives should not be overlooked. It is true that their absolute power is limited by the chairman's casting vote and ultimately by the general meeting, but Germans hate such conflicts and strain to avoid them. (Sometimes the employee members actually push for a vote knowing it will be adverse, just to show colleagues they did their utmost, or to create an impasse which it would be appropriate to settle in the courts.) The employee members can use their position to bargain for other advantages. For example, by threatening to vote down an appointment to the Vorstand they may secure some concessions elsewhere; in fact. However, if they feel strongly that a person should not be appointed to the Vorstand, he is unlikely to go forward. On the other hand they have been known to acquiesce peaceably in the appointment of a hard man when the circumstances clearly required one. We have noted elsewhere the modern tendency for the Vorstand and the shareholder members of the Aufsichtsrat to caucus together before a full meeting to iron out points better not raised in front of the employee representatives in case management authority might be undermined.

The employee representatives sometimes bring an otherwise comatose Aufsichtsrat to life, typically in enterprises dominated by the family or a parent company. In such cases there is often a danger of the Aufsichtsrat being purely nominal, as the family or parent company will control the Vorstand directly and bypass it. The fact that the Aufsichtsrat does have legal duties and that the employees have rights can stop this happening; management must at the very least prepare its case and justify its proposals (and the accounts).

When looking at the German system it is the supervisory tier and union representation on it that tends to attract much of the attention. It is easy to overlook the important part played by the works councils. Through them flows a stream of information which enables the employee representatives on the Aufsichtsrat to play a fuller, proper part in its deliberations. Many major proposals for change will necessarily have been discussed in the works councils, so that by the time the matter reaches the Aufsichtsrat some difficulties will have been eased; many companies have special committees to help in this predigesting process. All this consultation may help but it does not necessarily produce agreement; Aufsichtsrat debates do go to genuinely contested votes. In describing the system the outside commentator has to guard against making it sound as if best practice is universally followed. The Germans themselves are clear it is not (see below).

The Aufsichtsrat is largely dependent for its information on what the Vorstand provides but it can investigate subjects directly which it wishes to consider more deeply. There are three main incentives for members of the Aufsichtsrat to take a keen interest in what is going on. The first is their personal reputation, which would suffer from association with failure. The second is that they (particularly banks' representatives) are often 'interested' in the technical sense through shareholdings or loans or in some other way, any of which mean that the prosperity and survival of the business would be of great importance to them or their employees. The third is the law—if they neglect their duties they may be personally liable.

In practice, they ratify proposals put before them by the chairman, who within the company will normally have consulted other members of the board and the Sprecher of the Vorstand. He may also consult interested parties outside the company, particularly the banks. Indeed, a good chairman of the Aufsichtsrat would regard it as a danger signal if a candidate looked too 'comfortable' to the management. In some companies, however, the boot is on the other foot. The Vorstand effectively selects the members of the Aufsichtsrat.

The members of the Aufsichtsrat other than the employee representatives are appointed by the general meeting of shareholders for a period of four years (but de facto, five). According to the 2003 Korn/Ferry International annual board of directors study (p. 8), the average size is sixteen members. In some companies the founding family still effectively have a power of appointment—even one as big as Siemens, where the family have 1% of the shares but 10% of the votes; as no one else has anything like as many they are able still to exercise a substantial power of patronage. Shareholders may have a statutory right to a board seat (which is not a rare case for founders, even though they may be minority shareholders) (Section 101, Stock Corporation Act). As to security of tenure, it takes a 75% vote of those cast to remove prematurely a member of the Aufsichtsrat. The reality is that many companies are controlled by a major shareholder who picks the members of the Aufsichtsrat to suit him; they are the objects of his patronage and there to do his bidding. They may formally pass all the tests of independence but their sense of obligation negates their freedom.

Committees of the board

It has always been free to appoint committees when it wished to do so, but now the Aufsichtsrat is told 'it shall form committees with sufficient expertise ... to increase its efficiency and the handling of complex issues'[GCGC 5.3]. Committee chairmen report to it. An audit committee is required (5.3.2) and its chairman should not be a former member of the Vorstand. But, whereas an audit committee is required ('shall') a remuneration committee is voluntary ('may') (5.3.4).

To those who have more shall be given

In Germany senior and respected members of the commercial community tend to collect numerous appointments, as they do elsewhere. Table 2.4, compiled by DSW in 2003, sets out their analysis of some of the leading personalities. Female directors are few and far between across Europe, 6.4% in Germany, 5.8% in the UK, which is the average. It is also illuminating to consider Table 2.5—the shareholder representatives on the board of Allianz (ages as of 31 December 2002) with DSW's view on their independence—half were independent—and then to consider the part they play on board committees alongside employee representatives.

Table 2.4. Leading personalities in German commerce

Name	SB mandates	No. of SB mandates (DAX30)	Effective committee chairs	Effective committee memberships	Assessed SB chairs ($\times 10$)	Assessed committee chairs ($\times 8$)	Assessed committee memberships ($\times 6$)	Simple SB memberships ($\times 4$)	Final (Former) score	CEO profession
Manfred Schneider	Allianz, Bayer (C). DaimlerChrysler, Linde (C), Metro, RWE, TUI	7	6	5	2	1	3	1	50	Former CEO of Bayer
Karl-Hermann Baumann	Deutsche Bank, E.ON, Linde, Schering, Siemens (C), ThyssenKrupp	6	6	3	1	4	1	0	48	
Ulrich Hartmann	Deutsche Bank, Deutsche Lufthansa, E.ON (C), Henkel, Münchener Rück (C)	5	3	4	2	0	2	1	36	Former CEO of E.ON
Gerhard Cromme	Allianz, Deutsche Lufthansa, E.ON, Siemens, ThyssenKrupp (C). Volkswagen	6	2	4	1	0	1	4	32	Former CEO of ThyssenKrupp
Martin Kohlhaussen	Bayer, Commerzbank (C), Infineon Technologies, Schering, ThyssenKrupp	5	1	3	1	0	2	2	30	Former spokesman of the management board of Commerzbank

Name	Mandates									Background
Henning Schulte-Noelle	Allianz (C), E.ON, Siemens, ThyssenKrupp	4	2	3	1	0	2	1	26	Former CEO of Allianz
Paul Achleitner	Bayer, Henkel, MAN, RWE	4	1	3	0	1	2	1	24	CFO of Allianz
Rolf-E. Breuer	Deutsche Bank (C), Deutsche Börse (C), E.ON	3	2	1	2	0	0	1	24	Former spokesman of the management board of Deutsche Bank
Friedel Neuber	RWE (C), ThyssenKrupp, TUI (C)	3	2	1	2	0	0	1	24	Former CEO WestLB
Jürgen Strube	BASF (C), BMW, Commerzbank, Linde	4	1	1	1	0	1	2	24	Former CEO of BASF

Note: C = Chairman.

Table 2.5. Shareholder representatives on the board of Allianz

Name	Ind.	Age[a]	Date appt.	Other positions[b]	Information on current/former profession
Dr Klaus Liesen	NO, as he has a relation with the company for more than 9 years	71	1983	E.ON AG, TUI AG, Volkswagen AG, Beck GmbH & Co. KG	Chairman of the Supervisory Board of E.ON AG
Dr Bernd W. Voss	YES		2002	Continental AG, E.ON AG, KarstadtQuelle AG, Quelle AG, TUI AG, Wacker Chemie GmbH	Member of the Supervisory Board of Dresdner Bank
Dr Dlethart Brelpohl	NO, as he is a former Management Board member	63	2000	Beiersdorf AG, Continental AG, KarstadtQuelle AG, mg technologies AG, KM Europa Metal AG, Banco Popular Espafiol S.A., BPI Banco Portogues de Investimente, Crédit Lyonnais, Les Assurances Générales de France (AGF), Euler & Hermes	Former member of the Managing Board of Allianz AG
Bertrand Collomb	YES	61	1998	ATCO, TotalFina Elf	President, General Director of Lafarge

Name	Age[a]	Since	Other board memberships[b]	Ind.	Current/former position
Jürgen Dormann	62	1998	Lion Bioscience AG, ABB Ltd., IBM Corp.	YES	Former CEO of Aventis SA, former CEO of Hoechst AG, now Chairman of the Supervisory Board of Aventis SA
Dr Uwe Hassen		2002	—	NO, as he is former member of the Management Board	Former member of the Management Board of Allianz AG
Dr Manfred Schnelder	64	1998	DaimlerChrysler AG, Linde AG, Metro AG, RWE AG, TUI AG	NO, as in 2002 he was CEO of Bayer in which Allianz holds a notifiable holding	Former CEO of Bayer AG, now Chairman of the Supervisory Board of Bayer AG
Dr Hermann Scholl	67	1998	BASF AG	YES	Managing director of Robert Bosch GmbH
Jürgen E. Schrempp	58	1998	NYSE, Sasol Ltd., Vodafone Airtouch plc.	YES	CEO of Daimler-Chrysler AG

Note: Ind. = DSW's view as to whether the director is independent.

[a] Age as of 31 December 2002.

[b] Not including other board memberships within the group, but membership in additional supervisory boards.

Table 2.6. Board committees of Allianz

Committee	Member	Shareholder/employee representative
Audit Committee	Dr Liesen	Shareholder representative
	Dr Breipohl	Shareholder representative
	Dr Cromme	Shareholder representative
	Prof. Dr Hickel	Employee representative
	Mr Meyer	Employee representative
Standing Committee	Dr Liesen	Shareholder representative
	Mr Ley	Employee representative
	Dr Schneider	Shareholder representative
	Mr Blix	Employee representative
	Dr Voss	Shareholder representative
Personnel Committee	Dr Liesen	Shareholder representative
	Mr Ley	Employee representative
	Dr Voss	Shareholder representative
Mediation Committee	Dr Liesen	Shareholder representative
	Mr Ley	Employee representative
	Dr Voss	Shareholder representative
	Prof. Dr Hickel	Employee representative

The Monopolkommission reports (op. cit. p. 568) covered links between board members of the top 100 companies (without prejudice to their directorships of other companies). In 2000 37 had members of the Vorstand who were on the Aufsichtsrate of other companies (59 of them). The total number of links through management organs was 139 (down from 152 in 1998).

The Vorstand and Aufsichtsrat—working together: committees of the Aufsichtsrat

Although the functions of the two organs of governance are clearly differentiated, the success of an enterprise depends on their working well together, and having open discussions (3.5). This is made clear both in 5.2 and also in GCGC 3, which talks in terms of close cooperation (3.1) about strategy, matters of material importance, and flows of information. The two bodies have to report annually on corporate governance (3.10). It is becoming common practice for the employers' side of the Aufsichtsrat to caucus with the Vorstand before a formal joint meeting. This enables the members to let their hair down without weakening the managers' authority. The resulting body is not very unlike a unitary board—executives and 'non-executives' sitting together. Another step on the road to convergence.

Besides the Aufsichtsrat and Vorstand themselves there are subsidiary parts of the structure which help create a series of interlocking relationships and assist the effective working of the system.

The use of committees of the board has increased in many countries and Germany is no exception. GCGC 5.3.2 mandates an audit committee (which the chairman of the Aufsichtsrat shall not chair) and points towards other committees such as remuneration and investment and strategy (5.3.3). As these are committees of the Aufsichtsrat, they have at least one employee representative on them.

Audit committees only meet about twice a year which casts a shadow on the control of risk within the company. This in turn exposes the board members to lawsuit and D&O cover is becoming more difficult to obtain, despite the fact that only the company can sue.

The Aufsichtsrat may well set up other small committees (Praesidium or Praesidial committees), which may well include employees' representatives (though they do not always do so). The composition is often the chairman and vice-chairman of the Aufsichtsrat (the vice-chairman always comes from the employees' side) and two or three others, including perhaps the chairman of the works council. This is a convenient forum for handling awkward issues before they reach the whole Aufsichtsrat. The Aufsichtsrat may also create other committees to report to it on certain aspects of the business, for instance, on matters of high technology. A Praesidial committee has the authority to summon members of the Vorstand before it; such a command is taken with the utmost seriousness and careful preparation. Banks in particular may have credit committees to sanction major loans recommended by the Vorstand: this type of committee meets almost every month. As has already been noted there are formal links between the works council and the Aufsichtsrat and the Praesidium.

Shareholders

The types of shares

It is only too easy to underestimate the importance of the formal arrangements under German law in respect of the German system of shareholdings. In GmbHs transfers are by contracts in notarial form, a formal and cumbersome procedure: share certificates are unnecessary and therefore uncommon. Shares in AG companies used to be nearly all in bearer form, but nowadays there are more registered shares especially among insurance companies. Lufthansa shares are registered. Bearer shares need proper custody and transfer arrangements (in which the Central Depositories, Kassenvereine, play an important part), but these technicalities are outside the scope of this chapter. There is, however, an important consequence for the exercise of voting rights. Banks used to act as depositories for bearer shares and this gave them de facto considerable voting power since in practice shareholders were content to let them vote as they chose. Times have changed. Most banks no longer offer such a service as it was unprofitable and the few that do have to get specific instructions before they can vote on behalf of an owner (see below).

Who owns what?

Some people consider that one of the dominant features of the German system is the ownership structure. It is far more concentrated than the UK and USA. Theoretically this means that the Berle-Means analysis does not apply. (They argued that dispersed shareholdings in effect left management unaccountable.) German commentators sometimes argue that although there is therefore less likely to be a conflict between shareholders and entrenched managers, it is more likely there will be conflict of another kind—between majority and minority shareholders. The Stock Corporation Act does provide some protection to minorities who can muster 10% of the voting equity.

The figures are not easy to obtain. In an analysis in the *Company Lawyer* in 2000 it was stated that 85% of German companies had at least one shareholder owning more than 25% of the voting shares; for 57% there is a majority shareholder; and for 225 the holding is big enough to form a blocking minority. Going a little further back in time Mulbert (1998) reported that in 81% of the 435 companies in the first tier of the stock market in 1996, the holding of the five largest shareholders was 50% or more.

Private shareholders are not major shareholders in Germany but over the last decade there has been greater interest in the stock market directly and indirectly.

The switch away from bank deposits has been noted; at the end of 2001 shares were held as in Table 2.7.

Other sources give a rather different breakdown, which is understandable, given that shares are in bearer form. Even so, all the series I have seen, including the Bundesbank numbers, present a different picture from other countries. Foreign holdings tend to be concentrated in the major companies. The average of 16.22% conceals the fact that in many companies 35–40% of the equity is held abroad. In the case of VEBA, for instance, it has reached 49%.

Table 2.7. Share ownership (%)

Private direct holders	14.5
Investment funds[b]	18.1
Companies[c]	31.0
Insurance companies	9.2
Banks[a]	12.3
The Federal and Länder governments	0.6

[a] Includes building and loan associations.
[b] Includes funds open to the general public.
[c] Down from 37.6% at the end of 1996.

Source: PROSHARE share ownership yearbook (2003), 122.

The Deutsches Aktieninstitut, making their own calculations from Bundesbank capital markets and financial accounts statistics, produced Table 2.8.

The pension funds and insurance companies are relatively insignificant with only about 12% between them. This is because German companies used to hold their pension funds on the liability side of the balance sheet of the company as accrued pensions and could use them as working capital. They are not obliged to create a separate trust (or equivalent) in which to house them, but pay a premium to the Pension Guarantee Association to insure these funds. In the public sector, pensions are unfunded.

The investments of pension funds ('Pensions Kassen') are subject to the same rules and regulations as insurance funds, including a limit of 20% of assets held against current obligations being in securities and not more than a 10% stake being held in the share capital of any one Company.

This was at first a consequence of the German Pension Insurance system. The law on the Supervision of Insurance Companies requires that the majority of assets (the so-called 'cover stock', i.e. assets held against current obligations) is subject to a limit of 20% in equity holdings. All assets have to be located in Germany, and there has to be 100% currency matching. Small wonder then that in 1989 German life insurers only had 9.3% of their assets in equities. That said, Allianz is in fact the biggest single shareholder in Germany, a position it consolidated by its purchase of Dresdner: if it takes more than 10% of a company's equity it usually wants a seat on the Aufsichtsrat. The shareholdings and therefore the potential influence of the insurance companies are growing rapidly. Taking all things together, however, it seems that

Table 2.8. Shareholder structure since 1991

Shareholdings of the sectors (€bn)

	Investment funds open to the general public	Direct ownership of shares by households	Enterprises	Government	Banks (incl. building and loan associations)	Insurance enterprises	Investment funds	Rest of the world	Total of all sectors
1991	8.8	143.3	328.0	15.0	88.0	32.1	27.7	73.8	707.9
1992	9.3	134.6	312.2	14.5	88.3	34.9	31.3	65.9	681.7
1993	17.9	190.8	423.7	17.4	121.8	58.7	53.2	89.1	954.7
1994	20.9	189.1	447.9	18.5	121.4	56.2	57.7	82.6	973.4
1995	22.1	203.6	499.0	18.7	147.2	65.6	64.9	85.7	1.084.7
1996	27.2	240.7	581.1	22.4	183.0	79.4	90.3	114.8	1.311.7
1997	48.4	321.3	715.1	35.2	243.9	133.7	153.8	175.2	1.778.2
1998	67.5	388.0	900.6	27.2	279.2	154.2	217.4	253.2	2.219.8
1999	123.7	478.5	986.7	19.7	366.7	219.9	357.4	395.3	2.824.2
2000	141.6	439.4	963.4	16.8	306.1	217.1	383.3	332.9	2.659.0
2001	115.2	348.6	890.0	15.1	279.1	225.8	320.8	341.7	2.421.1
2002	73.6	189.0	476.3	11.3	158.5	193.2	206.8	214.4	1.449.5
2003	89.7	244.7	573.1	15.4	158.9	232.3	238.6	302.2	1.765.2

1991	1.24	20.24	46.33	2.12	12.43	4.53	3.91	10.43	100.0
1992	1.37	19.74	45.80	2.13	12.95	5.12	4.59	9.67	100.0
1993	1.88	19.99	44.38	1.82	12.76	6.15	5.57	9.33	100.0
1994	2.15	19.43	46.01	1.90	12.47	5.77	5.93	8.49	100.0
1995	2.04	18.77	46.00	1.72	13.57	6.05	5.98	7.90	100.0
1996	2.07	18.35	44.30	1.71	13.95	6.05	6.88	8.75	100.0
1997	2.72	18.07	40.21	1.98	13.72	7.52	8.65	9.85	100.0
1998	3.04	17.48	40.57	1.23	12.58	6.95	9.79	11.41	100.0
1999	4.38	16.94	34.94	0.70	12.98	7.79	12.65	14.00	100.0
2000	5.33	16.53	36.23	0.63	11.51	8.16	14.42	12.52	100.0
2001	4.76	14.40	36.76	0.62	11.53	9.33	13.25	14.11	100.0
2002	5.08	13.04	32.86	0.78	10.93	13.33	14.27	14.79	100.0
2003	5.08	13.86	32.47	0.87	9.00	13.16	13.52	17.12	100.0

Table 2.8. (cont'd)

Growth of shareholdings of the sectors (% change from previous year)

	Investment funds open to the general public	Direct ownership of shares by households	Enterprises	Government	Banks (incl. building and loan associations)	Insurance enterprises	Investment funds	Rest of the world	Total of all sectors
1992	6.16	−6.07	−4.82	−3.33	0.34	8.72	13.00	−10.70	−3.70
1993	91.92	41.75	35.71	20.00	37.94	68.19	69.97	35.20	40.05
1994	16.89	−0.89	5.71	6.32	−0.33	−4.26	8.46	−7.30	1.96
1995	5.47	7.67	11.41	1.08	21.25	16.73	12.48	3.75	11.43
1996	23.10	18.22	16.45	19.79	24.32	21.04	39.14	33.96	20.93
1997	77.84	33.49	23.06	57.14	33.28	68.39	70.32	52.61	35.56
1998	39.50	20.76	25.94	−22.73	14.47	15.33	41.35	44.52	24.83
1999	83.31	23.32	9.56	−27.57	31.34	42.61	64.40	56.12	27.23
2000	14.53	−8.17	−2.36	−14.72	−16.53	−1.27	7.25	−15.79	−5.85
2001	−18.65	−20.66	−7.62	−10.12	−8.82	4.01	−16.31	2.64	−8.95
2002	−36.08	−45.78	−46.48	−25.17	−43.21	−14.44	−35.54	−37.25	−40.13
2003	21.85	29.47	20.32	36.28	0.25	20.24	15.38	40.95	21.78
Geom. Mittel	21.31	2.55	3.45	−2.54	5.49	17.72	20.05	10.18	6.73

Sources: Deutsche Bundesbank, Financial accounts for Germany; Deutsche Bundesbank, Capital Market Statistics. Supplement 2 to Monthly Report; own calculations.

German institutional shareholders, other than Allianz, are not generally in a position to play a leading role in corporate governance matters, though they may have an important role in particular companies. Even the investment funds have relatively small equity holdings (about 12.8% 1990, including 2.8% in foreign equities).

Legal proceedings

Shareholders have the right to fight in court decisions made at shareholders meetings, and this may delay changes for years in such matters as changes to the Articles, or equity issues or repurchases.

General meetings

General meetings are mandatory for AG companies. Ordinary meetings decide proposals concerning legal and business operations and, if the Vorstand requests it, proposals concerning the Aufsichtsrat. Extraordinary meetings deal with such matters as mergers or losses equivalent to half the share capital. Following the KonTraG law of 1998, the GCGC (2.1) stipulates 'one share one vote'—no multiple or preferential voting rights, 'golden' shares, or maximum voting rights. The company has to provide the necessary documents, including the report and accounts, and publish them on its Internet site together with the agenda. The meeting resolves on 'the appropriation of net income [2.2.1.] including the dividend and the discharge of the acts of the Vorstand and Aufsichtsrat and as a rule the auditors'. It also deals with the election of the members of the management board and the auditors and the discharge of members of both management and supervisory boards. Decisions are taken by simple majority of those present (but amendments to the company's constitution require a 75% majority). The chairman decides whether to accept a show of hands or have a ballot.

Shareholders holding more than 5% of the shares or a nominal amount of 500,000 euros can propose an additional resolution to the agenda. Counterproposals to a management proposal on the other hand can be lodged by anyone with a single share—but it must not exceed 100 words.

Individual shareholders have right to speak and ask questions (2.2.3) but in fact they seldom attend; however, as they have a right to appoint a proxy, generally a depository bank or shareholders' organization either of which has a duty to suggest how to vote and must follow the instructions they receive, a high proportion of the total voting power will be present in the

Table 2.9. AGM turnouts of the DAX 30 companies (1998–2003) (%)

Company	Included in DAX since/until	Actual listing	1998	1999	2000	2001	2002	2003	3-J-average
Adidas-Salomon AG	since 19.06.98	DAX	(35.10)	43.90	45.44	30.00	31.52	23.17	28.23
Allianz Holding AG		DAX/Eurostoxx	70.92	69.06	60.60	53.70	46.71	39.97	46.79
Altana AG	since 23.09.02	DAX		(76.00)	(71.71)	(65.21)	(~64.00)	63.00	~64.07
BASF AG		DAX/Eurostoxx	53.03	49.48	46.02	43.59	36.82	31.31	37.24
Bayer AG		DAX/Eurostoxx	47.53	44.79	37.53	35.90	33.21	36.00	35.04
Bay. Hypo- u. Wechselbank AG	until 19.06.98		88.20	—	—	—	—	—	—
Bayerische HypoVereinsbank AG[a]		DAX/Eurostoxx	64.10	59.10	51.99	53.48	57.39	55.56	55.48
BMW AG		DAX	73.00	73.00	64.40	64.04	66.57	65.84	65.48
Commerzbank AG		DAX	46.54	43.91	55.97	56.07	58.93	57.31	57.44
DaimlerChrysler AG[b]		DAX/Eurostoxx	63.97	39.02	39.00	36.92	38.25	38.84	38.00
Degussa AG[c]	until 23.09.02	MIDAX	69.51	70.86	82.82	75.86	76.24	—	—
Deutsche Bank AG		DAX/Eurostoxx	44.69	37.50	31.73	34.44	33.41	38.75	35.53
Deutsche Börse AG	since 2003	DAX						44.53	—
Deutsche Lufthansa AG		DAX	31.90	34.60	35.25	34.90	41.14	46.37	40.80
Deutsche Post World Net AG	since 19.03.01	DAX	—	—	—	76.18	77.37	79.35	77.63
Deutsche Telekom AG	since 18.11.96	DAX/Eurostoxx	85.61	82.67	75.86	69.52	56.45	59.47	61.81
Dresdner Bank AG	until 23.07.01	DAX/Eurostoxx	70.33	61.72	59.75				
E.ON AG	since 19.06.00	DAX/Eurostoxx	—	—	—	39.01	37.35	31.00	35.79
Epcos AG	until 2003	DAX	—	—	42.60	44.88	54.54	—	—
Fresenius Medical Care AG	since 17.09.99	DAX	(62.40)	(67.88)	64.79	61.06	62.59	64.97	62.87
Henkel AG (Vz.)		DAX	65.12	66.75	83.24	84.50	83.73	56.73	74.99
Hoechst AG	until 17.09.99		65.86	62.68	—	—			
Infineon Technologies AG	since 19.06.00	DAX	—	—	—	74.74	41.66	31.88	49.43

Karstadt-Quelle AG	until 19.03.01		64.90	65.65	68.46	—	—	—	—
Linde AG		DAX	59.00	56.46	54.40	53.67	54.19	50.08	52.65
MAN AG		DAX	61.00	59.81	55.80	50.62	52.80	48.41	50.61
Mannesmann AG	until 14.02.00		44.70	45.51	—	—	—	—	—
Metro AG[d]		DAX	78.49	77.72	87.53	66.93	66.38	65.86	66.39
MLP AG	since 23.07.01	DAX	—	(77.89)	(79.22)	75.38	51.41	59.50	62.10
Münchener Rück AG	since 20.09.96	DAX / Eurostoxx	75.80	72.33	69.80	65.60	53.45	57.49	58.85
RWE AG		DAX / Eurostoxx	75.01	67.15	63.90	65.09	66.08	39.06	56.74
SAP AG (Vz.)	since 15.09.95	DAX	59.77	53.36	56.70	50.85	55.37	58.04	54.75
Schering AG		DAX	43.16	47.01	43.33	37.40	37.00	34.84	36.41
Siemens AG	since 18.03.99	DAX / Eurostoxx	46.66	44.97	24.93	22.00	36.40	47.51	35.30
ThyssenKrupp AG[e]		DAX	58.74	55.90	64.13	61.26	59.97	61.60	60.94
TUI AG (former Preussag)	since 03.09.90	DAX	65.41	66.87	39.30	37.21	37.21	54.18	42.87
Veba AG[f]	until 17.06.00		45.33	46.44	40.41	—	—	—	—
Viag AG[f]	until 17.06.00		66.39	54.99	65.47	—	—	—	—
Volkswagen AG		DAX / Eurostoxx	43.70	37.62	34.39	36.99	32.98	29.01	32.99
Average peaks			60.95	56.36	54.85	53.03	51.23	49.14	50.94

[a] Since 1999, previously Bay. Vereinsbank AG.
[b] Since Dec. 1998, previously Daimler Benz AG.
[c] Since Dec. 2000, after merger with SKW, previously Degussa AG.
[d] Since 1997, previously Kaufhof AG.
[e] Since Dec. 1998, previously Thyssen AG.
[f] Since the merger of Veba and Viag, E.ON and Infineon have been included in the DAX 30.

hall. About 50% would be normal for an unexceptional meeting. The AGM turnout for DAX 30 companies 1998–2003 was as shown in Table 2.9.

The causes of decline are unclear, but probably include the growth of foreign holdings and the evolution of the bearer share system. It is the banks as custodians of deposited shares who are notified about GMs and they in turn notify the owners: conversely, a shareholder cannot attend and vote unless he has lodged his certificate with certain specified banks. Some decisions require 75% of the votes so a 25% shareholder has a power of veto. Because of the importance of the banks (see below) and the complexity of their relationship with the company, there is ample opportunity for them to make contact with management during the year. A demarche at a general meeting is therefore rare: meetings are seldom controversial, but may be protracted, with a wide range of general questions. A tendency has grown for special interest groups to use them for propaganda, for instance in former days on South Africa or on environmental issues. Such groups often purchase a minimal holding just to have the right to attend. They sometimes make use of a provision in German law which entitles them to introduce a counter-proposal (if they hold 5% of the share capital or a nominal amount of 500,000 euros) which the company must distribute with its proxy materials before the meeting. A recent example was the resolution put by DSW about the management of DaimlerChrysler. In fact counter-proposals seldom reach a vote because the management's own proposals must first be rejected and this is extremely rare. There have however been recent examples of shareholders at a general meeting taking positive action about a company going downhill. At the DaimlerChrysler AGM on 7 April 2004 for example DSW called for shareholders to vote against the discharge of both management and supervisory board members following disappointing figures and an inadequate share price. They also objected to payments of 'phantom stock'. The European Corporate Governance Service (ECGS) of which DSW is a member analyses companies in detail. In their 2003 report on Allianz for instance they review compliance with the GCGC, the composition of committees, and the long-term incentive programme (LTIP). They also look carefully at the members of the Supervisory Board to describe their connections and assess their independence.

There is no obligation on a GmbH to have an annual general meeting. It is up to the directors to call a general meeting of shareholders when they wish, but a member's resolution is required in certain circumstances (e.g. to raise more capital), or if more than half the capital has been lost in a given year. Members holding one-tenth of the share capital can require a meeting to be held. There is an interesting provision that where otherwise a meeting would have been necessary by law, a unanimous vote in writing of the shareholders may instead declare themselves agreed on the decision to be made.

The Market

General

The German public's agnosticism to the cult of the equity reflects German management's lack of enthusiasm for the stock market. With the most powerful economy in Europe and one of the strongest in the world, only 774 German companies were quoted at the end of 2001 according to data published by the Internal Market Directorate of the European Commission. The comparable figure for France was 808, for Spain 1,019, and for the UK 1,926. Furthermore there seems to be little enthusiasm to bring companies to the market (IPOs). The *Financial News,* quoting Dealogic in its issue of 22 March 2004, noted the decline from 97 in 2000 to 12 the next year, 4 in 2002, and none in 2003 or in 2004 up to that point. One deal—X-Fab—was pulled because of adverse market conditions. Even so 17 companies, mainly in biotech and technology, are said to be lined up for later in the year.

The total market capitalization of quoted companies was DM 596,476 million at the end of 1991; savings accounts exceeded DM 1,000 billion. Germany has a high savings ratio—12.2% of disposable household income in 1989—but the money does not seem to find its way into equities. In that year only 10 DM billion out of DM 150 billion of private-sector savings reached the equity market directly or indirectly.

In 2000 the ratio of stock market capitalization to GDP was 68% in Germany, 89% average in the EU, and 150% in the USA—the UK was 185%.

We noted earlier how concentrated ownership is; only 17.5% of German companies did not have a holder with at least 25% of the shares—the comparable figure for the UK is 84.1% Despite this concentration of ownership, delisting has become a live issue, not least to escape the GCGC, but the process can be extended if shareholders challenge the Stock Exchange's decision. The Supreme Court requires a shareholders' resolution carried by a simple majority but accompanied by a requirement to purchase minority shares. A special review procedure has been instituted for valuation (Spruchverfahren). At the time of writing some aspects of the new procedures were uncertain and unclear.

It is much easier to manage a German company if there is not a small rump of minority shareholders, and to facilitate the process of getting rid of them 'squeeze-out' procedures have been introduced. They only apply to a minority of 5% or less. There has to be a valuation, a reasonable cash offer with a bank guarantee that it will be paid, and a resolution at a shareholders' meeting. This procedure often proceeds delisting, which is much simplified thereby.

The relative size of some leading companies is as in Table 2.10 (DaimlerChrysler is quoted separately below) in terms of their turnover for 2003 quoted in *billions* of euros

At the other end of the spectrum, it was a different story. In the aftermath of the steep decline in the indexes across the world in 2001 (96% in Germany) the Deutsche Borse AG decided to close the Neuer Markt (September 2002).

Mergers

The European Union has been struggling for some years to facilitate cross-border mergers but the European Parliament turned down the proposals by the closest of margins on 4 July 2001. One of the key factors was German opposition—thus reversing their previous stance. It will not scotch takeovers altogether—after all Vodafone bought Mannesman under the old rules. The thrust of the directive was to strengthen the shareholders' position by making management consult them when faced with a hostile bid.

Also in the pipeline is a Directive on cross-border mergers between companies with share capital. This is aimed at smaller businesses, lays down the processes for ratification, and also protects employees' participation rights. It is still under consideration by the UK Parliament.

The most interesting merger in recent years is that between Daimler-Benz and Chrysler, not just because of its size (revenues in 1998 at the time of the merger were $132,064 billion) but because of the solution applied to cope

Table 2.10. Turnover of some leading companies 2003

	Turnover (€bn)	Number of employees
Siemens	74	417,000
EON	46	66,549
Allianz		173,750
BASF	33	87,159
Deutsche Bank	21	67,682

with the differences between the USA and Germany. The new entity follows the German two-tier model and incorporates formal employee membership of the supervisory board. There are two chairmen and two CEOs. The managing board has sixteen members, divided half and half, and the supervisory board has twenty members, half appointed by the shareholders, half by employees. The company returned group profits of $7.2 billion in 2003. Interestingly, the market capitalization on the last trading day of March 2004 was 34.4 billion euros in Frankfurt and $42.3 billion on the New York Stock Exchange.

The series of events involving Krupp show that the system may not be as rigid as first appears. Hoesch AG was absorbed in 1992 and five years later it bid for Thyssen AG (bigger than itself). Deutsche Bank was an ally (which aroused much wrath from the public, politicians, and organized labour). But serious talks continued and both supervisory boards agreed a merger in early 1998. One of the consequences was that the new entity was subject to the general co-determination law rather than the more stringent Montan law which now applies only to a handful of companies in the coal and steel industries. The case also illustrates the divided loyalties of bankers sitting on supervisory boards.

The takeover of Mannesman by Vodafone also illustrates points about the way the German market works. Mannesman had been a conglomerate but had felt secure when in a colder environment it might have deemed it wise to divest itself of some of its peripheral parts. That is indeed what Vodafone did after the merger. There was political interference at the highest level—Chancellor Schröder no less—and that brought in the UK Prime Minister, Tony Blair. Schroder is on record as saying, 'It is for the time being only an affair between companies', but the Mannesman CEO spoke out against government interference. In the end the German shareholders voted overwhelmingly to accept a much enhanced offer. The battle had been complex and tough, with Mannesman's board toying with the possibility of violating corporate law and the takeover code by announcing the intention to make two other alliances. In the event neither materialized.

Finally the security of tenure of board members under German law does not make life any easier for an aspiring bidder; the shareholders have no power to remove a labour representative.

The number of mergers has grown in recent years. Paper 12/847 produced by the Bundestag (12th term) shows there were 445 in 1975, 635 in 1980, 709 in 1985, and 1,348 in 1990. About 1,100 of the companies acquired were quite small, with a turnover of less than DM 50 million, but 55 had turnovers in excess of DM 1 billion and four had turnovers in excess of DM 12 billion. Figures from the Federal Cartel Office have a rather different classification but show a similar growth pattern, from 287 partial or full acquisitions in 1980 to 616 in 1988.

We can gain some idea of the volume of deals by reference to the lawyers conducting them (Table 2.11).

Friendly mergers often occur for normal commercial reasons such as lack of succession or synergy. Mergers also take place in circumstances in which one of the parties is troubled. If so they will be quietly negotiated. Companies go downhill as they do anywhere else in the world. The stock market itself is not the scene of remedial action when an Aufsichtsrat fails to arrest a company's decline. Germany has no long-stop mechanism of this sort, though it comes quite close to it when certain types of marriage are arranged (e.g. AEG–Daimler Benz). The banks play a leading part in such arrangements, as well they might, for they have much at stake.

The 1,348 mergers in 1990 were followed by over 2,000 in 1991, partly as a result of reunification. There is some concern that this process is causing the disappearance of highly effective medium and small businesses to the detriment of their productivity. The issue of greater concentration is worth a closer look.

Concentration

There has for many years been a tendency towards concentration by merger and organic growth. The Monopolkommission's 2001/2 report notes that the value added of all companies rose 4.19% between 1998 and 2000 but in the case of the 100 biggest companies the figure was 11.58%. The ten biggest had a share of 40.8% but this rose to 44.79% of the 100. Allianz AG had the most holdings in other companies—22.

Proposed mergers must be notified to the Federal Cartel Office if the firms concerned have worldwide sales of more than 500 million euros and one party has sales in Germany of more than 25 million euros. Its main criterion is market domination—that is, they will interfere if a proposed merger so weakens competition as to allow a company to dominate the market. In reaching their judgement they may take financial strength and vertical integration into account, as well as the structure of the market, that is, the size and number of competitors as well as other factors. Between 1973 and 1988 they scrutinized 9,500 mergers, of which fewer than 200 were prohibited. Such a policy by its very nature favours conglomerates since the purchase of a company in an unrelated business is less likely to offend the basic criterion.

Table 2.11. Volume of deals

	Rank adviser	1 Jan.–31 Dec. 2003 ranking value including net debt of target (US$m.)	Number of deals	Jan.–31 Dec. 2002 ranking value including net debt of target (US$m.)
1	Freshfields Bruckhaus Deringer	26,648.6	56	62,743.2
2	Clifford Chance	21,421.9	49	36,643.4
3	Shearman Sterling LLP	15,283.5	36	47,278.8
4	Jones Day	14,533.8	13	30,428.6
5	Linklaters	14,082.6	34	50,561.0
6	Hengeler Mueller	12,793.8	39	52,794.5
7	Allen & Overy	11,456.6	18	23,352.0
8	Herbert Smith/Gleiss Lutz/Stibble	10,675.5	18	27,574.3
9	Simpson Thacher & Bartlett	10,159.2	4	10,005.0
10	Sullivan & Cromwell	9,881.3	4	22,512.4
11*	Cravath, Swaine & Moore	8,098.3	1	11,188.4
11*	Morris Nichols Arsht & Tunnell	8,098.8	1	—
13	Fried Frank Harris Shriver & Jacobson LLP	7,621.2	3	—
14	McDermott Will & Emery	6,122.8	5	1,596.5
15*	Heuking Kuehn Lueer Heussen Wojtek	6,121.1	2	
15	Mayer Brown Rowe & Maw	6,121.1	3	149.5
17	LeBoeuf Lamb Greene & MacRae	5,654.9	2	15,025.5

Table 2.11. (cont'd)

	Rank adviser	1 Jan.–31 Dec. 2003 ranking value including net debt of target (US$m.)	Number of deals	Jan.–31 Dec. 2002 ranking value including net debt of target (US$m.)
18	Cleary Gottlieb Steen & Hamilton	5,316.3	11	22,840.5
19	White & Case LLP	4,718.9	11	12,887.9
20	CMS	3,402.9	39	3.9
21	Debevoise & Plimpton	2,887.2	4	17,806.7
22	Davis Polk & Wardwell	2,452.3	3	1,795.7
23	Lovells	2,094.6	18	3,915.9
24	Mannheimer Swartling Advokatbyra	2,056.0	5	450.8
25	Simmons & Simmons	1,998.3	7	4,624.7
Subtotal with legal adviser		54,014.3	347	125,603.9
Subtotal without legal adviser		7,709.6	831	11,786.3
Industry total		61,723.9	1,178	137,390.2

Source: *Acquisitions Monthly* (Feb. 2004).

The significant feature of the German system is that virtually none of the very large number of mergers would be classified as 'hostile' in the USA or UK, that is, none was preceded by an open market bid over the heads of the management of the target company: they were all negotiated. There are, however, 'hostile' takeovers, very often with the support of one or several banks which may have built up a controlling block of shares secretly, for years if necessary. Secret purchases, if big enough, do move the market by the sheer pressure they exert. The bid for Hoesch by Krupp was an example of this kind. 'Hostile' bids of the 'open market' variety used to be unknown, but no longer.

It is now necessary to disclose a significant stake. The Securities Trading Act of July 1994 requires investors to disclose to the Financial Supervisory Authority if they amass more than 5%, 10%, 25%, 50%, and 75%; the public is notified. The Stock Corporation Act itself requires investors to notify the company on 25% of the equity or 50% of the votes. The company has to tell the public who the investor is and what the holding is.

The EC directive foresees registration at 10%, 20%, 33%, 50%, and 66.1%, or lower thresholds, and includes shares held or controlled directly or indirectly. The state of German law technically leaves German companies exposed to foreign purchasers who may themselves be protected by stringent disclosure rules, as in the UK. In the meantime, the takeover of Hoesch by Krupp shows how the German rules currently favour a bidder, because the target cannot marshal defences and the bidder can buy in the market secretly without the bid premium factor coming into play.

Interestingly the Kodex covers the subject in GCGC 6 under the title 'transparency'. Management is required to disclose—presumably to the Aufsichtsrat, though it does not say so, and it might have meant 'directly to the Stock Market'—any facts that would materially affect the stock price. This includes the news that an individual acquires, 'exceeds or falls short of 5%, 10%, 50% or 75% of the voting rights' (6.2).

The examples of hostile takeovers used to be so rare that everyone quoted the same cases. A major battle took place between 1990 and 1992 over Pirelli's unwelcome bid for Continental, and this involved court actions and the removal of the Sprecher of Continental's Vorstand. Acrimonious struggles with or without the building of clandestine stakes is still counter to the prevailing ethos, which remains strongly opposed to open market hostile bids. There are many other reasons why they are difficult to mount, for example:

- The founding family still has a strong position in many companies; or there may be a sizeable but supportive shareholder. Franks and Mayer (1994) looked at 171 quoted companies and concluded that 85.4% of them had a shareholder with 25% of its voting capital (this would include a family group).

- The accounts of German companies tend to be relatively opaque so that unfriendly bidders would be taking great risks even though the general tendency is for balance sheets to be conservative.
- The banks effectively control a large proportion of outstanding shares through deposited share voting rights.

The whole atmosphere, however, is one in which the stock market is far less at the centre of the stage. The Germans used to find it odd that the evening BBC broadcast to Germany at peak time included a long financial report, identical or similar to the one London receives as part of the national 6 o'clock news.

The Banks

General

In any description of German corporate governance after 1945 it was necessary to mention the banks in many different contexts. In other countries it would not have been important to single out the banks for their shareholdings and board membership as well as for their key role in providing working capital and other services. One of the cardinal features of the last decade is how greatly the role of the banks has diminished.

It is not as if Germany were short of banks. There are 1,800 cooperative banks, 550 Sparkassen, 11 Landesbanken, 15 insurance companies, 8 leasing enterprises, and about 100 commercial banks. The Landesbanken, as their name suggests, are tied into the Länder and enjoy a state guarantee. This makes them an excellent credit risk and enables them to compete with commercial banks. The EU competition rules are about to put a stop to this and life will be much tougher for them from 2005. Reports of the ratings agencies views (*Financial News*, 28 June 2004) suggest that some ratings will be too low for some banks to sustain their business models. Doubtless these banks will react to maintain their position even if it means changes to the balance sheet or finding new partners or both. Many of the other banks are relatively small and local. Consolidation is in the wind, sometimes with foreign banks. The big three have shrunk to two since Allianz bought Dresdner—and they have plenty of competition, and relatively small shares of the total credit market.

The banks as lenders

In the early days of industrialization, Germans starting business had no choice but to look to the banks for long-term money. For companies without access to the capital markets this remains the case. The banks for their part approach their lending from the inception on the basis that it will be long term. This approach means that both parties realize that they are in together for the long term: in modern parlance it implies 'relationship' not 'transaction' banking, which in turn requires the bankers to understand their customers and the industries in which they are engaged. The consequence of this is the need not only for a good flow of information from company to bank, but for a good cadre of well-trained personnel within the banks to understand and evaluate the intelligence they receive.

Small German companies appear to depend more heavily on bank finance than some European counterparts. Those with a turnover of less than £7 million only have 14% of their balance sheets accounted for by their own capital (France = 34%). The bigger companies with a turnover of > £40 m. are pretty much the same across countries. But insolvencies rose sharply in 2002 even though German productivity was greater than its competitors (Germany 101, Italy 89, UK 69). (Source: German Statistics Office; the European Observatories for SMEs.)

Large companies are a different matter. Most of the data is rather old but it showed clearly that the banks were not a major supplier of working capital to them. Bundesbank figures for 1992 drawn from a sample of 1926 large firms suggest that bank finance only accounted for 7.6% of total assets in 1989.

Universalbanken

With a customer base securely tied to them on long-term arrangements, the banks set about developing a wider range of services as a means of improving profits (for relationship banking is expensive), and for cementing relationships by broadening the opportunities for contacts. Entrepreneurs are lonely men and the banks were able to provide valuable counsel when needed; and they were trusted. This has proved significant in the eastern Länder where young companies run by people quite unused to a market system need intense care and nursing. What the banks provide is a cross between counselling and management consultancy. Much of the structure and dynamics of this relationship between the banking system and industry still applies across a wide swathe of German industry. The major banks have developed into what the Germans describe as Universalbanken—a term applying to the range of services they provide rather than their geographical spread (deposits; lending; all aspects of investment; foreign exchange).

The banks are still very important players, and their interest in corporate governance does not depend on any leverage they might obtain from the loans they make and the services they render.

The banks as shareholders

The German banking system has not set out as a matter of policy to acquire shares in its customers' companies. Even so, by 1975 the banks had become substantial shareholders, owning by that time 9% of AGs (14% if financial companies are excluded). Many of their holdings were acquired *faute de mieux* from impecunious companies which could not repay their debt and had nothing else to offer. Sometimes the companies failed and the shares became worthless; sometimes, however, they prospered mightily and the banks found themselves holding shares which could not be sold without incurring a serious tax charge. This changed from 1 January 2002 when the divestiture of such stakes became tax exempt. When the tax law changed, banks—often themselves in need of more liquid assets—sold most of their holdings. Today they have few shares apart from Deutsche's holding in DaimlerChrysler. The criticisms of the banks' shareholdings by the Monopolkommission and the Kartellamt in the 1980s are now of historial interest only.

The banks as proxies

As German shares are still predominantly in bearer form they are negotiable and valuable; receipt of the dividend requires production of a coupon. German shareholders generally lodge the instruments with banks authorized to do all the necessary work. As noted earlier the banks found this service unprofitable and only four now do it. Holding the instruments gave the banks de facto power of the voting rights—deposited share voting rights (DSVR). Nowadays depositary banks and shareholder organizations are obliged to submit suggestions to the beneficiaries on how to exercise their votes, as well as following their instructions. They do this by means of a fifteen months' proxy form covering all a shareholder's holdings. Shareholders are then sent the agendas for companies as they are issued, together with a bank's views on how to vote. In the absence of a contrary instruction the bank will then exercise the proxy in the way indicated. Very few shareholders bother to respond (as might be expected, since few issues are controversial).

An example some years ago was Deutsche's advice to abstain from voting on motions arising from Volkswagen's currency tribulations. A bank may go further and inform owners that it will not, on a controversial issue, exercise votes on their behalf; in that case the owners themselves must cast their votes if they wish an opinion to be registered. Banks would easily be put into an invidious position were this not so; for instance, if one of their clients were in negotiation with another. Institutional shareholders, like insurance companies, generally leave it to their depository bankers to vote (though this is illegal for investment companies). Business is usually uncontentious; if, however, they wish to register opposition the banks will generally require them to do it themselves.

Except in a few cases banks' direct shareholdings are not a significant factor in corporate governance. Their effective control of a large number of shares they do not own through DSVR has shrunk from a total of 36% of the votes of the 100 largest companies according to the 1978 Monopolkommission report to an average of 8.5% (Edwards and Nibler, October 2000, in *Economic Policy*, 248). Even so, this means that their aggregate holdings sometimes rose to 20–30%— sometimes larger than any other single holder. There is a dearth of evidence about whether they act in concert, but if they did they might be a real influence in corporate governance.

In recent years some German institutional shareholders have become more active. Deutsche Asset Management, part of the Deutsche Bank Group, publishes a quarterly statement on corporate governance and socially responsible investment. 'Engagements' in the third quarter of 2003 include accounts of meetings with:

Intertek—mainly on remuneration;
Scottish and Southern Energy—mainly on remuneration;
GlaxoSmithKline—mainly on remuneration;
BskyB—mainly on the succession to Rupert Murdoch;
Vodafone group—on social responsibility and the environment;

Deutsche Bank is a leader in investment banking and topped the table in 2004 Q1 with a net revenue of $234.6 million; its nearest rival was UBS with $185.6 million (*Financial News*, 29 March 2004).

Bankers on boards

Historically the banks' pre-eminence as suppliers of capital and the range of their services gave them the opportunity to establish strong personal links with smaller companies at working levels. These links, which themselves ensure influence and information, were reinforced more formally in quoted companies by a bank taking a seat on the Aufsichtsrat. As we have seen, the value to a company of these links is enhanced by the company's being able to draw on its bank's logistic support in the form of research and analysis.

The Bundesverband Deutsche Banken report of 1989 noted that,while in the mid-1970s the banks held between 10% and 20% of the total seats on the boards of the top 100 companies, by 1988 the figure had fallen. By 2000 it had fallen further to 78 out of 1,543 seats—about 5% (Schmacke/Jaeckel, 'Die Grossen 500', www.yaaz.de/d/35) Edwards and Nibler (2000) note the distribution in their sample.

The position is more complex still. The big banks have advisory boards on which industrialists sit. These industrialists also sit on the boards of other industrial companies. There is a whole range of secondary links which commentators have attempted to measure. The figures suggest linkages of one sort or another between the big banks and perhaps 3,000 enterprises.

To be more specific, a study of some major companies reveals the following numbers of bankers on their boards:

BASF	4 bankers out of 22
Bayer	3 bankers out of 20
BMW	1 banker out of 21
Hoechst	2 bankers out of 20
Siemens	4 bankers out of 22
Volkswagen	2 bankers out of 20

It should not be supposed from this, however, that representatives of the banks force themselves on the boards of unwilling or even reluctant companies. Companies are glad to have them and they are generally glad to serve. The company benefits from their considerable personal skills and experience, the intelligence network they can tap, and their contacts. Besides they can often provide specialized advice, financial knowledge, and information (often with the help of an assistant at their bank). The banks gain by cementing the relationship with the company, by adding to their sources of information, and by the kudos board positions give them, not to mention the money, which generally they keep. 'We have day to day involvement in a functioning network of information. We are necessarily well informed and owing to our swift access to information are in a position to give management boards proper advice. That is why we are so often asked to serve on supervisory boards' (F. W. Christians, Deutsche Bank, writing in *Die Zeit*, 1987). With such an interwoven series of relationships the banks are in a position, if they choose, to act as monitors of companies, not in any formal, methodical sense, but informally when they judge that their influence is needed to nudge a company back on track, or in extreme cases to put it under some other company's wing. Banks do act in this way and many a company's survival and many a merger have depended on a bank's quiet initiative: it is a role which banks accept and in which, in important cases, their own board may be involved.

In his 1993 study Baums felt that one of the more important parts of their role was the ability of bankers on boards to contribute to discussions on managerial performance, although it appears that monitoring activities seem to be limited anyway.

It is remarkable that at the time of the 1992 study the question of conflict of interest was never raised. Even so a banker on an Aufsichtsrat must often find himself in a difficult position. To whom does he owe allegiance, the bank or the company? With increasing activity in the takeover market, bankers on boards may easily find themselves in an awkward position and indeed a conflict of interest. Precise figures are not readily available, but my impression is that there tends to be more industrialists and fewer bankers on supervisory boards.

Summary

The combination of direct ownership, DSVR, length of lending, and breadth of services together used to imply:

- Deep firm relationships between company and banks, not lightly put aside. At best banks become counsel and guide to proprietors and the relationship lasts for decades.
- A massive flow of information into the banks about individual companies and sectors of industry which can be used to customers' advantage.
- The development by the banks of well-trained staff capable of sustaining the relationships described above.
- The knowledge, motivation, and authority to exert influence on company management.

However, for all the reasons stated plus the emergence of the market as a significant influence, the influence of the banks has greatly diminished and is diminishing but it is far from extinct, especially in times of difficulty. They used to be such a significant part of the total machine that this affects its running. Influence as well as power abhors a vacuum. Where has it gone?

The Basic Principles

Entrepreneurial drive

The driving power in many small and medium German enterprises comes from the people who founded them and their successors. Many highly successful companies even in international terms have payrolls of a few hundred, but their niche products, sold by the proprietor personally, have a valued place in world markets.

In bigger companies, as we have seen, the Vorstand is entrusted with the task of driving the business forward. We know that its members are not inhibited by fear of hostile takeover, or by concern about government interference. As far as the law is concerned, they do not stand in fear of private lawsuit, but nevertheless have regard to the duties that are placed upon them; the state could take them to task if they did not. Their employees too would take them to court were they to disregard the proper processes in which the works councils are entitled to participate.

Within the Vorstand the drive may come largely from the Sprecher or chairman or general membership, according to the relative strength of the personalities and the company's tradition. Some Vorstands operate in a more collegiate way than others, and of course some companies have more drive than others, as they do the world over. The main point is that there is nothing within the German system to constrain this drive harmfully and there is a great deal to encourage it. The ethos and culture within which my interlocutors work seemed to encourage long-term thinking, planning, and investment with a conspicuous interest in quality and technical excellence.

Accountability

We have already seen that in a formal sense the Vorstand is accountable to the Aufsichtsrat; that its effectiveness is affected in some ways for the better by having employee representatives on it; that bankers have a key role on and off the Aufsichtsrat; and that the threat of a hostile takeover, although marginally greater than it was, is still not sufficiently pressing to act as a goad to management and cause them to think less long-term. The question is, does the system really work? Is the Vorstand's accountability nominal or real?

One thing we can say from the start: there can be no real accountability without a flow of information. In the UK and USA information to the outside directors flows through the chairman/CEO. In the German system the employee representatives have a flow of information through works councils, to the point where they may well be the best-informed people on the Aufsichtsrat. There is, however, the question of technical and particularly financial knowledge. Do the employee members have enough? If not, are they trained? On the shareholders' side, bankers will have external flows of information from their own contacts with the company, from colleagues, and often from their research departments, both about the company and its sector. It is these supplementary flows which make many Aufsichtsrat meetings important. Where they do not exist, because works councils are weak or there are no bankers, an Aufsichtsrat will depend almost exclusively on the power and personality of its members, particularly the chairman. If there is a dominant shareholder (even with a minority stake) the other members may prove mere cyphers. Sometimes it is not up to the mark, a mere rubber stamp. A better flow of information gives the Aufsichtsrat a chance to be effective, but does not guarantee it. Management will prepare the ground better if it has to explain and argue the reasons for a proposed course of action. The mere fact of having to present figures quarterly and justify them is a discipline in itself—and they go far beyond the information presented to shareholders quarterly or half-yearly.

The bankers on the Aufsichtsrat are often not alone in reading the runes and asking the penetrating question. Many experienced senior industrialists serve on them, and even if they hesitate to embarrass managers in front of their employees at joint meetings, they may very well take up the cudgels informally on other occasions. As a matter of fact, companies are divided about having bankers on their Aufsichtsrat. Some like the connection (not to mention the information flow and contacts), but others feel they can get all they need from their bankers anyway without having to have them on their supervisory tier—they might, for instance, put them on an Advisory Committee. As noted above the proportion of bankers seems to be diminishing.

In fact, even when a company's main banker is not on the Aufsichtsrat, he has every chance to assess management both from personal contacts and from the figures, and he is in a position to exercise influence on a day-to-day basis if necessary. It is impossible to assess precisely how important the influence of the German banks is on companies, for evidence only breaks surface in troubled times. It must, of course, depend on a company's relative strength. If it is cash rich and prospering its Hausbank will have neither the cause nor the power to intervene. But if a company is troubled the banks' combination of information and voting power—plus perhaps a place on the supervisory board—strengthens the authority their position as lenders would normally provide.

Critics of the Aufsichtsrat contend that a group which meets quarterly at most cannot really understand a business, particularly if it is big and complex. A good Vorstand will in fact make sure its Aufsichtsrat is properly informed, and a strongly led Aufsichtsrat will ensure this is so (appointing special committees for the purpose if necessary). As noted above, many Aufsichtsrate are very well informed from various sources. Besides, the chairman of the Aufsichtsrat and some members of special subcommittees usually have much closer contact with the firm. He may even have an office in the company; in some cases he will come in often, even daily. The potential authority of the Aufsichtsrat should not be underestimated. The shareholders' representatives will generally be experienced industrialists or bankers. Members of the company's Vorstand will themselves serve on the Aufsichtsrat of other companies. The practical effects are to provide companies with an excellent flow of intelligence and guidance and to create a significant personal network.

Although the role of the Aufsichtsrat is formally limited, its members' experience is tapped by the Vorstand either at formal meetings or outside them, in a way which a US/UK non-executive director would find familiar: it is not true therefore to say that they are only supervisors and do not contribute. In smaller companies the articles may prescribe a wider range of subjects on which the Aufsichtsrat must be consulted.

On boards of companies of all sizes, personalities count as they always do. The balance of power in the Vorstand will be influenced by the strength of its chairman, just as the effectiveness of the Aufsichtsrat will depend heavily on its chairman. If there is a poor Vorstand and a weak Aufsichtsrat a company will flounder. Sometimes an Aufsichtsrat can see what needs to be done and be slow about doing it. (There is a striking similarity here to the UK and USA, where exactly the same is true if there is a poor CEO and weak outside directors.) Significant companies with strong Vorstands often seek strong and experienced Aufsichtsrate which can make a positive contribution to the company.

Some German critics of their own system regard Aufsichtsrate as otiose. It is true that some meetings are short and perfunctory ('two hours followed by lunch and a pleasant afternoon' as one man said), but this is not necessarily because they are neglecting their duties (though of course they may). If a company is palpably going really well there may be no cause to intervene. There are, however, signs that Aufsichtsrate are getting tougher—quicker to act when things go radically wrong. The Volkswagen currency scandal some years ago was a spur in this direction. It will be interesting to measure in due course the effects of governance on the frequency and duration of meets as well as the changes in their scope.

The supervisory element in the two-tier system should not be regarded as the invigilation of a regular series of examinations. It is concerned with establishing and maintaining standards, and to the extent that it succeeds remedial action is unnecessary. Sometimes, however, it fails. What if things really do start to go wrong? If the Vorstand as a whole is competent, inadequate individuals will be dealt with quietly; poor performers will be tolerated temporarily or eased out, depending on age and the degree of incompetence. The Aufsichtsrat will only intervene if it thinks the Vorstand is being slow or wet—and even then it will try to avoid a public fracas in front of the unions. One element, though not a major one, is that the degree to which the Aufsichtsrat is ready to take drastic action will depend to some extent on the degree of its involvement in the original appointment of the manager concerned. It will in all cases have had to approve the appointment, but if the name had been originally proposed by the management board the Aufsichtsrat may feel rather less committed to it than if it had been directly suggested by them. To sack their own candidate would be an admission of failure, though it does happen. Banks incidentally do not claim any special knowledge except for the company's financial management. Their own credibility might come into question were they to presume to exercise special judgement on people from spheres like design or engineering where they have no special knowledge.

A far more difficult circumstance arises when the Vorstand as a whole appears to be performing poorly. My general impression is that the Aufsichtsrat can be slow to take remedial action. This partly reflects the general attitudes mentioned earlier: management is often given the benefit of the doubt, and a further chance to redeem itself. Reciprocal appointments are prohibited by Section 100 of the Stock Corporation Law, that is, A serving on B's board and vice versa. Other cross-appointments are permitted and frequently exist, for example, A on B's board, B on C's, and C on A's. This is not an act of deliberate policy but simply the result of the fact that there is a coterie of suitable people who are natural candidates and are therefore chosen. Between such people there may be an instructive and unspoken non-aggression pact on the principle 'There but for the grace of God go I'. Even in cases when an Aufsichtsrat has steeled itself to act, it may choose to ride out the storm, particularly if the media are involved, and then move quietly but effectively when it has abated. It can only make matters worse if the Vorstand was slow in producing the information—and this happens too. Even when the information is timely and the Aufsichtsrat skilled, keen, and determined, it can make mistakes. The Aufsichtsrat of Karstadt did not veto the disastrous purchase of Neckermann, nor did the Volkswagen Aufsichtsrat stop the purchase of Triumph-Adler which lost them DM 1 billion. No system is or ever could be perfect.

The major weapon in the hands of the Aufsichtsrat is its power to appoint or dismiss. In this as in other matters, the chairman has to build a consensus for action; the company and indeed the country looks to him to play his part when circumstances require it. Sometimes he fails. Action in regard to the Vorstand of AEG is commonly regarded as having been dilatory to say the least: the management had their appointments renewed several times when (in the view of commentators) some might well have been replaced. The Aufsichtsrat's role is bound to be less important in times of prosperity, especially as it is not in the German nature to try to buy short-term prosperity without proper consideration for the longer term. If a German company looks prosperous today, there is a reasonable inference that there is little to be served by interfering. If, however, the evidence of decline is accumulating, the influence of the Aufsichtsrat becomes potentially greater, so that ultimately it can steel itself for action. But 'ultimately' is the crucial word. Germans are like their competitors elsewhere in being reluctant to remove those who have served a company well until the evidence of their diminished capacity has become irresistible.

There is another factor which may come into play. It used to be a not unusual sequence for the chairman or Sprecher of the Vorstand to join the Aufsichtsrat when he retired, often as its chairman. This progression is now regarded with disfavour, but the Kodex goes no further than saying that only two members may be promotees from the Vorstand (5.4.2). Meanwhile, he will have had a major part in picking his own successor. The complications can be imagined. If his successor fails he will feel responsible, and in any event his propensity to intervene will, at least to begin with, be considerable. The German system may look as if relationships and responsibilities are clear cut, but the reality is often more blurred.

A 1991 takeover case illustrates the system at work. The Aufsichtsrat of Continental, chaired by Horst Urban, disagreed with its Vorstand about the appropriate response to a bid by Pirelli. But as the contest progressed trading conditions worsened and the Aufsichtsrat ditched Urban in order to open serious negotiations. What was interesting about this case, apart from the light it shed on German takeover laws, was the role of the Aufsichtsrat, clearly playing a major part in determining a strategic issue.

Summing up the balance on accountability, the judgement of most of my interlocutors was that it was reasonably effective and consistent, with banks and employees/unions playing an important part in making the supervisory tier function adequately. It is undoubtedly a system that depends heavily upon networks and they in turn only function effectively (even with abundant interlocking directorates) because cooperation is seen as the proper mode. There were fewer examples than in some other economies of power-hungry industrial moguls running amok in an excess of megalomania: given the success of German industry over the years, the absence of such characters is rather remarkable. Perhaps accountability is mainly about how one feels;

my impression is that the German system does induce this feeling to a considerable degree in major public companies. In private businesses where the boss is still very much the boss, accountability in a formal or narrow sense is probably not so much in evidence, but even then the influence of the banks may be considerable and a sense of social obligation general. In any company, quoted or not, large or small, a major shareholder on the supervisory board will make the accountability of the management real enough—unless he has 'lost the plot'. Sadly, families do not always produce able people unto the third and fourth generation.

The Developing Scene

An economic sea change?

In 1982 the combination of factors, in particular, the availability of a well-motivated and trained workforce, technical competence, stable macroeconomic climate, and effective governance system, had together enabled German industry to prosper even though its currency had firmed and the hours worked by its labour force had declined (37-hour week). (It was said to be easier to reach a British or American executive on a Friday afternoon than it was a German.) By 2004 the picture had changed. *The Economist* refers to a 'Wirtschaftblunder' and *Der Spiegel* wrote a cover story 'Deutschland, die Lachnummer' (Germany, it's a joke). It is not within the scope of this book to attempt economic appraisal but the great engine does appear to have slowed down. Part of this can be attributed to 'social on-costs', part to the bill for reconstructing East Germany (estimated at 250 billion euros), and part to structural rigidities. German growth rates have declined to below the European average, as has its per capita GDP. The savings ratio has, however, stood up and at over 10% is one of the highest in Europe.

Demographics are an important element, not least because of the effect on the cost of pensions relative to the active workforce. The state pension costs 12% of GDP and there was a deficit in 2002 of 72.3 billion euros. Various ideas have been tried like the 'Reister' scheme for personal pensions. Although it is said to be complicated, 500,000 contracts were signed in 2003. Companies normally still keep their occupational scheme on the balance sheet but this is changing. More now use professional managers. Some big companies like Commerzbank have axed company pensions, and most small Mittelstand companies cannnot afford a stand-alone scheme.

The strains on the corporate governance system have been recognized. Many have been discussed above. Even so, it is worth considering its main components one by one.

The two-tier system changing?

There is a trade-off between the clear definition of function that a two-tier system provides and the specialization of the supervisory function among board members of the unitary system where everyone has the same legal duties. Actually both systems fudge the issue. The members of a German Aufsichtsrat do not have a stand-off from management, but all sorts of informal ways and some machinery to get close enough to them to make sense of the business; we have noted the increasing tendency for the employers' side to caucus with management which makes the resulting body look superficially much more like a unitary board: both systems have their conflicts of interest. The Aufsichtsrat can be attacked from either flank, as too distant and out of touch, or, rarely, as too intrusive and interfering. On the whole the view still seems to be 'We would not create a system like this were we given a blank sheet of paper today. But we have it and we make it work. It does have benefits and the hassle of changing it would be excessive.'

The test of any system is how good it is at accommodating individual idiosyncrasies: does it, despite all the variations, broadly get the balance right between entrepreneurial thrust and accountability? Perhaps because of the basic German approach referred to earlier the answer to this question is generally positive. No Germans I encountered foresaw radical change. What some see is a gradual evolution in the role of the Aufsichtsrat. In her Stockton Lecture Schneider Lenne said, 'In the course of the years, the focus of the supervisory board's work has begun to shift more and more towards advising and counselling the board of managing directors. The rationale of monitoring companies' management is no longer perceived to be a question of detecting past mistakes but rather of preventing them from being made in the first place.'

There seemed a little more pressure to change the basic rules of co-determination. Perhaps the unions have advanced as far as they are going to, but they are not in retreat. A position of some stability has been reached, but there is increased unease on the management side.

The basis from which German industry viewed the world—'make everything at home'—has certainly changed, and there are more plants being established and more components being sourced abroad under the pressure of rising wage costs, social costs, and a hard currency. Even Germany's legendary productivity may not be enough to stop some products becoming uncompetitive. In the field of corporate governance one obvious consequence is the effect on representation on the Aufsichtsrat. Should co-determination in future be applied to the overseas operations of German companies irrespective of their nationality? After all, the

Vorstand or Aufsichtsrat may take decisions which affect plants abroad. The Daimler-Chrysler solution may not necessarily establish a pattern.

More market influence?

At the present moment the stock market, though more important to German savers than it used to be, is not near centre stage as it is in the USA and UK. The German stock exchanges regret this (they would, wouldn't they?), but there is little sign of a change in sentiment or behaviour.

Since 1992 there have been important changes in the Exchanges' structure to make them more competitive internationally. The Frankfurt exchange became a holding company, Deutsche Borse AG, which acquired both the Deutsche Terminborse (futures and options exchange) and the Deutsche Kassenverein (clearing and settlement house) as well as the other regional stock exchanges. Trading, clearing, and settlement are linked electronically, while regulation and management has been centralized.

The private investor seems rather less content with less risky investments than equities, but may well continue to be risk averse. The fight against inflation has transferred from the Bundesbank to the European central Bank. A major change could come if more pensions were funded, and there are some signs of a drift in that direction through Speziäl Fonds etc., but it is a very gradual one. Although it is surprising that such a powerful economy as Germany's has so few quoted companies, the advantages and benefits of the market seem not to have lured many more companies into it; indeed some have delisted. The obligations of more open and transparent governance are not to everyone's taste.

As we have seen the German view of the purpose of companies gives shareholders an interest and a role, but not such a pronounced one as in the UK. They are important—much more so than a decade ago—but are still further down the pecking order. Private shareholders, other than proprietors, do not constitute a large proportion of the market anyway. The gradual decline in holdings by companies and banks may weaken dominance of the 'jam tomorrow' management school. In Germany as elsewhere arguments about maximizing shareholder value tend to beg the question of time scale. Thinking long has become so ingrained that it is unlikely to change; and in many industries it is still indispensable for success.

Takeovers: the 'discipline of the market'

Even though there are now more cases of hostile takeovers, and a greater awareness of potential pressures from disappointed shareholders, there does not seem to be any great concern within Germany that the general absence of threat of takeover is harmful. On the contrary such pressures as there are, coupled with the greater disciplines imposed by the GCGC, suggest that companies prefer where possible to keep out of the clutches of the market. The failure of the Neuer Markt reinforces such a view.

As it is, companies that do consistently badly may well come under pressure from some shareholders and from their bankers. Vorstands are not wholly insensitive to a declining share price when it is clear that it signals specific market disapproval: nor are Aufsichtsrate. It is not clear, however, that the absence of greater pressure has done much damage. The country has so far managed to live with a rising currency—though not to keep intact without subsidies the heavy industries, like coal, iron/steel, and shipbuilding, which are in general decline in the West. What the absence of general stock market pressures has undoubtedly assisted is the Germans' natural tendency to think in the long term and invest accordingly. A substantial part of the German economy is in the hands of private companies, but even where shares are quoted, German shareholders are said to take a long-term view—slow steady increases in real earnings, and heavy reinvestment leading to an increase in real assets employed, rather than a high level of distribution. Perhaps the picture may be changing with dividend payments becoming a more important measure of a company's health. In any event, low inflation has made it easier for Germans to see what the real picture is.

It is easy to oversimplify as regards investment and the time scale of returns, but it does seem highly probable that the absence of pressure from the German stock market reinforces the natural tendency German management would have anyway to set the balance at the point they feel right to equal the best foreign competition. If this is true one would expect the German system to show to good advantage internationally in areas where the balance needed to be set long-term, like engineering. Observations suggest this is so. In industries where the time scale is naturally shorter the comparative advantages are likely to be less marked—and so it seems. But this balance seems on the whole satisfactory to the Germans and there is little urge to change it unless returns are so poor as to excite the growing band of overseas investors in quoted companies into some sort of action.

Cooperation or confrontation?

The prevailing ethos is still one of cooperation rather than confrontation. It is demonstrated in the relationships between sections of the German economy—proprietors, professional management, employees generally, the financial sector, government, and academia. The dangers of exploitation inherent in cooperation are held in check partly by German institutional arrangements, partly by a sense of duty to the community. The question is whether a lack of 'constructive tension' will lead to inefficient cosiness. There are those who believe that the German system has led to inefficiency and structural over-rigidity which greater global competition has penalized. The absorption and rebuilding of the eastern Länder cost more and took longer than many had predicted. Unemployment remains high, but inflation was controlled and the evidence seems to be that the governance system still hangs together, even though the banks' role is less important and the market's is greater.

The law

I could detect no change in the basic attitude to the law described earlier, but there is a cloud on the horizon. Law has become a popular subject for study. There are now as many law students in training as there are lawyers. If they stay in the profession (which of course many may not), how will they all make a living, except by greater general litigiousness?

A change in the role for the banks

The banks are vitally important to the system, especially to unquoted companies. If it were ever true to say that 'their power depends on their shareholdings' it is so no longer. Besides, companies often have more than one bank and can change bankers if they choose. It is moreover more difficult for them to mobilize votes through the DSVR system—even if they wish to do so. Their position in a hostile bid for instance can no longer be taken for granted. It would be premature to write off their influence and there is no way in which to measure it. It is regarded as being there still, but much diminished.

There has been a tendency for major German companies, often cash rich, to do in-house many of the operations previously carried out by the banks for them—highly sophisticated treasury operations, for instance. In any case an exclusive relationship with one bank is now uncommon for big companies. Indeed, they may well have half a dozen main banks and use others for particular purposes. It is felt that the principle of relationship banking will survive, but there are other factors. Some major companies are immensely cash rich. And the market comes into play far more than it did—though still with a relatively small number of companies. There are of course giants among them.

The impression I had at the time of the first edition of *Keeping Good Company* was that the German system fitted its traditions well and worked effectively in the circumstances then prevailing. Internal and external developments have put pressure on it, but its main provisions remain intact. The factors for change have been the diminishing role of the banks, the international governance codes and principles, and the international capital markets. Even small companies like GPC Biotech have obtained a quotation on US Nasdaq which brings in its train the requirements of the Sarbanes-Oxley Act. If German companies wish to attract foreign capital, or a quotation abroad or both, there is no escaping the markets' requirements.

At the heart of the system—of any system—is its capacity for renewal. Can it ensure that management is 'refreshed' when necessary? ('Refreshed'—replaced.) On this criterion the jury is out—only the next few years will tell whether the changes work. Dr Cromme's commission is wise to give itself time to review progress and see whether the changes are actually productive; it is not enough for them to satisfy the press, politicians, rating agency, commentators, and management itself. Everything we ever wanted from companies—good competitive products, profits, concern for shareholders of all kinds, a responsible attitude towards society—depends on their governance. It remains to be seen whether recent developments represent progress as well as cost. The Germans seem optimistic about this.

Annex 2: *The German Corporate Governance Code**

1. Foreword

This German Corporate Governance Code (the 'Code') presents essential statutory regulations for the management and supervision (governance) of German listed* companies and contains internationally and nationally recognised standards for good and responsible governance. The Code aims at making the German Corporate Governance system transparent and understandable. Its purpose is to promote the trust of international and national investors, customers, employees and the general public in the management and supervision of listed German stock corporations.

The Code clarifies the rights of shareholders, who provide the company with the required equity capital and who carry the entrepreneurial risk.

A dual board system is prescribed by law for German stock corporations:

The Management Board is responsible for managing the enterprise. Its members are jointly accountable for the management of the enterprise. The Chairman of the Management Board coordinates the work of the Management Board.

The Supervisory Board appoints, supervises and advises the members of the Management Board and is directly involved in decisions of fundamental importance to the enterprise. The chairman of the Supervisory Board coordinates the work of the Supervisory Board.

The members of the Supervisory Board are elected by the shareholders at the General Meeting. In enterprises having more than 500 or 2000 employees in Germany, employees are also represented in the Supervisory Board, which then is composed of employee representatives to one third or to one half respectively. For enterprises with more than 2000 employees, the Chairman of the Supervisory Board, who, for all practical purposes, is a representative of the shareholders, has the casting vote in the case of split resolutions. The representatives elected by the shareholders and the representatives of the employees are equally obliged to act in the enterprise's best interests.

In practice the dual board system, also established in other continental European countries, and the internationally widespread system of management by a single management body (Board of Directors) converge because of the intensive

---

* Deustscher Corporate Governance Codex. Published by Kind permission, as a 'convenience translation' by Regierungs Kommission

interaction of the Management Board and the Supervisory Board, both being likewise successful.

The accounting standards of German enterprises are oriented on the 'true and fair view' principle and represent a fair picture of the actual conditions of the asset, financial and earnings situations of the enterprise.

The recommendations of the Code are marked in the text by use of the word 'shall'. Companies can deviate from them, but are then obliged to disclose this annually. This enables companies to reflect sector and enterprise-specific requirements. Thus, the Code contributes to more flexibility and more self-regulation in the German corporate constitution. Furthermore, the Code contains suggestions which can be deviated from without disclosure; for this the Code uses terms such as 'should' or 'can'. The remaining passages of the Code not marked by these terms contain provisions that enterprises are compelled to observe under applicable law.

For Code stipulations relating to not only the listed company itself but also its group companies, the term 'enterprise' is used instead of 'company'.

Primarily, the Code addresses listed corporations. It is recommended that non-listed companies also respect the Code.

As a rule the Code will be reviewed annually against the background of national and international developments and be adjusted, if necessary.

2.   Shareholders and the General Meeting

2.1   Shareholders

2.1.1 Shareholders exercise their rights at the General Meeting and vote there.
2.1.2 In principle, each share carries one vote. There are no shares with multiple voting rights, preferential voting rights (golden shares) or maximum voting rights.

2.2   General Meeting

2.2.1 The Management Board submits to the General Meeting the Annual Financial Statements and the Consolidated Financial Statements. The General Meeting resolves on the appropriation of net income and the discharge of the acts of the Management Board and of the Supervisory Board. It elects the shareholders' representatives to the Supervisory Board and, as a rule, the auditors.

Furthermore, the General Meeting resolves on the Articles of Association, the purpose of the company, amendments to the Articles of Association and essential corporate measure such as, in particular, inter-company agreements and transformations, the issuing of new shares and, in particular, of convertible bonds and bonds with warrants, and the authorisation to purchase own shares.

2.2.2 When new shares are issues, shareholders, in principle, have pre-emptive rights corresponding to their share of the equity capital.

2.2.3 Each shareholder is entitled to participate in the General Meeting, to take the floor on matters on the agenda and to submit materially relevant questions and proposals.

2.2.4 The chair of the meeting provides for the expedient running of the General Meeting.

2.3 Invitation to the General Meeting, Proxies

2.3.1 At least once a year the shareholders' General Meeting is to be convened by the Management Board giving details of the agenda. A quorum of shareholders is entitled to demand the convening of a General Meeting and the extension of the agenda. The Management Board shall not only provide the reports and documents, including the Annual Report, required by law for the General Meeting, and send them to shareholders upon request, but shall also publish them on the company's Internet site together with the agenda.

2.3.2 The company shall inform all domestic and foreign shareholders, shareholders' associations and financial services providers, who, in the preceding 12 months, have requested such notification, of the convening of the General Meeting together with the convention documents, upon request, also using electronic channels.

2.3.3 The company shall facilitate the personal exercising of shareholders' voting rights. The company shall also assist the shareholders in the use of proxies. The Management Board shall arrange for the appointment of a representative to exercise shareholders' voting rights in accordance with instructions; this representative should also be reachable during the General Meeting.

2.3.4 The company should make it possible for shareholders to follow the General Meeting using modern communication media (e.g. Internet).

3. Cooperation between Management Board and Supervisory Board

3.1 The Management Board and Supervisory Board cooperate closely to the benefit of the enterprise.

3.2 The Management Board coordinates the enterprise's strategic approach with the Supervisory Board and discusses the current state of strategy implementation with the Supervisory Board in regular intervals.

3.3 For transactions of fundamental importance, the Articles of Association or the Supervisory Board specify provisions requiring the approval of the Supervisory Board. They include decisions or measures which fundamentally change the asset, financial or earnings situations of the enterprise.

3.4 Providing sufficient information to the Supervisory Board is the joint responsibility of the Management Board and Supervisory Board.

The Management Board informs the Supervisory Board regularly, without delay and comprehensively, of all issues important to the enterprise with regard to planning, business development, risk situation and risk management. The Management Board points out deviations of the actual business development from previously formulated plans and targets, indicating the reasons therefore.

The Supervisory Board shall specify the Management Board's information and reporting duties in more detail. The Management Board's reports to the Supervisory Board are, as a rule, to be submitted in writing (including electronic form). Documents required for decisions, in particular, the Annual Financial Statements, the Consolidated Financial Statements and the Auditors' Report are to be sent to the members of the Supervisory Board, to the extent possible, in due time before the meeting.

3.5 Good corporate governance requires an open discussion between the Management Board and Supervisory Board as well as among the members within the Management Board and the Supervisory Board. The comprehensive observance of confidentiality is of paramount importance for this.

All board members ensure that the staff members they employ observe the confidentiality obligation accordingly.

3.6 In Supervisory Boards with codetermination, representatives of the shareholders and of the employees should prepare the Supervisory Board meetings separately, possibly with members of the Management Board.

If necessary, the Supervisory Board should meet without the Management Board.

3.7 In the event of a takeover offer, the Management Board and Supervisory Board of the target company must submit a statement of their reasoned position so that the shareholders can make an informed decision on the offer.

After the announcement of a takeover offer, the Management Board may not take any actions outside the ordinary course of business that could prevent the success of the offer unless the Management Board has been authorised by the General Meeting or the Supervisory Board has given its approval. In making their decisions, the Management and Supervisory Boards are bound to the best interests of the shareholders and of the enterprise.

In appropriate cases the Management Board should convene an extraordinary General Meeting at which shareholders discuss the takeover offer and may decide on corporate actions.

3.8 The Management Board and Supervisory Board comply with the rules of proper corporate management. If they violate the due care and diligence of a prudent and conscientious Managing Director or Supervisory Board member, they are liable to the company for damages.

If the company takes out a D&O (directors and officers' liability insurance) policy for the Management Board and Supervisory Board, a suitable deductible shall be agreed.

3.9 Extending loads from the enterprise to members of the Management and Supervisory Boards or their relatives requires the approval of the Supervisory Board.

3.10 The Management Board and Supervisory Board shall report each year on the enterprise's Corporate Governance in the Annual Report. This includes the explanation of possible deviations from the recommendations of this Code. Comments can also be provided on the Code's suggestions.

4. Management Board

4.1 Tasks and Responsibilities

4.1.1 The Management Board is responsible for independently managing the enterprise. In doing so, it is obliged to act in the enterprise's best interest and undertakes to increase the sustainable value of the enterprise.

4.1.2 The Management Board develops the enterprise's strategy, coordinates it with the Supervisory Board and ensures its implementation.

4.1.3 The Management Board ensures that all provisions of law are abided by and words to achieve their compliance by group companies.

4.1.4 The Management Board ensures appropriate risk management and risk controlling in the enterprise.

4.2 Composition and Compensation

4.2.1 The Management Board shall be comprised of several persons and have a Chairman or Spokesman. Terms of Reference shall regulate the allocation of areas of responsibility and the cooperation in the Management Board.

4.2.2 At the proposal of the committee dealing with Management Board contracts, the full Supervisory Board shall discuss and regularly review the structure of the Management Board compensation system.

Compensation of the members of the Management Board is determined by the Supervisory Board at an appropriate amount based on a performance assessment in considering any payments by group companies. Criteria for determining the appropriateness of compensation are, in particular, the tasks of the respective member of the Management Board, his personal performance, the performance of the Management Board as well as the economic situation, the performance and outlook of the enterprise taking into account its peer companies.

4.2.3 The overall compensation of the members of the Management Board shall comprise a fixed salary and variable components. Variable compensation should include one-time and annually payable components linked to the business performance as well as long-term incentives containing risk elements.

All compensation components must be appropriate, both individually and in total.

In particular, company stocks with a multi-year blocking period, stock options or comparable instruments (e.g. phantom stocks) serve as variable compensation components with long-term incentive effect and risk elements. Stock options and comparable instruments shall be related to demanding, relevant comparison parameters. Changing such performance targets or the comparison parameters retroactively shall be excluded. For extraordinary, unforeseen developments a possibility of limitation (Cap) shall be agreed for by the Supervisory Board.

The salient points of the compensation system and the concrete form of a stock options scheme or comparable instruments for components with long-term incentive effect and risk elements shall be published on the company's website in plainly understandable form and be detailed in the annual report. This shall include information on the value of stock options.

The Chairman of the Supervisory Board shall outline the salient points of the compensation system and any changes thereto the General Meeting.

4.2.4 Compensation of the members of the Management Board shall be reported in the Notes of the Consolidated Financial Statements subdivided according to fixed, performance-related and long-term incentive components. The figures shall be individualised.

4.3   Conflicts of Interest

4.3.1 During their employment for the enterprise, members of the Management Board are subject to a comprehensive non-competition obligation.

4.3.2 Members of the Management Board and employees may not, in connection with their work, demand nor accept from third parties payments or other advantages for themselves or for any other person nor grant third parties unlawful advantages.

4.3.3 Members of the Management Board are bound by the enterprise's best interests. No member of the Management Board may pursue personal interests in his decisions or use business opportunities intended for the enterprise for himself.

4.3.4 All members of the Management Board shall disclose conflicts of interest to the Supervisory Board without delay and inform the other members of the Management Board thereof. All transactions between the enterprise and the members of the Management Board as well as persons they are close to or companies they have a personal association with must comply with standards customary in the sector. Important transactions shall require the approval of the Supervisory Board.

4.3.5 Members of the Management Board shall take on sideline activities, especially Supervisory Board mandates outside the enterprise, only with the approval of the Supervisory Board.

5. Supervisory Board

5.1 Tasks and Responsibilities

5.1.1 The task of the Supervisory Board is to advise regularly and supervise the Management Board in the management of the enterprise. It must be involved in decisions of fundamental importance to the enterprise.

5.1.2 The Supervisory Board appoints and dismisses the members of the Management Board. Together with the Management Board it shall ensure that there is a long-term succession planning. The Supervisory Board can delegate preparations for the appointment of members of the Management Board to a committee, which also determines the conditions of the employment contracts including compensation.

For first time appointments the maximum possible appointment period of five years should not be the rule. A re-appointment prior to one year before the end of the appointment period with a simultaneous termination of the current appointment shall only take place under special circumstances. An age limit for members of the Management Board shall be specified.

5.1.3 The Supervisory Board shall issue Terms of Reference.

5.2 Tasks and Authorities of the Chairman of the Supervisory Board

The Chairman of the Supervisory Board coordinates work within the Supervisory Board and chairs its meetings.

The Chairman of the Supervisory Board shall also chair the committees that handle contracts with members of the management Board and prepare the Supervisory Board meetings. He should not be Chairman of the Audit Committee.

The Chairman of the Supervisory Board shall regularly maintain contact with the Management Board, in particular, with the Chairman or Spokesman of the Management Board and consult with him on strategy, business development and risk management of the enterprise. The Chairman of the Supervisory Board will be informed by the Chairman or Spokesman of the Management Board without delay of important events which are essential for the assessment of the situation and development as well as for the management of the enterprise. The Chairman of the Supervisory Board shall then inform the Supervisory Board and, if required, convene an extraordinary meeting of the Supervisory Board.

5.3 Formation of Committees

5.3.1 Depending on the specifics of the enterprise and the number of its members, the Supervisory Board shall form committees with sufficient expertise. They serve to increase the efficiency of the Supervisory Board's work and the handling of complex issues. The respective committee chairmen report regularly to the Supervisory Board on the work of the committees.

5.3.2 The Supervisory Board shall set up an Audit Committee which, in particular, handles issues of accounting and risk management, the necessary independence required of the auditor, the issuing of the audit mandate to the auditor, the determination of auditing focal points and the fee agreement. The Chairman of the Audit Committee should not be a former member of the Management Board of the company.

5.3.3 The Supervisory Board can delegate other subjects to be handled by one or several committees. These subjects include the strategy of the enterprise, the compensation of the members of the Management Board, investments and financing.

5.3.4 The Supervisory Board can arrange for committees to prepare Supervisory Board meetings and to take decisions in place of the Supervisory Board.

5.4 Composition and Compensation

5.4.1 For nominations for the election of members of the Supervisory Board, care shall be taken that the Supervisory Board, at all times, is composed of members who, as a whole, have the required knowledge, abilities and expert experience to properly complete their tasks and are sufficiently independent. Furthermore, the international activities of the enterprise, potential conflicts of interest and an age limit to be specified for the members of the Supervisory Board shall be taken into account.

5.4.2 To ensure the Supervisory Board's independent advice and supervision of the Management Board, not more than two former members of the Management Board shall be members of the Supervisory Board and Supervisory Board members shall not exercise directorships or similar positions or advisory tasks for important competitors of the enterprise.

5.4.3 Every member of the Supervisory Board must take care that he/she has sufficient time to perform his/her mandate. Members of the Management Board of a listed company shall not accept more than a total of five Supervisory Board mandates in non-group listed companies.

5.4.4 The election or re-election of members of the Supervisory Board at different dates and for different periods of office enables changing requirements to be taken into account.

5.4.5 Compensation of the members of the Supervisory Board is specified by resolution of the General Meeting or in the Articles of Association. It takes into account the responsibilities and scope of tasks of the members of the Supervisory Board as well as the economic situation and performance of the enterprise. Also to be considered here shall be the exercising of the Chair and Deputy Chair positions in the Supervisory Board as well as the chair and membership in committees.

Members of the Supervisory Board shall receive fixed as well as performance-related compensation. Performance-related compensation should also contain components based on the long-term performance of the enterprise.

The compensation of the members of the Supervisory Board shall be reported in the Notes of the Consolidated Financial Statements, subdivided according to components. Also payments made by the enterprise to the members of the Supervisory Board or advantages extended for services provided individually, in particular, advisory or agency services shall be listed separately in the Notes to the Consolidated Financial Statements.

5.4.6 If a member of the Supervisory Board took part in less than half of the meetings of the Supervisory Board in a financial year, this shall be noted in the Report of the Supervisory Board.

5.5 Conflicts of Interests

5.5.1 All members of the Supervisory Board are bound by the enterprise's best interests. No member of the Supervisory Board may pursue personal interests in his/her decisions or use business opportunities intended for the enterprise for himself/herself.

5.5.2 Each member of the Supervisory Board shall inform the Supervisory Board of any conflicts of interest which may result from a consultant or directorship function with clients, suppliers, lenders or other business partners.

5.5.3 In its report, the Supervisory Board shall inform the General Meeting of any conflicts of interest which have occurred together with their treatment. Material conflicts of interests and those which are not merely temporary in respect of the person of a Supervisory Board member shall result in the termination of his mandate.

5.5.4 Advisory and other service agreements and contracts for work between a member of the Supervisory Board and the company require the Supervisory Board's approval.

5.6 Examination of Efficiency

The Supervisory Board shall examine the efficiency of its activities on a regular basis.

6. Transparency

6.1 The Management Board will disclose without delay any new facts which have arisen within the enterprise's field of activity and which are not known publicly, if such facts could, owing to their impact on the asset and financial situations or general business development, substantially influence the price of the company's registered securities.

6.2 As soon as the company becomes aware of the fact that an individual acquires, exceeds or falls short of 5, 10, 25, 50 or 75% of the voting rights in the company by means of a purchase, sale or any other manner, the Management Board will disclose this fact without delay.

6.3 The company's treatment of all shareholders in respect of information shall be equal. All new facts made known to financial analysts and similar addressees shall also be disclosed to the shareholders by the company without delay.

6.4 The company shall use suitable communication media, such as the Internet, to inform shareholders and investors in a prompt and uniform manner.

6.5 Any information which the company discloses abroad in line with corresponding capital market law provisions shall also be disclosed domestically without delay.

6.6 The purchase or sale of shares in the company or of related purchase or sale rights (e.g. options) and of rights directly dependent on the stock market price of the company by members of the management board and supervisory board of the company or is parent company and by related parties shall be reported without delay to the company. Purchases based on employment contracts, as a compensation component as well as immaterial purchase and sale transactions (EURO 25,000 in 30 days) are excepted from the reporting requirement. The company shall publish the disclosure without delay.

Corresponding information shall be provided in the Notes to the Consolidated Financial Statements. The shareholdings, including options and derivatives, held by individual Management Board and Supervisory Board members shall be reported if these directly or indirectly exceed 1% of the shares issued by the company. If the entire holdings of all members of the Management Board and Supervisory Board exceed 1% of the shares issued by the company, these shall be reported separately according to Management Board and Supervisory Board.

6.7 As part of regular information policy, the dates of essential regular publications (including the Annual report, interim reports, General Meeting) shall be published sufficiently in advance in a 'financial calendar.'

6.8 Information on the enterprise which the company discloses shall also be accessible via the company's Internet site. The Internet site shall be clearly structured. Publications should also be in English.

7. Reporting and Audit of the Annual Financial Statements

7.1 *Reporting*

7.1.1 Shareholders and third parties are mainly informed by the Consolidated Financial Statements. They shall be informed during the financial year by means of interim reports. The Consolidated Financial Statements and interim reports shall be prepared under observance of internationally recognised accounting principles. For corporate law purposes (calculation of dividend, shareholder protection), Annual Financial Statements will be prepared according to national regulations (German Commercial Code), which also form the basis for taxation.

7.1.2 The Consolidated Financial Statements will be prepared by the Management Board and examined by the auditor and Supervisory Board. The Consolidated Financial Statements shall be publicly accessible within 90 days of the end of the financial year; interim reports shall be publicly accessible within 45 days of the end of the reporting period.

7.1.3 The Consolidated Financial Statements shall contact information on stock option programmes and similar securities-based incentive systems of the company.

7.1.4 The company shall publish a list of third party companies in which it has a shareholding that is not of minor importance for the enterprise. The trading portfolios of banks and financial services companies, on which voting rights are not exercised, are disregarded in this context. The following shall be provided: name and headquarters of the company, the amount of the shareholding, the amount of equity and the operating result of the past financial year.

7.1.5 Notes on the relationships with shareholders considered to be 'related parties' pursuant to the applicable accounting regulations shall be provided in the Consolidated Financial Statements.

7.2 *Audit of Annual Financial Statements*

7.2.1 Prior to submitting a proposal for election, the Supervisory Board or, respectively, the Audit Committee shall obtain a statement from the proposed auditor stating whether, and where applicable, which professional, financial and other relationships exist between the auditor and its executive bodies and head auditors on the one hand, and the enterprise and the members of its executive bodies on the other hand, that could call its independence into question. This statement shall include the extent to which other services were performed for the enterprise in the past year, especially in the field of consultancy, or which are contracted for the following year.

The Supervisory Board shall agree with the auditor that the Chairman of the Supervisory Board will be informed immediately of any grounds for disqualification or impartiality occurring during the audit, unless such grounds are eliminated immediately.

7.2.2 The Supervisory Board commissions the auditor to carry out the audit and concludes an agreement on the latter's fee.

7.2.3 The Supervisory Board shall arrange for the auditor to report without delay on all facts and events of importance for the tasks of the Supervisory Board which arise during the performance of the audit.

The Supervisory Board shall arrange for the auditor to inform it and/or note in the Auditor's Report if, during the performance of the audit, the auditor comes across facts which show a misstatement by the Management Board and Supervisory Board on the Code.

7.2.4 The auditor takes part in the Supervisory Board's deliberations on the Annual Financial Statements and Consolidated Financial Statements and reports on the essential results of its audit.

3

Japan

Introduction

The main features: obligation, family, consensus

There are marked differences in culture between Japan and all the four other nations studied and some of these have an important bearing on corporate governance. Experts are divided on their importance, some believing them to be great, others feeling that they are less significant than the special factors affecting Japan's economic development in the post-war period. Wherever the truth lies I am sure we should not neglect them. It is not a long list and some are more significant than others. We need to consider briefly what these are.

It is not necessary to delve too deeply into history or geography though both are important, and as time goes on it is impossible to ascribe precise causes and origins to what exists today. Suffice it to rehearse briefly the main factors that everyone knows. Geographically Japan has a large population on a series of extended islands without good natural resources and with much of its usable land mass subject to earthquakes. Spiritually it has tolerated many faiths and has woven into the fabric of thought and principle many threads of Confucianism and Buddhism: politically and economically its modern history starts with the convulsion of the Meiji restoration over 125 years ago.

The three main general features that affect Japanese attitudes towards corporate governance are their concepts of 'obligation', 'family', and 'consensus', and all are linked.

'Obligation' does not derive from broad general principles as it does in Judaeo-Christian cultures but from specific causes. This may be to return a service for one rendered or it may derive from a more general relationship, for example, to one's family or old alumni, or one's company (or ministry) or the country. This sense of particular obligation is common elsewhere but it feels stronger in Japan.

So does the sense of 'family', which is part of the same approach. In the context of this study it certainly seems stronger in regard to the company than in other countries. It is not just a case of paternalism but of common membership of an enterprise which envelops one's life to an unusual degree. In his book *Corporate Governance: What can be Learnt from Japan* (2002) Simon Learmount speaks of 'a community of employees' (chapter 6): the company commands the allegiance and prime attention of everyone from top to bottom. They in turn expect to be treated as befits a member of the family. The type of group of companies known as Keiretsu, which are described later, is felt to be more than a simple economic concept (important as the economic aspects are); it is a family. The very word 'Kaisha' has this flavour—it is much nearer to 'company' than 'corporation'. Families are not all equal and companies are not, either. The big companies expect to provide more than smaller or weaker ones, which can afford less. There are, in this respect, two Japans.

The third element is that of consensus. The adversarial approach is uncommon. Immense efforts go into building a consensus in every walk of life, and this is particularly evident in corporate governance. Building a consensus does not mean that all parties to it are equal—often they are very unequal, but the Japanese feel it best (even at the cost of a slow and often cumbersome decision-making progress) to try to win the hearts and minds of people whenever possible, rather than to proceed by diktat. Of course, there are exceptions, but consensus is the norm in a way most other countries would find strange, and it is not an obvious element, especially as the Japanese give seniors much deference.

These concepts mean much mutual and reciprocal help for those within a 'family', but almost by definition much different treatment for those outside. It is not always difficult to get inside and many a foreigner has done so satisfactorily—and indeed, has found it virtually imperative. Getting in deeply is, it appears, more difficult for all sorts of reasons, of which perhaps individualism and language are the two best known. Language is obvious enough and real, but it can also be an excuse as well as a reason; given enough training and practice foreigners do become highly proficient. Individualism is very well illustrated in a book entitled *You Gotta have Wa* by Robert Whiting (1990), which describes how difficult US baseball stars, who were much wanted, found it to integrate into Japanese teams which had a more collegiate approach. It may be argued that to some extent all organizations have to work in a collegiate way: it is just that it is much more the norm in Japan, and much more heavily emphasized.

The emphasis on 'family' has certain other effects. Although foreigners work happily in many Japanese companies (and vice versa), there seems to be a limit on how far they can go. Japanese companies are most assuredly not alone in this; the road to the top is not entirely open in many other countries, either. It will, I believe, present a growing problem generally as multinational companies account for an ever-increasing proportion of business, and it will therefore matter greatly to the Japanese. There may be few nationals of any country who are ambitious enough to make the changes to their lives necessary to qualify for the top places in a company, if it requires moving to a distant location, absorbing a strange culture, and learning a difficult language to a high degree of proficiency. But that road needs to be open to those who are brave enough to take it and competent enough to warrant advancement: one or two Japanese companies like Sony have shown the way. The merger between Nissan and Renault seems to have been a conspicuous success in which the absorption of French nationals into the company in Japan has played an important part.

The concept of family seems to have affected the way in which the market economy has developed. One interlocutor described the Japanese system as being based on 'community logic' against the US system which is based on 'market logic'. In the UK and USA the tendency has been for the market to operate freely and in recent times for the state to pick up the social consequences, for example in unemployment pay and national assistance. In Japan, the tendency has been to regard it as preferable to prevent and delay potential tears in the social fabric and for government to act to mitigate the effects of any changes that cannot be avoided. This seems true at both company and national level and what it boils down to is belief that 'the family' comes first. Put another way, the fabric of society should not be wantonly or carelessly torn and if necessary the state should step in to prevent it.

We can set aside the reconstruction period after the war where it was a case of husbanding scarce resources and determining priorites—a task filled brilliantly by MITI and other government departments (though one should dismiss the idea of this acting in concert; they were often at loggerheads) and Japan is not so very different from other countries in protecting uneconomic industries for social reasons; think of the EEC Common Agricultural Policy. The Japanese rice producers would have much in common with the European beet sugar industry. As normal trade patterns were re-established the government, like others, faced problems of decline. The concept of family meant that it focused on damage limitation by redeployment and retraining rather by trying to buy its way out of the inevitable.

The concept of 'family' is by definition limited; outsiders do not enjoy its protection. So in a downturn small companies that have no 'family protection' may go the wall more easily. There are degrees of closeness in a company's family and that can be painful for its more distant member.

The company in society

Firms in Japan grow, fail, and merge as they do elsewhere, but the notion of 'the company in society' is generally present; to put it another way, there is concern about the social fabric. This probably reflects basic societal attitudes anyway, but my interlocutors believe it was accentuated by the war and its aftermath which required the aims of business to be plural—not just the generation of profit but the healing of economic and social wounds by policies that recognized their significance.

Of course profit matters and is essential for survival, but to the Japanese it is not all that matters—even in these days when the importance of 'shareholder value' has become a sort of religion elsewhere. Japanese companies are far less ready to 'downsize' than their US/UK counterparts if it means throwing people out of work. This can of course affect 'the bottom line' but then so do many policies which reflect 'corporate social responsibility'. Quite apart from the effect on shareholders' pockets, these policies may impair the allocative process in which money tends over time to flow to the places that offer the best returns. That said, there are indications that dividends are rising. Some people describe this as the 'China effect'; others attribute it to foreign raids on cash-rich Japanese companies (for instance by Steel Partners) which forced management to increase distributions.

As an indication of all the tensions and inherent contradictions we need not look beyond the passage from the 2004 paper by the Tokyo Stock Exchange entitled 'Principles of Corporate Governance for Listed Companies', reproduced below (p. 114).

The role of government

The traces of government policy in the post-war period, during which it inspired and controlled the recovery of the economy from the disastrous effects of the 1941–5 war, are still with us. Some of the arrangements live on, like the role of some sponsoring ministries, for instance those concerned with the construction industry where they still operate a system of 'guidance' (having largely shaken off bribery scandals). The principal department in the early years was MITI, the Ministry of International Trade and Industry, but this has now evolved into METI—the Ministry of Economy, Trade and Industry, whose primary focus is macroeconomic. It has no need to prompt or cajole the new industries like IT in the way it did the old like shipbuilding. Many companies are big enough and rich enough to stand up for themselves. Guidance for the finance industry has been transferred from the Ministry of Finance to the Financial Services Agency.

One recent development (2003) has been the establishment of the Industrial Revitalization Corporation of Japan (IRCJ). Its task is to keep companies afloat that are worth saving, keeping creditors, including the banks, at bay whilst it develops a financial strategy for the business. It had a capital of 50,507 million yen and 130 employees in August 2003. By August 2004 it had helped twenty-one companies; one of the reasons for its creation was the weaker position of the banks themselves, which made them unable or unwilling to mount a rescue from their own resources.

There is more to the IRCJ than mere rescue—like preserving a valued brand name. Thus it bailed out Kanebo in February 2004 to stop Japan's second biggest cosmetics maker from falling into the hands of KAO Corporation; as the *Japan Times* of 30 August 2004 put it, 'This effectively short circuited the market while putting tax payers' money at risk'. At that time there was speculation that the retailer Daiei might go the same way to keep out of the clutches of Wal-Mart, a prospect feared by competitors Aeon Co. and Ito-Yokado Co. and also by the supporters of Daiei's money-losing baseball team the Daiei Hawks, concerned for their heroes and the stadium. By the time October arrived, there were second thoughts. The London *Financial Times* reported on 13 October that IRCJ had withdrawn, refusing even to revalue Daiei 's assets. At that stage the IRCJ had not definitively and finally left the scene. Whatever the outcome, it was a most unusual and public drama; it was not possible to complete the story at the time of going to press but the latest information there was that IRCJ would become involved—to the great satisfaction of the press.

The IRCJ is seen as a temporary expedient. It has, in other words, a finite life, being scheduled to disband in two or three years' time. It has however proved its value as a temporary stopgap to plug the hole left by the banks' reluctance to participate after their spate of balance sheet adjustments they had to make in order to face up to non-performing loans. One wonders whether the French dictum 'rien dure que la provisoire' will find a new application.

The Kanebo Case is so illuminating that I have included the Press Release of summer 2004 as annex 3C.

What the Japanese authorities have created is an organization that has some of the elements of US Chapter 11 (the procedure under which, with the consent of the court, management continues to run the company whilst there is a moratorium on debt) and some of those of the Bank of England's 'London Approach' (in which the banks involved voluntarily keep their facilities in place whilst the problems are addressed). The aim in all cases is to assist a company's survival, but only the Japanese include all injection of public money, albeit to be repaid.

Litigation

Americans see 'due process' as cementing together disparate peoples; they are equal before the law and in judicial process. The Japanese consider litigation between themselves as a shameful failure of human relations, though they keep their powder dry to deal with foreigners (and employ lawyers to deal with ordinary legal formalities). There have however been two dramatic changes during the last few years which have transformed the position:

1. Japanese companies are now bringing matters to the courts in a way previously unknown. The takeover battle for UFJ between Mitsubishi and Sumitomo is a case in point.
2. A change in the law lowered the threshold for people who wished to launch a derivative suit. Directors (who stand to be sued) are concerned if they fully understand the threat to them. This will not encourage people to take up directorships. A little kudos is a poor counterbalance to potential ruin, even though Japanese companies are making use of D&O insurance.

The unions

It is no disrespect to Japanese unions to have left them till last. They are not trade-based but enterprise-based. The great spring offensive for the annual pay claim is nearly genuine, but all companies have the same settlement date, which gives the government and employers a chance to produce a common stance on the prevailing economic facts. The result is to establish clearly in people's minds where the band of expectation lies within which settlement is likely.

This short account of union activities is not intended to belittle their contribution. Although there were some fierce struggles immediately after the war, the unions became much more responsible from the mid-1950s onwards. There are occasional instances of confrontation, for instance at Nissan and Fujitsu—which certainly damaged Nissan for some time. Generally speaking, the relationship between union and management is not bedevilled by folk memories of bitter battles and a long history of sour antagonism. Instances of confrontation are now rare. Commentators ascribe the reasons for the improvement to the better education and training the workforce receives, which make the relations with management easier to handle, and to a more accommodating attitude on both sides. Management has made increasing efforts to make sure that the workforce understands its policies. The unions have reciprocated by trying to understand the companies' needs. There is as a result greater unity of purpose than there was; leaders of unions sometimes find themselves appointed to the board on retirement (quite common in the banking industry). In general it seems that although unions of course push their members' claims, they are *au fond* concerned with the company's prosperity and, given that dividends are meagre, there is less room for argument about how the cake should be cut. Indeed, there have been examples when the union has played a leading part in causing a president to stand down. When it comes to mergers and takeovers they do not seem to have much of a say.

The weakening of the 'lifetime employment' system has resulted among other things in a growing incidence of part-time work, in which employees are more vulnerable. There does not appear to have been any determined effort to recruit them for their better protection.

Whose company is it anyway?

Before we leave the background to Japan and its concept of 'family first' we ought to consider one particular effect of this attitude—the idea of 'society first' fits well with the doctrine of 'shareholders last'. There seems little doubt that to most Japanese, employees and suppliers are 'in the family'— they depend on the company and have a strong relationship with it. Shareholders on the other hand may be here today and gone tomorrow (quicker if it is a hedge fund). They are seldom the original people who did subscribe their savings with the long term in mind and might on that account be counted as 'family'. Arguments that neglecting shareholders' interests vitiates the market system seem remote. After all, despite shareholders being neglected Japanese companies have thrived—to the point where foreigners bustle to buy into them.

When the Tokyo Stock Exchange (TSE) came to produce its 'Principles of Corporate Government for Listed Companies' in March 2004, it had to reflect the distaste of Japan Business Federation, the Keidanren, for the whole subject. (They could see clearly enough that better governance means more accountability and circumscribed personal power.) No wonder that the following paragraph appeared:

The profit-pursuing activities of enterprises are not fulfilled in modern economic society without complicated coordination of interests among various concerned parties (shareholders or investors, management, employees, suppliers, creditors, and local communities). As the areas of corporate activity are expanding, corporations face a growing need to take into account the values of different cultures and societies. As such, enterprises will have to engage in their profit-pursuing activities with a greater awareness of their social responsibilities, with greater transparency and fairness in accordance with market principles, while accepting full accountability to the entire economic community as well as shareholders and investors. The relationship with every concerned party bears an influence on corporate governance. From the perspective of the capital market, its focus centers primarily on relations between shareholders (including potential shareholders) and management.

Two forces have been at work these last years to push shareholders up a notch or two. The first is the gradual increase in the holdings of savings institutions, which need a better income stream to meet their obligations. The second, and more militantly, is foreigners, who now on average own about 18% of Japanese companies, which naturally means that in some companies they own much more—perhaps even a majority.

The TSE's governance principles reflect the fierce but largely submerged debate that might be titled 'Whose company is it anyway?' In other words, who owns it? Like many other such questions, it is probably misplaced. A better one would be 'What claims are there against the company and what is their relative priority?' Viewed like that, it is not at all difficult to put employees and creditors at the top of the list—what becomes inexplicable is the decision of many managements to accumulate funds when all their claims have been handsomely met, to the point where cash piles up. Do the shareholders not have a claim to at least part of such surpluses? They should not be surprised if predators cast envious eyes on the cash mountains that such policies produce. It is not as if dividends were stratospheric—the Tokyo Stock Exchange Fact Book from 2002 shows (p. 105) an average yield of 1.14% on first division stocks. (compared with 0.72% five years before (1996) and 4.20% forty years earlier (1962)).

The Pension Fund Association set out its policy for voting proxies on 20 February 2003. There is a marked difference in emphasis from the Tokyo Stock Exchange's compromise noted above, as is shown in the following extract:

Significance of stock investment
Companies are the main entities which create profits. The continuous prosperity of companies is a basis for the stable management of pension plans. For the benefit of pension plan participants and pensioners, it is necessary for companies to operate with the highest respect to the interests of shareholders and secure stable corporate profits for a long term. For that purpose, it is essential that corporate governance in companies functions efficiently.

Basis of corporate governance
The most important thing in corporate governance is to establish an internal procedure within companies to check corporate management from the standpoint of shareholders' interests. From this viewpoint, it is necessary that the functions of execution and supervision should be segregated within companies, and the board of directors should carry out properly the function of supervising management from

the viewpoint of shareholders' interests. To ensure that this supervisory function is fulfilled effectively, it is essential to appoint an outside director(s), who is independent and who has no interest in the company. In addition, accountability to shareholders concerning company management should be implemented by sufficient disclosure in both quality and quantity.

In reality, in many Japanese companies the segregation of function is barely visible as the traditional insider system, led by wise management, was felt capable of handling both. This notion has been more severely tested as contingency risks have grown in periods of slower growth.

The Law

Studying corporate governance in any country means examining the law. We need to know the framework in which companies operate since they are not creatures of nature but of statute. We may also accept that the laws of economics will prevail. In a market economy there are a thousand roads to success but only a limited number of ways to fail. One of the differences between countries lies in the province of the behavioural sciences. We find that structures and processes both reflect and emphasize a particular society's normal patterns of behaviour. The extent of the boss's powers (whatever his title) is a case in point and so is the desire for checks and balances on the use of those powers. And one of the insights the Japanese constantly provide is that human beings adapt slowly. Keeping society together therefore requires a policy of gradualism. And in the development of corporate governance that is precisely what we find, as we shall see.

There are three sets of laws that companies must consider. Those concerning tax need not concern us here. There is a law governing disclosure, rather on the US model, which is administered by Japan's Securities and Exchange Commission; this covers financial statements. The main law governing companies, however, is the Commercial Code (CC) of Japan and the version referred to in this chapter is the one published in 2004 by Nishimura & Partners. Individual articles of the code will be identified at the appropriate places in the course of the chapter. The Diet passed a new law on 30th june 2005 see page 152.

The different types of company are identified as:

- Partnership Companies (Gomei-Kaisha) (CC 62–145);
- Limited Partnership Companies (Goshi Kaisha) (CC 146–164);
- Joint Stock Companies (Kabushiki Kaisha) (CC 165–230);

This chapter is concerned solely with the last of these.

The basic structure of a joint stock company is the one familiar in the western world—shareholders, directors, and managers. It follows therefore that the chain of accountability is similar—but not identical as the Commercial Code now draws a distrinction between 'large' and 'small' companies, in relation to auditing requirements (Law No. 22 of 2 April 1974 as amended). These are defined in Article 1.2.

A recent change in the law provides for an alternative structure to the traditional one which includes statutory auditors. A company may now instead opt to be a 'Company with Committees'. If it does so it must have (CC article 21.5 in Section 4) a nominating committee, an audit committee and a compensation committee, and one or more executive officers. This structure and its committees are considered in more detail below.

Accounting and auditing

Japan has not escaped the international movement towards the convergence of accounting standards. Talks started in October 2004 between the International Accounting Standards Board and the Accounting Standards Board of Japan to reduce differences between them.

Companies: The Japanese Universe

Introduction

At the end of the financial year 2001 the *Japan Almanac* tells us there were 2,607,923 companies of which 452,145 were in manufacturing industry. Between them they employed 36,950,000 people. Of all these companies 2,174 were listed at the end of 2003 (according to the Tokyo Stock Exchange's yearbook), substantially more than in 1992 (1,651).

Financing

Japan Securities Research Institute 2002 (pp. 4 and 9) sheds some interesting light on companies' sources of funds. Table 3.1 shows comparable figures, in percentages for 1980 and 2000.

Viewed from the other end, so to speak, Table 3.2 shown how individuals' financial assets were composed.

The Bank of Japan's figures do not vary significantly from those shown in the tables, which I have retained to ensure comparable samples.

Table 3.1. Companies' sources of funds (%)

	1980	2000
Borrowings	54.7	38.4
Securities	8.1	36.5
Inter-business credits	37.2	16.6
Of the securities:		
Equities	4.8	30.8

Table 3.2. Composition of financial assets (%)

	1980	2000
Securities	15.6	8.5 (6.5 equities and 2.0 bonds)
Insurance	13.3	28.1
Time deposits	51.4	42.7
Cash	11.4	11.9

Groups of companies

It is usual in many countries for companies which are in law separate entities to be bound to other companies by some sort of linkage, either formal or informal. Formal linkages include wholly owned subsidiaries, and associated companies in which another company has a minority shareholding. There are also satellite companies whose goods or services mainly go to a single customer. Japan provides many examples of all these arrangements.

One of the features of industrial reorganization after the Meiji restoration was the development of Zaibatsu—combines usually built round a bank. By 1941 they controlled 32% of the national investment in heavy industry and nearly half of Japan's banking resources (Clark 1979: 43). Four of the most prominent were Mitsubishi, Yasuda, Sumitomo, and Mitsui. Their structure was a holding company controlled by the founding family which in turn controlled a dozen or so core companies including the bank, the trading company, the trust company, and the insurance company, and round them clustered other associates, affiliates, and subsidiaries.

After the war the Occupation authorities dismantled the Zaibatsu, and although nothing quite like them has emerged, as noted earlier, Japanese industry is in effect two nations, the big companies and the rest. It is possible—and indeed it has often happened since the war—for a small company to grow and make the transition; among the most significant features of big companies are the capacity and resources to offer recruits a lifetime career with all the diversity and security that implies. In recent years the pressures on even the top companies have risen, but are being met by various means. These include passing on as much pressure as possible down the chain, cutting back on bonuses, out-posting and 'gardening leave', reducing the hours for part-time workers, reducing recruitment, and natural wastage.

Since the war two distinct types of group have developed, which foreigners often lump together under the generic title 'Keiretsu', which means, broadly speaking, 'Association'. The more usual of these to UK/US eyes is the vertical Keiretsu, in which subcontractors and sub-subcontractors (unto the fourth layer) service a main manufacturer like Toyota. A variation of this theme occurs when, at the other end of the chain, a manufacturer controls retail outlets.

The organization theory that lies behind this kind of arrangement is that entrepreneurial talent is more likely to flourish in independent subsidiaries (which may, if good enough, market their wares elsewhere) than in divisions. 'Partnership sourcing' is a convenient title for a common arrangement in which a big company develops a long-term relationship with a supplier; this involves deep contact at an early stage of the product cycle so that designs are developed together, and it implies that the purchaser nurtures the supplier (as well as squeezing him hard on quality, delivery, and price). Outsiders complain that such arrangements make it difficult to break in. Certainly they have to be good enough and have to get in whilst the door is open, often some years before the order is finally placed.

It is in the horizontal Keiretsu groups that the memories of the pre-war Zaibatsu echo most loudly. These are a version of conglomerate in which companies in often dissimilar industries are grouped together, frequently with a bank at the centre, but sometimes more industrially centred: Mitsubishi, Mitsui, Sumitomo are examples, though these groups include important banks too. This second trio are basically family groups with common trademarks and are the direct heirs of the pre-war Zaibatsu. Banks are said to have encouraged the formation and development of groups of this kind, as a source of mutual strength and reciprocal help. The Fair Trade Commission in 1992 reckoned that 188 companies were in these Keiretsu groups and that they accounted for 17% of the capital, 19% of the assets, and 16% of the sales of all quoted companies (and their definition of a group was reckoned to be narrow). Companies in a horizontal Keiretsu group are often linked by cross-holdings.

What then are the benefits of belonging to a group? The main one is accomplished through meetings of the company presidents, but the list is extensive:

- exchanges of information;
- deployment of business experiences and know-how;
- dnhancing credibility through the corporate brand;
- corporate management assistance;
- financial assistance (including extending credit dates and the acceptances of new shares);
- loans to affiliate from a financial company.

Cross-shareholdings

A survey by Fumio Kuroki of the Financial Research Group sheds an interesting light on cross-shareholdings at 31 March 2002. The banks had long been at one end of these transactions with business companies at the other. The banks, however, had to make sure their holdings did not exceed Tier 1 capital and the Bank of Japan's share purchase programme helped them sell off 6.4 trillion yen of shares. Companies did not necessarily reciprocate.

The survey covered 2,674 companies. Cross-shareholdings did not imply balanced reciprocity. The market value of cross-held shares dropped sharply between 2001 and 2002—from 27.6 to 17.6 billion yen. Even so the latter figure exceeds the market capitalization of listed banks—16.3 billion yen. The financial institutions were large net sellers; the long-term shareholding ratio dropped 3.1% to 27.1% by value and by 4.5% by volume; 2,281 companies (85%) were still cross-shareholders and that includes the 1,615 who do not have a shareholder with more than 20%. Indeed, 93% of these are confirmed cross-shareholders.

The seventh survey of the Fair Trade Commission (18 May 2001) covered six major groups. These covered 151 companies excluding banks. Their position in the Japanese economy has been declining since 1989 though they still accounted for 13.15% of total capital, 11.21% of total assets, and 10.82% of sales. The leadership of a group rests either with a bank or a trading company, which will hold shares in most of the constituent companies within it.

The government stepped in twice, creating the banks' shareholding purchase programme (BSPP) in February 2002 and the Bank of Japan's share purchase programme (BJSPP) that November. The BSPP could not buy bank shares from corporations after the BJSPP started operations. A revision of the law in 2003 allowed business corporations to sell bank shares to the BSPP up to over half of the value of the shares held reciprocally in the companies by the bank concerned.

What all this seems to mean is that cross-shareholdings between banks and companies are melting, but far faster on the banking side.

Fumio Kuroki of the Financial Research Group in a publication on 18 November, 2003 gave the figures shown in Table 3.3.

Looking at the cross-shareholding relationships of 2,441 business corporations listed on stock exchanges in fiscal year-end 2001 and 2002, we find that of the confirmed cross-shareholdings with large bank groups at the end of fiscal 2001, bank groups reduced their stake in 45% of cross-shareholdings during fiscal 2002. Thus business corporations retained their bank shares, but were still unable to keep banks from unilaterally unwinding reciprocal shareholdings. At least 70% of business corporations whose shares were unwound by banks chose not to unwind any of their reciprocal holdings of bank shares. For the majority of companies, the unwinding of cross-shareholdings with banks was thus one-sided, and on the side of banks. As it happened, bank shares appreciated sharply during this period.

In fact, Shareownership Survey results by industry show that business corporations (including unlisted companies) still own 31.4% of all bank shares, down only 1.2% from the previous fiscal year.

Here are two examples of cross-shareholdings taken at random from the *Japan Company Handbook*, Autumn 2004:

Sumitomo Rubber Industries
Sumitomo Electric	27.9%
Sumitomo Corp.	3.9%
Sumitomo Mitsui Banking	2.1%

Mitsui Chemicals
Sumitomo Mitsui Banking	2.3%
Mitsui Life Insurance	2.2%
Mitsui & Co	2.1%
Chuo Mitsui Trust & Banking	2.0%
Mitsui Sumitomo Insurance	1.9%

Looking at the complete list of minor holdings in companies in the handbook, one is struck by the extent of cross-shareholding that still exists and not just in the groups, though the figure at 6.7% is far less than that for groups—20.25% as quoted above.

It is interesting to consider why the change is occurring. We have already noted the increased pressure on banks' capital; to this can be added the pressure of changes in the accounting rules. Now that such investments have to be marked to market, there is an increased balance sheet risk.

Table 3.3. Unwinding of cross-shareholdings by banks and business

	1977	1981	1987	1989	2002
Cross-shareholdings of banks business corporations				3,506	
of which, cross-shareholdings unwound by banks				1,577	(45%)
of which, business corporations who:					
also unwound cross-shareholdings				1,127	(71%)
did not unwind cross-shareholdings				222	(14%)
unwinding status is unknown				228	(14%)
Average shareholding[a]	2.19	1.78	1.52	1.42	1.38
Former Zaibatsu	2.16	2.05	1.70	1.57	1.46
Bank related	2.22	1.51	1.33	1.27	1.29
Cross-shareholdings[b]	23.86	25.48	22.65	21.64	20.25
Former Zaibatsu	28.86	32.16	28.93	27.46	
Bank related	18.85	18.75	16.36	15.82	

[a] Average shareholding: average shareholding of one company in any other one company belonging to a Keiretsu presidents' meeting club (%).

[b] Cross-shareholdings: the percentage of shares in other club companies owned by member companies of a presidents' meeting club.

Source: Fair Trade Commission, 'Company Groupings' (1992 and 2002).

Another factor is the pressure on institutional investors for greater income — which often does not sit comfortably with shareholdings whose main function was to support a business relationship.

Shareholders

Who owns what: the statistics

The most significant group of shareholders is the financial institutions with 39.1%. Next come business corporations, with 21.5%; third, individuals, with 20.6%; and fourth, foreigners, with 17.7%. The financial institutions total includes:

Trust banks	21.4%
City banks & other banks	7.7%
Life insurance companies	6.7%
Annuity trusts	5.8%
Investment trusts	4.0%

(*Source*: *Tokyo Stock Exchange Fact Book* 2004)

Looking behind these numbers we find that individuals only put 8–12% of their financial assets into securities. Sources differ about the precise number whilst the Pension Fund Association for Local Government Officials records that only 22.7% of the assets are in equities—13.4% domestic and 9.3% foreign; 64.1% are in domestic bonds. This mix is slowly changing.

Table 3.4 shows that individuals have just about held their share of the market at around 20%, that foreigners have increased theirs to about 22%, that business corporations at 22% are diminishing, as are financial institutions—mainly the banks and life insurance companies. This squares with anecdotal evidence of unwinding cross-shareholdings.

Shareholders

These are some examples of holdings above 5% taken at random from the Autumn 2004 *Japan Company Handbook*.

Yokohama rubber (p. 52)

Foreign	12.3%
Japan Trustee Services Bank	9.3%
Master Trust Bank of Japan	5%
Furukawa Electric	5.8%
Zeon Cpn	5%

Table 3.4. Distribution percentage of market value owned by type of shareholder

(Units: %)

Survey year	Govt. and local govt.	Financial institutions	LTCB city, and regional banks	Trust banks	Investment trusts	Annuity trusts	Life insurance cos.	Non-life insurance cos.	Other fin. institutions	Business corps.	Securities companies	Individuals	Foreigners (cos. + indiv.)
1970	0.6	31.6	15.8	—	2.1	—	10.0	3.7	2.1	23.9	1.3	37.7	4.9
1975	0.4	35.5	19.0	—	2.2	—	10.2	4.4	2.0	27.0	1.4	32.1	3.6
1980	0.4	38.2	19.9	—	1.9	0.4	11.5	4.6	2.3	26.2	1.5	27.9	5.8
1985	0.3	39.8	20.9	—	1.7	0.8	12.3	4.1	2.4	28.8	1.9	22.3	7.0
1986	0.9	41.5	14.9	7.3	1.9	1.0	12.8	4.0	2.5	30.1	2.1	20.1	5.3
1987	0.5	42.5	14.9	8.6	2.6	1.1	12.4	4.0	2.6	30.3	2.3	20.4	4.1
1988	0.4	44.1	15.7	9.8	3.1	1.0	12.6	4.1	2.0	29.0	2.3	19.9	4.3
1989	0.3	43.5	15.7	10.2	3.7	0.9	11.8	3.9	1.9	29.5	2.0	20.5	4.2
1990	0.3	43.0	15.7	9.8	3.7	0.9	12.0	3.9	1.6	30.1	1.7	20.4	4.7
1991	0.3	42.8	15.6	9.7	3.4	1.0	12.2	3.9	1.4	29.0	1.5	20.3	6.0
1992	0.3	42.9	15.6	9.9	3.2	1.2	12.4	3.8	1.2	28.5	1.2	20.7	6.3
1993	0.3	42.3	15.4	10.0	2.9	1.4	12.1	3.7	1.1	28.3	1.3	20.0	7.7
1994	0.3	42.8	15.4	10.6	2.6	1.6	12.0	3.7	1.1	27.7	1.2	19.9	8.1
1995	0.3	41.1	15.1	10.3	2.2	1.8	11.1	3.6	1.0	27.2	1.4	19.5	10.5
1996	0.2	41.9	15.1	11.2	2.0	2.4	11.1	3.6	0.9	25.6	1.0	19.4	11.9
1997	0.2	42.1	14.8	12.4	1.6	3.8	10.6	3.5	0.9	24.6	0.7	19.0	13.4
1998	0.2	41.0	13.7	13.5	1.4	4.7	9.9	3.2	0.8	25.2	0.6	18.9	14.1
1999	0.1	36.5	11.3	13.6	2.2	5.0	8.1	2.6	0.9	26.0	0.8	18.0	18.6
2000	0.2	39.1	10.1	17.4	2.8	5.5	8.2	2.7	0.7	21.8	0.7	19.4	18.8
2001	0.2	39.4	8.7	19.9	3.3	6.0	7.5	2.7	0.7	21.8	0.7	19.7	18.3
2002	0.2	39.1	7.7	21.4	4.0	5.8	6.7	2.6	0.7	21.5	0.9	20.6	17.7
2003	0.2	34.5	5.9	19.6	3.7	4.5	5.7	2.4	0.9	21.8	1.2	20.5	21.8
High (Year)	0.9 (1986)	44.1 (1988)	20.9 (1985)	21.4 (2002)	4.0 (2002)	6.0 (2001)	12.8 (1986)	4.8 (1979)	2.6 (1987)	30.3 (1987)	2.3 (1988)	37.7 (1970)	21.8 (2003)
Low (Year)	0.1 (1999)	31.6 (1970)	5.9 (2003)	7.3 (1986)	1.4 (1998)	0.4 (1982)	5.7 (2003)	2.4 (2003)	0.7 (2001)	21.5 (2002)	0.6 (1998)	18.0 (1999)	2.7 (1978)

Notes: The number of shares has been calculated on a 'unit-of-share' basis since 1985 survey; the number of trust banks is included in that of LTCB, city, and regional banks in and before 1985 survey.

Yushin Precision Instrument (p. 766)
Korani LP   17.4%
Mayumi Kurani   14%
Foreign   10%
Yushin Industry   5%

Hankyu Department Stores (p. 1245)
Hankyu Department Stores Kyoeikai   17.5%
Japan Trustee Services Bank   10.5%
Foreign   12.7%

Sitowa Sangyo (p. 167)
Itochu Shokuryo Hanbai   9.6%
Nissho Iwai   6.3%

Japan General Estate (p. 1440)
Foreign   27.7%
Makuto Nishimara   17.2%
Isami Suzuki   7.4%
Morgan Stanley International   5.2%

Although I used 5% as a cut-off point the full list in every case included smaller holdings by varied financial companies, often with between 1 and 2%.

Table 3.5 gives a list of the largest shareholders in Japan.

Shareholders' activism

There are signs that there is less than universal consent that shareholders should be relegated to the end of the queue when a company has prospered to the point where it has stacked up cash. US buy-out fund Steel Partners took stakes in two such companies, Sotoh and Yushiro Chemical with a hostile takeover bid in mind. Yushiro jacked up its dividend from 13 to 200 yen *and* pledged to pay a further 300 yen over the next two years. Steel Partners withdrew, savouring capital gains on their investment in the two companies of 2.7 billion yen.

More subtly and less aggressively there are signs that highly regarded institutions like the Pension Fund Association (PFA; with its US$80,000 million under management) are looking for more dynamic dividend policies from companies that can afford it. At the same time they resent profligacy, like paying bonuses when the company is still in the red. But PFA does not accept the argument that a company need not explain its dividend policy because it does not belong to the shareholders anyway, and they subject proposals for stock repurchase to close scrutiny.

Table 3.5. Largest shareholders in Japan (March 2003)

Shareholder	Amount held in billion yen
Japan Trustee Services Bank	2,380 Custody Bank (Sumitomo Mitsui)
Master Trust Bank of Japan	1,942 Custody Bank (Mitsubishi UFJ)
Ito-Yokado Co. Ltd.	1,687
Chase Manhattan Bank NA, London	658
Dai-ichi Life Insurance	572
State Street Bank and Trust	567
Mizuho Corporate Bank	470
Roche	448
Nomura Securities	426
Nippon Life	398
Aeon	389
ExxonMobile	278
Matsushita Electric Industry	229
Mitsubishi Corporation	229
Trustee and Custody Services Bank	191 Custody Bank (Mizuho)
Sekisui Chemicals	177
Canon, Inc.	175
Meiji Yasuda Life	164
Sumitomo Mitsui Bank	161
The Shell Petroleum Company	156
Moxley and Co.	149 ADR Depository (JPMorgan)
Yasuda Fire and Marine Insurance	137
MC Retail Investments (Mitsubishi Corp)	134
UNY Co Ltd.	134
Bank of Tokyo-Mitsubishi	131
Mellon Bank	122
Ken Enterprise (Softbank)	120
UFJ Bank	116
Kirin Brewery Company Ltd	105
Daiei, Inc.	102
Tokio Marine & Fire	92
Mizuho Trust & Banking	77
BNP Paribas Securities	68
Norinchukin Bank	64
Mitsui Life	62
Robert Bosch	61
SumitomoCorp	59
Sumitomo Electric Industry	53
Mizuho Bank	52

The PFA has for some years regarded voting as part of its fiduciary duties: it now recommends fund managers, trust banks, and fund management companies to follow its guidelines so that there is a recognized reason for an abstemption or negative vote. Its record of voting results as of June 2004 is as in Table 3.6.

Investor relations programmes are improving though some presidents complain they are a waste of time because the percentage they see 'only care about the share price and do not care a fig about the company'.

The PFA is concerned with the long-term return on equities and therefore with shareholder value. It resents dividend policies that do not reflect profits and cash reserves and the underlying attitude that a company does not belong to its shareholders so the board does not have to explain. They had started a fund to invest in companies with good corporate governance—an opposite kind of focus fund to those who look for badly governed companies with a view to reforming them. It intends setting up a list of conforming and performing companies to set an example. It will be interesting to see whether this carrot works better than the stick. Shareholders are reluctant to act together; it is costly and time-consuming to set up a proper programme.

Quite apart from individual forays by speculators into the Japanese equity market designed to prod management into greater generosity with the dividend, there are signs of a more general attack from elements in the

Table 3.6. Voting result by PFA in June 2004

	For	Against	Total
Allocation of profit/loss	919	337	1,256
Election of directors	523	536	1,059
Election of corporate auditors	903	107	1,010
Amendment of article of association	1,194	12	1,206
Payment of retirement allowance to directors/corporate auditors	441	615	1,056
Reviewing remuneration amount to directors/corporate auditors	109	0	109
Issuance of stock subscription right for option plan	159	65	224
Appointment of independent auditors	35	0	35
Approval of corporate restructuring	58	4	62
Other items	135	7	142
Shareholders' proposals	14	60	74
	4,490	1,743	6,233

USA. The Californian State Employees—CalPERS—has long been in the van of the better governance movement at home. Now it has set out principles for the Japanese market the main points of which are:

1. Shareholders have a duty to exercise responsibilities as corporate owners.
2. Japanese corporate boards should consider the interests of, and strive for accountability toward, all shareholders.
3. Japanese corporate boards should use the corporate governance principles developed by the corporate governance forum of Japan as a benchmark of their duties and responsibilities to shareholders. Of these, CalPERS views the following principles as most significant:

   A. Corporate boards should include directors who are truly independent from the corporation and its affiliates.
   B. The size of Japanese corporate boards should be reduced to enable effective and efficient decision-making regarding the company's strategic plan and executive performance.
   C. Japanese corporations should appoint auditors who are truly independent from its affiliates.
   D. Development and periodic review of best practice guidelines should continue and reviewing bodies should include investors based outside Japan.
   E. Best governance practices in Japan should include elements that strengthen management accountability to corporate owners through the director–shareholder relationship.

A further example of shareholder activism comes from another US firm, Taiyo & WL Ross, which has set up a fund for the purpose of prodding companies into better strategies. In the case of NIFCO it was to cause it to improve its focus—and it has stakes of more than 5% in seven other companies. They assert they do not wish to bully, but are not convinced they have always converted targets to better governance: 'In general, the mindset is not so much "I've been converted to governance" but "I'm afraid of being taken over so I've got religion!"'

Even Sony has been attacked: 38% of the stock is in foreign hands. Shareholders proposed at the last AGM that individual directors' salaries should be disclosed. The board decided not to do so, even though the resolution mustered 30% of the role. There are details about Sony's regime in the Annex 'Sony's Distinctive Approach to Corporate Governance' (Annex 3E).

There does not yet seem to be any highly developed sense among some institutions, including insurance companies, that they should always cast their votes, and do so in a way that furthered their interest as shareholders (and therefore as Fiduciaries for their policy holders).

Japanese Companies: The Top Command

Titles often confuse the unwary. The person with top executive authority is called the president, sometimes president and chief executive, sometimes CEO; the revised commercial code strengthens their power. The directors are now only appointed for a year, which gives the president the opportunity to evaluate them. Presidents are known as Shacho. Their duties are not defined by law. They will invariably be 'representative directors'.

The presidents are in a strong position, but the normal Japanese practice of collective decision-making means that they are less likely to be personally exposed unless they get their personal relationships wrong and fail to ensure harmony. There are occasions when it becomes clear their leadership leaves something to be desired. Although they may be more dedicated to their company and less to themselves than their Western counterparts (few hit the headlines; conspicuous consumption is for gangsters—they are less likely to go on an ego trip), they like power as much as any CEO in the world. Even so, Japanese self-discipline has its limits. If the president is the kind of person who is attuned to the views of colleagues he or she will sense from the tone and substance of questions at the top management committee or the board that they are dissatisfied. And if it is clear that their dissatisfaction is deepening presidents may feel that they owe it to the company to stand down. Even if they do not, eventually they may find it hard to resist other influences that build up within the company, for example, from the chairman, or past chairmen and presidents, especially if they are still advisers, and especially if they have a proprietary interest. (There are tales of the founders of business still calling the shots long after they had ceased to hold a formal position; generally, however, this is not so.)

If, however, presidents do not want to listen, and have a dominant personality, the Japanese themselves seem to regard it as particularly difficult to get rid of them even though they has palpably gone off the boil and company results are deteriorating, until such time as trouble is well developed. The Itoman case is a classic example. The president, Kawamura, who was ultimately dismissed (itself unusual as we have seen), is alleged to have made most major decisions on his own. According to the London *Financial Times* (June 1992), this was the first formal sacking of the president of a listed Japanese company since 1982. In less dramatic circumstances, restraint and respect for authority make hinting embarrassing (to those who do not wish to listen), and more drastic action wholly unpalatable. It is in practice very difficult for a Japanese board to unship such a president unless they have external help. Occasionally it is the unions which act, as was noted earlier, and help bring the crisis to a head. There are cases of their intervening effectively.

Thanks to Booz Allen Hamilton, the consultants, there are now some figures (reported in the London *Financial Times* on 17 May 2004.) Apparently nearly 13% of Japanese presidents retired voluntarily the previous year compared with only 0.6% being dismissed and a similar number being displaced by merger. In Europe CEOs were more likely to be fired—4.6%—with another 2% going because of a merger.

Not all companies have a separate chairman nowadays but those who do have often promoted a retiring president. Among those which have a separate chairman are Hitachi, Showa Shell, and Sony. Among those who do not are Nippon Telegraph & Telephone, DoCoMo, and Mizuho. The president will have played a major part in choosing his successor, so when he is 'kicked upstairs' he will wish to support him, if only to show how good a choice he made. If his successor disappoints, the chairman may feel it part of his duty to whisper into his ear that he should step aside. Such moves are naturally hidden from the public eye and can only be deduced from events.

Whilst the board remained a cypher, and power lay with the Jomukai(a small inner committee), which the president chaired, the chairman would in normal circumstances only have had a ceremonial role—sometimes scarcely that. It remains to be seen whether this will change as boards shrink in size, outsiders are recruited, and real decisions are taken. In some companies chairmen may be sidelined, but in others they begin to resemble the chairman of a UK or US board. And where a company has adopted the 'three-committee' system the chairman will generally be a member of the nominations and compensation committees but not the audit committee.

The role of chairmen is not defined in law. They are referred to as the Kaicho. Their power and influence vary from company to company. They may be given a special role in respect of appointments and they may have a representative role in trade or industry bodies and serve on their committees.

Many companies have advisers, though fewer than formerly, especially in the financial sector, where the Ministry of Finance opposed them. It was always necessary to enquire carefully about what part an adviser really played. Sometimes it was a sinecure, a way of providing an office and logistic support to a retired executive. Sometimes it was for a wise person whose sage advice might be sought. And sometimes it was for a specialist. An adviser might have real influence—or none.

The Board of Directors

The law

The Commercial Code, subsection 2, articles 254.2–272 deals with directors' appointment, removal, and powers. There must be at least three (CC 255) and they are appointed by shareholders, initially for a period of one year and thereafter for a maximum of two years (CC 256). They may be reappointed. Article 260 puts the management of the corporate affairs of the company into the hands of a 'Representative Director' plus other directors given representative powers by board resolution—such directors have to report quarterly to the board. Significantly, this section 260–3 covers the rights of Corporate Auditors (see below) to attend board meetings.

Recent changes: the 'three-committee' system
The Commercial Code was recently amended to offer companies an alternative to the traditional structure (article 21.5 *et seq.*). To adopt this system a company must have a nominating, audit, and compensation committee plus one or more executive officers. It may not have 'corporate auditors' as well—not to be confused with the external auditors (see below).

In the event it appears a relatively small number of companies have taken up this choice—although some of them are among Japanese industrial leaders. Sony's latest report is reprinted below. At the last count the number of 'three-committee' companies was about thirty and rising slowly; one has tried it and reverted.

Boards of directors have changed significantly and are continuing to do so. Taking first the traditional structure complete with corporate auditors (see below), it was commonplace fifteen years ago to find them composed of several layers of senior executive directors headed by the president (or CEO) and usually by a chairman. There were no outsiders—the role of the board was seen as mainly 'ceremonial', as might be expected of a 40–50-strong body. Important business was conducted by a small committee called the Jomukai and decisions passed to the board for ratification.
The principal developments are that

1. Boards have reduced in size, and significant discussion and decision rest with them. At the same time some companies have introduced an operating executive officer system, thus removing some executives with operational responsibilities from the board. Such officers are known as Shikko Yakuin.
2. Boards often contain outside directors.
3. The role of the Corporate Auditors has increased in importance as an organ or governance (see paragraphs below on Kansayaku).

4. The Jomukai still functions, and is important but does not now usurp, as it were, the authority of the board.

More recent figures and a longer sample from Nihon Keizai Shimbun, quoted by the Japan Corporate Auditors' Association in September 2004, say that 630 out of 2,108 listed companies have come to appoint outside direct-ors—an increase of 28% from 2003. The number of such directors has risen from 916 to 1,065, and 20% of companies with the traditional structure have outsiders. In thirty companies outsiders form a majority on the board. What proportion of the outsiders could be classified as 'independent' it is difficult to say.

Change is continual, so given the differences in the sample both sets of figures may well be accurate. What matters more than being precise about numbers is that the tendency is clear enough. The outside forces on Japanese boards are strengthening, an outcome much desired by shareholders as we shall shortly see.

In practice the president chooses executive directors, generally after nomination by or consultation with the person's superiors (who will be on the board already) and other colleagues, and the recommendations will be rubber-stamped, first by the board and then by the general meeting of shareholders. With such a well-structured system there will be few surprises (any more than there would be in promotion to the upper ranks of a civil service). People's track records and quality will be well known in the organization. Promotion thereafter largely depends on the president, who may seek advice from some company elders (who are perhaps advisers) and the chairman. Presidents also nominate their own successors, but generally consult no one about this, though they may tell the chosen person in order to give them time to prepare for office. The done thing is to receive prefer-ment with surprise—'This is a very sudden asking—most unexpected', as it was put to me. It is extremely rare for a nominee not to be appointed: in one case it took a combination of the unions and main bank to stop a nomin-ation and work out a solution that avoided too much loss of face. If somehow the succession fails because a president is sacked or dies, the chairman will coordinate the search for the successor: if there is no chairman the board will organize itself to find the right person. The chairmanship is usually filled by a retiring president. Toyo Keizai Shinposha (1991) put some figures to the process. The decision in the choice of president was taken as follows:

by the president alone	48.3%
in consultation with the chairman and advisers	32.9%
in agreement with the board	22.1%

taking account of parent or related companies   11.1%
taking account of the company's bank(s)   1.4%
other   2.6%

In normal times the choice of people for the board and especially of the president are entirely internal matters. No one outside the company is consulted, though certain privileged people may be informed as a matter of courtesy, for instance, the presidents of the main banks, and shareholders, suppliers, and customers. In some Keiretsu-type groups some top appointments may require consultation with the lead company. In industrial companies which have built up a network of subsidiaries and divisions top appointments in them are generally made by head office. No company admitted to consulting a government department, though sometimes they too were informed as a matter of courtesy: it is rare but not unknown for an official very informally to give guidance about a particular person. The government does, however, retain formal powers in respect of appointments to the board of certain industries which once lay in the public domain.

All this will change in companies that adopt the 'three-committee' system as one of these is the nominations committee.

Examples: the traditional system
Taking a handful of successful companies at random we find:
Showa Shell Sekiyo KK
A chairman (representative director)
A president (representative director)
Six directors
Two full-time and one part-time corporate auditor

NTT DoCoMo
A president and CEO. The board is gradually shrinking—now it has twenty-four directors (three senior executive vice presidents, eight executive vice-presidents and thirteen senior vice-presidents), four full-time and one part-time corporate auditors. It also has an advisory board that meets monthly and questions management vigorously. It contains ten experienced CEOs, of a calibre to be independent directors; balancing the long and short term is a major topic for the advisory board and the board itself.

NTT
President and CEO (representative director)
Eleven directors (three senior executive vice-presidents who are also representative directors plus 8 other vice-presidents)
Five corporate auditors

The Three-Committee System

Hitachi
Chairman
President and CEO (representative director)
Two directors with executive duties
Ten other directors, some of whom are from outside Hitachi. It is they who exclusively form the audit committee and also serve either on the nomination or the compensation committee.

Hitachi provide a full background note on the director's background. This is at Annex 3B.

Sony
Chairman (Representative Director)
President (Representative Director)
Four directors with executive duties
Eight outside directors

Sony's progress report in 2005 makes informative reading. An example of the classical kind of board may be seen in one of its most successful companies. The details are in Annex 3E.

Table 3.7 shows some June 2004 figures about some companies in Section 1 of the Tokyo Stock Exchange—interesting because of what they reveal about the size of boards and the number of outside directors in them.

Kansayaku

There have already been several references to this organ of governance, which is unique to Japan, and is variously translated as 'Statutory Auditor' or 'Corporate Auditor'. The latter term is preferred by the Japan Corporate Auditors' Association (JCAA) and is therefore used here. It should not be confused with the external auditors, whose function is much the same in Japan as elsewhere. The Kansayaku themselves work as a board.

In the narrative below it is suggested that what Kansayaku actually do varies from company to company. There is no doubt, however, that the amendments of 2001 significantly strengthened their position by

- forcing the president to seek the approval of the board of Kansayaku before putting proposals to shareholders;
- extending their team of office from three to four years;
- requiring large companies to appoint at least half the Kansayaku from outside;

Table 3.7. Number of directors and outside directors

Number of directors	Number of outside directors	
8	3	Hitachi Plant Eng. & Cons.
14	4	Niws
8	5	Kanebo Ltd
8	3	Hitachi Chemical Co Ltd
9	4	Toyama Chemical Co.
11	6	Eisai Company Ltd
12	4	Konica Minolta Holdings Inc.
8	4	ST Chemical
6	3	Hitachi Metals Ltd
11	2	Asahi Tec
8	3	Hitachi Cable, Ltd
6	3	Hitachi Powdered Metals
8	3	Hitachi Construction Machinery
7	2	Hitachi Kiden Kogyo
11	3	NSK Ltd
14	4	Hitachi, Ltd
14	4	Toshiba Corporation
12	5	Mitsubishi Electric Corp.
5	3	Kokusai Electric
16	8	Sony Corporation
8	4	Nippon Columbia Co.
8	3	Hitachi Maxell
9	4	Sumida Electric (OTC)
6	3	Hitachi Medical
7	3	Shin-Kobe Electric Machinery
8	5	Hoya Corporation
10	3	Fuji Seal
6	2	Nissei Sangyo
7	4	Shaddy

Japanese companies at a glance

Based on data prepared by J-IRIS Research, June 2004, from 1,557 companies listed on 1st section of Tokyo Stock Exchange.,

Board of Directors (of 1,557 companies)

Average number of directors per company	10.5
Average number of outside directors per company	0.6

Box *cont.*

Number of companies with more than one outside
director   523
> (Two-thirds is of companies are without an outside director)

Average number of outside directors per company
with outside director   1.7
>> (Definition of an outside director: any board member who has never
>> been an employee of the same company or its subsidiaries, and who is not
>> responsible for the management of business (Commercial Code Article 188-
>> 2.7.2))

Board of Corporate Auditors (of 1,514 companies on TSE 1st section)

Average number of corporate auditors per company   3.9

Average number of outside corporate auditors per company   2.3
>> (Responsibilities of a corporate auditor: to review financial statement, to
>> monitor business execution by the management.
>> Definition of an outside corporate auditor: any member who has not been an
>> employee of the same company for five years immediate to the appointment,
>> rule will be revised in 2006.)

Three-committee system (adobted by 43 companies out of 1,557)

Average number of directors per company   9.2

Average number of outside directors per company   4.2
>> (Three-committee system: First introduced in 2002 commercial code review; a
>> companiy can abolish board of corporate auditors if it decides to set up three
>> board committees: audit, nominating and compensation. It must appoint at
>> least two outside directors, and at least one 'executive officer' to perform the
>> role of a CEO.)

Traditional management model with corporate auditors (retaineable 1,514
companies)

> Companies with a non-statutory executive officer (Shikko-yakuin)   500

> Companies with voluntary audit committees

> (mainlydealing with risk management and compliance)   550

Board independence

Percentage of directors originating in	All directors	Outside directors only
dominant shareholder (holding more than 33%)	4.9	13.6
other major shareholders	6.0	19.4
keiretsu companies	3.0	11.6
more than seven years	28.7	8.9

close family members	3.1	0.7
banks	4.7	4.5
ministries and public entities	2.2	2.3
employees of the same company	76.3	0.0
Companies with more than 21 directors		57
Companies reducing number of directors from previous year		302
Average reduction		2.7
Companies increasing number of directors from previous year		347
Average increase		1.5
Companies with non-statutory executive officers		50
(abolishing Jomu-kai)		536

- requiring the directors to seek the agreement of the Kansayaku when there is a proposal to limit the directors' liability.

The Commercial Code is succinct (Article 274):

1 A corporate auditor shall audit the directors' execution of their duties
2 A corporate auditor may at any time request the directors and the managers or other employees to provide a report on the business operations or may investigate the status of the corporate affairs and assets of the company.

The succeeding paragraphs cover his term of office, duty to report, right to investigate subsidiaries, duty to examine and report matters to be put to the shareholders' meeting, and his right to tell a director to desist from an action that breaches a law or regulation if it might significantly damage the company.

As we have seen, Japanese companies must either have corporate auditors or else opt for the 'three-committee' system and the vast majority have so far stuck to the traditional system. Their role has been interpreted in 2002 by the JCAA to mean that there is in effect a double function. The first is a compliance audit—are the directors observing the law and the company's Articles? The second relates to the discharge of the directors' duties—an 'appropriateness' audit. This appears to mean that decisions should be properly taken, in other words that there is a sound process of decision making (something courts in other countries have tackled e.g. *Smith* v. *Van Gorkom* in the USA). Providing the process is sound, the statutory auditors' duties do not extend to double-guessing decisions. Put another way, the directors can rest on the business judgement rule. Even so the Kansayaku have no mean task, which includes attending board meetings. A JCAA survey in 2001 which covered 3,625 individual members showed that 89% of companies had either three or four Statutory Auditors, and that in fifty leading companies just over half had been 'insiders', i.e. previously employed by the company.

The evidence suggests that the Kansayaku now take their duties with great seriousness. In more than half the companies sampled by the JCAA they attended the Jomukai, the top management committee, as well as the board. The proportion rose from 63% in 1996 to 71% in 2001—though not all the Kansayaku necessarily went.

That said, the seriousness with which the Statutory Auditors take their task does vary. Anecdotal evidence is that at one end of the spectrum the duties are performed perfunctorily. It is an agreeable (and paid) place in which to park wholly retired employees. More and more, however, it appears that their role is seen as a useful organ of governance—the JCAA calls it a 'horizontal two board structure', an expression which should be seen against a background in which boards are nearly or wholly executive. It would seem to me that this system is a halfway house between a German type of two-tier board and the UK unitary board where a significant number of independent directors also man the audit and other committees. It is difficult to see how the systems could coexist in a company, but many statutory auditors might well prove satisfactory independent directors if a company adopts the three-committee system. One of the consequences of the change in the Commercial Code offering companies a choice of governance system is to cause them to turn their minds to a subject which some regard as threatening and many feel to be superfluous. Be that as it may, if they decide to stay with the traditional system with Kansayaku they have to consider afresh what their role is.

The system is stricter in larger companies, of which there are about 9,000 and they must have three Kansayaku, of whom one must be full-time, who constitute a board. None of them may be a director at the same time and they serve for a four-year term. At least half must be 'outsiders', i.e. not a past employee or director of the company. The Kansayaku board is appointed by and reports to the shareholders. In practice they work closely with directors. They cooperate with the external auditors, who are required to report 'inappropriate acts or violations of the law' to them; they in turn monitor and manage the external financial audit.

A full list of the powers of the Board of Corporate Auditors and the power of Corporate Auditors is at Annex 3A and it shows how extensive they are. As to the reality, there seems to have been a move towards making this authority real, though doubtless in some smaller companies things will be different.

Finally, there are some statistics from the JCAA corporate auditor survey (which pre-dated the introduction of the three-committee system, and reflects that all companies were obliged to have Kansayaku). In fifty leading companies rather more than half of the Kansayaku came from within the business. Of the 'externals' 57% were ex-chairman or presidents from other companies, 20% were lawyers, and 14% academics or ex-government officials. Note that after a five-year 'cooling off' period, an ex-director or employee may qualify to be an outsider.

The long arm of Sarbanes-Oxley

The consequential rule changes which followed the Sarbanes-Oxley Act have caused problems. Section 301 on audit committees simply does not fit the Kansayaku system, as the Keidanren pointed out in October 2002. Discussions continue on how to resolve the differences.

Amakudari

Literally translated, Amakudari means 'descent from heaven' and it refers to the practice, common until recently, of officials joining commercial companies, usually as directors, after retirement. Directors' origins are stated in the comprehensive list, in Japanese, which covers all companies, so their provenance is not secret. The process by which their descent is arranged is arcane. It may be an offer a company cannot refuse—without causing offence ('Have I got a director for you!'). It may be the other way round, a company seeking to ingratiate itself with a ministry. Indeed, critics have sometimes associated Amakudari with corruption.

Amakudari is now no longer prevalent in companies in the financial sector except in the rare cases where the ministry of Finance decides to strengthen top management, e.g. by nominating the president of Yokohama Bank. In some industries the practice is still commonplace, e.g. construction, energy, and transportation. Two big construction companies, Obayashi and Kajima, each have five and DoCoMo has three. Several of the appointees came from relevant departments but some clearly did not—they were top people from Japan Railways, which says a lot for the quality of the people they had recruited.

The Amakudari have little direct effect on governance except that they swell the size of the board if there are several of them. And the impression I was given is that their descent was not always a matter of pride for someone who has reached the board by that route, even if chosen not for their connections but their ability. Having said that the practice ensures that some first-rate talent is used constructively that might otherwise be wasted. Some officials, however, are subject to a five-year cooling-off period before they can serve with a firm which had connections with their department.

Annual General Meetings

The law

The Commercial Code requires them to be held annually at or near head office (CC 134 & 233).

They are in fact heavily concentrated on a single day in June. Figures for 2002 of 2,542 companies were July, 9; August, 25; September, 19; October, 6; November, 17; December, 40; January, 19; February, 43; March, 154; April, 34; May, 132; June, 2,044.

This is a leftover from the days when *sokaiya*—gangsters—used to use AGMs to extort money from managers by blackmail. It is now illegal to make such payments but the memory lingers and so do occasional scandals. But the choice of 4 June is related to the fact that most companies' fiscal year ends on 31 March and that makes June a natural time for the AGM.

How long meetings last is related to the size of the company. Of 2,529 companies, those with assets of more than 500 billion yen had meetings which mainly went on for more than 2.5 hours. In the highest category, 50 out of 87 companies had meetings lasting more than 5 hours. At the other end of the range, companies with assets of not more than 20 billion yen generally finished the meeting within an hour. Of 596 companies in this range, 393 had meetings that lasted less than 40 minutes. Generally, the length of meetings is increasing.

One thing has changed recently: the hurdle for shareholders to get something on the order paper. It is now 1% of the voting rights or 300 voting shares held for six months (Article 232.2). If shareholders do attend an AGM the directors and corporate auditors are bound to explain relevant matters put to them; if they have received written notice well in advance, they must explain. And the shareholders can appoint an inspector to examine matters submitted by the directors and corporate auditors (238).

Even if AGMs were held on different dates boards could reasonably expect support from their allies (through 'friendly' holdings), whether or not these were strictly reciprocal. In any event shareholders round the world tend not to intervene when the price is headed north.

A recent survey attempted to assess the ratio of stable shareholders, without specifying too closely what that actually meant. Of the 1950 companies asked, 107 returned no reply. Of the rest, the assessment was as shown in Table 3.8.

The formal functions of the AGM include the appointment of directors and the approval of the dividend. They are also increasingly used to ventilate feelings about directors' remuneration (though by Western standards this is still small as a multiple of average earnings in the company).

It is not the style of Japanese institutional investors to seek a demarche at an AGM. They would rather do it privately if at all, but that does not stop them.

Foreign shareholders

Foreign shareholders are using their voting rights more than they did. The Commercial Law Centre records that from July 2001 to June 2002 the percentage voting against company proposals had risen to 29.7 (585 companies). This was mainly in respect of director's retirement benefits or earnings, but also extended to the election of directors and Kansayaku (and their retirement benefits). The voting process is complex and involves agents and global custodians. Proxy solicitors are now in evidence.

Shareholder resolutions

It has never been difficult for shareholders to propose resolutions and from 2005 it will become easier. They will need to be lodged with the company six weeks beforehand—eight weeks for foreign holders. The Keidanren opposes this change (CC 232.2) as it will make it more difficult to the company to prepare its defence.

Table 3.8. Ratio of stable shareholders (%)

	All companies	Biggest	Smallest
Less than 10	1.2	1	—
10–20	8.2	9	—
20–30	11.5	17	2
30–40	19.6	12	5
40–50	25.6	11	6
50–60	26.6	8	8
60 +	5.7	9	4

Note: Biggest had assets of 1,000 bn. yen, smallest of up to 5 bn. yen.

Many resolutions are on peoples' pet topics—for example, against nuclear reactors at an electric utility's AGM or to pursue an environmentalist agenda.

Rehearsals

Many Japanese boards take their AGM so seriously that they rehearse for it; 10% do not. Of the rest some have as many as four or five rehearsals. In 94% of cases the president attends them and in 92% the Kansayaku do too. So, often, do the company's lawyers.

The Banks

The important role Japanese banks have played in financing their industry is well understood and widely documented in quantitative terms. History repeated itself. Both in the establishment of industry in the second half of the nineteenth century and in its re-establishment after 1945, the banks were the most convenient way of channelling savings–and the most controllable by government in terms of direction, quantity (by fiscal incentives), and price (by interest rates). Even if the situation has now changed for bigger companies, it will be remembered that numerically more than 99 per cent of Japanese companies are unquoted and they look to the banking system as the only source of external capital.

There should, however, be no misapprehension that the role of the banks as the main source of long-term primary capital meant they were or are an easy source. One now hugely successful entrepreneur said he had been refused by thirty-two banks before he found one to back him. As he pointed out ruefully, collateral is of great importance and significance to the banks when considering applications for loans (and it figured prominently in Ministry of Finance guidance). This led to real problems for the banks in the 1990s when the value of property collapsed and local bankers, with no yardstick other than collateral, found it impossible to take decisions. The result was to push lending decisions upwards, which slowed them greatly.

It used to be the normal pattern for companies to have a 'main' bank which had the largest share of the company's business (although there are prudential limits imposed by the authorities on a bank's exposure to any individual company or group). The main bank saw itself as having a special relationship with particular obligations, notably to provide or coordinate support for the company in times of trouble. The value of this relationship to the bank was its profitability because of its hold on the customer for a wide range of its services. To the customer it was a convenience and an insurance policy, and he was often likely to pay a price for it, for instance, by depositing money with the bank at cheap rates. The 'insurance' aspect is crucial. One financial house said they would still not deal with a company which had no main bank. Another source said that some companies with big cash balances still maintained an overdraft with a lead bank to keep the relationship. All the evidence is that such a policy is justified. If a company has a main bank the umbrella stays up longer.

The obligations inherent in the customer/main bank relationship can bear heavily on the bank itself as is illustrated by the case of Ataka, a trading company which got into major difficulties in late 1975 at a time when, in the aftermath of the first oil crisis, the Japanese economy was under some strain. Because of the potential systemic implications of a failure by Ataka, the Bank of Japan became involved and a merger of Ataka with another trading company, C. Itoh, was arranged. As a condition for the merger, however, Sumitomo, Ataka's main bank, was obliged to take on liabilities not only of Ataka but also of related companies which amounted to several times its original exposure to the company itself. Ataka was saved from formal bankruptcy. Similar, though less far-reaching, cases of rescue operations to avert bankruptcy can be cited, for instance, Tateho Chemical Industries. Taiyo Kobe and six other creditor banks organized a restructuring of the company which lost $22 billion in Zaitech operations (actually government bond futures). The top management was replaced. A lead bank will try to rally support from any other banks or non-bank lenders, but it may have to take the lead by some sacrifice of its own rights, for example, by reducing its own rates of interest and charges to the customers. Such support operations are part of the system but even so may be difficult to set up and finalize. They may take a long time to bring to fruition: with banks themselves under increasing pressure the need to 'share the pain' may become more widespread.

The lead bank concept rests upon an important foundation–Japanese banks, whether long-term credit banks or city banks, view themselves as being in long-term relationships. To use the modern jargon, they are relationship not transaction oriented. Although some Japanese banks have the privileged position of borrowing and lending long-term money, other types of banks have found ways of moving into such operations even before the formal breakdown of the barriers now being organized by the authorities. The long-term business has some attractions, and although not by any means the only source provides a good flow of information. Some banks have extensive computer links between head-quarters, local headquarters, functional departments, and branch managers, as a means of storing and making available the commercial intelligence they garner.

The long-term approach of Japanese banks affects staffing and training levels at the banks. As they expect to visit companies (nearly) daily, and aim to get to understand their business 'exactly well' as one banker said, and to know their people, the contact demands both time and knowledge; even so the switch away from collateral-based lending in the early 1990s is posing problems. Their basic concept, however, is to be able to provide some value added as well as funds: to assist in this, banks organize themselves to collect and dispense a flow of intelligence (gleaned from its client network) which its customers find invaluable about the economy in general but more especially about their own industry.

A gulf seems to have developed between the top third of quoted companies and the remainder. The top third have largely relinquished the 'main bank' system, but the rest have not, and matters remain much as they were, except that the banks cannot always afford to be as supportive as they used to be. The pressures on them have been very great. As lending was usually based on collateral and they were left with a mountain of bad debt when its value (particularly property) collapsed. It is the official objective that non-performing loans would be reduced to 4% of a bank's loan book by March 2005. Some heavy losses have been declared like Mizuho's record 2 trillion yen in fiscal year 2002. But recovery is now well on the way.

Summing up the banks' role as *lenders* it appears that they are *not* an easy touch; they place much weight on collateral, take a long-term view, and do not, judging by the number of bankruptcies, bail all companies out. At times of trouble, they may assume some responsibility for a company and its employees. The extent of their commitment will depend on many factors, not least but decreasingly that their relationship with a company may have been buttressed by reciprocal shareholdings.

In former days, when banks were prosperous, they could afford to act the patient nursemaid more often. Now pressure on their resources has made them more discriminating and they have tended, consciously, to sort out their customers into four categories:

1. those whose relationship they want to enhance;
2. those whose relationship they wish to maintain;
3. those to whom they want a reduced commitment;
4. those they wish to leave altogether.

The bursting of the bubble left a trail of devastation and this reduced the banks' capacity to lend; it nudged bigger companies in a direction they might have chosen anyway–the use of the financial markets. The figures are quoted earlier. Smaller companies have relied more on internal sources of finance. There has also been a major restructuring in the banking sector reducing the number of entities, but as far as we could discover with as little disturbance as possible to pre-existing relationships.

Technical developments have presented the banks with a different range of problems. Sophisticated experts are now needed to handle some areas of business, for instance some of the more complex structured derivatives; this to some extent cuts across the all-embracing bank–client relationship entrusted to a particular banker. These relationships have however survived and not, I believe, just for economic reasons; the sense of continuity and value of enduring relationships with a lot of history in them are key factors. Learmount 2002 cites instances of banks going to great lengths to subordinate their internal arrangements to the clients' needs and preferences. The one aspect one seldom sees discussed in all this is profitability. Again the shareholders are far down the line—if they are in it at all.

The banks as shareholders

German banks became substantial shareholders in industry mainly because a particular company was so distressed that its debt was turned into equity as a last resort. It was not an act of deliberate policy to take stakes in industry. In Japan, however, banks took such stakes partly to remedy the shortage of savings after the war and partly to cement their relationship with customers (especially when they were disintermediating). One of Learmount's interviewees confirmed this orientation of the investment—it was not to make money. It was also useful to strengthen their position if the company encountered difficulties and they had to exercise influence. Nowadays they are limited to 5% of the stock of any one company, but this does not preclude affiliates having holdings too.

Regulations have come into force which limit the banks' holdings of shares in other business enterprises within their Tier 1 capital. This makes them more selective in what to hold. The government set up an organization for the acquisition of bank-held shares to take the strain off the market. The terms of its operation need not concern us. It is, however, a far cry from the days when banks felt that they would be betraying customers to sell their shares, and sought permission to do so at the same time as trying to park them in friendly hands.

This book is not about the capital markets or the banks per se but about their influence on the governance of companies. As far as the banks are concerned it can be summed up simply; it was great, is much less, and is diminishing. The principal reason is the condition of the banks themselves, most of which have required some form of restructuring, often after or with a merger. Their troubles have undermined both the confidence and the dominating position they once enjoyed, critics have raised questions about their governance and the role of banking supervisors. It would not be so easy for the banks even if they wished it, to edge out weak management from one of their customers. They are no longer the force in Japan's governance system they once were, and this has left a gap. Are companies pleased or sorry? It is difficult to say; a safety net has gone. A bulwark against shareholder pressure (and even takeover) is far less secure than it was. In terms of historical perspective however an economy as strong as Japan's does not generally count its banks as among the key players in its corporate governance system.

The problem of non-performing loans still looms, even if the worst is now over. The *Financial Times* of 2 September 2004 (2) reports Gomi, the new head of Japan's Financial Services Agency as urging banks to reduce their exposure to large problem borrowers. This target is that by March 2005 not more than 4% of outstanding loans should be classified as bad.

There is a technical point of some importance. The Japanese authorities now require companies including banks to mark assets to market. This means disclosing hidden reserves where assets have appreciated or marking them down and taking the loss when they have declined in value. This change will have many effects, not least in mergers.

Finally, there are many references in this chapter to companies' conservative dividend policies. The banks have always seen it as in their own interests to encourage these, so as to preserve their cover.

Mergers and Hostile Bids

Mergers between two willing companies have long been a feature of the Japanese industrial scene. Recent years have seen marked consolidation, not least in banking, prompted or at least encouraged by the authorities.

'Hostile' bids were unknown and considered an alien idea, which would disrupt or even destroy notions of 'family' whatever immediate gains might have accrued to the shareholders of the target company. Cross-shareholdings were a fortification against aggression. A beneficial effect of their immunity was management's ability to take the long-term view without being harried or threatened. On the other hand, inferior management was in no danger of being displaced—its position was indeed strengthened after the banks' monitoring role diminished and virtually vanished.

The rise in foreign holdings, coupled with an aggressive stance by specialist firms (mainly US), reduced this feeling of security. We have already noted that some have made good money by pushing miserly managers into distributing part of its hoard to shareholders.

A more conventional case is that of Wal-Mart's bid for ailing retailer Daiei. This was no 'get rich quick' raid but an attempt by the US company to consolidate its position in the retail market. Chauvinism is however far from dead, and the Japanese authorities may choose to invest funds into Daiei via the IRCJ rather than allow Wal-Mart to sort it out (possibly with support from Goldman Sachs). The outcome of this very complicated situation, which may well involve restructuring, was undecided at the time of writing, but whatever it may be, the case does show that change is, slowly, on the way.

A sign of change was the battle between Mitsubishi Tokyo Financial Group and Sumitomo-Mitsui for UFJ, which was in poor shape. Not only was this, unusually, a public contest, but it went to the courts, a very rare occurrence between Japanese firms. There is some talk of Japan's Financial Services Agency seeking a criminal penalty from individuals who are said to have set up a parallel set of books and to have destroyed evidence sometimes in front of the inspectors' eyes! The FSA does now have funds to inject into banks that need a capital boost. A fund of 2,000 billion yen became available in August 2004 (Gomi, head of the FSA, reported in the *Financial Times* on 2 September 2004).

The financial press had a field day—the Asian *Wall Street Journal* of 9 September 2004 reported developments in detail including the fact that UFJ had taken the most unusual step of sending its shareholders an open letter explaining its preference for Tokyo-Mitsubishi. H. Takenaka of Mitsui remarked, 'Japan is becoming part of a borderless financial system—it's becoming more like America.'

The saga unfolded dramatically. On 10 September Mitsubishi-Tokyo announced an agreement that they would invest 700 billion yen into UFJ by way of a purchase of preferred shares—the hors d'oeuvre to a 'basic management integration agreement' of 12 August. Integration was to be accomplished by 1 October 2005. It predicated substantial savings by branch closures, slimming head office, and by integrating IT systems.

The *Financial Times* of 13 September revealed that UFJ board members were undertaking a campaign to convince shareholders they should back the deal. In the course of the struggle UFJ bank (an unquoted subsidary) introduced the first ever Japanese 'poison pill'. At the time of writing the

legality of this move had not been determined. The issue was UFJ's responsibility to its shareholders (30% of which are foreign institutions). There is
another dimension to this battle—it is a Tokyo v. Kansai contest. Eventually
Sumitomo-Mitsui withdrew from the contest.

Poison pills

Some commentators did indeed describe the MTFG injection of cash into UFJ
as a kind of 'poison pill'. Simultaneously on 10 September METI announced
the setting up of a committee to investigate the introduction of poison pills as
a way of thwarting hostile takeover bids. The impetus for this comes from the
unwinding of protective cross-shareholdings plus the growing proportion of
foreign-held shares, some in the hands of aggressive buy-out funds or ginger
groups. In 2005, moreover, bidders will be able to offer paper as well as cash.

This move aroused criticism from those who saw it as a step backwards
from market disciplines. I have not been able to trace anything in Japanese
law that would stop poison pills now. As a matter of fact that is true of UK
law too, but they are prohibited by the Takeover Panel's rules.

The government's initiative may seem unimportant, but that is not how
the Japanese press saw it. It made the headlines in the leading newspaper
Nihon Keizai Shimbun on 9 September 2004. What is more, it was not the
only device being considered. Others were:

- special tax advantages for long-term shareholders;
- the issuance of new stock to dilute the purchases made by corporate raiders;
- the encouragement of employee share ownership plans (ESOPs).

Meanwhile another 'hostile' takeover startled the Establishment—a bid for
Nippon Broadcasting (NBC) by Livedoor (President Mr Horie). NBC tried
to defend itself by transferring its 20% stake in Fuji TV (which Livedoor
wanted). The terms in which the Courts decided against NBC are important.
NBC's machinations were clearly designed to protect incumbent management, but the Court ruled that it was shareholders' interests that were
paramount. The case had not been finally settled at the time of writing
(April 2005), but it was widely recognized that the issues it exposed went
to the heart of the Japanese system of corporate governance-in particular the
supremacy of shareholders interests. The *Financial Times* (London, 23 March
2005, p. 15) commented (perhaps optimistically):

Regardless of the outcome, the battle over control of NBS has laid the groundwork for a more
dynamic M & A market and better corporate governance in Japan by highlighting the
significance of shareholder value, clarifying the rules and educating the public on the issues.
As such, it is a landmark in Japan's transition from a system that rewards insiders to a more

open capitalism in which shareholders including many viewers of TV talk shows, can expect a larger say in how companies are managed.

Summary

Progress in improving corporate governance in much of the Western world has not come by a considered programme of reform, but rather as a spasmodic reaction to scandal or incompetence. The root cause in many cases is greed coupled with a lack of integrity. Yoshizo Saijyo writing in *Viewpoint* in the middle of 2003 attributes Japanese scandals to a different cause—the desire to protect profit and a company's reputation. In this chapter I have identified the ways in which Japanese corporate governance has changed over the last decade or so. In no particular order they are:

1. The role of the banks has much reduced—so have their holdings of industrial shares.
2. Cross-shareholdings have reduced and are still reducing.
3. Boards have shrunk and are no longer mainly 'ceremonial'. Independent directors are no longer a rarity. Developments in this sphere appear to have lagged behind other elements of governance like disclosure, transparency, and internal risk management systems.
4. The law now permits a company to adopt 'the three-committee system' instead of having Kansayaku; few have yet converted.
5. The role of Kansayaku has been enhanced in the vast majority of companies that maintain the traditional system.
6. There are increasing pressures on companies that can afford to do so to improve dividends—not least from foreign shareholders who had over more than 20% (on average).
7. There is some awakening among Japanese shareholders to their obligations. Voting is more usual. There is still a long way to go.
8. Government interference (and guidance) has diminished, though it will still intervene if it deems it necessary, for example

   - The big bail-out fund for banks
   - The Industrial Reconstruction Company.

9. There is less lifetime employment than there was.
10. The post-war consensus is weakening.

These changes suggest a change in effective accountability (the second criterion of sound governance in any country). The important part the banks played has greatly diminished. In its place there are now better structured boards, more effective company auditors, and occasionally more active shareholders. An increase of interest, and, where appropriate, action on their part, might restore the balance that the banks' withdrawal from the scene has impaired.

Some issues have not changed significantly:

1. Despite recent cases, hostile takeover bids are counter-cultural and rare.
2. Shareholders are still at the end of the queue.
3. The company is viewed as a social as well as an economic construct.
4. The fabric of society still matters greatly.
5. Japanese management still meets the fundamental criterion of dynamism that is not unnecessarily fettered.
6. The maintenance of a protective screen against foreign encroachment. No sooner was the protection afforded by cross-shareholdings waning than the authorities started to look to 'poison' pills to shore up the defences, but there are signs that the screen is not as impenetrable as it was.

A corporate governance ranking

Institutional Shareholder Services are reported in *Business Week* on 17 May 2004 to have produced the rankings for some Japanese companies shown in Table 3.9. Because of the 'unquantifiables'—elements of the dynamics, any system of direction and control—we can but admire the brave attempt to put numbers to any analysis of a company's corporate governance, because they imply precision. In Japan's case the attempt is heroic.

The Japanese world, it seems, is bent on such measures. The 2004 Corporate Governance Survey by the Japanese Corporate Governance Research Institute resulted in the following scores among the top thirty companies that responded and also gave permission for their JCG index score to be quoted. Top came Toshiba with 83, followed by Teijn with 81, and Omron and Sanyo Electric both with 79. At the other end were Anritsu and Komatsu, both with 65, Showa Shell, Hoya, and Marubeni all with 64; Yamaha with 63, and Yokogawa Electric with 62.

C'est magnifique, mais ce n'est pas la guerre.

The Future

For an economy as powerful as that of Japan isolation has long ceased to be an option, and globalization has an increasing effect. The effects of the resurgence of the Chinese economy will be profound. The intense national concern for the fabric of society will tend to slow the pace of change to what can be assimilated without damage. But there are many voices within Japan

Table 3.9. A corporate governance ranking

	Corporate governance quotient	Market cap ($ m.)	% change in stock price (one year)
Nomura (diversified financials)	92.9	33,923.3	52
Sony (consumer durables)	85.7	37,127.5	47
Disco Co. (semiconductors & semiconducts equip.)	83.7	1,618.8	33
Orix (diversified financials)	81.7	8,874.9	115
Hoya (technology hardware & equipment)	78.8	11,947.8	69
Daito Trust Constr. (consumer durables)	78.3	4,646.9	64
Aucnet (retailing)	78.1	166.6	123
Nisshin Seifum (food, beverage & tobacco)	77.7	2,219.8	25
Hitachi Chemical (materials)	76.9	3,423.3	87
Daiwa Securities (diversified financials)	76.9	10,605.2	77
Kissei Pharmaceutical (pharmaceuticals & biotech)	17.1	1,270.9	78
Toyo Ink Mfg. (materials)	17.1	1,159.3	48
Tokyu Corp. (transportation)	17.1	6,222.3	71
Tohu Co. (media)	17.1	3,010.0	63
Toei Co. (media)	17.1	579.2	44
Teikoku Oil (energy)	17.1	1,587.6	66
Takashimaya (retaining)	17.1	3,713.6	150
Daio Paper Co. (materials)	17.1	1,051.7	17
Sumitomo Realty (real estate)	17.1	5,257.9	218
Shikoku Electric Power (utilities)	17.1	4,693.5	−5

raised in favour of better discipline within the corporate governance system—even without the raucous pressure of foreigners aching to make a quick buck from what they see as the illogicalities of the market. What will emerge ten years and more hence will look and feel more Western, certainly in respect of the board/Kansayaku system. It is a great and benign paradox that notions of corporate social responsibility elsewhere will, in their own way and in different language, come closer to the Japanese view of the 'Company in Society'; and the Japanese will find it in their own interest— not least those of their savers, to accord to shareholders a warmer place in the land of the rising sun.

Implementation of the
new Company Law

During the production of this book, a bill was passed at the Diet on 30 June, 2005, introducing a new Company Law in Japan. It is intended to enhance the competitiveness of Japanese companies, both domestic and international. In fact, the 'Company Law' has never existed in Japan, as all rules prescribing company matters were included and scattered around the Commercial Law, Special provisions for the commercial law, and other laws relating to smaller sized companies. The new law integrates these rules into one. It also summarizes the corporate restructurings, stock based incentive plans, committee-based management style, and many other rules, which made commercial law complex as the result of frequent changes over recent years. The new Law is written in modern Japanese replacing the original archaic expressions first adopted in 1899.

The new law extends companies' autonomy by easing rules on by-law (articles of association) amendments. Companies will have variety of ways to reorganize themselves to maximize value by swift decision making. They will be furnished with wider selection to reward shareholders and to grant incentives to management. For example, directors will be able to decide on the profit appropriation plan matters previously reserved for shareholders' approval. And, if directors decide to do so, they will have to be elected every year by shareholders, to improve accountability.

Under the new Company Law, companies will be subject to more intensive scrutiny by shareholders and stakeholders at large. Directors will be further accountable to shareholders by explaining their policy plans and performance. They will be required to set up internal controls and monitor their effectiveness.

Annex 3A: *Powers of Corporate Auditors*

Powers of the Board of Corporate Auditors and Powers of Corporate Auditors

Powers of the Board of Corporate Auditors

1. Right of consent to proposals related to the election of an external financial auditor (Law on Exceptions to the Commercial Code Article 3(2))
2. Authority to propose issues and to present proposals on the election of an external financial auditor (Law on Exceptions to the Commercial Code Article 3(3))
3. Right of consent to proposals on not reappointing the external financial auditor (Law on Exceptions to the Commercial Code Article 5–2(3))
4. Authority to propose not reappointing the external financial auditor (Law on Exceptions to the Commercial Code Article 5–2(3))
5. Right of consent to proposals related to the dismissal of the external financial auditor (Law on Exceptions to the Commercial Code Article 6(3))
6. Authority to propose the dismissal of the external financial auditor (Law on Exceptions to the Commercial Code Article 6(3))
7. Authority to dismiss the external financial auditor (Law on Exceptions to the Commercial Code Article 6–2(1))
8. Election of a corporate auditor to report the dismissal of the external financial auditor to the shareholders' meeting (Law on Exceptions to the Commercial Code Article 6–2(2))
9. Election of a provisional external financial auditor (Law on Exceptions to the Commercial Code Article 6–4(1))
10. Authority to receive reports from the external financial auditor (Law on Exceptions to the Commercial Code Article 8(1))
11. Authority to receive financial reports and attachments from directors or a liquidator (Law on Exceptions to the Commercial Code Article 12(1,2), Article 19(1); Commercial Code Article 420(1))
12. Authority to receive audit reports from the external financial auditor (Law on Exceptions to the Commercial Code Article 13(1))
13. Authority to receive reports on the results of auditors examining the audit report of the external financial auditor (Law on Exceptions to the Commercial Code Article 14(1))
14. Authority to prepare corporate auditor reports (Law on Exceptions to the Commercial Code Article 14(2 or 4))
15. Right of consent to proposals related to the election of corporate auditors (Law on Exceptions to the Commercial Code Article 18(3))

16. Authority to propose issues and to present proposals on the election of corporate auditors (Law on Exceptions to the Commercial Code Article 18(3))

17. Authority to receive reports from corporate auditors on the execution of their duties (Law on Exceptions to the Commercial Code Article 18–2(3))

18. Right of consent to proposals on relieving a director of responsibilities regarding the company (Law on Exceptions to the Commercial Code Article 19(1); Commercial Code Article 266(9, 13, 21))

19. Right of consent to auxiliary intervention by the company to support directors in lawsuits (Law on Exceptions to the Commercial Code Article 19(1); Commercial Code Article 266(9), Article 268(8))

20. Authority to receive reports from directors (Law on Exceptions to the Commercial Code Article 19(1); Commercial Code Article 274–2)

21. Determination of corporate auditor guidelines, of methods for examining the business and financial conditions of the company, and of other matters related to the execution of corporate auditor duties. However, the authority of individual corporate auditors shall not be impeded (Law on Exceptions to the Commercial Code Article 1802(2))

The board of corporate auditors will consist of all corporate auditors (Law on Exceptions to the Commercial Code Article 18–2(1)). Decision-making will be based on a majority of all members. However, decisions on the dismissal of the external financial auditor, on consent to proposals on relieving a director of responsibilities regarding the company, and on consent to auxiliary intervention by the company to support directors in lawsuits will require unanimous agreement (Law on Exceptions to the Commercial Code Article 18–31(1)).

Powers and Duties of Individual Corporate Auditors (autonomous authority)

1. General Auditing Authority
   a) Auditing of the execution of director duties (Commercial Code Article 274(1))
   b) Auditing of financial reports, etc. (Commercial Code Article 281(2))

2. Examination Authority
   a) Authority to request business reports and authority to examine business and financial conditions (Commercial Code Article 274(2))
   b) Authority to request business reports of subsidiaries and authority to examine business and financial conditions of subsidiaries (Commercial Code Article 274(3))
   c) Authority to request reports from the external financial auditor (Law on Exceptions to the Commercial Code Article 8(2))

3. Authority Related to Shareholders' Meetings and Board of Directors Meeting
   a) Duty of explanation to shareholders' meetings (Commercial Code Article 237–3)
   b) Duty to attend and state opinions at board of directors' meetings (Commercial Code Article 260–3(1))
   c) Duty of reporting to board of directors' meetings (Commercial Code Article 260–3(2))
   d) Authority to request the convening of or to convene a board of directors' meeting (Commercial Code Article 260–3(3,4)
   e) Duty to examine and report on proposals and documents to be submitted to shareholders' meetings (Commercial Code Article 275)

4. Authority Related to the Position of Corporate Auditor
   a) Authority to state an opinion on the appointment or dismissal of corporate auditors (Commercial Code Article 275–3)
   b) Authority to state an opinion on the resignation of a corporate auditor (Commercial Code Article 275–3(2))
   c) Consultation on the compensation of each corporate auditor (Commercial Code Article 279(2))
   d) Authority to state an opinion regarding compensation (Commercial Code Article 279(3))
   e) Authority to request auditing expenses (Commercial Code Article 279–2)
   f) Authority to elect full-time corporate auditors (Law on Exceptions to the Commercial Code Article 18(2))

5. Authority Regarding Initiating Management-related Corrective Measures
   a) Authority to request the suspension of illegal acts by directors (Commercial Code Article 275–2)
   b) Authority to bring various lawsuits and to declare procedures (Commercial Code Article 247, Article 280–15(2), Article 380(2), Article 381(1), Article 415, Article 428(2), Article 431(1), Article 452(1))

6. Other Authority
   a) Authority to examine the procedures of company founding (Commercial Code Article 173–2)
   b) Right to represent the company in lawsuits between directors and the company (Commercial Code Article 275–4)

Annex 3B: *Hitachi AGM*

Taken from the notice of HITACHI from its 2004 annual General Meeting.

Item No. 2   Election of 14 Directors due to expiration of the term of office of all Directors

Due to expiration at the close of this Meeting of the term of office of all the present Directors, it is proposed that Directors be elected. Election of Directors shall not be made in accordance with cumulative voting, in conformity with the provision of the Articles of Incorporation of the Company.

Candidates for Directors are as follows. All candidates have agreed to take office as Directors assuming that they are elected at this Meeting.

No.	Name (Date of Birth)	Principal Occupation	Brief Personal History	Outstanding Shares of Hitachi, Ltd. Owned shares	Conflict of Interest
1	Tsutomu Kanai (Feb. 26, 1929)	Chairman of the Board, Hitachi, Ltd.	5/1958 Joined Hitachi, Ltd. 6/1985 Executive Managing Director 6/1987 Senior Executive Managing Director 6/1989 Executive Vice-President and Director 6/1991 President and Representative Director 4/1999 Chairman of the Board and Representative Director 6/2003 Chairman of the Board	76,500	None
2	Etsuhiko Shoyama (Mar. 9, 1936)	Representative Executive Officer President, Chief Executive Officer and Director, Hitachi, Ltd.	4/1959 Joined Hitachi, Ltd. 6/1991 Director 6/1993 Executive Managing Director 6/1995 Senior Executive Managing Director 6/1997 Executive Vice-President and Representative Director 4/1999 President and Representative Director	69,000	None

(Continued)

Table *cont*

No.	Name (Date of Birth)	Principal Occupation	Brief Personal History	Outstanding Shares of Hitachi, Ltd. Owned	Conflict of Interest
			6/2003 Representative Executive Officer, President, Chief Executive Officer and Director		
3	Yoshiki Yagi (Feb. 27, 1938)	Director, Hitachi, Ltd.	4/1960 Joined Hitachi, Ltd. 6/1991 Director 6/1993 Executive Managing Director 6/1997 Senior Executive Managing Director 4/1999 Executive Vice President and Representative Director 6/2003 Representative Executive Officer, Executive Vice President, Executive Officer and Director 4/2004 Director	68,250	None
4	Kotaro Muneoka (Oct. 30, 1940)	Director, Hitachi, Ltd.	4/1964 Joined Hitachi, Ltd. 4/1999 Senior Vice President and Director 4/2001 Director 6/2001 Corporate Auditor 6/2003 Director	24,000	None
5	Takashi Miyoshi (Sep. 25, 1947)	Senior Vice President and Executive Officer, Hitachi, Ltd.	4/1970 Joined Hitachi, Ltd. 6/2002 General Manager, Finance Department I 4/2003 General Manager, Finance and Finance Department I	17,000	None

No.	Name (Date of birth)	Position	Career history	Shares held	
			6/2003 Executive Officer 4/2004 Senior Vice President and Executive Officer	shares	None
6	Ginko Sato (Jul. 6, 1934)	President, Japan Association for the Advancement of Working Women Director, Hitachi, Ltd.	4/1958 Joined Ministry of Labour (currently Ministry of Health, Labour and Welfare) 6/1985 Ministerial Councillor, Ministry of Labour 1/1986 Director-General, Women's Bureau, Ministry of Labour 7/1990 Assistant Minister of Labour 10/1991 Ambassador Extraordinary and Plenipotentiary of Japan of Kenya 7/1995 Commissioner, Securities and Exchange Surveillance Commission 7/1998 Chairperson, Securities and Exchange Surveillance Commission 8/2001 President, Japan Association for the Advancement of Working Women 6/2003 Director, Hitachi, Ltd.	2,000	None
7	Hiromichi Seya (Oct. 7, 1930)	Senior Corporate Advisor, Asahi Glass Company, Limited ("Asahi Glass") Director, Hitachi, Ltd.	4/1954 Joined Asahi Glass 3/1985 Director 3/1987 Managing Director 3/1988 Representative Director Executive Vice President 3/1990 Representative Director Senior Executive Vice President	4,000	None

(Continued)

Table *cont.*

No.	Name (Date of Birth)	Principal Occupation	Brief Personal History	Outstanding Shares of Hitachi, Ltd. Owned	Conflict of Interest
			3/1992 Representative Director President		
			6/1998 Representative Director Chairman & CEO		
			6/2002 Representative Director Chairman of the Board		
			6/2003 Director, Hitachi, Ltd.		
			3/2004 Senior Corporate Advisor, Asahi Glass		
8	Akira Chihaya (Mar. 6, 1935)	Representative Director and Chairman of the Board, Nippon Steel Corporation Representative Director and President, Tekko Kaikan Co., Ltd. Director, Hitachi, Ltd.	4/1957 Joined Yawata Iron & Steel Co., Ltd. (currently Nippon Steel Corporation)	2,000	Note(1)
			6/1987 Director		
			6/1991 Managing Director		
			6/1995 Representative Director and Executive Vice President	2,000	Note(1)
			4/1998 Representative Director and President		
			4/2003 Representative Director and Chairman of the Board		
			6/2003 Director, Hitachi, Ltd.		
9	Toshiro Nishimura (Apr. 10, 1933)	Attorney at Law	4/1961 Member of the First Tokyo Bar Association	1,000	None

No. Name (Date of birth) / Position	Career	Shares held	Notes
Director, Hitachi, Ltd.	5/1966 Senior Partner of Nishimura & Partners 6/2003 Director, Hitachi, Ltd. 1/2004 Founder, Senior Counsel, Nishimura & Partners		None
10 Isao Uchigasaki (Jan. 2, 1939) Hitachi Group Executive Officer, Hitachi, Ltd. Chairman of the Board, Hitachi Chemical Co., Ltd. ('Hitachi Chemical')	4/1962 Joined Hitachi, Ltd. 4/1963 Joined Hitachi Chemical 6/1991 Board Director 6/1993 Executive Managing Director 6/1997 President and Representative Director 4/2003 Chairman of the Board and Representative Director 6/2003 Chairman of the Board 4/2004 Hitachi Group Executive Officer, Hitachi, Ltd.	10,000	None
11 Takashi Kawamura (Dec. 19, 1939) Chairman of the Board and Representative Executive Officer, Hitachi Software Engineering Co., Ltd. ('Hitachi Software Engineering') Director, Hitachi, Ltd.	4/1962 Joined Hitachi, Ltd. 6/1995 Director 6/1997 Executive Managing Director 4/1999 Executive Vice President and Representative Director	Shares 37,000	Note(2)

Table *cont.*

No.	Name (Date of Birth)	Principal Occupation	Brief Personal History	Outstanding Shares of Hitachi, Ltd. Owned	Conflict of Interest
			4/2003 Director 6/2003 Chairman of the Board and Representative Executive Officer, Hitachi Software Engineering		
12	Yoshiro Kuwata (Sep. 1, 1936)	Chairman of the Board and Representative Executive Officer, Hitachi High-Technologies Corporation ('Hitachi High-Technologies') Director, Hitachi, Ltd.	6/1961 Joined Hitachi, Ltd. 6/1993 Director 6/1997 Senior Executive Managing Director 6/1995 Executive Managing Director 4/1999 Executive Vice President and Representative Director 6/2003 Representative Executive Officer, Executive Vice President Executive Officer and Director Chairman of the Board and Representative Executive Officer, Hitachi High-Technologies 4/2004 Director	27,700	Note(3)
13	Hiroshi Kuwahara (Nov. 23, 1935)	Chairman of the Board and Representative Executive Officer, Hitachi Maxell, Ltd. ('Hitachi Maxell')	4/1960 Joined Hitachi, Ltd.	31,600	Note(4)

	Name	Career summary	Shares	
	Director, Hitachi, Ltd. 6/1991 Executive Managing Director	6/1989 Director 6/1993 Senior Executive Managing Director 6/1995 Executive Vice-President and Representative Director 6/1999 Vice Chairman of the Board and Representative Director 1/2001 Executive member of Council for Science & Technology Policy, Cabinet Office 1/2003 Vice Chairman of the Board and Representative Director 4/2003 Director 6/2003 Chairman of the Board and Representative Executive Officer, Hitachi Maxell		
14	Masayoshi Hanabusa (Oct. 10, 1934) Chairman of the Board, Hitachi Capital Corporation ('Hitachi Capital') Director, Hitachi, Ltd.	4/1957 Joined Hitachi Sales Corporation 8/1960 Joined Hitachi Credit Corporation (currently Hitachi Capital) 6/1977 Director 6/1983 Executive Managing Director 6/1987 Senior Executive Managing Director 6/1991 President and Representative Director	8,050	None

Table *cont.*

No.	Name (Date of Birth)	Principal Occupation	Brief Personal History	Outstanding Shares of Hitachi, Ltd. Owned	Conflict of Interest
			6/2001 Chairman of the Board and Representative Director 6/2003 Chairman of the Board Director, Hitachi, Ltd.		

Notes:

(1) Mr. Akira Chihaya is the Representative Director and Chairman of the Board of NIPPON STEEL CORPORATION ('NSC'). Both NSC and the Company conduct businesses in the area of power and industrial systems. Additionally, the Company has continuous transactions with NSC, including purchases of steel products of NSC through trading firms and sales of rolling mill control systems and electric machinery to NSC. The amount of such business is negligible, in comparison to the revenues and procurement costs of both companies. The Company has no special interest in Tekko Kaikan Co., Ltd., for which Mr. Chihaya serves as Representative Director and President.

(2) Mr. Takashi Kawamura is the Representative Executive Officer of Hitachi Software Engineering. Both Hitachi Software Engineering and the Company conduct businesses in the area of information & telecommunication systems. Additionally, the Company has continuous transactions with Hitachi Software Engineering, including purchases of software from Hitachi Software Engineering and sales of computers to Hitachi Software Engineering. The two companies also have dealings with each other in the form of loans under the Hitachi Group's centralized financial management system.

(3) Mr. Yoshiro Kuwata is the Representative Executive Officer of Hitachi High-Technologies. Both Hitachi High-Technologies and the Company conduct businesses in the areas of sales of information systems and medical equipment, etc. Additionally, the Company has continuous transactions with Hitachi High-Technologies, including purchases of information system equipment and electronic components from Hitachi High-Technologies and sales of information system equipment to Hitachi High-Technologies. The two companies also have dealings with each other in the form of loans under the Hitachi Group's centralized financial management system.

(4) Mr. Hiroshi Kuwahara is the Representative Executive Officer of Hitachi Maxell. Both Hitachi Maxell and the Company conduct businesses in the area of digital media related products. Additionally, the Company has continuous transactions with Hitachi Maxell, including purchases of batteries from Hitachi Maxell and sales of components for computers and software to Hitachi Maxell. The two companies also have dealings with each other in the form of loans under the Hitachi Group's centralized financial management system

(5) Ms. Ginko Sato, Mr. Hiromichi Seya, Mr. Akira Chihaya and Mr. Toshiro Nishimura are candidates who fulfill the qualification requirements to be outside directors as provided for in Article 188.2.7–2 of the Commercial Code of Japan.

Annex 3C: *The Role of the IJRC*

Problem Loan Issue

From the point of view of the lending financial institution a problem loan is a problem asset, whereas from the borrower's point of view it is a problem liability. The IRCJ's role is to support revitalization of the borrowing company, so in that sense the IRCJ is contributing to the resolution of the problem loan issue.

Microecnomic approach

The IRCJ provides models and prescriptions for individual businesses, and aims to help create a business revitalization market that will contribute to the ongoing flow and vitality of economic activity. The IRCJ operates within a limited time frame— two years for the acquisition of liabilities, and five years in total including the disposal of liabilities acquired.

Private versus legal rehabilitation

The IRCJ acts within the framework of private rehabilitation to preserve the value inherent in businesses. The key strength of this approach is the rapid resolution of problems. The key strength of rehabilitation using the legal system, on the other hand, is the fairness resulting from third party adjudication. When the IRCJ participates, normal commercial credits are protected to help preserve corporate value, and appropriate corporate rehabilitation schemes are developed in each cash, taking the above into account.

The main bank and other creditors

In corporate rehabilitation cases where financial creditors have difficulty resolving issues, the IRCJ aims to act as a neutral and fair third party in order to generate a solution that is equitable to all concerned parties.

The necessity for true revitalization

The IRCJ has no interest in creating illusory turnarounds that merely extend the life of a moribund business by a year or two. Our objective is to revitalise businesses so that they can compete and succeed in tough and competitive markets over the long term. To achieve this the IRCJ starts with a thorough analysis of the business, proposes a realistic business restructuring plan and based on this constructs the required financial strategy.

Annex 3D: *IJRC and the Kanebo Case*

IRCJ approves application for assistance for Kanebo, Ltd

Tokyo, March 10, 2004—The Industrial Revitalization Corporation of Japan ('the IRCJ') today approved an application by Kanebo, Ltd and related companies under Article 22, Clause 3 of the Industrial Revitalization Corporation Act of 2003.

Note: The abovementioned decision to provide assistance incorporates two applications for assistance. The first concerns Kanebo, Ltd and its 34 group companies: the second concerns Kanebo Boutique Co., Ltd.

1. **Outline of business approved for assistance**

Company names	(1)	Kanebo, Ltd (hereafter, 'Kanebo')
	(2)	Kanebo Boutique Co., Ltd (hereafter 'Kanebo boutique')
Dates of establishment	(1)	1887
	(2)	1975
Capital	(1)	31.34 billion yen (As of the end of September 2003)
	(2)	450 million yen (As of the end of March 2003)
Head offices	(1)	3-20-20 Kaigan, Minato-ku Tokyo 108–8080
	(2)	3-20-20 Kaigan, Minato-ku Tokyo 108–8080
Representatives	(1)	Mr Takashi Hoashi
	(2)	Mr Masahiro Fujita
Number of employees	(1)	Consolidated basis—14,027 Non-consolidated basis—2,618 (As of the end of Sept 2003)
	(2)	28 (As of October 2003)
Outline of businesses	(1)	Cosmetics, Home Products, Textiles, Food, Pharmaceuticals, and other businesses including new materials and electronics.
	(2)	Manufacture and sale of textiles and accessories. Sale of cosmetics, pharmaceuticals, and food.

2. **Name of financial institution or other party jointly submitting application**
   Sumitomo Mitsui Banking Corporation

3. **Outline of business revitalization plan and rationale for IRCJ involvement**

Outline of business plan

1. *Overall direction of business revitalization plan*

Each Kanebo business that is deemed to be struggling will, as soon as possible, undergo drastic 'selection and concentration'. In businesses targeted for restructuring, there will be a complete review of their strategy and a thorough reform of their management, business organisation, and human resources. Whenever necessary, strategic alliances with third parties will be rapidly considered and implemented as appropriate.

2. *Reorganisation of company and business*

The management structure of the whole Kanebo Group will, as quickly and as thoroughly as possible, be divided up by business unit in order to crystallize management responsibilities.

The first step in this plan will be for Kanebo to spin off quickly its cosmetics division through a transfer of its operations. This is Kanebo's healthiest business and the one that risks being damaged the most over time. Kanebo's other divisions will remain listed and, under the IRCJ's support, will each be thoroughly considered for potential selection, concentration or spinning off as appropriate.

3. *Fundamental reforms to financial structure*

Funds obtained from the transfer of the cosmetics division will be used by Kanebo to offset capital losses from asset appraisal losses and restructuring costs. The value of the business and assets of the other divisions will then be thoroughly audited.

Asset appraisal losses and restructuring costs from reducing the closing unprofitable businesses following this audit will be assessed, and additional losses sustained through asset-impairment accounting will be determined.

Should these additional losses exceed the funds generated from the transfer of the cosmetics division and lead to Kanebo's excessive debt burden not being resolved, or, should Kanebo's debts be deemed to be excessive in the light of the real value and profitability of Kanebo's other divisions, financial support and a reduction and subsequent increase in capital will be necessary to restore Kanebo's financial soundness. In that respect it may therefore be necessary to seek financail support.

1 Business Plan

1. Strengthen cosmetic division

After spinning off Kanebo's cosmetic division, the risk of this business being damaged will greatly diminish. The new structure will also facilitate independent and flexible management. Raising new capital will loosen existing constraints on the company's investment and other programs, and will allow competitiveness to be improved.

Specific measures the company will take are as follows:

- Rebuild brand portfolio (concentrate existing brands, create new brands)
- Spend strategically on marketing and advertising
- Revise channel distribution policies
- Lift operational efficiency (distribution, logistics, etc.)
- Improve management infrastructure (invest in IT systems, etc.)

2. Review unprofitable businesses

There will be a thorough and rapid selection and concentration of Kanebo's other divisions. As part of this, a comprehensive financial plan will be created that can be introduced as promptly and as broadly as possible. The creation of this plan will involve giving advance consideration to the necessity, rationality, and appropriateness of any capital that is assessed as likely to be required for restructuring and other measures.

A comprehensive restructuring plan will also be created and implemented for those businesses earmarked for concentration. This overall plan will include strategies for individual businesses that take into account their operational arenas and management structures.

3. Improve organization structure to improve profitability

Implementation of this business revitalization plan is aimed at creating a new business organisation that will enable revitalization of the entire Kanebo Group. Specific structural measures in the plan include the following:

- Reforming the management structure (including external hiring)
- Considering shifting to a committee system
- Examining options for reorganising and integrating Group businesses
- Reviewing the internal company structure
- Reducing surplus employee numbers
- Strengthening corporate governance

2 Business restructuring

Kanebo will separate its core cosmetics division and, to maintain its value and make the most of future growth opportunities, will transfer the business to Kanebo Boutique, a wholly owned subsidiary. Ahead of this transfer Kanebo Boutique will receive investment from the IRCJ, and Kanebo's investment ratio in Kanebo will then drop to 14%.

The transfer of the cosmetics division will clarify that division's value, and generate funds for Kanebo that will significantly improve its financial position. After the transfer, Kanebo will still hold some of the shares of Kanebo Boutique and so will continue to own some of the value of the business. Kanebo will also retain the right to purchase at market value some of the shares the IRCJ owns in Kaneo Boutique.

3 Outline of financial support

The IRCJ will at a later date carry out a thorough audit of the value of the businesses and assets of Kanebo's other divisions to determine the amount and terms and conditions of any financial support. The IRCJ will also coordinate any debt resolution required to implement the transfer of the cosmetic operations from Kanebo.

4 Implications for management

All eight directors of Kanebo, including the current President and Chairman Takashi Hotari, will resign. The management of Kanebo Boutique will also resign.

5 Implications for shareholders

The audit of the assets of Kanebo's other divisions has not yet been completed, so the necessity and nature of any financial support required therefore remains to be determined. Once the audit by the IRCJ has been completed, any implications for shareholders will also be decided.

Kanebo Boutique is currently an indirect wholly owned subsidiary of Kanebo, and so any implications for shareholders of Kanebo Boutique will be borne by Kanebo. As mentioned above, implications for holders of Kanebo shares will be determined after completion of the audit.

Kanebo Boutique effectively has only one shareholder, Kanebo. Following the capital injection from the IRCJ and the transfer of the cosmetics business from Kanebo, this capital relationship will be completely revised and the existing shares that Kanebo holds in Kanebo Boutique will be cancelled without compensation.

6 IRCJ rationale for providing assistance

Kanebo operates mainly cosmetics, home products, textiles, food and pharmaceuticals businesses. The core cosmetics business has 9,000 employees, customers in Japan and 47 other countries, and a top-level market share in its industry in Japan. Financially, however, the company's debt burden has become excessive because of business diversification. In the six months to September 30, 2003, Kanebo posted debts of 62.9 billion yen because of losses from closing businesses and costs from reducing staff.

Kanebo's core cosmetics business however has a strong business base. Separating the business from Kanebo quickly will avert the risk of damaging the business's value (its brand), while developing and implementing an appropriate business revitalization plan will, the IRCJ believes, make it possible to increase its corporate value.

Furthermore, the IRCJ believes that Kanebo can use the profit from the sale of the cosmetic business to improve the finances of its other divisions, cut the number of unprofitable operations, and reduce personnel.

7 Comments from the State Minister in Charge of Industrial Revitalization and Administrative Reforms and the minister relevant to the company seeking assistance

1. With regards to the application from Kanebo:
   Comments from the Minister in Charge of Industrial Revitalization and Administrative reforms and from the minister relevant to the company seeking assistance, and a convening of the Industrial Revitalization Committee will be made after the audit of Kanebo's other divisions has been completed and following the process to decide the details for the business revitalization.
2. With regard to the application from Kanebo Boutique[1]
   None expressed.

8 Debt repurchase application period[2]

1. The application period for the repurchase of debt from Kanebo is from March 10, 2004 to June 9, 2004.
2. The application period for the repurchase of debt from Kanebo Boutique is from March 10, 2004 to March 31, 2004.

9 Request for temporary cessation of demands for credit repayment

Under Article 24, Clause 1 of the Industrial Revitalization Corporation Act, financial institutions and other creditors of Kanebo have been requested not to recover loans or exercise any other rights they may have as creditors before the end of the debt repurchase application period as per item 5 above.

---

[1] Note on comments from ministers: The IRCJ is a quasi-governmental organisation. As such it is IRCJ policy to obtain comments about decisions to assist private-sector companies from the government ministries that regulate the industries in which these companies operate.

[2] The debt repurchase application period is a period established for the purchase of consensus building between the financial institutions concerned and the IRCJ in regard to debt repurchase and the revitalization plan. This plan is so named because, where agreement is achieved in legal terms, the financial institutions concerned apply to the IRCJ for debt repurchase etc.

10 Treatment of trade and other creditors

The decision to provide assistance concerns only the request for financial support made to financial institutions in regard to amounts lent to the assisted business and has no effect on the claims of trade and other creditors.

For more information, please contact
Corporate Planning Department
The Industrial Revitalization Corporation of Japan
Tel. 03-6212-6437

About the IRCJ:
The IRCJ was established jointly by the public and private sector on April 16, 2003, with the aim of providing revitalization assistance beneficial to both the industrial and the financial sectors in Japan. It targets assistance at companies that have sound business fundamentals but are unable to thrive because of excessive debt levels or other factors. The IRCJ has approximately 130 employees and is based in Tokyo. For more information please visit www.ircj.jp

Annex 3E: *Sony's Distinctive Approach to Corporate Governance*

In order to further strengthen corporate governance, regulations for the Sony Board of Directors include requirements in addition to those mandated by the Japanese Commercial Code. For example, there are rules to ensure the independence of the board of directors, a supervisory body, from the execution of business activities. There are also rules to ensure that appropriate actions and decisions are taken by the statutory committees.

Certain provisions in Sony's corporate governance regulations are unique to Sony and are based on the specific views of the company. For example, one regulation requires that the Board of directors, a supervisory body, consists of between ten and twenty members, and that at least five of these directors also must be Corporate Executive Officers. In general, a system that stipulates a minimum number of internal directors is unusual given the importance attached to separating the supervisory and executive roles within a company. Nevertheless, Sony believes that the participation of more than just a minimum number of internal directors on the board of directors is critical, based upon the belief that specific areas of the executive functions, such as accounting, finance, legal affairs, and other internal control functions, should be directly linked to the supervisory side of corporate governance. In the event of the discovery of a problem related to the business execution within a company, a framework that completely separates corporate oversight from business execution could increase risk, due to a lack of communication or the existence of an inadequate interface between the two sides. For this reason allowing part of the internal control functions belonging to the business execution side, led by the Group CEO, to be an extension of the board of directors, allows for the creation of a direct link between business execution and corporate oversight. Within this corporate governance framework, potential problems discovered within the scope of business execution can be reported directly to those responsible for corporate governance, allowing the latter to respond more rapidly to any potential problems. We therefore seek to avoid risks associated with the complete separation of corporate oversight from business execution, including the risk that information involving executive actions is not being properly communicated to the directors. Through this corporate governance system, Sony is able to strengthen the supervisory function of the board of directors and delegate greater authority for business execution to the Corporate Executive Officers, enabling the continued sound and dynamic management of the Sony Group.

The adoption of this system has facilitated even more lively deliberations among the board of directors. Previously, most executive decisions were made by the board of directors, the highest-level decision making body. However, under the new system, the board has delegated greater authority to Corporate Executive Officers, in the process entrusting them with a broader range of executive decisions. The introduction of this system has led to the clear division of these two corporate governance functions. Corporate Executive Officers execute business operations by making decisions within the scope of authority delegated to them by the board of directors, and the board of directors oversees their decisions. As a result of this structure, executives responsible for the execution of business operations are required to explain with even greater clarity to the board of directors the reason behind their business decisions.

Some commentators have observed wryly that Sony's performance has deteriorated since its governance had improved, and questions have been raised about CEO Idei staying on so long!

SONY'S Corporate Executive Officers

Nobuyuki Idei
Chairman and Group CEO;
Representative Corporate
Executive Officer.

Kunitake Ando
President and Global Hub
President, Representative
Corporate Executive Officer
Officer in charge of Personal
Solutions Business Group.

Howard Stringer
Vice Chairman & COO
(in charge of Entertainment
Business Group), Sony Group
Americas Representative.

Shizuo Takashino
Executive Deputy President &
COO (in charge of IT & Mobile
Solutions Network Company &
Professional Solutions Network
Company).

Keiji Kimura
Senior Executive Vice President
NC President, IT & Mobile
Solutions Network Company.

Fujio Nishida
Executive Vice President,
Officer In charge of Marketing and
Corporate Communications.

Yasunori Kirihara
Senior Vice President,
Officer in Charge of
Corporate Human Resources.

Ken Kutaragi
Executive Deputy President &
COO (in charge of Game Business
Group, Home Electronics
Network Company (HENC) &
Semiconductor Solutions Network
Company (SSNC), NC President
SSNC.

Teruo Masaki
Executive Deputy President & Group General Counsel.

Katsumi Ihara
Executive Deputy President & Group CSO & CFO.

Ryoji Chubachi
Executive Deputy President & COO (in charge of Micro Systems Network Company (MSNC) and EMCS), NC President, MSNC.

Tsutomu Niimura
Executive Vice President, NC President, HENC.

Takao Yuhara
Senior Vice President, Officer in Charge of Finance and Investor Relations.

Nobuyuki Oneda
Senior Vice President, Officer in Charge of TR60, Corporate Planning & Control, Accounting & Information Systems.

Nicole Seligman
Group deputy General Counsel.

Annex 3F: *Toyota AGM* *

AGM

June 7, 2004
President Fujio Cho
TOYOTA MOTOR CORPORATION
1, Toyota-cho, Toyota City, Aichi Prefecture

Notice of Convocation of FY2004 Ordinary General Shareholders' Meeting
(Unless otherwise stated, all financial information has been prepared in
accordance with generally accepted accounting principles in Japan)

Dear Shareholder,

Please refer to the following for information about the upcoming FY2004 Ordinary
General Shareholders' meeting. We hope that you will be able to attend this meeting.

If you are unable to attend the meeting, it would be appreciated if you could find the
time from your busy schedule to vote 'yes' or 'no' on the enclosed ballot form, sign
the form, and return it to us after reviewing the enclosed documents no later than
Tuesday, June 22, 2004. Thank you very much for your cooperation.

1. Date and time:	10:00 a.m., Wednesday, June 23, 2004
2. Venue:	Toyota Head Office, 1, Toyota-cho, Toyota City, Aichi Prefecture
3. Meeting Agenda Report:	Reports on business review, unconsolidated balance sheet and statement of income fro the FY2004 term (April 1, 2003 through march 31, 2004)

Resolutions:
Resolutions 1 to 6 Proposed by the Company

Proposed Resolution 1:	Approval of Proposed Appropriation of Retained Earnings for the FY2004 Term
Proposed Resolution 2:	Amendment of the Articles of Incorporation A summary of this resolution appears among

---

* English translation from the original Japanese-language document

the 'Reference Documents Pertaining to Exercise of Voting Rights,' on page 29 to follow.

Proposed Resolution 3: Election of 27 Directors

Proposed Resolution 4: Issue of Stock acquisition Rights without Consideration to Directors, Managing Officers and Employees, etc., of Toyota Motor Corporation and its Affiliates

A summary of this resolution appears among the 'Reference Documents Pertaining to Exercise of Voting Rights,' on pages 36–38 to follow.

Proposed Resolution 5: Repurchase of Shares

A summary of this resolution appears among the 'Reference Documents Pertaining to Exercise of Voting Rights,' on page 39 to follow.

Proposed Resolution 6: Award of Bonus Payments to Mr. Iwao Isomura (decreased), Former Representative Director and Vice Chairman, and to Retiring Directors.

4

France

Introduction

The system by which companies are managed and controlled in France is influenced by a number of features that are specific to the country: the role and influence of the government, the limited role of equity investments, the recruitment of managers from among a narrow côterie of students drawn from the *grandes écoles*, the concept of corporate interest, which, from a legal standpoint, has to be the criterion for decisions of managers and boards of directors.

Weight of the state: Colbertism and interventionism

Since Colbert, the principle that power should be concentrated at the centre and that it should be strong seems to be pivotal in French assumptions about the organization of society. It was this superintendent and later controller-general of the finances of Louis XIV, a collaborator of the King for twenty-two years in strengthening the powers of the state, who was the founder of the principle we now refer to as 'Colbertism'. It is reflected both in the constitution, in the authority of the President, and up to very recently, in corporate governance, in the authority of the Président Directeur Général (PDG) or chairman. A strong central power is inclined to be *dirigist*. It is also interventionist. Furthermore, since the eighteenth-century economists, France has been a country in which difficulties and problems tend to be addressed to the government and where it appears normal that the main economic and social services are publicly controlled: transport, energy, etc. Following the first nationalizations after the Second World War, and the second wave in 1982, it was not until 1987 that nationalized companies forming an essential element of the competitive sector, were privatized: banks, insurance companies, and major industrial groups. Further privatizations occurred in 1994. Later, the capital of public sector companies was opened up: France Telecom, Air France, etc., leaving just a few major public utilities such as Electricité de France and Gaz de France in public hands, and these may be open to private shareholders in 2005. Certain will remain in the public sector: the SNCF (National Railway system), the RATP (Regional Transport), and the Post Office, etc.

However, the state has not restricted its interventionism to public companies. Several recent transactions carried out under a centre-right government illustrate the strong interest of the state in keeping companies in the right hands: in November 2002, when Vivendi wanted to sell shares in Véolia to reduce its debt, it was two public shareholders, GDF and EDF, and Groupama, an insurance company with a government representative on its board, which acquired the shares. The press rightly remarked that as a result an undervalued Véolia had not fallen into foreign hands. When the government auctioned its shares in Crédit Lyonnais in November 2003, it opened the auction on a Friday evening asking that bids be sent in by the following morning. This effectively barred the way to foreign banks.[1] The refinancing of Alstom in 2003 and 2004 was negotiated with banks at Bercy (headquarters of the Ministry of the Economy and Finance).

Can the state take sides and influence takeover bids? My belief is that, today, while it can demonstrate its opposition, it cannot really impose its will. The extent of the influence of the state depends solely on how the company that launches the bid assesses the nuisance value of the public authorities for its future business. At the time of Sanofi-Synthélabo's bid for Aventis, the Finance Minister summoned the heads of both companies and asked them to reach an agreement, but was unable to force them to do so. Although the government had no real power, it nevertheless clearly indicated that it wanted a Franco-French outcome. Novartis was dissuaded, but was it really interested in the first place? A pharmaceutical company might fear an adverse reaction in view of the government's extensive control over the industry: authorization for the launch of new products and fixing of prices (although decisions are increasingly taken at the European level). If a bid concerned a tobacco retailer (for example Altadis), as tobacco retailers collect taxes (positive for their cash flow), if the government disliked the outcome of the battle, it could impose conditions on the foreign raider with negative consequences for cash flow.

A study made over the period 1986–2004 shows that 85% of foreign bids for French assets were approved, even in 'strategic' sectors such as banks, insurance, and high technology.[2] A French solution prevailed over a foreign

---

[1] UBS: State tradition versus family tradition. Philippe Tibi, 8 October 2003.

[2] UBS Investment Research. French Equity Strategy. 'French State Intervention: Not Exactly what you Think', November 2004.

bid in only 8% of bids. Only 4% of bids from abroad were vetoed outright by the state.

The powerful role of the state can be seen in the constant temptation to legislate on each and every subject. French law can enter into fine detail, covering areas which in other countries are dealt with by professional self-regulation or industry and company negotiations. Consequently, new laws have to be voted to deal with fine points, not dealt with in previous legislation. For example, the law on New Economic Regulations (NRE law) made publication of the remuneration of company directors mandatory in company annual reports. It required a new law to exonerate unquoted companies from this obligation. The NRE act limited the number of directorships to five and chairmanships of quoted companies to one, although the limitation on the number of company mandates was only a recommendation in the Higgs report.

Capitalism without capital

The omnipresence of the state has meant that the equity market has only become significant over the last twenty years. Nevertheless, this 'significance' is quite relative. French stock-market capitalization represented 1,147 billion as of 31 December 2004, i.e. 78% of GDP compared to 133% in Great Britain and 139% in the United States. Why is France in this position?[3] The French know the answer very well. France is a 'capitalist country without capital'. Although the ratio of equity financing has increased significantly, from 8.3% in 1982 to 14.5% in 1995, it remains quite low by OECD standards.[4] This situation has always existed. Saving has never been managed from a long-term standpoint. The pension system is public and based on a pay as you go system. It is not a funded scheme. It has only been interesting from a tax standpoint to manage pension savings via funded schemes since the spring of 2004. Consequently, pension funds have never emerged. In 1982, in an attempt to extend the period of savings, tax advantages were introduced for life insurance, although the minimum holding period was still eight years. Life-insurance products with a minimum eight-year holding period were launched to profit from the tax advantage but they were associated with guaranteed returns which only bond investments could secure. The only source of long-term savings was therefore invested in the bond market. Investments started being diversified very recently. Institutional investors,

[3] World Federation of Exchanges members (domestic market capitalization) and OECD (GDP).

[4] R. Deeg and S. Perez, 'International Capital Mobility and Domestic Institutions: Corporate Finance and Governance in Four European Cases', *Governance: An International Journal of Policy and Administration*, 13/2 (April 2000), 119–53.

the Caisse des Dépôts et Consignations and insurance companies (which held a very significant proportion of the stock market's capitalization until the 1980s), as well as mutual funds, now represent 30%. The mutual funds themselves have only invested 17.4% of their funds in equities.[5] At the time of the privatizations in 1987, the lack of domestic savings prompted the government to create the concept of 'stable shareholder groups' or so-called 'hardcore' shareholders ('noyaux durs'), in other words, cross-shareholdings consolidated into a bloc for several years (five to seven) designed to protect companies suddenly thrown into the competitive world of predators. Cross-shareholdings represented 58% of total share ownership in 1994 (see table in annex).[6] This phenomenon explains the 'consanguinity' evident in French company boards of directors. Gradually, these investments have been unwound, with foreign investors taking an increasingly significant position. Foreigners now possess 40% of France's stock market capitalization compared to only 7% for US quoted companies. In January 1999, foreign investors were responsible for 85% of all transactions in the CAC 40.

The corps of the 'grandes écoles': a narrow source of management

Another feature specific to France is its system of *grandes écoles*: Polytechnique (X) and the Ecole Nationale d'Administration (ENA). Among their graduates, the elite of Polytechnique's *corps d'application*, i.e. members of the 'mines', 'bridges', and 'telecoms' corps and, for ENA, the 'Inspection des Finances' and 'Conseil d'État', supply the majority of PDGs and company directors for CAC 40 companies. A study carried out in 1997 by researchers at the CNRS (National Scientific Research Centre) and Boyden shows that, in 1996, 30% of the heads of the 200 largest French companies came from one or other of the two *grandes écoles*, ENA and Polytechnique, and that 66% of multiple board memberships (with a seat on at least two CAC 40 companies) were held by alumni of the two *grandes écoles*.[7] In addition, as, until 2001, the number of directorships was only limited to seven, chairmen could find themselves board members in at least six other major quoted companies, not to mention subsidiaries in their own group (which are not taken into account in the maximum allowed). One chairman of a major bank was a member of seventeen boards of directors at the same time. The recruitment of directors from within a narrow elite, associated with cross-shareholdings

---

[5] *Financial News*, 8–15 March 2004: 'Asset allocation of French OPCVM as of February 29, 2004'. (Bonds: 17.5%; Money Market: 36.9%; Diversified: 22%; Guaranteed return: 6.2%).

[6] Ibid.

[7] CNRS and Boyden. Directors and Managers in the CAC 40. Michel Bauer and Bénédicte Bertin-Mourot. September 1997.

in newly privatized companies, has increased consanguinity in boards of directors. So much so, that among the limited number of recommendations in the first Viénot report of 1995, was a recommendation to limit director-ships to five. In this same year, around 300 seats on the boards of CAC 40 companies were held by just 75 individuals.[8] Since then, the principles of sound governance have increasingly prevailed and boards have introduced more independent members and reduced the number of multiple director-ships. Nevertheless, if one examines companies in the SBF 120, in 2004, of the 120 heads of major companies quoted on the Paris stock market, 60% came from major Parisian *grandes écoles*, of which 27 (22.5%) came from Poly-technique, and 18 (15%) from the Ecole Nationale d'Administration.[9] Changes are afoot however, as in 2003, only 34.7% of company directors in the CAC 40 had a Polytechnique or ENA background compared to 42% in 1996. However, it is still rare for boards to be open to persons outside a restricted circle of top managers and who are not already PDGs or CEOs. In 2004, 13% of board members continued to hold 20% of company director-ships in the CAC 40 (these figures were 8% and 22% the previous year), while 23% hold 44% (22% the previous year).[10] Intellectuals or foreign personal-ities are preferred to operational managers and finance directors, etc.

Furthermore, as Polytechnique only opened its doors to women in 1968 and ENA first and foremost forms senior civil servants (only admitting its first woman Inspecteur des Finances in 1975), there are still very few women PDGs and very few women board directors among the very largest com-panies, with the exception of women that have inherited family companies. A recent study showed that in France women have only 6% of board seats.[11] while 60% of French companies have at least one woman on their board of directors, only 20% have *more than* one woman on their board of directors. Of 41 women directors, 20% are representatives of shareholder families and 24% staff representatives. A statistic from Korn/Ferry International puts the presence of women in CAC 40 companies at 8% in 2003.

Corporate interest before shareholder interest

The stakeholder/shareholder debate has never really existed in France as it is 'corporate interest' which must guide corporate management. This concept contrasts with the Anglo-Saxon approach in which managers act in the interest of shareholders, to whom they have a fiduciary duty and to whom

[8] *Financial News*, Report France, 6–12 October 2003.
[9] La lettre de l'Expansion. 8 November 2004.
[10] Korn Ferry, 2004.   [11] Euro-Baromètre EPWN 2004.

they have to report as representatives. Corporate interest is distinct from shareholder interest. It is a sort of reification of the corporate entity:

Corporate interest, which should not be confused with that of shareholders or directors of the company, cannot be reduced to the various interests just analysed. Nor is it simply their sum. Both an economic reality and a social reality, situated at a crossroads, the company is a forum for a multitude of interests. To simply lump these interests together does not enable us to define the interest of the company as a whole.

This definition of corporate interest, clearly formulated by the Paris Appeal Court on 22 May 1965, is still a norm in French substantive law, whether in civil law, in the area of abuse of majority or minority positions, or in criminal law in the context of misuse of power and corporate assets. The Viénot report of 1995 took this French specificity into account, recalling that

corporate interest can be defined as an interest overriding that of the corporate entity itself, in other words, the company considered as an autonomous economic entity pursuing its own ends, distinct in particular from those of its shareholders, employees, creditors, including the tax authority, suppliers and clients, but which reflects their common interest, which is to ensure the prosperity and continuity of the company.

The Bouton report, recognizing this French specificity but also the necessity in France of taking into account to a greater extent the interests of share-holders, ascribed a dual objective to boards of directors, saying that 'a Board has to be a judicious balance of skills, experience and independence, serving the interests of the company and its shareholders'.

In his book *Corporate Governance, or the Uncertain Foundations of a New Power*, Jean Peyrelevade, former Chairman of Crédit Lyonnais, uses strong words to criticize the 'alibi' of corporate interest, which, according to him, 'provides a justification for autonomy, giving management leverage to arbitrate among various interested parties'.

The Legal Framework

Legislation

Since 2000, the corpus of corporate legislation has been grouped together in the Commercial Code. The aim of the codification is consistency: the Commercial Code contains matter of a legislative nature and precludes everything of a regulatory nature; it also harmonizes terminology, using more modern or more precise terms.

The three basic laws governing the organization of companies are the law on Commercial Companies of 24 July 1966, which sets out the legislation which applies to companies; the Nouvelles Régulations Économiques—the law on New Economic Regulations (NRE Act) of 15 May 2001; and the law on Sécurité Financière— the Financial Security Act (LSF) of 1 August 2003. They were supplemented by a ruling (ordonnance) of 24 July 2004, which governs securities. The last two laws were drawn up and voted in response to the need for 'good corporate governance' which has developed in France since 1995. The NRE Act introduced important reforms in the organization of governance. It overcame a basic weakness of the 1966 Act which attributed the same areas of responsibility to the chairman of the board of directors and the board of directors itself. It introduced the possibility of separating the functions of chairman and CEO, the latter becoming head of operations whereas in a traditional structure with a Président Directeur Général, he was just the chairman's deputy. The Act extended obligations with respect to accountability, and in particular made it compulsory to publish the remuneration of executive directors and policy with respect to allocation of stock options. (Later, this obligation was restricted to executive directors of listed companies and of their subsidiaries.) It limited the number of concurrent directorships, reducing the number of board positions in companies not belonging to the same group from eight to five for one individual. It would seem that this has led to a reduction in the number of board members on boards of directors rather than a redistribution of positions or the opening up of boards to new personalities. It also gives more power to small shareholders (holding less than 5% of the capital).

The law on Financial Security, LSF, was prepared and voted on after, and on the basis of, the US Sarbanes-Oxley Act. The Act focuses on improving the accountability of quoted companies and regulating financial markets. It led to the creation of the Autorité des Marchés Financiers—the Financial Markets Authority (AMF), the result of a merger between the Conseil des Bourses de Valeurs (CBV) and the Commission des Opérations de Bourse (COB). It reformed the status of auditors, strengthening their independence. In terms of governance, it made transparency the absolute priority of quoted companies. It made it easier for board members to obtain information. It increased obligations with respect to provision of information, making it compulsory for the chairman to issue a special report to shareholders (attached to the report of the board of directors) on the preparation and organization of the work of the board of directors (activity of the board of directors; composition, committee tasks, and activities); on internal control procedures introduced by the company; and on any limitations on the powers of the CEO imposed by the board of directors. It made the chairman responsible with regard to internal controls, and the board of directors and the Audit Committee responsible with regard to the accuracy of the company's accounts, urging the board to 'implement all the controls and verifications that it considers appropriate'. It enlarged the possibilities of class action available for minority shareholder associations.

Among other matters, the ruling of 24 July 2004 extends the powers which the shareholders' general meeting may give to the board of directors and the CEO as regards capital increases and share buybacks. It creates 'preference shares' and substitutes them to various types of priority shares which existed before.

'Soft' laws

In November 1994, the professor of law André Tunc wrote in the bulletin of the Commission des Opérations de Bourse (COB):

France seems to have been spared the cultural revolution that has unfolded in the United States and the United Kingdom. What special privilege allows this situation to persist in France? American collective savings (pension funds) have flexed their muscles, demanding accountability and sometimes changes in business leaders in the United Kingdom, Australia, Sweden, Switzerland and even Japan. It seems certain that French companies will have to bend to their demands if they want to benefit from foreign capital.

Shortly afterwards, the subject began to be talked about in symposiums and debates. As a result, the Conseil National du Patronat Français (CNPF), the French equivalent of the Confederation of British Industries, and the Association des Entreprises Privées (AFEP), Confederation of Private Companies, ended by asking a committee chaired by Marc Viénot, chairman of the Société Générale, 'to examine the main problems related to the composition, responsibilities and working methods of Boards of Directors of quoted companies'. The first Viénot report was dated July 1995. It clearly indicated its limited scope in its title, 'The Board of Directors in Quoted Companies'. It was followed by a second Viénot report in July 1999 entitled 'Report of the Committee on Corporate Governance' and the 'Bouton report' named after Marc Viénot's successor to the chairmanship of Société Générale, entitled 'For a better governance of quoted companies', published in September 2002.

The Viénot report was a response to the issues under debate. In general, the proposals were low key, contrasting with recommendations regarding corporate governance in Great Britain. The choice of words here is important. In its first report, the committee chaired by Marc Viénot 'considered desirable that each Board of a quoted company comprise at least two independent Board members'; it recommended 'that each Board should have at least a Board member selection committee, a remuneration committee and an audit committee'; it indicated that 'when a Board member exercised the functions of Chairman or CEO, he should not accept more than five Direct-orships in French or foreign quoted companies outside his group'. All these suggestions have been widely implemented by the main companies in the CAC 40 as the statistics presented below indicate, with the exception of 'Board evaluation': 'each Board has a dual obligation to examine periodically its composition, organisation and operations and to provide information to shareholders on any positions or decisions it has taken'. This dual obligation only began to be applied in the years 2002–3.

The second Viénot report tried to limit the government's proposed law on the publication of directors' remuneration and the dissociation of the func-tions of chairman and CEO. The report's reticence over the first point was disregarded by the NRE Act, which made publication of the remuneration of company directors mandatory in company annual reports. It was listened to on the second point, as the NRE Act left boards of directors the choice of opting for a structure based on separate or combined chairman and CEO functions, depriving shareholders from making the choice themselves. The second report went further than the previous report regarding recommen-dations concerning independence of committees and certain obligations concerning accountability. It even recommended abandoning the use of delegations of authority given to boards of directors enabling them to increase capital at the time of takeover bids by eliminating preferential subscription rights.

The Bouton report is more like a code of conduct. In some ways, it is a guide to 'best practices' in corporate governance. Although it is directed at quoted companies, only the very largest seem to use it as a code of conduct. It quite rightly insists in its introduction on the fact that practices have to be based on 'the fundamental principles of personal responsibility, accountabil-ity and integrity in business affairs'. Rules as regards the composition and functioning of boards and committees are made more precise. The verb 'should', and incitements to take action, become more frequent. The report also makes reference to the framework in which stock options should be attributed and exercised. It provides support for the independence of audit-ors and the transparency of financial information.

Two other studies in the Paris market were premonitary although they had little impact: in 1993, a working group chaired by Yves Le Portz (on behalf of the COB and the Compagnie Nationale des Commissaires aux Comptes— National Association of Auditors), worked on the independence and object-ivity of auditors working in a group. In 1995, the Lévy-Lang report on stock options, commissioned by the CNPF and AFEP, defined certain best practices concerning the subject, such as information to be provided in the annual report on the number of options granted, the total number of beneficiaries, the exercise price and price discount, and the number of options exercised during the year.

The Autorité des Marchés Financiers

The Autorité des Marchés Financiers (Financial Markets Authority) (AMF) is the result of the merger of the COB, the Conseil des Marchés Financiers (CMF) and the Conseil de Discipline de la Gestion Financière (LSF law of 1 August 2003). It plays an important role in the area of corporate governance through two of its tasks that were previously devolved on the COB: the protection of savings and investor information. In particular, it verifies that quoted companies publish comprehensive high-quality information in a timely manner.

In furtherance of this, the COB had as early as 1987 defined standards for annual financial information, since that time referred to as the 'reference document'. It was used as a model for defining the European prospectus. The COB also wanted to encourage harmonization of the content of annual reports and improve the quality of information.

The reference document can either be a specific document provided by the company at the time of a share issue, or the annual report if it fulfils the information standards demanded by the COB. Every reference document must be filed with the AMF, where, since 2002, they are subject to an 'a posteriori' check. Standards are reviewed every year to take into account new legislative obligations and areas requiring improvement identified by the AMF as a result of its analysis of documents received during the year.

Information standards cover areas of corporate governance such as:

- rules of procedure of the board and its committees ('règlement intérieur');
- mandates and functions exercised by directors;
- regulated agreements between the company and any of its directors and also with any shareholder that possesses more than 5% of voting rights;
- remuneration and benefits in kind paid directly or indirectly to any director; stock options, etc. They also concern other aspects of corporate governance: by-law details such as conditions governing access to and voting at meetings; the stock price movements and volume of transactions over an eighteen-month period;
- recent litigation and important facts;
- risks: market, legal, industrial and environmental; coverage by insurance; other risks such as labour conflicts.

In 2003, 350 reference documents had been filed. Those of nineteen companies were the subject of a rectification request by the COB.

Table 4.1. Changes in the number of reference documents by market

	Number of reference documents filed		Number of quoted companies		% rate reference documents	
	2001	2000	2001	2000	2001	2000
Premier marché	127	124	426	454	29.8	27.3
Second marché	80	89	347	354	23.0	25.1
Nouveau marché	119	89	165	158	72.1	56.3
Bond market	22	16				

Source: AMF.

Governance

Legal structures

There exist three main forms of legal structure for commercial companies in France: the Société Anonyme or SA, the Société à Responsabilité Limitée or SARL, and the Société par Actions Simplifiée or SAS. Derived from the SARL, there is the Entreprise Unipersonnelle à Responsabilité Limitée or EURL, and from the SAS, the Société par Actions Simplifiée Unipersonnelle, or SASU. Another one, the Société en Commandite par Actions, is rare but needs to be mentioned as it is the legal structure chosen by many well-known companies such as the Lagardère Group, Michelin, and Lazard for their principal holding company. Other forms of company such as Société en Participation, Société en Nom Collectif, and Société Civile are not relevant to the subject under discussion.

The Société Anonyme

The Société Anonyme (SA) is the equivalent of the public company, similar in concept to the AG in Germany or the PLC in the UK. To create a Société Anonyme at least seven shareholders are required. In 2003, there existed around 160,000 SAs, of which 739 were quoted. This chapter only deals with those that make public issues and hence are subject to tougher regulations: more complex formation formalities and operating procedures. The minimum capital required for companies that make public issues is €225,000 whereas it is only €37,000 for other public companies. These companies obviously have to comply with specific procedures with regard to publicity for shareholder meetings as well as operations concerning their capital and merger and divestments transactions. They are under the control of the AMF when they make public issues and are therefore obliged to publish a 'reference document' that complies with the standards outlined above.

The Société en Commandite par Actions

It offers the same possibilities as a Société Anonyme (raising of outside capital), and is particularly suitable in situations in which the founders of the company want to control it closely, enabling management control and control over the capital to be dissociated. There exist two types of associate in these companies, the 'commandités'—general partners, indefinitely and jointly and severally liable for the debt of the company, and whose rights in the company are not freely transferable—and the 'commanditaires'—limited partners, whose liability is restricted to the amount of their investment in the company, in the same way as shareholders in a limited company. The by-laws can freely determine the conditions governing the appointment, removal, and remuneration of managers. There are only a few thousand Sociétés en Commandite par Actions, as with two levels of management and indefinite joint and several liability of the 'commandités', their functioning is more complex.

Société à Responsabilité Limitée

As in an SA, the liability of a shareholder in a Société à Responsabilité Limitée (SARL) is limited to the amount of his investment. The capital of a SARL is freely determined in the company's by-laws and divided into 'parts sociales'—'company units' (rather than shares). The units are not freely transferable. This explains why this type of structure is inappropriate for large companies. With the SAS, the SARL is the only type of company that can be created by a single shareholder, in which case it is called an Entreprise Unipersonnelle à Responsabilité Limitée (EURL). Contributions in kind can be made in exchange for rights (unlike SAs). SARLs are managed by one or more managers and do not need to have a board.

Société par Actions Simplifiée

The Société par Actions Simplifiée (SAS)—simplified joint stock company—has a very flexible structure, as to a large degree its functioning depends on decisions made by its members. There is no minimum number of directors, no rules regarding maximum number of directorships and no need to hold shareholder meetings for decisions exceeding the powers of directors, etc. This type of company has grown very rapidly since 1999. It is very attractive for small to medium-sized companies, 100%-owned subsidiaries of groups, and group holding companies. There were around 4,500 SAS companies in 2000 compared to 225,000 SAs. In 2003, there were more than 100,000 SAs compared to 160,000 SAs. Considered in the beginning as an appropriate structure for joint ventures, in fact it has been used very little for this purpose. When created with foreign partners, it is important to check that the by-laws do not conflict with the provisions of international law.

An SAS can be created by individuals or corporate entities and only have one shareholder. Members of an SAS can freely determine in the by-laws the nature and functions of management bodies and the conditions and way in which collective decisions are taken. However, certain decisions have to be taken by shareholders themselves. These concern, *inter alia*, decisions regarding company capital, mergers, divisions, dissolution, appointment of auditors, approval of annual accounts, and distribution of profits. An SAS has to be represented by a chairman authorized to commit the company. Third parties (banks, suppliers etc.) can participate in the functioning of the company through rights of control and vetoes over certain decisions.

The Société par Actions Simplifiée Unipersonnelle (SASU) has developed rapidly as it is very handy in company groups. It is an SAS whose only shareholder can be a person or a corporate body ('personne morale'). It is more flexible than the EURL as there is complete freedom in organizing the functioning of the company and the relationships between partners. Sale of one's equitable interest ('droits sociaux') is very easy.

The structure of the board and its operations

The management of a Société Anonyme can be of the 'unitary' type with a board of directors and a Président Directeur Général or 'two tier' with a supervisory board and management board. Since 2001, the board of directors can have a non-executive chairman and a CEO in charge of operations. Companies can switch from one structure to another by making changes to their by-laws. The new by-laws must be approved by a General Shareholders' Meeting. Events have shown that modifications usually reflect the changing needs of managers and correspond to a new stage in relations between managers and the company. The most frequent change is the shift from a two-tier structure to a unitary structure. (See division of CAC 40 companies between these various structures as of 30 December 2003 in the Annex.)

The 'unitary' structure

Until 1940, the most common method of functioning of the SA, governed by a law of 1867, was very similar to the current situation in Great Britain: a board of directors elected by a General Shareholders' Meeting which elects a chairman from among its members and delegates the management of the company to a CEO separate from the chairman. (In the UK, the chairman of the board was often the CEO as well. This practice is now less frequent). In 1940, either in reaction to capitalism, scandals, and collective irresponsibility of directors, or out of concern to restore moral values and emphasize personal responsibility, three successive decrees in 1940 and 1943 led to the creation of the position of Président Directeur Général—chairman and CEO. The board of directors appoints a chairman from among its members. Thus, contrary to the United States, the chairman is never elected by a Shareholders' Meeting. He is chosen by the directors from among the directors. He is responsible for the General Management of the company. The two positions of chairman and CEO are consolidated into a single person, the PDG (Président Directeur Général). It is the most common structure: twenty-five companies out of forty in the CAC forty were organized in this way as of 31 December 2003.

The 'two-tier' structure

Since the 1966 law, a two-tier structure has been possible. It is based on the German system. The company is administered by two bodies: a Supervisory Board, whose main role is to appoint and remove members of the management board and control their management, and a management board in charge of administering and managing the company. The management board can have up to five members. In general, this structure is chosen when two companies of approximately the same size merge. The chairman of one of the companies (in general the oldest, or the chairman of the absorbed company) becomes chairman of the supervisory board, and the other, chairman of the management board (Aventis, after the merger of Rhône-Poulenc and Hoechst). Practice has shown that when this choice is made to preserve appearances, it rarely lasts very long: LVMH and Suez for example quickly returned to a unitary structure, the absorbing company obtaining the position of PDG. An organization based on a supervisory board and management board is also chosen by companies with a family shareholding structure: the chairman of the supervisory board is a member of the family and the chairman of the management board an external manager (Publicis, Pinault Printemps Redoute (PPR) until spring 2005, PSA Peugeot Citroën). It is also adopted when a PDG retires but wants to retain the function of management board supervision (Air Liquide). In total, seven companies in the CAC 40 had chosen this structure at as of the end of 2003. In terms of responsibility and corporate governance, the position of members of the supervisory board is very different to that of directors in companies with a board of directors. For example, members of a supervisory board are only responsible for their individual misdeeds. Unlike directors, they cannot be held responsible for the management of the company or its results in the event of bankruptcy. The remuneration committee of a supervisory board cannot determine the remuneration of members of the supervisory board and make a proposal to the board; only the chairman of the management board can determine remuneration. The supervisory board can only make suggestions.

The 1999 law on 'New Economic Regulations' also makes it possible for companies to adopt a structure where the chairman is non-executive and the CEO is the only executive manager ('structure dissociée'). Every Société Anonyme has to choose in its by-laws whether to adopt a unitary structure with a PDG or separate the two functions. The by-laws are subject to a shareholder vote. However, only the board of directors can decide which of the structures should be selected. Currently, six companies in the CAC 40 have opted for a dissociated structure. In at least half of these cases, the chairman was formerly PDG in the same company: BNP Paribas, Cap Gemini, Lafarge. It will require several more years before an external non-executive chairman is recruited by a headhunter or from among independent directors. The Financial Security law also makes it compulsory to define the respective powers of the chairman, CEO, and board of directors in the company's rules of procedure.

The development of corporate governance

The first reaction of the French to the development of corporate governance was fairly cold, and ultimately defensive. Although the subject was familiar to major international companies, it was not until 1995 that a committee of business leaders headed by Marc Viénot, former chairman of Société Générale, explored the issues. The subject was approached from its narrowest angle, the organization of the board of directors. The committee made a few recommendations (see the on soft laws, page section 185), but above all insisted that there should not be any new legislation, and that the 1966 law provided an adequate framework for governance issues. This was despite the fact that several weaknesses in corporate governance had been patent for some time, all of them connected to the passivity of boards of directors comprising friends and close relations. For example, the age at which certain chairmen resigned: nearer 80 than 70 (Antoine Riboud at Danone and Ambroise Roux atCompagnie Générale des Eaux, now Vivendi); and how their succession was arranged: contrary to all expectations, Antoine Riboud had his son appointed as chairman. More recently Alcatel modified its by-laws to allow its present PDG to stay until 70. PDGs that were contested or even indicted were only removed by their board after months of dithering(Alcatel (Suard), Vivendi (Messier)). Forced resignations on account of poor performance are very recent: France Télécom, Rhodia, and carrefour in 2005. All the same, a further step in this direction was recently made at the General Shareholders' Meeting of Eurotunnel in 2004, which went as far as removing the whole of the management of the company from office.

Matters changed quickly however. After the 1995 Viénot report, and above all since the 1998–9 period, the boards of major quoted companies have gradually implemented recommendations concerning corporate governance: an end to cross-shareholdings, the appointment of independent directors, the introduction of board committees and, more recently, board evaluation. A study made by Korn/Ferry International on the application of corporate governance recommendations in CAC 40 companies shows that while only 37% of them had adopted such measures in 1995, 100% have adopted them today. The process has been voluntary as regards the organization of committees and the presence of independent board members but forced by legislation, it has to be admitted, as regards transparency of remunerations and the role of auditors. Statistics do not exist for all quoted companies, but it is nevertheless clear that many are moving firmly towards better systems of governance. On the other hand, the rights of shareholders (elimination of anti-takeover measures, respect of minority shareholder rights, one share = one vote), have not really changed. Nevertheless, countervailing powers have been emerging as we will see in the chapter on shareholders.

Organization of the company and board responsibilities

Mission of the board of directors

The mission of the board of directors is very clearly defined in the NRE law of May 2001. The board of directors must participate in strategic decisions, oversee and control the management of the company, and ensure members of the board are accountable to shareholders.

The main characteristics of the company and its operating methods are written into the by-laws.

The Articles of Association ('Statuts')

They should indicate the form, term, name, head office, purpose, and capital of the company. However as legislation sets out in detail how commercial companies operate, the by-laws can be simple, except for SAS and unquoted companies. For SAS companies, the by-laws are important as they have to provide details on the respective powers of the various bodies, their scope and how they are exercised. In unquoted companies, the by-laws define how shares are transferred between shareholders, registered or bearer shares, etc.

Rules of procedure ('règlement intérieur')

The by-laws can be completed by an additional document, the rules of procedure, publication of which is not compulsory but which a number of companies make public nevertheless, as the Bouton report makes the rules of procedure (including the directors' charter) an important tool of corporate governance and accountability. The Bouton report recommends that rules of procedure specify the role of the board in strategic decisions, indicating those that must be submitted to it, and detailing how board members can gain access to information, and board member responsibilities with regard to confidentiality. It is also useful for rules of procedure to outline the scope and operations of the various specialized committees. It must also provide details on the aims and methods of the annual board evaluation process.

The rules of procedure of a board of directors generally also includes the following matters:

- organization of meetings of the board of directors;
- responsibilities of the board of directors;
- the division of responsibilities between the chairman and CEO (or between the supervisory committee and the management board);
- delegations of authority to the PDG (or CEO in the event of a two-tier structure) covering investments and divestments, financing and indebtedness;
- determination of specialized committees and, for each of them, composition, minimum number of annual meetings, mission, resources and reports;
- the methods and frequency of board evaluation.

Certain rules of procedure also give details on the fundamental rights of shareholders (financial, information, and expression) and the organization of relations with them (shareholder meetings, behaviour in the event of a takeover bid).

The directors' charter

Included or not in the rules of procedure, there is a directors' charter (which may be made public); this provides details on the rights and obligations of directors. In general, the directors' charter deals with the following issues:

- knowledge, skills, training and information of a director;
- defence of corporate interest, loyalty;

- the obligation to speak out and be independently minded;
- confidentiality;
- availability and assiduity;
- conflicts of interest;
- holding of a minimum number of shares;
- observance of rules concerning share transactions;
- if necessary, criteria governing the granting of directors' fees.

Thirty-five of the forty companies in the CAC 40 possessed a directors' charter in 2003.

Accountability to shareholders

Recent legislation such as the NRE and LSF has increased legal requirements in the area of corporate accountability. The AMF is responsible for organizing the process (see p.187). Legislation makes it compulsory for companies to inform their shareholders in their annual reports of the risks they run, the social and environmental consequences of the business, the functioning of committees, and corporate control processes. In all these areas, one has to remark that, legislation goes into an astonishing wealth of detail which is peculiar to France. If a company is quoted and carries out financial market operations, it has to indicate the risks it runs in the event of changes in interest rates, currency rates, stock market prices, and how it limits these risks and protects against them. In social affairs, the company has to provide information on the organization of work, time worked, subcontracting, etc. As far as the environment is concerned, companies have to provide information on water, energy, and raw materials consumption, waste disposal, and provisions and guarantees for pollution risks. The LSF wanted shareholders to have a better understanding of the functioning of corporate committees and control processes. Accordingly, the chairman of the board of directors or of the supervisory committee now has to describe in the annual report presented to the shareholders' meeting how the work of the board is organized and what internal control procedures have been set up within the company (this information is normally presented in a chapter entitled 'sustainable development' in the annual report, see p.213). The first report is generally entitled 'corporate governance' and describes the composition of the board, the number of meetings, the composition of committees and the number of meetings held, their tasks etc. The second report on internal controls has not yet been fully defined. A debate is ongoing between companies and the AMF on its content. Companies, supported by the Ministry of Justice (Garde des Sceaux), want to restrict the report to a description of existing control procedures. The AMF would like information on the effectiveness of the controls. Managers must also inform shareholders on transactions related to company securities that they or their family or friends hold.

The composition of the board of directors

French boards of directors have made progress both in terms of composition and functioning. The usual criticism levelled at the composition of French boards of directors is their 'consanguinity'. This is the result of two features of French society: the weight of the *grandes écoles* and the implications of a capitalist system without capital (introduction p.180). When in 1987, the government wished to protect companies that it was privatizing from raiders, it established groups of core shareholders using the instrument of cross-shareholdings. Core shareholder groups, in exchange for an advantageous purchase price, have accepted that the sale of their shares be subject to control. The cross-shareholdings went hand-in-hand with a reciprocal presence on the boards of directors of the companies concerned. Today, these investments have been unwound and, in the majority of companies, but not all, directorships are no longer reciprocal. Nevertheless, in large companies, the majority of directors come from the same background: the Polytechnique or ENA, and belong to a narrow milieu where everyone knows each other.

In terms of number of directorships, length of directorships and proportion of independent directors, France now conforms to international standards. An individual can only be the PDG of a single company (or two if the second is associated and unquoted). A director cannot have more than five directorships in French Sociétés Anonymes (leaving him the possibility of taking up the directorships in foreign companies or SAS companies beyond this quota). A recommendation has been made to reduce the length of directorships to three or four years (legislation authorizes six years) and to no longer consider a director as independent when he has been on the same board for nine years. The by-laws determine the age limit for directors. Legislation requires that the number of directors of more than 70 years of age should not exceed one-third of the board of directors. Although the average age has fallen, a few companies still remain where the founder is more than 75 years old, and still PDG. In 2003, the average age of directors was 60 in CAC 40 companies (Korn/Ferry International International).

In terms of functioning, boards are increasingly forums for discussion even though their size makes this a difficult task. The size of boards of directors is extremely variable. A quoted company cannot have less than three directors or more than eighteen. However, boards of directors of major French companies are often fairly large with seats for independent directors, employee representatives, as well as representatives of the Company Council and sometimes even censors. Many boards have more than fifteen persons around the table, with only two executive directors, the PDG and the CEO.

The activity of boards of directors, if it can be measured by the number of meetings, has more than doubled since 1995, as Table 4.2 indicates.

In general, meetings last around two-and-a-half to three hours. In the largest companies, a longer meeting is held every year for a presentation and discussion on strategy.

Independent directors

There is a real debate on the definition of and the necessity for independent directors in France. Concern about conflict of interest is recent but could be keener, although a law of 1966 already required that agreements between a company and executive directors or directors be approved by the board of directors and subject to a vote of shareholders on the basis of a special auditor's report. However disclosures have never succeeded in avoiding conflicts of interest; for example, company bankers have traditionally had a seat on the board. Company lawyers and investment bankers may have an ineluctable conflict of interest—at its worst when they advise two rival companies. Recently there has been a marked unwinding of cross-participations and a reduction in the number of cross-directorships. As regards the presence and proportion of independent directors, France has not gone as far as the Sarbanes-Oxley Act. The definition of independence is the same: 'A Director is independent if he has no relationship of any sort whatsoever, with the company, group or management, that might compromise the free exercise of his judgement.' But, as regards proportions, the Bouton report, which is the most demanding, only recommends a majority of independent directors on the boards of directors and various committees. It would seem that no company goes beyond this requirement, except if it is quoted on the NYSE. The AMF requires that the annual report provide information on the background of the directors and their independence. In any event, the role of independent directors continues to be closely tied to the personality of

Table 4.2 Board meetings

	2004	2003	2001	1999	1997	1995
Average number of board meetings	7	7	6.4	5.6	5	3

Source: Korn/Ferry International 2004.

each one. In no way is it collective. There is no Lead Director as in Great Britain, although this role is sometimes informally fulfilled by a director representing a significant shareholder and therefore not always independent. There are no meetings of independent directors either alone or in the presence of the chairman.

Composition of boards of directors

A distinctive feature of French boards of directors is that they have to include in their meetings, on a consultative basis, one or two representatives from the company's work council. This situation has several consequences. The board is decreasingly a forum for trade union representatives when the social climate in the company is strained. The board can also lose its role for strategic debate for fear of leaks or to avoid the offence of 'trade union obstruction'. This expression characterizes a situation in which decisions having an impact on the personnel are taken before consulting the company council. It is an offence for which they may be taken to court. To avoid this situation arising, strategy is often discussed in a strategy committee comprised solely of directors.

In nationalized companies that have been privatized such as Arcelor, BNP Paribas, Renault, Société Générale, and Thomson, two to four directors are directly elected by employees to represent them on the board of directors. Nationalized companies had a board comprising, depending on their size, five or six government representatives, five or six qualified personalities, and five or six staff representatives elected by the staff. When the companies were privatized, senior management wanted to maintain this representation and included it in the by-laws. However, since there is a will to reduce the size of the Boards, and since employees are not considered independent directors, Société Générale and BNPParibas have very recently decided (2005) to suppress one of the two Board seats dedicated to employees. More recently, the law on social modernization provides for one seat on the board of directors when employee shareholders in the company, grouped into an association, hold at least 3% of the capital. The employee representatives are not considered as 'independent'.

Lastly, there also exists the position of 'censor'. This very special status corresponds to that of a person who participates in the work of the board but without voting rights. He is not a director. Director liability is not applicable to censors. In general, censor positions are created when the board no longer has any room for directors but wants one or two other persons to participate.

Additionally, the auditors who certify the accounts have to participate in board meetings held to close the accounts, in other words, four times a year in very large companies.

According to Korn/Ferry International (2004), the average CAC 40 board comprises fifteen directors (fourteen the previous year) of which five are independent, three are non-French, and one is a woman (but more than one-third of boards in the CAC 40 have no female representation). The average age is 60. Since 1996, the most significant changes have concerned the reduction in the number of directors who are related to a shareholder or a business partner, the concomitant increase in the number of independent and non-French directors, the reduction in the number of directors coming from Polytechnique or ENA (although latest figures do not confirm it), and a slight increase in women representation.

Analysing proposals from new directors of major company boards in the spring of 2004, a lead writer for *Les Échos* (Yves de Kerdrel, 5 April 2004) concluded that 'it will not be this year that Boards of Directors open up to really new faces chosen from outside top management circles...Goatee capitalism ('I hold your beard, you hold mine...') has reappeared as quickly as it was put into the cupboard by the Viénot and Bouton reports.'

Indeed, a certain number of boards have reintroduced reciprocal director-ships and directors belonging to the same inner circle. The journalist ex-plained it by the 'shop-window effect' of boards. Made up of well-known personalities, they are more 'credible' to the market. Is France really any different from other major countries?

Table 4.3. Board composition (%)

Origin	2004	2003	2001	1999	1996
Linked to a shareholder or partner		37	46	47	63
Management representative		20	20	17	22
Representative of an individual or minority shareholder		0	1	1	1
Employee representatives		6	7	8	8
Independent Director	42	37	25	27	6
Educational background					
Polytechnique or ENA	33	31	32	37	42
Nationality					
French	75	76	78	80	93
Non-French	25	24	22	20	7
Men	92	93	94	95	98
Women	8	7	6	5	2

Source: Korn/Ferry International 2004

Board committees

The board of directors is a body that has to take its decisions collectively. The specialized committees of the board cannot in any circumstances replace the board. The committees which are a by-product of the board can only make proposals and prepare decisions.

With the exception of remuneration, the committees date from the first Viénot report of 1995. Since 1966, directors' remuneration has to be decided by the board. Consequently, to avoid a debate on the subject in front of members of the Company Council, the remuneration committee meets before the board meeting. During the board, the chairman of the committee simply informs the board that the subject has been dealt with and nobody dares ask awkward questions. The decisions are then appended to the minutes of the board without the latter deciding or understanding how the decisions were reached despite a court ruling that a board should vote on the matter.

Today, it is recommended that all quoted companies have an audit committee, a remuneration committee and a nomination committee. All the companies in the CAC 40 have an audit committee and 95% have a remuneration committee.

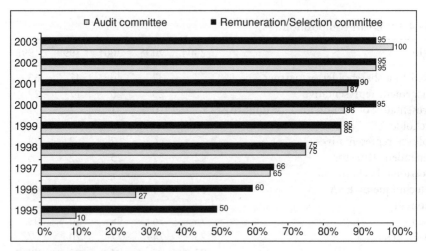

Source: Korn/Ferry International, 2003

Figure 4.1.   Specialized committees—CAC 40

The audit committee

The audit committee must have a majority of independent directors. Its tasks are the same as in Great Britain or the United States but its responsibilities are not comparable to those laid out in the Sarbanes-Oxley Act. In France, it is the managers that are blamed if the accounts are inaccurate. Nevertheless, over the last few years, audit committees have taken their role seriously: in principle, they meet one or two days before the board closes the accounts. The audit committee suggests the names of the auditors. Besides establishing the accounts, the audit committee examines the remuneration of the auditors for audit and non-audit work. The audit committee must, in particular, approve any additional tasks entrusted to the auditors and give its opinion to the board. It follows up on internal control issues and reports. The Financial Security law (LSF) established the principle of separation of audit and board functions. It explicitly proscribed situations in which conflicts of interest could arise, leaving it to the profession's code of conduct to define the term conflict of interest and to the audit committees to ensure that the auditors are independent and objective when they belong to a group also involved in consultancy work.

The auditors

In this area, France has a specific requirement. Every quoted company has to have two auditors from different firms. This requirement is the result of successful lobbying by the profession in France. A 1966 law makes it compulsory for all French companies which raise capital from the public to be controlled by at least two auditors, elected for six years minimum. Similarly, companies that have subsidiaries or investments and have to publish consolidated accounts, must also use two auditors.

The Financial Security law followed the path opened up by the Sarbanes-Oxley Act. It strengthened control over the auditing profession, creating the High Council of Auditors with the job of identifying and promoting best practices in the profession. It made it compulsory for auditing staff to be changed at least every six years. It also made it compulsory for information on the remuneration of auditors to be provided to shareholders.

The internal control report

The Financial Security law also makes it compulsory (1) for the chairman of the board to prepare a report for the General Shareholders' Meeting on internal control procedures in the company and (2) for auditors to present a report on that part of the chairman's report concerning procedures for financial and accounting information, a more restricted area than that described in the chairman's report. The AMF has been given responsibility by legislation to determine what the chairman's report should contain. In January 2004, it indicated that the evaluation process should enable 'an opinion to be formed on the adequacy and effectiveness of internal control procedures'. However, in June, following the recommendations of many companies, the Ministry of Justice indicated that the report should 'describe procedures without having to evaluate them or assess their adequacy or effectiveness'. The AMF in its 'règlement général' recently clarified its requirements. In the meantime, the first reports have been inconsistent. For lack of a definition of internal controls, companies refer to the Anglo-Saxon definition provided by the 'COSO', which defines internal control as 'a process put in place by general management, management and staff, and designed to provide a reasonable assurance that three objectives have been fulfilled: optimisation of operations, reliability of financial information and conformity with laws and regulations in force'. The subject has given rise to a number of debates that are far from over: legislation makes it the responsibility of the chairman to draw up the report. Is he the best placed to do so when he is not CEO. In such a case should it not be the responsibility of the CEO? Should the report be descriptive, as all chairmen wish, or analytical? Is it reasonable that its scope be so wide, almost limitless? Should it not be restricted, as in Sarbanes-Oxley, to financial and accounting information?

The remuneration committee

The remuneration committee comprises a majority of independent directors. Usually it is also the appointments committee. As in other countries, it determines the remuneration of directors and sometimes that of senior executives. It is also responsible for organizing top executives' succession within the company. All this is carried out in conjunction with the chairman, who may or may not be a member of the committee. The subject of remuneration has created the same stir in France as in Great Britain, Germany, and the United States. Since 2001, when all quoted French companies had to publish an annual report on the remuneration of their directors, the newspapers have established comparative lists for CAC 40 companies commenting on them in detail. To avoid any further temptation to regulate, the MEDEF (Mouvement des Entreprises de France—French Companies' Association) and the AFEP (Association Française des Entreprises Privées—French Association of Private Companies) have turned to the MEDEF ethics committee to define the principles and rules that should govern the remuneration of directors (see Annex 4A). A parliamentary committee took up the subject but did not come to the conclusion that additional regulations were necessary. The situation of stock options has already been dealt with by several pieces of legislation. In France, a director cannot borrow from a company he manages. Furthermore, stock options schemes have to be authorized by an extraordinary shareholders meeting which reaches its decision on the basis of a report by the board of directors or supervisory board and a special auditor's report that gives an opinion on the methods used to determine exercise prices. The shareholders' meeting has to decide on the methods employed to determine the exercise price and period. In addition, in order to benefit from the advantageous capital gains tax regime and not be taxed at the income-tax rate, the beneficiary of options has to keep the options at least five years. However, only shareholders can really curtail excesses. They have not been able to prevent certain directors from voting themselves substantial amounts of stock options when prices were very low (up to a thirtieth of their value) when a previous scheme had collapsed and stock prices could only rise.

The nomination committee

This is part of the remuneration committee. It is rare for French directors to be recruited by a recruitment firm on the basis of specific requirements provided by the board. On the other hand, recruitment firms are used to finding foreign directors. Co-opting is still mainly based on relations drawn from within top management circles. Exceptionally, an academic is called on to demonstrate originality and independence. In principle, the committee has to deal with questions of succession. It would seem that the subject is at last beginning to be dealt in a more timely manner.

Evaluation of the board of directors

Although the Viénot report had recommended as early as 1995 that the functioning of the board of directors be the subject of an evaluation, only Renault embarked on such an adventure, in 1998. The first evaluations of other CAC 40 companies occurred in 2003. According to a survey by Leaders Trust International,[12] sixteen companies had not carried out a formal evaluation, nine companies had carried out an in-depth evaluation with the help of an outside consultant, and fifteen had used a self-managed questionnaire. In the last case, the evaluations are based on a questionnaire filled in, anonymously or otherwise, bearing on all aspects of the composition and functioning of the board and committees, but not entering, or very little, into an evaluation of the contribution of each director and the effectiveness of the

[12] June 2004

board in carrying out its tasks. Generally, the questionnaire is analysed by the board secretary. The results are discussed in the following meeting. The evaluations have enabled a reassessment of the frequency of meetings, better targeting of information provided, improved organization of debates and their content, and have enabled suggestions to be made on the size of the board, and the age and nationality of directors. It would seem that frequently directors have requested that more time be spent on a discussion of strategy. Suez claims to have disbanded its strategy committee following an evaluation, replacing it by a general discussion by the board as a whole. It is not clear, however, that these evaluations have yet led to a reassessment of the composition of boards.

Company Shareholdings

The shareholders

The shareholding structure of French companies has profoundly changed since the 1980s. After the first wave of nationalizations in 1982, and the second wave from 1987 to 1994, major portfolio companies such as Suez and Paribas disappeared. Suez became an industrial company active in two businesses, energy and water. Paribas merged with BNP, has been totally integrated into it, and its portfolio has been substantially divested.

Many French companies have shareholdings that are family-based or dominated by a major shareholder ('actionnaire de reference'). They can also include employee shareholdings, which can be as much as 10%. The share of non-resident investors has increased considerably since 1993. At the end of 2003, 40.5% of the capital of quoted companies was in the hands of non-resident investors. In 1993, it was 25%. According to a Bank of France study, this is the highest proportion among industrialized countries with the exception of the United Kingdom. At the end of 2000, foreign shareholders held 26.6% of the capital of French companies compared to 11.4% for US companies, 14.8% for German companies, 18.2% for Japanese companies, and 37.2% for UK companies. In 2002, the proportion was 29% for French companies, 38% for quoted companies, 23% for family companies, and 42.4% for CAC 40 companies. Over the period 1999–2003, French origin funds only represented 35% of funds invested in unquoted companies.[13]

With the exception of Crédit Lyonnais, banks have only been minor shareholders in companies recently. Between 1989 and 1993, the newly privatized bank deliberately adopted the strategy of German banks, 'Rhine

---

[13] Source: *Les Échos*, Wednesday, 3 March 2004 : Barclays Private Equity France/Triago.

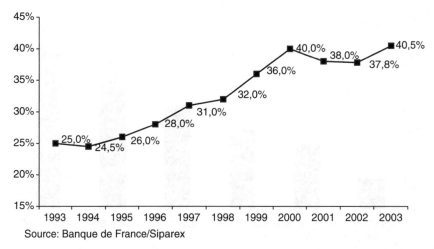

Figure 4.2. Non-resident investment in French listed equity as % total, 1993–2003

capitalism', wishing to transform itself into an investment bank, both a shareholder and a lender (with disastrous consequences for French taxpayers, who had to absorb more than €60 billion in losses in the government's budget). In the past, banks that had taken small minority shareholdings in unquoted companies that were their clients often found themselves stuck with the investments or had to keep them to protect family shareholdings. For example, the Société Générale and Pernod Ricard: Société Générale holds 3.4% of the capital of Pernod Ricard. Banks have participated in core group shareholdings but have unwound their cross-shareholdings and sold the majority of their industrial shareholdings.

Family shareholdings remains an important feature of French capitalism (Figure 4.3).

When the CAC 40 was created in 1988, there were twenty family-controlled companies. Today there are seventeen. Six of them are managed by the children of the founders: Martin Bouygues, Franck Riboud, Arnaud Lagardère, Édouard Michelin, Patrick Ricard, and François-Henri Pinault. Of the twenty non-family companies, eleven have been sold compared to only five family companies. A recent study shows that family companies have performed better than others, with faster growth, well-managed mergers, little diversification, and a refusal to give way to fashion.[14]

In mid-2004, the shareholding structure of CAC 40 companies was as follows: seventeen companies were controlled by a family, sometimes via a

---

[14] UBS : 'State Tradition versus Family Tradition'. Philippe Tibi, 8 October 2004.

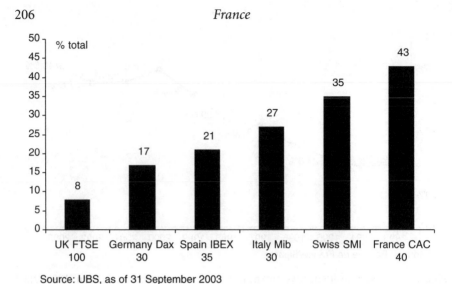

Source: UBS, as of 31 September 2003

Figure 4.3. Family firms in the leading European indices (%)

cascade of holding companies (LVMH (Bernard Arnault), PPR Pinault Printemps Redoute, Casino (Jean Charles Naouri)), fifteen companies were totally or partially privatized (for example the government still holds 15% of the capital of Renault), four are conglomerates or spin-offs of conglomerates, two are controlled by mutual companies (Crédit Agricole et Axa) and three have had a widely diversified shareholding structure for some time.[15] Of the sixteen companies privatized since 1986, ten have undergone profound transformation. Certain have been absorbed by French or foreign companies: among insurance companies, UAP has been absorbed by AXA, AGF by Allianz; Pechiney by Alcan; Aventis, the results of the merger of Rhône-Poulenc and Hoechst, has just been the target of a takeover bid by Sanofi Synthélabo.

At the end of 2004, other public companies had been or were due to be privatized. The French government has just fallen below the 50% ownership level in France Telecom and intends to divest at least 30% of its Areva shares on the stock market. The government also intends to privatize Snecma by merging it with Sagem.

In 2004, the number of individual shareholders was 6.4 million or 6.7 million if one includes employee shareholdings (5.2 million in 1999, 7.2 million in 2003 at the peak). Air Liquide is the only company to have kept more than 40% of individual shareholders, the other major corporations

---

[15] Philippe Tibi, UBS Investment Research, July 2004.

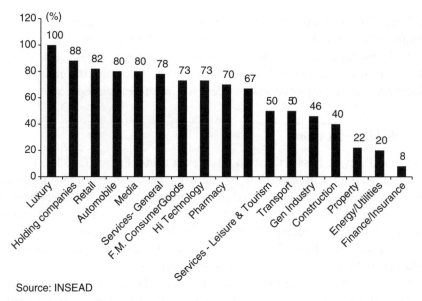

Source: INSEAD

Figure 4.4. SBF 120: Family ownership of individual sectors (% total), 1998

have a maximum of 20%. COB regulations (now the AMF) were (and still are) designed to protect the 'Carpentras widow', in other words the least informed private shareholder. (Carpentras is a small city in the south-east of France. The expression was used in the 1980s by a managing director of COB and is much in use.)

Other shareholdings are held by unit trusts and mutual funds, which generally have very short-term investment horizons. As of 12 October 2004, the number of French investment management companies was around 509, which bears little relation to the relatively limited number of US companies, and serves to explain why they have so little influence on corporate governance.

Employee shareholdings are another characteristic of the French market. Employee shareholdings have been encouraged by the creation of employee savings funds and strengthened at the time of the privatizations, in the form of private shareholdings. The privatization law of 1987 required that 10% of the government's shares be reserved for employees or former employees in the event of total or partial privatization. In such situations, employees benefited from a more favourable share price than that offered other private shareholders, free shares, and exoneration of social charges and taxes on capital gains generated from employee saving schemes—provided the shares were untouched for a period of five years. For example, the employee savings scheme of Saint Gobain holds 7.4% of the capital of the company and 11.4% of the voting rights; employees in Vinci hold 9.2% of the capital of their company. Renault employees hold 3.3% and France Telecom employees 2.1%. During the attempted takeover bid by BNP for Société Générale, the resistance of Société Générale employee shareholders to the project played a role.

Shareholder associations

The possibility of class actions does not exist under French law. The LSF Act made a step in this direction by allowing small shareholders to group together in associations and exercise the same rights as shareholders holding at least 5% of the company's capital. These rights include, among others, initiating legal proceedings to defend the interests of investors, having a shareholders meeting called, bringing liability actions against directors, asking questions in writing to the board of directors.

Since the beginning of the 1990s, three quite different organizations have been working to obtain 'an improvement in the functioning of joint stock companies'. These are ADAM (the Association for the Defence of Minority Shareholders), Deminor, and Proxinvest.

ADAM was created at the end of 1991. The association is financed by contributions from its members. Its means are very limited, although its chairman Colette Neuville has a high profile. Until recently, it rarely won its court cases. Nevertheless, they have drawn the attention of the market authorities to the issues, helping regulations to evolve in key areas of concern for ADAM: information, equitable treatment for shareholders, particularly during takeover bids, value creation, and fundamental shareholder rights. Sometimes, following criticism from ADAM, companies change resolutions proposed to General Shareholders' Meetings or the terms of bids.

Deminor was created in 1990 in Belgium and has had a very active office in Paris since 1994. The company is structured as a partnership. The cases it takes on are remunerated by its clients. Its vocation is similar to that of Adam: to create value for minority shareholders by assisting them in managing their minority stakes; to promote higher standards of transparency and accountability between corporations, management and shareholders; to maximize fair and equal treatment of shareholders; and to maximize the long-term value of minority stakes. In one of the cases it dealt with, Deminor forced Accor to considerably increase its offer for Compagnie Internationale des Wagons-Lits (1990–4). More recently, at the time of the acquisition of Sidel by Tetra Laval, Deminor, convinced that the information provided by the chairman of the company was false (1998–2000) and had misled investors, took the issue to the COB to protect minority shareholder interests. The association filed a class action suit against the company and its management. A thousand shareholders gave it a mandate to defend their interests by all legal means. In January 2002, ten months after the opening of the case, Deminor obtained compensation of around 20 euros per share for a thousand Sidel shareholders who had suffered damage after investing in the company on the basis of false declarations by its chairman.

Proxinvest describes itself as an 'expert in shareholder voting'. The company advises investors on shareholder value and vote management. Created in 1995, it assists major French and foreign investors in 'managing the decisions they are presented with at shareholder meetings'. It establishes voting criteria that reflect the management style of the investor and applies these criteria to each resolution presented. It publishes two annual reports, one on General Meetings and the other, in partnership with Hewitt Associates, on the remuneration of executive directors. Proxinvest acted strenuously, but in vain, against the provision in the 2001 NRE law on shareholders' identification requirements. These regulations require a 'wet' signature for proxy votes, and give excessive power to the company chairman to validate or invalidate the votes of foreign shareholders. In addition, the provisions allow the chairman to deprive foreign shareholders who he considers have not been adequately identified from receiving dividend payments or exercising voting rights for up to five years. Finally, the provisions allow the company chairman to keep secret the name of 'friendly' foreign shareholders allowed to vote. Among the association's scoops, it regularly denounces shortcomings in the principles of good governance. Gradually, it has enlarged its client base. The Association Française des Sociétés de Gestion (AFG) is one of its clients. One can be justified in thinking that the new requirement contained in the LSF law requiring investment management companies to vote on resolutions proposed to shareholders at General Meetings will result in this type of service growing.

The various categories of shares

Since the wave of privatizations in 1987, shares have been dematerialized, in other words they are no longer represented by paper but instead registered by computer on the share account of their owners. Shares can be either registered or bearer. Bearer shares are immediately transferable. Registered shares have to be converted into bearer shares before being transferred. On the other hand, to be able to vote in a General Meeting owners of shares have to convert them into registered form.

In France, if the by-laws of the company permit it, shares may, contrary to the demands of advocates of better corporate governance, have different rights attached to them. Legislation enables a wide variety of different share categories to be created: shares with priority dividend rights but without voting rights, and, lastly, investment certificates, very closely controlling the rights attached to them (financial rights, representation on management bodies and veto rights over important decisions) and denying them voting rights. Since a ruling (ordonnance) of 24 June 2004, preference shares, with or without voting rights, can be created: 'The rights attached to such shares are defined by company by-laws in accordance with legislation on voting rights. Voting rights can provide for a determined or determinable time period. They can be suspended for a determined or determinable period, or eliminated.'

Shares can have double voting rights and/or higher dividends attached to them. Usually, this advantage is designed to increase shareholder loyalty. It is given to holders of shares who hold them for a number of years, often a minimum of two. It is also a useful method for maintaining family control over companies (double voting rights), at the same time providing additional remuneration for members of the family (higher dividends).

In addition, contrary to what proponents of good governance request, eight companies of the CAC 40 are implementing restrictions in voting rights at General Meetings.[16] Most of these restrictions were introduced in the late 1990s or in 2000, in order to prevent one or a few shareholders taking control of a company during a General Meeting where participation of shareholders is low. In some 2005 AGMs, Proxinvest opposed such restrictions in the by-laws, sometimes successfully.

Shareholders' General Meetings

General meetings do not yet make the accountability of the board more real—which would require much more penetrating questions. They are still very much question and answer sessions. Representatives of shareholder associations may be present to ask one or two questions. In addition, shareholders can send their questions in writing to the meeting. Legislation requires that the board of directors approve the text of the answers to them, which have to be read during the General Meeting. Nevertheless, for many large companies, General Meetings are an opportunity to present the company's achievements, involving the projection of a film and an explanation of the results of the company based on a slide show (sometimes including an explanation of changes in the remuneration of directors). General Meetings

---

[16] Alcatel, Danone, Lafarge, Pernod Ricard, Schneider, Société Générale, Total, Vivendi Universal.

of major CAC 40 companies last around three to five hours (those of unquoted companies may only last a few minutes).

The meeting normally comprises individual shareholders representing only a small percentage of the capital. For major companies, there might be 500 or 600. France Telecom and Air Liquide attract a greater number of shareholders. The meeting can sometimes exceed 2,000 persons. Certain resolutions require a qualified majority. For the first notification, a qualified majority is never attained and the General Meeting is held after the second notification. Electronic voting is widespread among large companies. Proxies given to the chairman predominate. Nevertheless, better practices in corporate governance have been adopted, and management has become more sensitive to the differences in voting on the various resolutions. In particular, many institutional investors oppose resolutions designed to authorize in advance capital increases eliminating shareholders' pre-emptive rights or capital increases during takeovers. This has led many companies to abandon one or more resolutions proposed to shareholders.

The LSF law (2003) makes it compulsory for investment management companies to vote on resolutions proposed to General Meetings, or if they don't, to explain why. The AMF is discussing how to implement this requirement with professional organizations. Several difficulties still need to be overcome. The first concerns the freezing of shares for several days (often five days before the meeting). The debate over the move to a record date system has not been settled in more than ten years. It could be shortly and is likely to be three days.

The Stock Market

There are 739 quoted companies in France. The Paris stock market is managed by Euronext, which has taken over the Brussels, Amsterdam, and Lisbon stock markets.

The markets

From 2005, there will only be one regulated market, 'Eurolist by Euronext', instead of the three markets currently operated by Euronext, the 'Premier Marché' on which major stocks are traded, the 'Second Marché' for medium-size dynamic companies, and the 'Nouveau Marché', created in 1995 to boost the liquidity of small-cap technology stocks. The companies will be listed by alphabetical order and identified on the basis of their stock market capitalization: small capitalizations of less than €150 million; medium-size capitalizations of €150 million to €1 billion; and large capitalizations greater than €1 billion. The conditions that need to be fulfilled to be quoted are the same for all companies, as are disclosure requirements. This change reflects both the failure of the 'Nouveau Marché' after the financial bubble had burst, and new European regulations. The number of flotations on the Paris stock market was only six in 2003 and nine in 2002. In 2004, there were twelve.

Furthermore, 'a new structured and organized market, yet unregulated as defined by loi de modernisation des activités financières, loi MAF, 1996, which transposed the Directive on Investment Services', called Alternext, will be set up in 2005. It should enable companies that wish to raise capital gain access to the market on a simplified basis in exchange for undertakings with regard to accountability and investor protection. It will replace the 'marché libre', entirely unregulated, which small companies (who could not be quoted on a regulated market because too fragile and illiquid) used to raise capital and create liquidity in the shares.

Stock market indices

The main stock market indices are the CAC 40, the SBF 120, and the SBF 250. The CAC 40 is the official index of the French market. It comprises 40 of the largest stocks eligible for delayed settlement with substantial capitalizations and liquidity. Pernod Ricard and Publicis, two family companies, entered the CAC 40 in 2004. Publicis was selected in August 2004, based on daily turnover of its stock; although Essilor's capitalization was greater it did not enter until 2005). The SBF 120 comprises the 120 largest stocks in the first and second markets as well as the 40 stocks of the CAC 40. French managers also follow the Euro Stoxx 50 which comprises the 50 largest stocks quoted on euro-zone stock markets.

From February 2005, there will also be a new group of indices for medium-sized capitalizations weighted on the basis of their float: one for medium-size companies; one for small companies; and one that combines both. A new index will also be created for dynamic technology companies.

What influences stock market prices?

Is it concern for corporate interest? Is it the importance attached to the value of companies for shareholders that influences stock market prices in France? Is it any different from other major countries? Stock market prices in France are of course influenced by analysts but even more by the shareholder structure of French companies. The majority of investors are foreign, and French institutional investors represent less than 20% of trades. Stock markets can be swayed by trends affecting Anglo-Saxon markets. French investment management companies change little and are not subject to much competition from boutiques as they rarely grow fast enough to represent a threat. In France, there are no pension funds. Private savings are managed by mutual funds which tend to turn over their holdings more often than pension funds do in other countries. In Europe, it is rare to find 'country' funds. Since the inception of the euro, portfolio managers select stocks by sector on a Europe-wide basis. There exist some hedge funds and a few investors (of which Bolloré is the most visible, although Guy Wyser Pratt and the Hermès fund also operate in France) which take advantage of the passivity of traditional managers acting as catalysts and unearthing anomalies in stock valuations.

As for hostile takeover bids, they have been part of the French stock market scene since 1997. Before, 'it wasn't done'. Danone was persuaded to abandon its takeover of Saint-Gobain in January 1969 by the financial market authorities of the time. Over recent years there have been a number of major stock market battles: the hostile takeover bid by Promodès for Casino and Rallye in September 1997, and the hostile takeover by François Pinault for Worms et Cie two weeks later (IFIL, the holding company of the Agnelli family arrived as the white knight). Total succeeded in a hostile takeover bid for Elf, a bigger company. In 1999, Société Générale launched a hostile takeover bid for Paribas, after which BNP launched a simultaneous hostile takeover bid for Paribas and Société Générale. In the end, Société Générale lost its takeover bid but kept its independence, and BNP merged with Paribas. Paribas' reference shareholder, AXA, played a decisive role in the success of BNP's takeover of Paribas. In 2003, Pechiney was taken over by Alcan following a stock market battle which caused the offer price to be increased. The same occurred in 2003 during Crédit Agricole's takeover of Crédit Lyonnais and in 2004 in Sanofi-Synthélabo's takeover of Aventis.

Sustainable Development, Stakeholders, Ethical Funds

The expressions 'sustainable development', 'socially responsible companies', and 'relations with stakeholders' are used by French companies to describe the theme of 'corporate social responsibility'. The expression that is most often seen is 'sustainable development' although it is probably not the most appropriate.

Since the NRE law of 2001, all quoted companies have to report on the social and environmental consequences of their business in their annual management report (see p.195: accountability to shareholders).

A considerable number of them lump together this often disparate information, as detailed as it is uninteresting (number of staff, energy consumption, waste disposal), and in any case quite different from one company to another, under the heading 'sustainable development'. Among the smallest quoted companies, those of the SBF 120, only 65% of them deal with questions of sustainable development in their annual report and only 27% of them (against 56% for CAC 40 companies—source: RSM Salustro Reydel, *La Tribune*, October 2004) have a clear position on the issue. This section of the annual report can include a discussion of relations between the company and its partners. Astonishingly, one sometimes finds a description of corporate governance in this section (compulsory since LSF), although clearly it merits a separate section of its own. Certain companies have a specific report on 'sustainable development'.

Many very large companies have adhered to the United Nations Global Compact and developed specific programmes relevant to their businesses. Lafarge, for example, is partnering with WWF for the protection of the environment and the rehabilitation of quarries that it has finished mining. Danone's policy in the area of social and environmental responsibility goes back to 1972. At first, it covered human and social objectives but later was extended to principles governing business conduct (corruption and conflicts of interest), the environment, quality control, and food safety. The company is well known for the intensity of its discussions with unions and the care with which it prepares restructurings. However, this did not stop a vigorous strike when it decided to close a plant in the Paris region in 2002.

No French company has a board committee in charge of monitoring, controlling, and orienting the company in the area of social responsibility. (In the UK some companies do). On the other hand, some of them indicate that they have been included in ethical funds and others that they have been rated by rating agencies such as Vigeo and CoreRatings.

Vigeo was created out of ARESE in 2002 (Agence de Rating Social et Environnemental des Entreprises, a pioneer in France created in 1997). It is an independent rating and evaluation agency[17] active in the area of corporate social responsibility. It provides two types of rating. The first is aimed at portfolio managers. It is based on publicly available corporate documentation and examines six areas of social responsibility: clients/suppliers, human rights, social involvement, the environment, corporate governance, and human resources. The second is requested by companies. It is carried out on site. It enables managers to measure their performance in terms of social responsibility. Vigeo also publishes the ASPI index (Arese sustainable

---

[17] However for its financing, the agency has companies as shareholders.

performance indice) which measures the stock market performance of 120 companies quoted in the euro-zone with the best performance in terms of sustainable development.

France's interest in sustainable development can also be measured in terms of investment in ethical funds. Total assets under management in funds that apply socially responsible investment criteria (SRI) were €2.9 billion at the end of 2003 compared to €920 million in 2001. This only represents 0.25% of the €851.7 billion invested in funds in France at the end of 2003.

Difficult Subjects

There are still a few difficult subjects that remain to be resolved. Liability cases against managers and directors are a subject of dissatisfaction for some because there are few convictions and a cause of alarm for others because criminal proceedings are a real threat in a large number of cases.

The remuneration of directors and the absence of any link, in certain cases, with the performance of the company continues to be criticized in the press and by shareholders. Another theme is whistle-blowing, which is gradually gaining ground but continues to be a delicate subject.

Liability of managers and directors

Managers and directors can be held liable if their actions have caused a loss of value for the company. Consequences can be loss of remuneration and possibly dismissal, compensation payments following civil proceedings, and criminal penalties. It has to be said that few managers have ever been really penalized through a decrease in their remuneration though the shares have declined in value: remunerations are far from being as variable as the stock market is volatile. The chairman of Alstom, Pierre Bilger, voluntarily returned his leaving package, albeit contractual, when he was replaced after leading the company to the verge of bankruptcy as a result of a disastrous acquisition. Press revelations concerning the package had caused an outcry. Jean Marie Messier, the chairman of Vivendi, received authorization from members of his board to receive his package. Only court proceedings prevented the payment. A Parliamentary commission examined the subject of remuneration in autumn 2003, but concluded that, rather than legislate on the subject, it was preferable to facilitate liability proceedings against management in the event of bad management.

Civil proceedings are rare. Therefore, there are very few judgements. Civil proceedings have to be paid for by the litigant and, because complex, are costly. It has to be demonstrated that there has been a fault of management and not just a simple error, and that the harm suffered was a direct consequence. The fault has to be 'separable from the function' and attributable to an individual. In practice, however, it is almost always the company that is held responsible. The harm suffered has to be personal in nature. A shareholder cannot complain of a wrong that affects all shareholders. Experts have to be appointed, therefore, and it is rare for the proceedings to come to anything. This is the reason why, in the Vivendi Universal case, the French shareholders have joined a class action in the USA.

On the other hand, directors can be held criminally liable for many reasons. 'It was a choice made by Parliament who, in adopting the law of 24 July 1966, 'criminalised' corporate law. More than 60 different crimes concerning company Directors were scattered throughout corporate law.'[18] The number has been reduced recently. An effort is made to substitute nullifications to criminal penalties in cases of technical breaches. However, presentation of false balance sheets, misuse of company property ('abus de biens sociaux'), etc. all represent situations of criminal liability, as do collective proceedings following bankruptcies. The law has tried to improve business ethics through the vehicle of misuse of company property, which has often resulted in tension between management and the courts. Employers are calling for a 'de-criminalization of business affairs'. It is not obvious that all parties want it, but it is clear that making it easier to institute liability proceedings against directors and forcing them to participate in the indemnification of victims, can be considered as 'the most effective way of making them more responsible'.[19]

Whistle-blowing

Whistle-blowing is a very sensitive issue in France as it is reminiscent of the Second World War period when French people would denounce Jews or opponents to the German occupation. Companies are slowly organizing it when they have to, either because they have to demonstrate that they are implementing procedures to prevent corruption or because they are listed on the NYSE. The French law (LSF) also obliges them to protect confidentiality and to protect employees who blow the whistle. In the few implementations known, companies advertise their procedure with great caution.

---

[18] Frédéric Peltier 'La Corporate Gouvernance au secours des conseils d'administration'. *Dunod*, April 2004, p. 118.
[19] Jean François Burgelin, public prosecutor in the Appeal Court. *La Tribune*, 3 November 2003.

Remuneration

The question of remuneration seems to be less controversial in France than the UK. There is no word in French for 'fat cats'. Apparently remuneration packages—fixed salary plus bonuses—are relatively lower than in the UK and Germany. On the other hand, there are three main criticisms levelled at French practices. First, there is an absence of transparency concerning sever-ance pay, additional pension rights paid by companies which are an exception to ordinary law, and which can enable retired directors to maintain practically the same salary that they had when in office, as well as many benefits in kind such as a secretary, a company car, and a chauffeur, etc. Second, there is a lack of transparency concerning methods of allocating the variable element of remuneration. Are they really designed to encourage a medium-term man-agement of the company? Are they not too generous? (Bonuses often repre-sent more than 150% of the base salary. They can be as high as 250% and sometimes more. Third, there is a disproportionate amount of stock options. Stock option grants are more generous in France than in any other European country. They are rarely linked to company performance and have become even more abundant with collapsing stock market prices. A prominent case in 2005 was the revelation that at a time when employees were pressing for higher pay, the dismissed PDG of Carrefour had entitlement to € 38 million.

The notion of independent director

The importance given to independent directors irritates many directors and business leaders. Some of this irritation can be found in the Bouton report when it says:

The first quality of a Board of Directors can be found in its composition: naturally, it should be made up of directors of integrity that well understand the operations of the company, are concerned by the interest of all of the company's shareholders, and are sufficiently involved in determining strategy... A Board of Directors needs to be a judicious balance of skills, experience and independence, serving the interests of the company and its shareholders... The position of independent Director does not imply any value judgement. Independent directors do not have qualities that are different from those of other directors, implying in some way that they act more in the interests of shareholders.

As already mentioned in the introduction, French corporate organization encourages the recruitment of directors from within a small circle of person-alities which considers that directors should have enough force of character to adopt independent positions and not participate in debates which concern them or their organization. Some suggest that the issue of the independence of directors be dealt with differently. As conflicts of interest are inevitable, and to avoid excluding the advice of those who have experience and skills in the sector, new procedures need to be introduced to avoid, deal with, and report on conflicts of interest in an entirely transparent manner. For example, the by-laws could provide for a director to leave the boardroom during any debate that involves him, and so on.

Annex 4A: *Corporate Governance in the CAC 40*

Corporate governance in the CAC 40 (as of 31 December 2003)

	Board of Directors	Management board + Supervisory board	Chairman + MD	Sté en commandite
1 Accor	1			
2 Agf	1			
3 Air liquide	1			
4 Alcatel A	1			
5 Arecelor			1	
6 Axa	1			
7 BNP Paribas			1	
8 Bouygues	1			
9 Cap Gemini			1	
10 Carrefour	1			
11 Casino Guichard			1	
12 Credit Agricole	1			
13 Dexia Sico.	1			
14 EADS	1			
15 France Telecom	1			
16 Groupe Danone	1			
17 L'Oreal	1			
18 LaFarge			1	
19 Lagardere				
20 LVMH Moet Vuitto	1			
21 MIchelin				
22 Pernod-Richard	1			
23 Peugeot		1		
24 PInault PrintemP		1		
25 Publics Groupe		1		
26 Renault	1			
27 Saint Gobain	1			
28 Sanofi-Avents	1			
29 Schneider Electr	1			

	Board of Directors	Management board + Supervisory board	Chairman + MD	Sté en commandite
30 Societe Generale	1			
31 Sodexho Alliance	1			
32 StMicroElec.Sico		1	7	
33 Suez	1			
34 TF1	1			
35 Thales	1			
36 Thomson			1	6
37 Total	1			
38 VeoliA Environne	1			
39 Vinci	1			
40 VivendI Universa	1	25		
Total	(62.5%)	(17.5%)	(15%)	

Source: 2003 Annual Reports, company Internet sites.

Annex 4B: *Chairman and Chief Executive Officer and Executive Directors Compensation*

MAY 2003

I Chairman and chief executive officer and executive directors compensation is currently giving rise to a broad debate concerning its mode of determination, level, trend and relationship with corporate performance. Long before the current media turmoil, MEDEF had recommended greater transparency for such compensation in listed companies and the creation of ad-hoc committees, while being aware of a risk of curtailment of individual liberties and insisting on the need to protect contractual freedom.

The Committee on Business Ethics considers that it is advisable that MEDEF states again its opinion on chairman and chief executive officer and executive directors compensation. Because this issue is a major component of corporate governance, the Committee on Business Ethics intends to propose a number of '*assessment principles*' in order to support the thinking and decisions to be made by compensation committees.

The report recently issued by the task force chaired by Daniel Bouton recalls and supplements the requirements defined in the VIENOT report concerning the compensation committee's composition and mandate, as well as its role vis-à-vis the board of directors. This report also recalls the rules under which stock options are awarded and exercised in France and states several recommendations in this respect. This document specifically concerns the compensation proper of chairmen and chief executive officers and executive directors, and not the terms and conditions in which such compensation is determined.

II The thinking on business ethics is not restricted only to the definition of what is appropriate or not. Indeed, such an approach would unavoidably result in a merely legal focus and would reduce each player's sense of personal responsibility. The committee has adopted a broader conceptual view, including values, the need for restraint, a concern for fairness and confidence, etc. The thinking developed on this issue by the Committee on Business Ethics has centred on the search for an "appropriate" behaviour based on balance and moderation. Indeed, this thinking might have been made in response to either of two different concerns, i.e. that of investors and shareholders fearing the payment of "excessive" remuneration or the sense of responsibility of officers themselves, their ethics and their will to deserve the confidence extended to them. It is this approach that prevailed when we set out to define the "assessment principles" detailed below.

The compensation paid must at all times be justified and justifiable in view of relevant criteria: competitive practices in the industry concerned, international comparisons for multinational enterprises, enterprise's size and complexity, etc. and must take into consideration risks incurred, knowing that each employee is facing risks[1]. The compensation policy must thus be moderate, balanced and fair and must strengthen solidarity within the enterprise. Vis-à-vis shareholders, it is also necessary to prove that compensation is fair and duly justified.

Furthermore, those hoping for excessive gains risk losing touch with reality. When there is no limit, officers no longer feel any need to factor in the facts of life. Recent scandals have proved this. Ethics must be based on moderation and control.

Finally, it also appeared, particularly in France, that society at large finds it hard to understand the compensation levels that have been reached. Possibly for cultural reasons, such a reaction is less prominent in the public opinion of Anglo-Saxon countries, unless there is an obvious distortion between compensation and results.

III Chairmen and chief executive officers and executive directors are not appointed following a call for tenders. Situations are specific to the country and industry concerned and to the enterprise's own features and management mode. The market serves as a benchmark, but other factors are to be taken into account. We note in this respect very sharp changes in the compensation of the same chairman and chief executive officer and executive director when he or she is recruited by another enterprise, for whatever reason.

The compensation of a chairman and chief executive officer and executive directors depends on the work done, on results obtained, but also on responsibilities assumed. A chairman and chief executive officer and executive directors may not be assimilated with an employee. They bear the ultimate responsibility for the management team. While the chairman and chief executive officer and executive directors form part of the management team (and this creates constraints), they also have a unique role which warrant the payment of a compensation markedly higher than that of other officers. However, this does not mean that no comparison is to be made between the compensation of the chairman and chief executive officer and executive directors and that of the other officers.

Chairman and chief executive officer and executive directors compensation must be a driver contributing to the achievement of the enterprise's goals, in

---

[1] It may happen that the compensation (broadly defined) of certain senior executives exceeds that of chairmen and chief executive officers and executive directors. Chairmen and chief executive officers and executive directors should pay close attention to this and rely where applicable on the principles they have used for their own compensation. It would be advisable to check whether, in each profession, such situations are justified by a very high skills level or by very exceptional living conditions, or whether such situations result from particular and abnormal market conditions and, if so, to determine how such conditions might be eliminated.

particular in terms of financial performance. It is however necessary to recall that, in most cases, compensation is not the only incentive. Factors, such as a project's appeal, the satisfaction given by the exercise of power and the achievement of results, social position, etc., also play a role. Along these lines, when these last factors are less powerful (ailing enterprises, less glamorous tasks, etc.), an additional compensation is to be paid.

IV As recommended by the Bouton report, it would be advisable to set up a compensation committee in those companies having a large number of shareholders. The committee's mandate would be to enable the board of directors to best exercise its freedom to contract:

1. in order to compensate and motivate the chairman and chief executive officer and executive directors by placing them in conditions most favourable to the discharge of their duties,
2. by ensuring to the greatest extent possible that the chairman and chief executive officer and executive directors interests are in line with those of shareholders, which may only be assessed over a sufficiently long term,
3. by maintaining social cohesion within the management team, the enterprise and its environment,
4. by fostering the greatest transparency, within the compensation committee and the board of directors, and vis-à-vis shareholders in the annual report and during general meetings. A statement made by the chairman of the compensation committee during the general meeting might prove useful, at least if questions are raised.

V In order to determine the appropriate level of compensation, it may be advisable to take into account the major principles below:

1. **Balance**: balance between compensation and performance, balance between officers' and shareholders' interest, balance between risk taking and legal protection (this may justify the execution of a liability insurance policy), balance between market practices and expectations of the public.
2. **Completeness**: compensation review must be exhaustive: fixed part, variable part (bonus), stock options, directors' fees, pension, termination payment, special benefits, etc. All of these components must be assessed as a whole, of course at a consolidated level, before any decision is reached.
3. **Benchmark market / Business line**: compensation must be seen by reference to the relevant business line and market. Enterprises in certain areas are more stable, while others depend more on those individuals who agree to lead them and on the teams they may form.
4. **Consistency**: Chairman and chief executive officer and executive directors compensation must be designed in a manner consistent with that of other officers in order to increase the solidarity of the management team. In addition, consistency serves as an example within the enterprise and vis-à-vis society at large.

5. **Simplicity and stability**: the performance criteria on which the variable part (which is often significant) relies should be easy to determine and to explain and should also be stable over time. Taking into account the position, these criteria should correspond to the achievement of the enterprise's overall goals. The same rule applies to the setting up of stock option plans and to the relevant awards (see below).

VI When defining each component of the compensation, the following elements may be taken into consideration, knowing that, in each case, reference is made to amounts before tax and that companies should in no event bear the personal income tax of the officers concerned.

1. **Fixed part**: This part may be structured differently depending on whether the officer has pursued a continuous career within the enterprise or is an outside recruit.

   It would be logical to revise this fixed part only after relatively long intervals (three years, etc.). The increase must be linked to specific events (appointment of a new officer deserving a staggered increase in his fixed compensation, change in the size of the company, etc.). The increase in fixed compensation must be consistent with the way in which performance is rewarded, generally through a bonus. Benefits in kind form part of the base compensation and are obviously not added thereto.

   Because of the increase in variable and deferred compensation, it may happen that fixed compensation only accounts for a rather small part of chairman and chief executive officer and executive directors compensation. While such a trend may increase motivation, it does not seem to support the long-term, transparent approach that should be the mark of chairmen and chief executive officers and executive directors. Neither does this move favour the determination of a compensation scheme that should have the value of an example. It would be advisable to return to greater moderation and stability.

2. **Bonuses (bonuses proper or variable part)**:[2] This component rewards short-term performance and progress made by the enterprise in the short or medium term. This part is not related to the share price. The relationship between bonuses and salary must be clear and be defined either as a warning signal requiring a renegotiation between the parties or as a cap related to the base salary. Either option must be adapted to the enterprise's business and leave room for an "*exceptional bonus*" under very specific circumstances The bonus may be awarded on the basis of quantitative and qualitative criteria that must always be specific and predetermined.

---

[2] In general, for chairmen and chief executive officers and executive directors, bonuses and stock options account for an increasing share of total compensation. It seems necessary to take a few precautions in this respect.

a) Bonus: ascertain whether aggregate bonuses correspond to a limited fraction of aggregate compensation and represent a reasonable share of profits.

It is advisable that certain criteria be common to the entire management team. The qualitative part, which must be measured, must take into account exceptional circumstances. In order to be simple, quantitative criteria must be few in number, objective and measurable without any artifice. It is a sound practice to regularly review these various criteria and to avoid ad-hoc revisions. The terms of payment of the bonus are open.

3. **Stock options:**[2] In the same manner as for performance-based bonuses, stock options have the considerable merit of bringing the interest of beneficiaries in line with that of shareholders, in particular under French law which focuses on medium- and long-term objectives. The award of stock options must of course comply with the recommendations inherent in this type of product (and in particular the recommendations recalled in the report of the working group chaired by Daniel Bouton) and must be exercised in keeping with the same objectives. Along these lines, share purchase options would be preferable to share subscription options (except if their recognition increases the volatility risk), and beneficiaries should not be allowed to hedge their risks. As regards chairmen and chief executive officers and executive directors, it should also be necessary to stipulate that part of the shares acquired through exercise of the options shall be held for a certain time (one or two years) and shall accumulate on an ongoing basis, according to a proportion that may take into account the overall compensation of the officer concerned.

However, stock options are affected by imperfections that are felt most specifically in the case of chairmen and chief executive officers and executive directors. Indeed, not only are options inherently very volatile, but also they play only in one direction, by offering a chance of gain without any risk of loss. This may prompt certain chairmen and chief executive officers and executive directors to expose shareholders and the enterprise in general to excessive risks. This is why it would be interesting to link part of the options to the achievement of performance targets over one or more

2b) Stock option plans: suggested policies:
- the aggregate of awarded options must be defined as a multiple of annual compensation.
- aggregate stock option plans must account for a small share of the capital, and the right balance must be struck, depending on the benefits that shareholders derive from the CEO's management talent. Dilution must be closely monitored.
- plans must be issued at a fixed date, after publication of the financial statements, and probably each year in order to mitigate the volatility impact.
- a choice must be made between (i) the dilutive consequences of subscription options and (ii) purchase options which give a right to existing shares but may generate a loss or gain for the company upon exercise of the option.
- stock options must be issued without any discount, and their price may not be revised.
- stock options must be held by the chairman and chief executive officer and executive directors for a certain time period, and part of the options must be accumulated on an ongoing basis according to a proportion that may be based on the total compensation of the officer concerned.

years. For those who are responsible for deciding on and preparing the financial statements, it might also be envisaged, subject to simple but indispensable tax adjustments, to replace options, at least in part, by the distribution of shares restricted for a sufficient time period.

4. **The retirement terms** offered to the chairman and chief executive officer and executive directors should not extend to the retirement period the highly special benefits that were granted to him because of his exceptional responsibilities. Pension benefits should be carefully monitored by compensation committees, and their determination or review must take into account the position of the group employing the chairman and chief executive officer and executive directors. It is logical to calculate pension benefits on a pro rata basis of the length of the term of office.

5. **Termination payments** would raise fewer difficulties if they were, from the outset, defined by contract as a proportion of the base salary (a special definition might also apply in the event of a change of control). Such payments would only be excluded in the event of termination with cause. The contract might also provide for the status of outstanding stock options. It is clear that no chairman and chief executive officer and executive directors may be awarded any stock option upon termination of his office. Because of the need to provide for all of these terms immediately upon recruitment, it is necessary to recommend amending the laws governing the legal status of chairmen and chief executive officers and executive directors, so that their position may be clarified in a contract upon their being recruited as officers.

Chairman and chief executive officer and executive directors compensation is an issue for all enterprises, whether large or small, listed or unlisted. However, constraints are different for each category of enterprise. Listed companies must publish such compensation, while the smallest enterprises probably have less freedom to determine levels of compensation. In each case, chairman and chief executive and executive directors compensation is the result of a negotiation between the existing or future chairman and chief executive officer and executive directors and the compensation committee (or the equivalent body whose status must be formalised). MEDEF's Committee on Business Ethics recommends that these discussions be conducted in a responsible, transparent, moderate and civic manner. Based on the principles and policies developed in this document, these negotiations must provide a justification for all components of aggregate compensation.

5

The United States of America

Introduction

Like the rest of this book this chapter is about publicly held companies. The recent reforms led by the Sarbanes-Oxley Act (SOX) apply directly only to them and their audit firms and not to privately held companies though these and not-for-profit companies will be affected by parallel changes in Federal or state laws and rules. (A special committee of AIPCA was established under Chairman James G. Castellano to carry such business forward.)

In reality SOX will reach beyond publicly quoted companies partly through its general influence even in not-for-profit organizations, and partly because some of its provisions like the falsification of documents actually apply. Some states have passed or are intending to pass SOX 'clones' that do not limit its application to publicly held companies but also cover other companies and not-for–profit organizations.

We have already seen in each country studied how corporate governance holds up a mirror to society in general. The USA is no exception. To understand the greatest of the democracies, therefore, we need to remind ourselves of what the relevant laws, assumptions, and attitudes are, so similar to those of others in many ways and yet so different. Societies in market economies have much in common, but who else would offer as two of their guiding principles 'sunshine and due process'?

Federal and state laws

Ever since independence the states have fought to limit the role of the Federal government. Even today the basic laws governing company structure are state laws, with some significant differences between them. Wherever a company operates it may choose any state in which to incorporate, and the states compete for its business. Concerns have been expressed that competition between these states is 'not one of diligence but of laxity' (Justice Brandeis

1933), or, in Professor W. L. Cary's words, a 'race for the bottom' (he had been chairman of the SEC) (Cary 1974: 663). The example of New Jersey is often cited. In 1913 its legislature reintroduced a restrictive approach to corporations. The law lasted only four years because by that time most corporations had transferred to Delaware. Few returned.

Delaware, not an industrial centre by any means, is at the moment the clear winner, with about half of the top 500 companies registered there, partly because of its statutes, partly because the courts and lawyers there have long specialized in governance issues. The Delaware Chancery Court established in 1792 is undoubtedly the pre-eminent judicial tribunal in the realm of company law. Delaware's statute is not substantially dissimilar from the Model Business Corporation Act (which was itself originally based on Illinois legislation) suggested by the American Bar Association and which a number of states use in whole or in part. (For the text see Soderquist and Sommer 1990.) That said, there is competition between states which may favour management's interests, since management decides where to incorporate. The states' legislatures try to attract them. State legislation is subject to some rather loose constitutional limitations, but the key point is a dislike of Federal intervention. Indeed, if a political head of steam builds up in Washington which might lead to Federal intervention a non-legislative solution is found wherever possible; sometimes however the pressure does become too great—as the Sarbanes-Oxley Law has shown.

An example of proceeding by non-legislative means was the incorporation in its listing requirements by the New York Stock Exchange in 1978 of a rule that companies should have audit committees composed of outside directors. Deregulation is part of the same strand of thought, that is, rolling back the boundary of the central government's authority. There is a widespread feeling that those who govern least govern best. Of course, even this principle can be dented to protect vital interests, and there was a time before 1986 when there was pressure on the Congress to control or prohibit hostile takeovers. But this evaporated after the Supreme Court decision in *CTS* v. *Dynamics Corporation of America* restored states' rights in this area.

The issue of states rights coupled with a general disinclination among politicians to wish to interfere on corporate governance issues means that the subject tends to be addressed only in the wake of scandals. As in the United Kingdom they are sometimes addressed by non-legislative means. The scandals that led to the setting up of the Treadway Commission did not produce a change in the law, but led to a requirement that companies appoint audit committees composed of non-management directors. The sanction was the Stock Exchanges, first New York and then the others—companies that did not comply would not be listed. The weakness of using the SEC as a back door to producing a sort of Federal legislation is that its mandate is concerned with markets. Its mandates reach thousands of publicly owned but not exchange-listed companies, but privately owned companies are beyond its reach. California has adopted a SOX clone.

A series of large-scale corporate failures beginning in 2001, most notably the bankruptcy of energy giant Enron Corp., resulted in the loss of billions of dollars in shareholders' equity. Federal intervention quickly ensued when the Sarbanes-Oxley Act was signed into legislation on 30 July 2002. SOX is mentioned on several occasions in this chapter, notably in its creation of the Public Company Accounting Oversight Board (PCAOB)—see below. SOX, in Title III (Corporate Responsibility), mandates certain governance practices for public companies (section 302). It imposes for example a requirement that a quoted company's annual and quarterly company reports be certified in stringent terms by those signing them off, by declaring

A   That they have reviewed the report
B   It contains no untrue statements of material facts
C   The financial statements . . . fairly present . . . the financial situation . . . and the result of operations. It places on the signatories the duty of establishing and maintaining internal controls: and they must report on their effectiveness. What is more they must have reported to the board or its audit committee 'Significant deficiencies . . . in internal controls', and also on all frauds by employees who have a significant role in internal controls.

There may still not be a Federal Companies Act as there is in the UK for instance, but SOX moves a long way down the road, at least in regard to quoted companies. There have been acidic comments on the cost on companies of implementing SOX—not least in the extra work required to enable executives to justify reassuring statements about internal controls. Some commentators have even wondered whether the SOX requirements will prevent other Enrons.

The SEC

The chief but not all-powerful machine for exerting Federal pressure is the Securities and Exchange Commission (SEC) which regulates many of the processes affecting companies, shareholders, and the market, and the traffic between them. Its staff are traditionally activist, and since its creation in 1934 it has been regarded as an 'elite' Federal agency. There are elaborate and important rules on what information must be provided, when and how it must be lodged, or whither sent and to whom. Although SEC regulation, particularly SEC rules promulgated pursuant to SOX, goes close to the heart of corporate governance because it largely controls information, substantive issues relating to, among other things, the fiduciary duties of directors remain with the states, and the Supreme Court (in *Green* v. *Santa Fe*) has prevented the SEC encroaching. The SEC, for instance, rules on the disclosure of executive remuneration and states do not. While generally state laws govern what issues must be put to shareholders for approval, it is the SEC which arbitrates whether a shareholder proposal may be excluded from the company's proxy materials.

The SEC looks at the top 100 quoted companies annually (they account for 90% of the market) and looks at the rest on a three-year cycle. This will extend to 500 companies by 2005. Its powers are substantial, including preventing directors serving on other boards. The SEC (item 106) now requires companies to disclose whether they have adopted a code of ethics—to be published and made available to anyone who wants it.

The law

'Due process' has always been a crucial part of the US system, perhaps because it was a way of welding together people of many different races, traditions, and backgrounds. The legal system provided a common basis for them. Access to the system is facilitated by contingency fees (banned centuries ago in England as 'maintenance and champerty'), by class actions, and by derivative suits. The number of lawyers is high; recourse to the law is a normal part of life; and people do not move far without a lawyer at their elbow. This has a profound effect on corporate governance as it does on many aspects of US life. It is also expensive, as all legal costs are borne somewhere in the price of goods and services.

The king

The United States have not of course had a king for 200 years, but the image of George III lives on in the tradition of distrust for a centralized governmental power and a desire for checks and balances; it has been reinforced by waves of immigrants with memories of truly despotic governments. For most of the last forty years—but not at the present day—the President's party has not controlled the Senate and House of Representatives—whether intended or not, a triumph for checks and balances over efficiency. The constitution was concerned with public not private power, but a similar concern about concentrated power surfaces elsewhere from time to time, and has in the past led to legislation about monopolies, banks, banking and insurance operations, and bank and insurance holdings in industrial companies. Whenever cabals threaten, hackles rise. These are the eyes through which some of corporate America views the potential power of institutional investors.

Size and natural wealth

Just as Japan's lack of usable land affects so many aspects of Japanese behaviour, the sheer spaciousness of America and the fact that it has so many industrial centres is reflected in US attitudes. To have such a rich and vast economic unity, with geographical diversity, encourages people to move. The attitudes of the old frontier have not yet gone. Those who move often must make friends quickly, and the basic assumptions are still of openness and hospitality. The possibility of renewal is always present. Failure is a setback but unshameful; Lincoln had failed in business twice, Truman once. It has been a world of vision, of risk-taking, of adventure. Perhaps, as the memory of the frontier dims, and the lawyers close in, the spirit of regeneration and adventure will falter. Americans fear both this and the decline of the entrepreneurial spirit and independent self-reliance. And the minerals are not inexhaustible.

Diversity

The plurality of US society is most striking in its ethnic mix. Unlike many other countries it cannot delve deep into its past to define the origins of its basic inhabitants. Those who originally lived there were largely dispossessed or annihilated, and the Europeans, who came from many countries, were *sub specie aeternatis*, a recent phenomenon. No one group could claim to be 'it', so all are equal (and the US constitution so decrees), though some, particularly the WASPs (White Anglo-Saxon Protestants), are more equal than others. The Lowells may yet speak only to the Cabots, but neither would think of telling other immigrant groups to 'go back where you belong'—they belong there. Minority religious groups like Catholics and Jews did not take long to be emancipated, because they had never been as disadvantaged as they might have been elsewhere. The balance between the aristocracy of the blood and the plutocracy is different from countries in which there used to be or still survives a formal aristocratic structure, often linked to the land. The USA by and large has an aristocracy of wealth, to which all can aspire. Having said that, being a member of an 'old' family with 'old' money still counts for something and it also colours assumptions and thinking. The USA of course lacks an honours system which confers recognition without cash, and this has important consequences (as indeed does the retention of such a system in the UK).

The old order is changing in that the new waves of immigrants do not see the need to accept the British/US inheritance and its values, and some even baulk at the language. Hispanic influences have grown at an amazing speed, and Spanish is the second language in very many places, the prime language for many, and the only language for some. The demographic centre of the USA has now for the first time shifted west of the Mississippi river.

It would not be surprising to find unevenness or some intolerance in such a heterogeneous society and as a consequence to find pressures from groups who feel disadvantaged on account of race, colour, language, disablement, sexual proclivities, age, and sex—*inter alia*. This can give rise to egalitarian pressure for 'democracy' in many walks of life—at one end bilingualism in schools, and at the other representation on company boards. Today's motto is 'PC'—Politically Correct; curricula, for instance, in some universities are not allowed to concentrate on European cultural antecedents.

The UK inheritance

The USA inherited, of course, the English language, the common law, a dislike of despotic systems of government, and, above all, a confrontational and individual approach, not a cooperative or collegiate one. What the USA did not inherit was UK envy. Perhaps this is because the country is so much richer that there is less cause for envy. Be that as it may, Americans do not resent success because they would rather use their energies trying to attain it. The unions want a bigger slice of a bigger cake and so can identify with the prosperity of the business. They have never seen themselves as the storm troops of socialism. But even though their industrial power is waning, they can and do exercise considerable political power.

The USA discarded monarchy and aristocracy and substituted a wealth-measured meritocracy. There are 'old boy' networks all over the place and the buddy system is considered by some to be the bane of boards. The Americans are so secure in their individuality that they can become great joiners without fear of impairing it. And boards are among the bodies they join, potential lawsuits notwithstanding.

The emphasis on individuality sits well with a pioneering entrepreneurial society, which needs heroes however tough, and powerful leadership what-ever its darker aspects. The typical CEO is heavily personalized by the media (which, in contrast to Japan, find it more profitable to make stories about personalities than products). The style at the top of US companies has been more presidential than collegiate—but the balance is shifting. We consider CEOs' pay below, but it is worth noting here that US heroes in any sphere tend to be exceptionally well rewarded.

The political system

This is no place for a lengthy critique of the system as a whole and the salient features that affect corporate governance can be stated quite briefly:

- The division of power between states and Federal government noted above.
- The two party system, Democrat and Republican.
- The lesser importance of party and party programmes.
- The crucial importance of individuals' campaign funding, which often means they enter office burdened with obligations, and leaves them exposed to multifarious pressures.
- The major role of lobbyists. In recent years, divergent interests have mobilized support so effectively that in some areas an impasse has been reached, that is, 'lobbying gridlock'—for instance, on tort reform. Traditionally, the business community has had a powerful voice – but as enactment of the Sarbanes-Oxley Act of 2002 proved, legislation in the area of governance can occur in the right circumstances.

US commentators have remarked that there is a lack of deference towards central government. Even if it is much less respected than elsewhere (and that is unproved), some opprobrium attaches to large corporations that disregard its laws. Helped by their control of the media, use of expensive lawyers, and funding of political campaigns, power in the USA now largely rests with these large corporations. But the entrepreneurial spirit has not been extinguished, so that if a big business in an industry is afflicted by bureaucratic sclerosis it will in time let in new thrusting companies who will take their share of power along with profit.

Openness

The 'sunshine' referred to above means openness. The Freedom of Information Acts in the USA give access to government papers that would be locked away elsewhere. The Government in the Sunshine Act (5 USC 552b) gives the public access to agency meetings. Openness pervades the atmosphere. The German and Japanese way of operating quietly and effectively behind the scenes to influence company management would strike Americans as underhanded and wrong (and the lawsuits would start flying). American television programmes are amazingly frank and unrestrained by UK standards. Their laws of defamation do not seem inhibiting. The fear of adverse publicity in the media is a powerful prompter of self-restraint.

'Openness' affects behaviour but not human nature. The USA has its fair share of fraudsters, but they have to work on the assumption that discovery will be inevitable. Warren Buffett, on taking the chair at Salomon, told the staff they should not do anything they would be unhappy to see on the front page of the *New York Times*. The fear of clandestine groupings, of conspiracy and cabals, is extreme and is strengthened by fear of ensuing lawsuits. The SEC rules permit up to ten shareholders to meet to discuss a company in which they have invested and about which they are concerned; they have seldom done so, however, for fear of the possibility that they may be sued for an alleged infringement of another SEC rule requiring disclosure by persons holding an aggregate of more than 5 per cent of the company's stock who agree to act together—even if the meeting decided in the event not to take common action. This particular situation was changed by the SEC in the second half of 1992 (see below). To take another example of openness, Schedules 14 D-1 (and 14 D-9) of the SEC regulations require both sets of advisers in a takeover to file details of the fees; if fees are to be fixed by a formula this must be stated.

Academia

The weight of literature coming from North American universities should not be underestimated. There are sophisticated articles and papers on many aspects of corporate governance. The measurable is measured, the rest described. The angle of approach varies—economic, legal, behavioural. Academia is more closely interwoven with the commercial world than in some other countries and is apparently influential, though advice tends to vary and some influences have not necessarily proved beneficial. Alongside the learned pieces (often complete with the mandatory algebra) are the popular books, apparently well researched, written like novels, but with better stories. *Barbarians at the Gate* (Burrough and Helyar 1990) and *The Predators' Ball* (Bruck 1988) are examples. Alongside these are serious and sometimes polemical works like *Power and Accountability* (Monks and Minnow 1991), *Bidders and Targets* (Herzel and Shepro 1990) and *Recurrent Crises in Corporate Governance* (Millstein and MacAvoy 2003). This last urges an independent board of directors and the separation of the CEO and chairman's role. It must never be forgotten that the lifeblood of academics is publication. In other words, the trees are numerous and the undergrowth tangled: to discern the wood, let alone describe it succinctly, is a far more difficult task than for other countries.

National power

The author happened to be in New York at the time of the Cuban missile crisis in 1962. What was most striking was the feeling that decisions on war and peace would be made right there. This was the centre of power. Since then US military and economic hegemony has strengthened, particularly since the collapse of the Soviet empire. Even so there have been moments of doubt and introspection. In the economic sphere for instance it came as quite a shock in the mid-1980s to see so many Japanese and German cars on the streets—an affront to what had seemed a dominant industry. A spasm of modesty caused thoughtful commentators to enquire whether there was any ingredient of such importance that might be worth examining—their corporate governance systems for instance.

The pessimists were confounded about the US economy, which proceeded to boom—in contrast to Japan where the property bubble burst and the economy was in the doldrums. The Nikkei index, which had been over 40,000, declined to less than 9,000. Germany in the aftermath of reunification found itself coping with structural problems in which rigidity and high social costs contributed to a lacklustre performance and high unemployment. In other words, the grass on the other side of the fence that had looked green in the mid-1980s now looked less inviting. This gave Americans reassurance among other things about the relative merits of their governance systems. And US productivity still marched ahead.

But the USA had a bubble of its own—'dot.coms'. This was especially damaging in the USA because so many people had rushed in. It would have been bad enough if firms had simply failed, but what happened was that many managements tried to put off the evil day by cooking the books (fraud, misleading accounting, market manipulation, and misfeasance) on an unprecedented scale: $7 trillion of market value was wiped out. Why did boards and managements act like this? Some contend that it was a response to pressures to create shareholder value by forcing up the share price and that on the basis of quarterly reporting—and this affected a great swathe of corporate USA, not just dot.coms. Pro-forma earnings in the hands of some analysts became a shackle rather than a goal to the point that companies strained every nerve to satisfy their expectations. The analysts themselves may have been models of objectivity, but optimism did suit some at least—if the investment banking side of their institutions could obtain or retain investment banking business. Top US lawyer Martin Lipton writing in *M&A Lawyer* in July 2003 in the course of a convincing analysis referred to remarks by Daniel Vasella in *Fortune* (18 November 2003):

The practice by which CEOs offer guidance about their expected quarterly earnings performance, analysts set 'targets' based on that guidance, and then companies try to meet those 'targets' based on that guidance, is an old one. But in recent years the practice has become so enshrined in Wall Street culture that the men and women running public companies often think of little else. They become pre-occupied with

short term 'success', a mindset that can hamper or even destroy long-term performance for shareholders. I call this the tyranny of quarterly earnings.

The events of 9/11 shook the USA to the core, as well they might. Their
consequences will be with the world for years to come. It is difficult even now
to define the causes. What has been cruelly exposed are the limitations of
power even in the hands of the country with the greatest military supremacy
the world has ever seen. It cannot defend itself against individuals prepared
to be killed for a 'cause'; it cannot police the whole world. The Iraq disaster
was unresolved at the end of 2004 with appalling costs in terms of life,
property, and military expenditure. Will it inhibit the USA taking such an
advanced foreign policy stance in future unless its own territorial integrity is
threatened?

Meanwhile other great nations are stirring. China is set to catch up with
the USA economically sometime between 2020 and 2030. The exact timing
matters not, for there will be others in the race, notably India and Russia.
Such grandiose speculation seems a million miles away from the practical
consideration of systems of direction and control of individual enterprises,
but it is not so. The greater international competition becomes, the more
each of its elements will matter.

The Governance Machine at Work

The basic framework

As noted earlier there is no Federal Companies Act; companies incorporate
under the laws of the state of their choice and rather more than half have
chosen Delaware. The main features are, however, common to all and
familiar to the UK: namely, a board of directors elected by the shareholders
and responsible to them for seeing that the company is properly run. Other
common features include the directors' and officers' duties of loyalty, care
and good faith to the corporation, and the right of any shareholder to sue on
the corporation's behalf for breaches of duty, subject to certain procedural
hurdles. The USA has many more listed than unlisted companies, but this
chapter is confined to companies that are quoted on one of the US stock
exchanges or on NASDAQ. We will now examine each of the parts of the
machine starting with the Chief Executive Officer, but before we do so we
ought to examine briefly one of the most powerful lobbying organizations in
the world of US governance—the Business Round Table (BRT)—since its
influence is so great and directly affects many of the issues that are exercising
commentators around the world. It describes itself as 'An Association of

Chief Executive Officers committed to improving public policy'. It interprets this role as meaning resistance to attempts to encroach on the CEO's authority. It has not, for instance, espoused the idea of requiring the separation of the roles of CEO and chairman of the board (though it does not rule it out); it does not warm to the idea that the non-executives on the board should have a recognized leader; and it resists moves to make it easier for outsiders to nominate directors. Their work is a useful reminder that governance is about power and all parties to it regularly 'speak their own book'.

The Chief Executive Officer

When examining corporate governance in the USA, the place to start is not the board but the Chief Executive Officer. To quote Herzel and Shepro (1990):

A reader unfamiliar with American company boards who walked into a board meeting [after reading our discussion of directors] might be surprised and disappointed. Under ordinary circumstances, what would be going on in the boardroom would correspond very little to the Delaware and other state law procedures. The CEO would probably be the chairman of the meeting and completely in charge. Generally, he controls both the agenda and the flow of information to the directors. He dominates the meeting and the board plays a quite secondary role.

Shareholders and the market are far more interested in CEOs than directors. When we read about big businesses in the financial press, CEOs usually are the centre of attention and directors are obscure. In fact, under normal circumstances very little attention is paid to directors by shareholders, the market, or the press.

The change in the balance of power—and how it affects the CEO

What the above quotation confirms is that US companies are run by their chief executives (whatever the formal title). The form of leadership is much more individual than collegiate. The balance of power between CEOs and their non-executive colleagues will naturally depend on the personalities. In most cases the CEO's position is far more exalted than theirs, in the CEO's own eyes, in theirs, and in the eyes of the world at large. The universal acceptance of CEO's supremacy has a profound effect within their organization, not least in regard to their relationship with subordinates and their own aspirations. As noted earlier, they are frequently the outward and visible symbol of the business and treated as such by the media—a fact they usually enjoy and are sometimes seduced by. Their pre-eminence is reflected in their pay. The second-highest-paid person gets substantially less than the CEO.

Viewed through a CEO's eyes such statements about their power might seem extreme. Their tenure of office is generally about six to eight years, and shorter therefore than that of many outside directors. Many are conscious of their vulnerability and do their best to make real colleagues of their board members. The reality seems to be, however, that it is generally accepted as the norm by all the parties concerned that on the spectrum which runs from individuality to collegiality, the place of the CEO is firmly at the end of individuality, and much of what follows, for better or worse, flows from this simple fact.

The overwhelming dominance of CEOs has been challenged over the last few years, while boards' influence has increased. In former times they could after entering office slowly mould the board to their will through their power of patronage. The advent of nomination committees has whittled away this power, so that new appointees need not feel personal allegiance to them. So it can no longer be considered disloyal for appointees to convene without the CEO. And the CEO cannot depend on their personal loyalty transcending their duty to the company.

Direct responsibility has been sharpened by the requirement for the CEO, and the CFO, to certify personally in quarterly and annual SEC reports that as far as they knew there are no untrue statements or omissions of material facts that might be misleading; and that the financial condition and results have been fairly presented. They also have to make a statement about internal controls.

CEOs' dominance was buttressed by their serving as chairman of the board as well. The chairman is in fact elected by fellow directors. Despite the BRT's views the separation of the roles has become a major issue following Sarbanes-Oxley. Government Metrics International (GMI) (29 November 2004) quotes R. Bernstein of Merrill Lynch & Co. as saying that companies with split roles outperformed the others (average return of 22% against 18%). Statistics on exactly how many companies have split roles seem to vary but in the GMI sample only 34% of the 1,154 companies have done so.

Compensation

There is a mass of data on what the British prefer to call remuneration, and the subject itself has become controversial, partly because CEOs are well compensated through thick and thin; this does not seem just, as judged by any standard the sum paid seems relatively and absolutely excessive. Much ink has been spilt on the subject, not least Graef S. Crystal's *In Search of Excess: the Overcompensation of American Executives* (1991) and Frank Partnoy's *Infectious Greed* (2003).

To some extent the figures speak for themselves. Watson Wyatt SCA analysis states that the median of CEO total direct compensation rose from $1.7 million in 1990 to $5.3 million in 2000. *Forbes Magazine*, 10 May 2004, lists the top ten US earners. The least of these, Todd S. Nelson, got $32,812,000; the top was Reuben Mark of Colgate Palmolive with $147,970,000. Michael Eisner of Disney was described as 'one of the worst performing US bosses' and he got $121,200,000. The articles go on to make comparisons with foreign companies. The boss of BP got $5.3 million, the boss of GlaxoSmithKline $4.6, and the boss of Nestlé $5.1 million. The top name in a long list was the boss of UBS, Peter Wuffli, with $6.8 million.

Such figures have given rise to much concern, starting with the explosion of the differential between average pay and the CEO's pay.

More importantly there is the perverse effect of linking pay to perform- ance, which sounds an obvious solution to the problem of appearing to over- reward CEOs in poor years. It appears that whereas salary accounted for a third of total compensation in 1990, this had shrunk to 15% a decade later. That in itself is not significant but the motivational effects of the timing of long-term incentives, and, worse, stock options, is. Especially if options are exercisable in the short term they positively invite executives to 'cook the books' so as to be able to cash in. They tempt executives to think of the short term rather than take a long-term perspective. In the autumn 2003 edition of the *Securities Reporter*, Professor Jeffrey N. Gordon writes, 'The managers' concern about the stock price can become pathological...managers will be strongly tempted to produce the financial results the market 'expects' through manipulation of the financial results. This was a major ingredient of some of the scandals.' Some commentators consider that options have always been a 'con' trick anyway, born of a failure to distinguish between a company and its stockholders. They appeared to be a way of rewarding executives at minimal cost to the company; this was because the money was coming directly from the existing shareholders by way of dilution— which had reached more than 12% of the shares in issue by 2000 (including 'overhang'). All other payments go through the P&L but options do not. To put it bluntly, they are a swindle. Gordon again: 'The interactive multiplier effect means that high-powered compensation like stock options raise special moral hazard problems in comparison to other forms of incentive based compensation.' Rewarding executives by real stock in order to align their interests with other stockholders is a different matter.

Criticism tends to be shrill to command attention. It is not clear yet where the debate will end. There are pressures for *better* information and for better reflection of results in remuneration. Some critics would focus on the structure of remuneration packages rather than the actual sums. Others argue that top talent is rare and it matters greatly to a company to attract and retain it in a competitive market: the American CEO is not especially secure and his removal from office may in the end be abrupt, public, and wounding (so comparisons with regimes abroad where there is no mobility and great security are unfair). The equilibrium which it is the function of the market to maintain depends upon information, and in the event this is often inappropriate or incomplete. The market for CEOs is in any case structurally imperfect and bound to be so. So almost everything depends upon judgements made inside and outside compensation committees. When all is said and done, however, there seems to be a widespread feeling that some judgements have failed to reflect the balance of interests which in the long run can only be disregarded at some risk to company and country.

The Business Round Table acknowledges that 'there are problems in a few corporations', but generally considers that its 1990 dictum remains valid: 'Select, regularly evaluate, and, if necessary, replace the chief executive officer. Determine management compensation. Review succession planning.' This is supplemented by the following five principles:

1. The committee of the board of directors designated to deal with executive compensation and share-ownership programmes should be composed solely of non-management members of the board of directors.
2. The overall structure of executive compensation and share-ownership programmes should directly link the interests of the executives, either individually or as a team, to the long-term interests of the shareholders.
3. Executive compensation and share-ownership programmes should be designed to attract, motivate, reward, and retain the management talent required to achieve corporate objectives and increase shareholder value.
4. Executive compensation and share-ownership programmes should be designed to create a commensurate level of opportunity and risk based on business and individual performance.
5. Proxy statement reporting of annual cash compensation should be done in a standard format for all corporations in a manner that is easy for shareholders to comprehend. Share-ownership programmes should be separately reported in the proxy in a similarly understandable format.

The Business Round Table's view is, broadly speaking, that shareholders already have all the powers they need including, as a last resort, replacing some or all of the board ; but as we shall see later this power is limited and it is understandable that shareholders should display dismay. Although in the past the SEC did not require management to include shareholder resolutions on executive remuneration in company proxy statements, in 1992 the SEC changed its position. Now, executive compensation is a frequent topic of shareholder proposals included in management's proxy statement.

Implementing performance-based pay and capping executive severance arrangements are amongst the most common shareholder proposals. Expensing stock options is now required.

The SEC's requirements concerning disclosure of executive compensation have broadened substantially; it now requires substantial disclosure of executive compensation under its proxy rules:

- Disclosure must be consolidated into several tables, designed to be clear, concise and easy to understand.
- A summary table must disclose all forms of compensation to the chief executive officer and the four other most highly paid executives for each of the past three years.
- The compensation committee (or the whole board) would issue a report explaining the specific factors and criteria considered in determining the compensation for each of the executives named in the summary table (and for NYSE and NASDAQ listed companies, the compensation committee must be comprised of independent directors).
- A performance graph is required to compare the cumulative return to shareholders over the past five years to the return on a broad market index such as the Standard & Poor's 500 Stock Index and to the return on an index for a peer group of companies.
- Various forms of compensation are broken down in the table.
- The table must distinguish between annual compensation and long-term compensation.
- Annual compensation consists of salary, bonus (which cannot be aggregated with salary), and other (such as perks, payments to cover taxes, restricted stock, stock appreciation rights (SARs), and stock option plans with above-market interest rates or preferential dividends, deferred earnings on long-term incentive plans, and preferential discounts on stock purchases).
- Long-term compensation consists of awards of restricted stock, accrued dividends on restricted stock, pay-outs under long-term incentive plans, and stock options and SARs.
- In addition to the summary table, there must be a table showing the potential values that can be realized by the named executive officers from the exercise of options and SARs, assuming various rates of appreciation of the price of the stock.

There has been a debate about 'expensing' options and a new Financial Accounting Standards Board (FASB) rule is on the way that will require this for their first fiscal reporting period after 15 June 2005. There is a more fundamental question about them, mentioned above (p. 239). If executives were to receive shares bought in the market, it would not arise. The cost would go through the profit and loss account and the shares would not be diluted. Furthermore, holding stock rather than options is a more accurate way of aligning shareholders' interests with those of the executives; they feel a drop in the share price more actively than an option going 'under water'. There would be tax consequences of such a switch. As to small high-tech companies, there are means of offering shares rather than options. As it is, the *Wall Street Journal* (14 December 2004) reported that the value of options had fallen 41% for CEOs and 53% for other staff between 2001 and 2003.

There has been criticism of CEOs' salaries for years. I referred earlier to Graef S. Crystal's 1991 book *In Search of Excess*. The National Association of Corporation Directors' (NACD) report in 2003 drew attention to 'the simple maths' (p. 7):

- The average total compensation for the CEOs in the S&P 500 was over $6 million in 2002.
- The Institute of Policy Studies in Washington DC reported that CEO pay in the 200 largest companies increased nearly 600% from 1990 to 2000. The federal minimum wage in that period rose by 37%.
- The ratio of CEO pay in the largest US companies to the pay of lowest paid employees was 25 × in 1970; 40 × in 1990; 360 × in 2002 (It has peaked in 2000 at 570 ×) (Kevin Murphy, University of Southern California).

The whole subject of executive compensation has attracted extensive analysis and comment—often hostile. A slow process of polarization in US society does seem to be taking place. The *Washington Post* on 20 September 2004 published some details of what it called 'A Shifting Landscape'. The top fifty of households now accounts (2003) for 49.8% of the nation's income compared with 43.8% in 1967.

Other aspects of directors' compensation are considered in their place below, including the role of compensation committees, outside directors' remuneration, and shareholder activism.

Directors and Boards

The structure of the company puts power into the hands of the directors who work together on a single-tier board, and makes them accountable to the shareholders for the way they use it. Their election by the shareholders and their accountability thereafter are the cornerstones of US corporate democracy. But it is a strange form of democracy and it is under state not Federal law. Under rule 14a–4 (and Regulation 14A) directors can be nominated singly, in clumps, or as a slate. They do not have to be elected every year—which leads to 'staggered boards'. And 'plural voting' is often allowed. (This means the shareholder can give all his/her votes to a single candidate.) It is common practice for the election of directors to be done that way, not individually. There is moreover no way the shareholders can vote against—they can only abstain ('withhold their vote') so abstentions may mean anything from downright opposition to a lack of interest. It is more like Soviet Russia than democratic America. So we can conclude that the shareholders' right to elect the board usually amounts to ratifying the board's nominations (which the CEO often plays an important part in formulating), but it can mean their proposing candidates or a full slate of their own. As election is by a plurality of the votes cast, it would be possible for a shareholder nominee to be elected, alongside the names on the slate that received a plurality of the votes. Shareholder nominees are rare and seldom elected. There are very few such nominations largely on grounds of cost. 'Official' candidates' costs are borne by the company, but others who seek nomination pay their own unless they are elected.

The SEC during 2004 was still pursuing its proposal to increase shareholders' ability to nominate directors. This has generated opposition, ferocious in the case of the BRT, and there is the possibility of its being challenged in court on constitutional grounds.

The reality for many years was that power lay with the CEO; what has happened recently is that the board has begun to become the organ of governance originally envisaged. And shareholders have at last begun to examine more carefully the performance of management and the directors' competence to monitor it.

The NYSE and NASDAQ requirements after SOX include regular executive sessions of the non-management directors without management being present. The name of the director presiding must be disclosed in the proxy statement or Annual Report (if there isn't a proxy statement) together with information about how interested parties can communicate with him/her, or with the group. If the group includes non-independent directors the independents must meet at least once a year.

At one time boards were dominated by executives, but the tendency over the past decade has been for 'outside' directors (the US term for 'non-executive' directors) to constitute a significant minority or, more usually, a majority. Today, US companies listed on the NYSE or NASDAQ must have a majority of 'independent directors'. Indeed, the CEO may be the only executive on the board. The CEO may, however, have fellow executives on the board too, typically the president or chief operating officer (COO), financial officer, or a senior vice-president. The nomenclature for the top executives varies a great deal. Boards have shrunk in size since 1972, the median for big companies having reduced from fourteen to about ten and for medium-cap companies from twelve to nine. Small companies have about seven. (The figures vary according to the criteria for describing company size. But the picture is clear enough.)

The Conference Board 2003 Blueprint on Corporate Governance best practices brings together (p. 11) the view of the American Law Institute (ALI), the Business Round Table (BRT), the NACD, and other relevant bodies. It states that the general board responsibilities should include:

- Approving a corporate philosophy and mission.
- Selecting monitoring...compensating...and if necessary replacing the CEO...and ensuring proper management succession.
- Reviewing the company's financial objectives...including significant capital allocation.
- Monitoring corporate performance against the strategic plans.
- Ensuring ethical behaviour and compliance with laws and regulation.
- Assessing its own effectiveness...

The NYSE rules require boards to conduct a self evaluation at least annually to determine whether the board and it committees are functioning effectively. The company may choose how to do this but must say how it proceeds. CB's blueprint pp 32/3 lays out the desiderata, and they are tough. It will be interesting to see how they are achieved in practice.

Outside and independent directors

The movement towards a greater proportion of outside directors accelerated in the late 1970s as a result of some cases of extensive misfeasance by executive directors. The response to this was that in 1978 the New York Stock Exchange made it a listing requirement that companies should have audit committees composed of outside directors.

The rules of the New York Stock Exchange and NASDAQ were amended in the wake of the Sarbanes-Oxley Act (having been approved by the SEC). Both now require a majority of independent directors. Independence is defined in the Act (sect. 301) but the rules have been elaborated to exclude people

- who in the last three years have had a material relationship with the company such that it might interfere with the exercise of independent judgement;
- whose firms have such a relationship;
- whose immediate family are employed by the company or its auditors.

This is not an exhaustive list, but it gives a flavour of the main criteria and illustrates why there is such a difference between being an 'independent' and simply a 'non-management' director.

The recent reforms address the board's processes and are far more prescriptive than before. The non-management directors (including the 'independents' of course) are enjoined to meet regularly without management being present. This marks a major change, as in days gone by such gatherings would have been felt by the CEO to be conspiratorial.

Companies must now have audit committees, nomination committees, and remuneration committees, each of which is considered below. Three-quarters have executive committees and there is a wide variety of other committees too, such as finance, public policy, planning, and human resources. The system still retains some flexibility. Executive committees are the most common and most important and can be used to deal with urgent matters arising between board meetings (there may be two- or three-month intervals between them) or as a sounding board on general management problems. By their very nature executive directors play an important part on them and may have about a third of the seats.

It is said to be getting rather more difficult for companies, especially big ones, to recruit outside directors, partly because of exposure to liability, partly because of the time the office takes, particularly in light of the enhanced expectations of directors under the recent governance reforms. Directors are generally protected from liability arising from business decisions under the business judgement rule. In addition, Delaware corporation law allows companies to eliminate or limit directors' liability for breaches of the duty of case—so long as they had acted in good faith and there was no breach of their duty of loyalty. The Delaware courts have recently focused on the duty of good faith and have indicated that such charter provisions will not protect directors who ignore known risks.

In any event, many companies protect their boards with Directors and Officers (D&O) liability insurance. They also usually have provisions for reimbursing directors and officers for expenses incurred in defending litigation, amounts paid out in a settlement of an action, or sometimes because of a judgement.

Nominating committees

The process of selecting director candidates has undergone changes over the past decade. The NYSE and NASDAQ now require listed companies to have nominating committees composed entirely of independent directors. This structure serves both to reduce the CEO's influence and to make choice more methodical. Some companies invite nominations from shareholders, or meet with large institutional investors to consult on potential candidates.

Nominating committees (which sometimes cover governance issues too and thus become nominating/governance committees) only existed in 46.3% of the companies covered by the National Association of Corporate Directors in their 2003/4 survey. Such committees met on average 3.6 times a year and meetings lasted two hours. Averages of course conceal extremes; in practice only a third of small-cap companies had such committees, whilst most of those in the S&P 500 did (96.2%—up from 85.0% in 2001).

Whilst nominating committees are not mandatory under SOX, the SEC rules now require companies to describe in their proxy statements how the committee works, if there is one, who is on it, its policy and standards, and the way it deals with shareholder nominations. If there is no committee the company must still describe the processes and who is involved in them; it must say why it does not have a committee. The rules for this reporting are elaborate. The process is a very long way indeed from reliance on an 'old boy network'. Even so professional search firms are only used in a minority of cases, which must mean that names are put forward by the chairman, CEO, other members of the board, and the company's advisers. Patronage may be more disciplined, but it is not dead.

Audit committees

Before we examine the role of audit committees we need to clarify a basic point about the audit itself. In the USA its function is directed at accurate market information, which is why the SEC, whose business this is, plays such a central role. In the UK by contrast the auditors are accountable to the shareholders and only to them (the Caparo judgment: see Chapter 6). The end result is often similar, but it is not identical. Furthermore, as US audit is market oriented, the SEC's regulatory authority does not extend to privately held companies. Delaware law does not oblige such companies to have their accounts audited, though as a matter of business practice they may need to so do if borrowing. The Inland Revenue Service (IRS) will expect to see the tax returns authenticated. But there is no company register as there is in the UK and therefore no requirement to file accounts.

Publicly held companies had long been required by the SEC to file audited accounts, but this did not prevent frauds (as elsewhere). It was to meet this problem that the New York Stock Exchange made audit committees a precondition of obtaining a listing as far back as 1978, and companies met this requirement. In the early days there was much scepticism about their effectiveness: the imposition of a piece of machinery did not of itself ensure it was useful.

In a 1988 survey (Report 914), the Conference Board found that times had changed. Audit committees' responsibilities had generally been broadened. They were credited with having 'brought about improvements in ... traditional core areas of their role—external audit, internal auditing, financial controls, and financial reporting. Many agreed that the committees' work has also improved both the full board's understanding of these matters and also its effectiveness. In particular, audit committees were thought to have improved the procedures, practices and effectiveness of internal audit.'

The Enron case and others illustrated the dangers of lack of independence when the auditors put management's interests first, often against a background in which they derived more income from non-audit work than from the audit itself and the more of such work they did the more they stood to lose from a spat with management.

Audit committees should have helped but often prove to be broken reeds. Towards the end of the Worldcom debacle, Cynthia Cooper, an internal auditor who had discovered the accounting mistreatment, went to see the head of the audit committee about it and suggested the committee be told. The chairman said he thought this was premature! The fact that Worldcom had, according to accounting rules, overstated its income by billions of dollars was still not told to the board. There are technical arguments as to whether the principles themselves made sense, but no argument for the lack of transparency to the audit committee and board.

The Sarbanes-Oxley Act has faced up to the problem. Section 301 requires exchange listed firms to have an audit committee with responsibility for the 'appointment, compensation and oversight of the firm's auditors'.

Members of the audit committee will be able to engage at the company's expense their own expert advice including, where appropriate, independent legal counsel.

The audit committee will be expected to delve into the auditors' qualifications, history, and record of problems and restatements. The Act and the NYSE's rules will oblige the auditor to tell the committee about alternative GAAP treatments discussed with management and about any disagreements. The committee must pre-approve all services provided by the auditor (audit and non-audit). It will make periodic reports to investors about its decisions to pre-approve non-audit services. Certain non-audit services are prohibited:

- bookkeeping, information systems design;
- appraisals or valuations;
- actuarial services;

- internal audits;
- management and human resources;
- broker dealing and investment banking;
- legal or expert advice unrelated to the audit.

The independence of auditors will be reinforced by new conflict of interest provisions and mandatory rotation of the lead audit partner and the audit review partner after five years. Furthermore an accounting firm will not be able to provide audit services to a public company if one of that company's top officials was employed by the firm and worked on the company's audit during the previous year (CEO, Controller, CFO, Chief Accounting Officer, etc.).

Sarbanes-Oxley requires audit committee members to be independent. One member must be a 'financial expert' as defined by the SEC. What this means is:

- a thorough education and experience as a public accountant or auditor or a principal financial officer;
- an understanding of generally accepted accounting principles and financial statements;
- experience with internal controls;
- an understanding of audit committee functions.

The duties, obligations, or potential liability of the person so designated and the other directors will not be affected (according to SEC rules—Regulation S-K, item 401).

In addition to its traditional duties, the audit committee must now hire and supervise the external auditor, oversee compliance programmes, and establish whistle-blower procedures. It will have an enhanced role in ensuring the adequacy of internal controls.

All this is on top of the normal range of duties such as

- recommending the auditors;
- reviewing the scope of the external audit;
- reviewing the results of the external audit with the auditors;
- reviewing the results of the internal audit with the internal auditors;
- reviewing the adequacy of the companies' accounting policies, practices, and systems of controls;
- reviewing the scope and adequacy of the internal audit.

This list is by no means exhaustive. The terms of reference—which are disclosed in the proxy statement or the annual report—may go into considerable detail and include various specific functions not mentioned above. Their essence is some reassurance about the effectiveness and integrity of the systems of financial control and information; a means of providing both internal and external auditors with a privileged and private forum in which to express doubts and concerns even (and perhaps especially) about top management; and a way of getting the outside directors closer to the business. The committee must have a charter and at Annex 5 we reproduce the requirement of the NYSE and NASDAQ.

Audit committees used to meet about three times a year on predetermined dates, but there were ad hoc meetings as well if necessary. Now the audit committees of S&P 500 companies meet on average 7.5 times a year; on other large companies the number is 6.8 times. In fact, committee meetings are usually attended by key executives or other corporate employees, some as a matter of routine and some on a 'when invited' basis, but all may be excluded by the committee chairman for items it would be inappropriate for them to attend. As directors often have to fly some distance to attend, it is frequent practice for an audit committee to meet within a day or two of the board. This can in practice cause duplication if the same matters are on both agendas—and the same people attend. Indeed, audit committees will have to make sure they are not dealing with matters that are the board's business. It is in practice only too easy to stray.

The committee is now required to establish procedures to cover complaints about accounting matters including controls and whistle-blowing on accounting and auditing matters.

The committee has, under Sarbanes-Oxley, the right to engage independent counsel and other advisers if they feel it necessary. It is understood that the outside auditors can request a private hearing with the committee when they want one.

Compensation committee

The NYSE and NASDAQ rules following SOX require companies to have compensation committees of independent directors; 94.2% of publicly held companies do so (NACD Survey, p. 21) and they meet about four times a year for an average of 2.5 hours. The NYSE requires them to have a formal charter which details what the committee must cover and how it should report, with particular attention to the CEO and his performance.

The committee's remit generally covers only senior management and executive directors including the CEO, but its role is generally broad and covers the company's remuneration policy and guidelines—which takes it into questions of performance. Judging by the volume of criticism about many top executive 'compensation packages', the compensation committees concerned have failed in their prime task of reconciling the interests of management and shareholders by producing a 'fair' solution. The Disney

250 United States of America

case (2004), for example, attracted widespread comment. Many reasons are suggested for their shortcomings, such as the indirect reciprocity between CEOs, which tempers the severity of their judgement because they dislike being harsh towards those who are in the same position as themselves, and the desire of consultants not to lose business by producing unpalatable advice.

The SEC requires companies to include in their proxy a report from the compensation committee or from the whole board if there is no committee, covering:

- a discussion of the compensation policies for the executive officers, including the extent to which they are performance based;
- an explanation of the reasons for repricing the exercise price of options granted to named executive officers, if such options were repriced during the last year; and
- disclosure of the identity of the members of the compensation committee, identifying any members that are employees or officers of the company or have certain other relationships with the company.

The board at work

Thirty years ago a distinguished academic could describe the outside directors as 'ornaments on a Christmas tree' (Mace 1971). This certainly is not the case now. Boards have become more assertive and SOX plus the ensuing rule changes have made it difficult for directors to avoid the burden of responsibility.

Directors who accept appointment to a board are not generally looking for trouble. They are not, one gathers, doing it primarily for the money. They are more motivated by status and interest. Americans, in discussing the director's role, used to turn to the old adage, 'If it ain't broke don't fix it.' The relationship between the CEO and the directors he has appointed, or who have appointed him, made this a natural attitude, but not now. They generally trust him and like him and do not want prematurely to oppose him, much less eject him: they want him 'to provide strong leadership to pursue economic gains'. They realize his job in the market place is tough enough anyway without the board holding him back. All this, of course, applies to female CEOs and directors too.

They are not unduly worried about this in normal times, will ask enough questions to satisfy their consciences, but accept the limitations imposed by their lack of information compared with the CEO. Such attitudes may change in the aftermath of Enron (and the Equitable in the UK). The message in both cases was that directors must push hard enough to make sure they really understand the games being played and the risks being run. They will have to face the fact that CEOs vary and the boards depend crucially on the role the CEO wants them to play. Some CEOs dominate and suppress; others encourage and create a collegiate style. It mainly depends on personalities and their interplay: two similarly structured boards can behave in entirely different ways. But Enron and the subsequent change in the law have now marked out the field of play differently. Most importantly, the directors will have to push when there are issues that are unclear. Having said that, they are still at the mercy of a devious or secretive CEO.

Directors will assert themselves more readily 'when push comes to shove'. In other words there may be a point beyond which even a weak board cannot be pushed. Readers of *Barbarians at the Gate* will remember this can be a long way down the track. We encounter in the USA the same phenomena described in other countries. First, that in times of trouble the tendency is to accord more, not less, power to the leader; second, that contrary to popular myth, there is no greater a tendency to fire the CEO prematurely in the USA than there is elsewhere. CEOs around the world tend to be given the benefit of the doubt for a long time, for reasons of inertia, cowardice, comradeship, and the sheer difficulty of organizing their removal and replacement. Many would go so far as to say (with the benefit of hindsight) that CEOs are often left in post too long.

So it is misleading to imply that US boards make little contribution. In many moments of crisis, including, for instance, the sudden death or resignation of a CEO, they may find themselves effectively in executive command for the interregnum. Their role is enhanced when takeovers threaten, not least because these have given rise to so much litigation. In the normal course of business, directors have little to fear from the courts because of the 'business judgement rule', that is, the courts are most reluctant to double-guess management decisions, providing directors have not breached their duty of loyalty, good faith, and diligence. In takeovers, however, the courts may well be heavily involved. As this is so, the directors are much more alert to the duty of due care. (*Vide* the judgment in *Smith* v. *Van Gorkom*.) Nowadays, outside professional advice is invariably sought. The balance of power often shifts sharply and suddenly when a company is under attack. Even so, it is not necessarily always easy for directors to reconcile their support for the CEO and the continued independence of the company with their overriding duty to the shareholders.

Those who serve on them assert that the USA has many excellent boards. This is surely true, and reflects the will of those CEOs to make them work properly. Even so, many Americans feel that there are few grounds for complacency about the general effectiveness of their system and particularly of the operation of the board. They know that they are faced with yet another manifestation of the agency problem. As E. B. Rock put it, 'Because directors do not generally have significant shareholdings and do not depend on the shareholders, they lack any significant economic incentive to discipline management. To the extent that they are economically or psychologically dependent on management, they have significant incentives not to act as the shareholders' champion...' (Rock 1991). It remains to be seen whether SOX will lessen this dependence.

A quite different problem arises if the board as a whole does not work, either because the directors cannot control the CEO when they should, or because neither he nor they are up to the mark and the whole apparatus is declining in a welter of reciprocal mediocrity. A poor CEO picks poor directors and vice versa. In these circumstances only the shareholders can address the problem. We shall examine their role a little later.

Boards: frequency of meetings

There are two significant features of US boards that are so familiar that they seldom excite comment: geography and frequency of meetings. Compared with the USA, all the other countries studied, the UK, France, Germany, and Japan, have relatively concentrated industrial bases. Any major US company is likely to be widely dispersed at home, let alone overseas. With so many different industrial centres and so much dispersal, it is obviously sensible for US companies to seek their outside directors to match, and so they do. As a matter of mere logistics this would lead one to expect fewer meetings than elsewhere, and so it proves. In addition US companies are obliged to report quarterly, so the amount of public information directors have is greater than elsewhere. All these factors affect what boards do and how they do it.

The Conference Board (CB) 2003 survey tells us that the number of board meetings in a year varies from 3 to 13 and that the median is 6. The bigger the company the more frequent the board meetings. There is no appreciable difference between manufacturing, financial, and services. As to duration, the median is four hours throughout—which does of course mask a considerable difference at the extremes—from two to eight hours or even longer.

The remuneration of the outside directors

There is a wealth of information in two surveys by the CB for 2003 and by the National Association of Corporate Directors (NACD). The salient points are:

- The bigger the company the more they pay.
- Some industries pay much better than others.
- Compensation is normally composed of these elements:

  (1) a retainer
  (2) committee fees
  (3) share grants or options.

These are average numbers from NACD (p. 6):

Smaller companies   Total$42,892
Medium companies   Total $96,191
Top 200   Total $155,575

Table 5.1 gives a closer look at these figures in these three groups (NACD, p. 7).

Looking at numbers by industry we find (CB 21) the following examples and median total compensations:

Building materials $42,702
Paper and allied products $56,750
Printing and publishing $71,500
Computer hardware & office equipment $90,375
Food, beverages and tobacco $123,330

CB reports a wide range of other benefits (p. 35). Apart from D&O cover there is often other insurance and sometimes matching charitable donations.

For the background of the outside directors we turn to the Korn Ferry International 2003 study(p. 8), which shows the percentage of boards with one or more of the following:

Retired executives from other companies   94%
Investor   89%
CEO/COO from other companies   83%
Women   79%

Table 5.1. Remuneration of outside directors

	Full value shares or stock options etc.(%)	Meeting and committee fees(%)	Cash retainers(%)
Smaller companies	45	29	26
Medium companies	54	22	24
Top 200	59	16	25

Former government official	59%
Academic	59%
Non-US citizen	16%
Commercial banks	31%

There are also figures for ethnic minorities.

Some post-SOX trends in the top 100 companies

(Source: Sherman and Sterling LLP 2004)

1. Forty-six of the 100 have exceeded the requirement for or a majority of independent directors—they comprise 75% or more of eighty-one boards.
2. The CEO is the only non-independent on thirty-five boards but in eighty-five he combined the role with that of chairman.
3. Forty-two companies disclosed the name of their finance expert on the audit committees and in seventeen companies all the committee members are experts!
4. Board meetings and committees meetings have become more frequent; so much so that forty-seven companies placed limits on the number of other audit committees their audit committee members might serve. More generally, only twenty-nine limit the number of other boards on which their directors may serve.
5. Eighty-six companies have a mandatory retirement age of directors—usually 70–2. Only five have limits on length of service.
6. Thirty-three have 'poison pills'.
7. There was a wide range of shareholder proposals on governance issues like splitting the chairman/CEO roles, or six-year terms for outside directors or a vote on poison pills. And there were numerous proposals about various aspects of compensation.

The Banks

As we have seen in the sections on corporate governance in Germany and Japan, the role of the banks was once central and is still important. The relationships between banks and companies in both countries are subtle and complex; each reflects the history of the development of the economy, as well as social and national attitudes and behaviour. Naturally, the role the banks play conditions the way they select, train, and deploy their staff.

There was a time when the USA might have developed on somewhat similar lines (though early on it had more developed capital markets), but the politico-social history of the USA worked out differently. Perhaps the decisive event was the market collapse in 1929–31.

Much of the blame for the intensity of the slump was attributed to financiers, and there was a reaction against their alleged abuse of power and influence. This led to legislative curbs on banks in the 1930s. It is unnecessary to give a blow-by-blow account of what occurred (Margaret Blair gives a short summary of the crucial elements in the *Brookings Review,* Blair 1991). The Glass-Steagall Act of 1933 prohibited banks from under-writing stock or affiliating with investment banks that do, but that has now been replaced. The Bank Holding Company Act of 1956 restricts bank holding companies from owning control blocks in companies not closely related to banking. Potential liability under trustee law encourages bank trust departments to diversify their holdings, and other rules make it difficult or impossible for the bank trust department to act in concert with other insti-tutional stock holders.

Banks therefore do not come into the corporate governance picture except in so far as their trustee departments manage shares for clients. These are the record-holders of a significant portion of shares as custodian or fiduciary, in which case their preference is for their clients to vote their shares. Elaborate procedures have been introduced to facilitate this (under the 1986 SEC regulations pursuant to the Shareholder Communications Act under which proxy materials must be forwarded to the beneficial owners).

Banks' own holdings are minimal because the law restricts them and they have few funds to spare; they neglect to use the influence they already have. Furthermore, their biggest actual or potential clients are likely to have credit ratings as good or better than their own and are therefore able to get money on better terms and without their help (disintermediation). This has meant that the industrial and commercial companies which do still borrow are usually not the best risks. Banks have, however, been prominent in supplying some of the funds for leveraged buy-outs (LBOs) or other take-overs (and costly this has proved when the overstretched borrower could not repay).

Some banks—the investment banks—have been key players, though not as shareholders. It is they who have acted as catalysts of change, not by assessing the quality of corporate governance but by analysing companies to see if the market appeared to undervalue them. If so they hawked the company around (having produced a 'book' on it) among potential purchasers to whose greed and egos they might confidently turn. To the extent that the market's valuation did reflect the inadequacy of management, the investment bankers were assuming the shareholders' proper role, though the remedy they ap-plied—a takeover—was often not as good for the parties as a straightforward change of management would have been. It suited the banks, of course, as takeovers and restructuring were infinitely more profitable to them than were changes of CEO or board. Investment bankers on the whole do not enthuse about really good boards or active shareholders, since both deprive them of an opportunity to make a killing by producing an inappropriate answer to a misguided question.

As if life were not already difficult enough for bankers, ingenious lawyers have exhumed the ancient Common Law concept of 'fraudulent conveyance' as a form of action against banks who loaned money to an LBO that failed. (See the *Revco* case, 1990/1, *Wall Street Journal* (3 January. 1991).) But such claims are rare.

Despite all these problems, a bank may still form a close relationship with customers, and some do. But 'relationship banking' depends on mutual trust and good information. It means a company being prepared to pay what is in effect an insurance premium for help in difficult times, and a bank giving its support if such times come. This goes against the grain when treasury departments are profit centres, straining to squeeze the last cent from every transaction. The trouble is that unless the board tells the treasury department to pay (within defined limits) the costs of relationship banking, it will not get it. Companies seldom think the price worth paying in good times and only regret the absence of an umbrella when the storm breaks. US banks, for their part, hemmed in by their law, seldom have the inclination, resources, and staff to try to sell the umbrellas—profitable though this might be. If a bank syndicates or securitizes debts, the tenuous connection between company and lender ceases to exist at all. In good times the company services its debt and repays when due. But if Humpty Dumpty falls off the wall there are likely to be so many pieces that even the marines cannot reassemble him. (See e.g. the *Federated Stores* case in Lowenstein 1991: ch. 2.) It is not just the company that may get damaged—as the weight of non-performing loans on banks' books shows. An interesting account of Citibank's policy is given in *Institutional Investor* (December 1991).

The banks may not play a part in governance issues, but they may nevertheless be key players in financial machinations that turn out to have facilitated breaches of sound principles of corporate behaviour. Enron is a case in point (Partnoy 2003: 301 *et seq.*). Enron lived on its traders' ability to borrow money and this in turn depended on the ratings accorded by the agencies. On 28 November they downgraded its debt below investment grade. Enron was virtually dead, and filed for bankruptcy on 2 December. This is not to place blame or praise on the banks involved, such as JP Morgan Chase and Citigroup, but simply to note their importance to the construction of the Enron edifice and the apparent disinterest in its governance.

The Public Company Accounting Oversight Board (PCAOB)

Title 1 of SOX set up the PCAOB, whose function is described in section 101 as being 'to oversee the audit of public companies that are subject to the securities laws . . . in order to protect the interests of investors and further the public interest in the preparation of informative, accurate, and independent audit reports for companies the securities of which are sold to, and held by and for public investors'.

Its main function is the control part of the accounting profession—which involves registering accounting firms that 'prepare audit reports for issuers in accordance with section 102'. It has the right to examine them, can fine them or even shut them down. It sets standards. By September of 2004 it had a staff of 237—scheduled to rise to 300.

Titles VIII, IX, and XI of SOX deal with fraud and introduce severe penalties for destroying 'audit and review work papers'. The PCAOB must adopt a standard of registered accounting firms to maintain audit working papers. They must be maintained for at least five years. The destruction of documents in a federal or bankruptcy investigation is made a felony with a maximum twenty years' sentence. The limitation for the discovery of fraud is extended to two years after the act and five years after discovery.

The PCAOB moved swiftly into action. On 26 August 2004 it published its reports on 2003 Limited Inspections of four major accounting firms. Before doing so it records that by the time of the Release 1271 firms had registered with the board. Its overview was as follows:

In 2003, the Public Company Accounting Oversight Board conducted inspections of public accounting firms for the first time. The Board inaugurated its inspection program with limited inspections of the four largest U.S. public accounting firms, including Ernst & Young LLP, the subject of this report. (There followed Reports on Limited Inspections of Deloitte and Touche LLP, KPMG LLP, and Price WaterhouseCoopers LLP.) In those inspections, the Board identified significant audit and accounting issues that were missed by the firms, and identified concerns about significant aspects of each firm's quality controls systems. The Board's inspection reports describe those issues. Each report refers to some 'nonpublic' pages ie matters the PCAOB chose not to reveal. Because Board inspections and inspection reports are new, however, the Board offers a few remarks by way of providing readers with a context for the observations described in this report.

The Board's statutorily prescribed mission is to oversee auditors of public companies in order to protect the interests of investors and to further the public interest in the preparation of informative, fair, and independent audit reports. To advance that mission, Board inspections take up the basic task that had been the province of the accounting profession's peer review system, but Board inspections do not duplicate the programs and approach of peer review.

Board inspections do, of course, examine technical compliance with professional accounting and auditing standards, but Board inspections also examine the business context in which audits are performed, and the ways in which that context influences firm audit practices. Among other things, the Board looks at firm culture, the relationships between a firm's audit practice and its other practices, and the relationship between a firm's national office and its engagement personnel in field and affiliate offices. Through this approach, the Board believes that it can help bring about constructive change in the types of practices that contributed to the most serious financial reporting and auditing failures of the last few years.

Toward that end, an essential ingredient of the Board inspection process is an unflinching candor with firms about the points on which we see a need for improvement. That emphasis may often result in inspection reports that appear to be laden with criticism of a firm's policies, practices, and audit performance, and less concerned with a recitation of a firm's strengths. That is because, from the Board's perspective, the inspection reports are not intended to serve as balanced report cards, rating tools, or potential marketing aids for any firm. The reports are intended principally to focus our inspection-related dialogue with a firm on those areas where improvement is either required for compliance with relevant standards and rules, or is likely to enhance the quality of the firm's audit practice.

The reports' emphasis on these criticisms, however, should not be understood to reflect any broad negative assessment. The four firms inspected in 2003 are made up of thousands of audit professionals, have developed multiple volumes of quality control policies, and perform audits for a combined total of more than 10,000 public companies. It would be a mistake to construe the Board's 2003 inspection findings as suggesting that any of these firms is incapable of providing high quality audit services.

Moreover, the Board does not doubt that the bulk of the firm's audit professionals consists of skilful and dedicated accountants who strive—at times against the competing priorities of the large and complex business of the firms—to make audit quality their top priority. The Board is encouraged by the increasing tendency of persons at the highest levels of the firms to speak of the need for a renewed commitment to audit quality as the firm's top priority. The Board is also encouraged by the firms' recognition of the value of the Board's inspection process. The Board will continue to use its inspection authority to focus the firms on aspects of their practice that may stand as an impediment to the highest quality audit performance.

The final standard for audits of internal control, adopted by the board on 9 March 2004, incorporated certain suggested changes and reflected certain basic principles on which the board members agreed:

- Audit quality would be best improved in integrating the auditor's examination of internal control into the audit of a company's financial statements.

- The costs of an audit of internal control must be reasonable, particularly for small and medium sized companies.
- Outside auditors may rely on the work of internal auditors and others, based on their competency and objectivity.
- An assessment of the effectiveness of a company's audit committee is a vital part of an audit of internal control and consistent with existing standards.

The by-laws and rules of the PCAOB as of 8 September 2004 deal with the question at some length (p. 140 *et seq.*) under the rubric 'Auditor's Objective in an Audit of Internal Control Over Financial Reporting'.

The firm of Arthur Andersen doubtless merited severe treatment after the behaviour of some of its partners, but the total destruction of one of the big five, which had wide international coverage, has in the opinion of many left the cupboard unhelpfully bare—as can be seen when investigating account-ants are needed and conflicts of interest can become difficult to avoid.

Shareholders

It is perhaps a sign of the times that one of the longest sections of this report is devoted to shareholders. For half a century commentators accepted the famous analysis by Berle and Means (1932) that the fragmentation of hold-ings had deprived shareholders of influence and power (in contrast to earlier days when proprietors retained enough stock to exercise both). The emer-gence of organizations which administer collective savings is gradually changing the picture, but there are many angles and complications, as we shall see. Before turning to the role, if any, of shareholders in corporate governance, we take in order:

- the form in which shares are held;
- annual meetings and the voting process;
- shareholders' duties;
- shareholders' diminishing rights;
- who owns what.

It is widely appreciated that the USA has what Michael Jacobs dubbed a 'Board Centred' model (1991). Evidence suggests, however, that boards are not always self-correcting and self-renewing and that the takeover market is not always the right remedy for persisting deficiencies. Attention has there-fore properly focused on shareholders in respect of the role they were originally designed to play—to ensure that the stewardship of their assets remained up to the mark, not by double-guessing management decisions, but by their interest in the composition of the board.

The form in which shares are held

American shares are issued in registered form. Many are held by brokers in nominee names ('street names'). In fact, 70% of all corporate stock was held in street name (by 1987), of which 30% was held in broker name and 70% in bank nominee name. The reasons for such arrangements vary from pure convenience to deliberate obfuscation. Arbs (Arbitrageurs) conceal; pension funds are held in trust. Whatever the cause the result is to complicate the process of voting proxies. There is no need in this chapter to examine all its intricacies, but the curious sounding 'NOBO' rules may be cited as an example. These were introduced by the SEC in 1985, requiring brokers to tell issuers the names, addresses, and security position of shareholders who do not object (Non-Objecting Beneficial Owners). Some shares are held as American Depository Receipts (ADRs).

For many years the New York Stock Exchange refused to list common stock of companies which had unequal voting rights (the 'one share, one vote' rule). Some major companies challenged this rule and the implied (or explicit) threat of their moving to another exchange put the NYSE under severe pressure. The SEC sought to standardize the one share, one vote rule for all quoted companies by adopting Rule 19C-4 in 1985, but the Court of Appeals for the District of Columbia ruled that this was beyond the SEC's authority. US companies often have other kinds of share in issue and many debt instruments. This chapter is concerned mainly with ordinary shares ('common stock'), because residual ownership attaches to them which provides their owners with potential influence on corporate governance. The issue of whether holders of senior securities should be enfranchised and if so to what extent lies outside its scope.

Annual meetings and the voting process: corporate democracy in action

As in most other countries the real business is not generally fought out at an AGM. J. K. Galbraith opined that 'The Annual Meeting of the large American corporation is perhaps our most elaborate exercise in popular illusion' (Galbraith 1967). But its very existence does produce certain consequences.

State law usually requires publicly held companies to convene a shareholders' meeting annually. The NYSE expects companies to make certain that at least a majority of the outstanding shares are voted (to ensure a representative vote), and this has resulted in the appearance of proxy solicitors whose task *inter alia* is to help companies ensure that meetings are quorate and to afford shareholders a convenient method of voting. The SEC requires companies to send search cards to brokers twenty days before the record date so that brokers can tell them how many sets of proxy materials they will need for distribution together with the annual report, which has to be made public not more than three months after the end of the financial year.

The proxy voting system in the USA is a more important part of the governance process than in any of the other countries studied. In the UK, which is closest to the USA in style and approach, proxy contests rarely occur. As far back as 1934, the SEC was given powers to regulate proxies (the Securities Exchange Act), and its extensive rules cover both the process and content of proxy solicitations. Schedule 14B, for instance, lays down the information which must be given about candidates in a directors' contest. More importantly, the SEC was permitted to vet all proxy materials before they are mailed and insists on wide disclosure about those concerned, costs, and the issues. There is a good account of the whole subject, with cases, in a booklet by R. E. Schrager (1986), which noted: 'In any given fight, each side spends enormous amounts of time, effort and money, conveying its message to shareholders.... Both managements and dissidents retain a supporting cast of lawyers, investment bankers, and proxy solicitors... and often hire public relations specialists.'

Unless shareholders come under the ERISA legislation (which broadly speaking covers pension funds in the private sector), they do not have to vote. If they choose not to, management may vote the proxies provided that it has indicated how it intends to cast its votes and the shareholder has signed and returned the proxy and 'marked the boxes' in regard to specific items. If a properly signed proxy is returned without an indication of how to cast the vote, management can choose how to do so. Shareholders can use the proxy system negatively, that is, they can resist management's proposals. They can also launch competing proposals of their own—including candidates for the board. Indeed, this is a way of getting control of a company without a takeover bid. Some candidates put themselves forward on a platform of putting the company up for sale or liquidating it. We noted earlier that the SEC is considering a rule change to make it easier to access the proxy statement and make nominations for the board.

Shareholders' access to the proxy statement is limited via an SEC rule that confines shareholder proposals to matters that are not 'ordinary business'. Until recently it was impossible to raise the issue of excessive executive compensation, for instance (the SEC is in the process of changing this prohibition). Shareholder proposals are in any case generally 'precatory', that is, they do not bind management, though it does appear that management often heeds and acts on shareholder proposals that are passed, or might pass, even though there is no formal legal requirement for them to do so. Until recently proposals tended to be on politico/social issues like the environment and South Africa. There were twenty-one resolutions on Northern Ireland in 1990 (the New York Comptroller's Office was the most active in leading them). It must be irritating for the board to find general meetings raking over such issues, but they have the consolation of knowing they pre-empt the time and attention that might more fruitfully be spent on governance issues.

The 1980s saw proxy contests become more prominent (but not more numerous), and they were used from time to time as a cheap way of getting control of the board. The data on this type of proxy contest for the twenty years till 1977 show that about twenty-five contests occurred annually and that the dissidents were successful in getting full control in 15% of cases or partial control in 32%: a rate of between twenty and twenty-five contests per annum is thought to have continued well into the 1980s. In 1983, for instance, there were twenty-five such contests, of which eleven were for full and four for partial control. Management won in 36% of the cases and the dissidents in 40%, an unusually high proportion. Proxy contests were also used in conjunction with a tender offer in an attempted takeover to put management on the defensive (e.g. AT&T/NCR), or were coupled with other takeover tactics, like 'putting a company into play': that is, the dissidents' purpose was to force up the share price by attracting bids or restructuring.

From the beginning the Annual General Meeting was the only regular appointment for all shareholders to face the directors (if they had all turned up in a big company it would have needed a baseball stadium). In keeping with national attitudes it was structured to be confrontational. It was more-over the only regular occasion on which resolutions could be launched at management.

This battlefield is still visible in the landscape but nowadays major share-holders and companies find that dialogue out of the limelight is more constructive. This is for instance the stance taken by TIAA-CREF, the largest institutional investor. The preliminary report by ISS (Institutional Share-holders Services) on the 2004 season is titled 'A Law Corporate Governance World: From Conflict to Constructive Dialogue'.

That does not mean the disappearance of shareholder resolutions—far from it: ISS reported that boards moved to implement more than 70 majority votes on previous shareholder resolutions. More than 40 companies took action on their poison pills while 50 moved to introduce the annual election of directors.

'Vote-no' campaigns became more frequent and pushed some companies into adopting governance reforms. Other companies kept ahead of the game by introducing changes—like the appointment of independent lead directors with real authority at Boise Cascade and General Electric Co. 'Withhold' votes on the re-election of directors reached new heights—in the Federated Department stores case it was more than 50%, and promptly ignored!

We may reasonably conclude that increasing and more effective shareholder activity, publicly or privately conducted, is part of the much wider movement towards improved accountability.

Shareholders' duties

In most countries shareholders have no duties once they have subscribed for their shares or bought them in the market. If they own the shares beneficially they may vote eccentrically or not at all. If they hold them as trustees they may still throw the papers away, and in the UK over 80 per cent of all holders routinely do so. In the USA the Labor Department requires the trustees of corporate pension plans which fall under the ERISA legislation (which covers most of them) to vote their shares or see that investment managers do so. Trustees must monitor their managers to make sure they comply; unless the trustees specifically reserve the voting rights for themselves the managers must vote. What is more, the votes must be cast in the interests of the beneficiaries.

Shareholders' diminishing rights

Shareholders' rights vary according to state statute, but usually include the right to elect directors as is general practice, as a slate not individually. The NYSE *Listed Company Manual* ensures a degree of uniformity and covers the frequency of reporting (§203). Most US public companies publish their results quarterly. They are not obliged to send copies to shareholders (except for the annual results), but usually do so.

Shareholders can bring a class action against the directors on behalf of all the shareholders (or those who bought or sold stock during a specified period). Alternatively they can bring a derivative suit—that is, they purport to sue on behalf of the company, which gets any ensuing benefits. Under Delaware law they generally need the board's consent to do this if it has a majority of disinterested directors—who can refuse if it is acting in accordance with the business judgement rule. If there is no such majority or if the action is not protected by the business judgement rule—for example, alleged waste of corporate assets—they do not need the board's permission to sue. If they win or settle the court may require the company to reimburse their costs where the action conferred a 'specific and substantial benefit' upon the company; but they may well fail, because when they reach the substantive issues they may butt up against the business judgement rule which is designed to let directors run businesses without having to worry about shareholders with the benefit of hindsight suing them for mistakes.

The waves of takeovers during the 1970s and 1980s were only possible because control could so easily be acquired through open purchases in the stock market (without even having to offer to buy more than a bare majority of shares). There were no protective banks or interlocking shareholdings to stand in the way as there are in other countries; the NYSE had long insisted on 'one share, one vote'; finance became even easier to raise; and accounts (which had to be produced quarterly) lacked that enveloping opacity that shrouds companies' assets in some other regimes.

As this is so, incumbent management sought to protect its own position, partly from a genuine desire not to see its life work broken on the wheel of financial opportunism and a belief that they knew better than the shareholders how to protect their interests, partly from personal fear, greed, and love of power. To achieve their ends management was obliged to seek shareholders' permission to limit or reduce their power: and shareholders often gave it. The courts, however, generally permitted management to introduce poison pills without consulting their shareholders first. The whole issue of poison pills is covered below p. 277 and 278.

The SEC in its laudable aim to regulate the flow of information has in some cases made it far more difficult for the shareholders to monitor a company and take effective action to correct poor management. When it comes to proxy battles, management holds all the money and most of the cards: it may even reduce the board and make access to shareholders' names and addresses difficult or hideously expensive.

Various state legislatures have moved to protect their own, for example, Boeing by Washington; Norton by Massachusetts; and Armstrong World by Pennsylvania. We shall consider this further in the section on takeovers: the point here is that the protection of management led inexorably to a diminution of shareholder rights. And they may be further threatened by states introducing 'other constituency' provisions. These provisions have muddied the waters by permitting directors to consider the interests of other constituents than the shareholders—which can provide a convenient excuse for putting their own interests first. An incompetent management that does not wish to be dislodged can argue that it was resisting a bid which would have been to the shareholders' advantage on the grounds that other interests would not have benefited or had been harmed by it. In the long run shareholders can only prosper if all the other main interests—customers, employees, and creditors—have been satisfied first, but there is no excuse for neglecting the shareholders' interests and thus removing one of their effective means of redress.

Of course shareholders still retain their right to sell in the market, but if they see a board quite clearly underperforming or milking the company remorselessly, they cannot easily change its composition and they may not even get a chance to accept the offer if a bidder appears. The price of protecting good management from the depredations of the takeover artists has been to bring the mediocre within the corral and disarm the shareholders.

One kind of shareholder has been singled out by law for special attention—mutual funds. In the 1930s some began to act as monitoring intermediaries, but the 1936 Tax Act and the 1940 Investment Company Act forced them to stop. There were many contributing reasons but the main one was the general suspicion of the financial sector and the fear of its power over industry. American public opinion has always been mistrustful of accumulation of economic power and feels safer when it is fragmented. Recently however, new SEC regulations were issued requiring mutual funds to disclose their proxy voting policies and actual proxy votes. One of the reasons given for the new regulations was to motivate funds to be more active as corporate shareholders.

SOX plus the NYSE rules are intended to boost shareholder confidence by ensuring greater transparency in SEC filing and in the report and accounts. There will have to be for instance an expanded MD&A disclosure. There will also have to be detailed discussion of critical accounting policies, off balance sheet transactions, and certain contingent obligations. 'Proformas' must be accompanied by more disclosure, including a discussion of what a closely related GAAP measure would be. The practical effect of these additional requirements will be to discourage the use of pro-forma information. Rules are being formulated to improve the information available to shareholders, for instance corporate governance guidelines, and the committees' terms of reference. Across the board a great deal of additional information will now become available to shareholders one way or another.

The CEO and CFO will have to certify that the company's financial statements are accurate and that internal controls are effective. If moreover a company is required to restate its financials because reporting requirements have not been met in a material way, management will forfeit any bonus or equity compensation. They in turn will demand comfort from the independent auditor and legal counsel. What this means in practice is that management will have to satisfy the board about the internal control structure, financial reporting, and compliance. The SEC advises that a special committee should monitor disclosures as well as the audit committee. A company's form 10-K will in the future include a report on internal control. All this is designed not only to improve transparency as between company and shareholder, but also to satisfy shareholders that appropriate checks and balances are in place.

Does all this mean that shareholder activism will be unnecessary? Unfortunately not. Flawless and honest governance is one thing and sheer commercial competence another. As always, shareholders will need to concentrate on this issue above all else.

Shareholders: who owns what?

According to Proshare's 2003 share ownership handbook, drawing on the ICI/ISA share ownership survey, 49% of all households had some type of equity—i.e. 52.7 million—and these had 84.3 million individual investors. Private shareholders and not-for-profit organizations held 36.7% of US equities in all, down from 50.7% in 1990. Many are totally passive; they are generally viewed as supportive of management, with good reason. They do not have to vote their proxies and management can usually do it for them.

Institutional investors, mainly pension funds, private, state and local, mutual funds, insurance companies, etc. have the lion's share of the rest, that is 46.1% of the equity market in 2002. This compares with 38% in 1981 and 53.3% in the 1990s

The breakdown is as follows:

Private pension funds	12.9%
State and local pension funds	8.5%
Mutual funds	18.3%
Life insurance companies	6.4%

According to the flow of funds accounts published by the Federal Reserve, institutional shareholders held 48% by the third quarter of 2003, with mutual funds at 21%.

Foreign holdings now account for 10.9%—up from 6.9% in 1990.

Some of the Management Buy-Out (MBO) funds perform the role of monitoring shareholders. There have recently been examples of funds being set up (like the LENS fund) with the avowed purpose of taking a large enough stake in underperforming business to influence management and secure improved performance.

The role of individual shareholders

Except for the mega-rich or the proprietor who retains a substantial proportion of the stock, the situation is still as Berle and Means (1932) described it. Even if they had the knowledge and motivation (which would be rare), individual shareholders would be faced with the problem that for them to be active would mean incurring a private cost for a public benefit. Others would stand aside, do nothing and yet reap benefits; this is called the 'free rider' problem. The only way the private shareholder can act economically is in concert with others. Of course, individual shareholders can perfectly well support the initiatives of others and this means the institutions. It is to their position we now turn.

The role of the institutions: the relationship between investment policy and corporate governance

It is quite wrong to suppose that anyone concerned with institutional investment wakes up in the morning with corporate governance in their mind as the determining issue in choice of manager, portfolio strategy, or stocks. What they want of course is profitable investment, and the traditional way of achieving it is through straightforward market operations. If a stock disappoints one sells (exit). This is the so-called Wall Street Walk.

In principle institutional shareholders face the same basic choices as private ones, with one exception—their fiduciary duties prevent their taking certain kinds of risk. The US private shareholder may put all his money into a handful of local companies and stick to them through thick and thin. The institutional shareholder must to some extent spread risk and this has led to a somewhat indiscriminate acceptance of the principle of massive diversification, in which the golden rule seems to be 'Nothing succeeds like excess.' It is not restricted by the capacity to understand; one public pension fund has, for instance, 1,400 stocks and does more than 8,000 stock transactions a year.

How far to diversify is a matter of policy and we know from O'Barr & Conley's (1992) study that the choice of policy depends more on 'inheritance' than on objective and deliberate selection. Fund managers tend to stick with their predecessors' policy (not necessarily with the actual stock selection). There seem to be five choices:

1. A passive portfolio (see 'index' funds below).
2. An actively managed heavily diversified portfolio.
3. A concentrated portfolio.
4. A 'target' fund.
5. Hedge funds.

Portfolio managers may choose any of them or indeed a combination of all of them. Each affects an institution's potential or actual role in corporate governance.

It seems gradually to be appreciated by owners or trustees that for fund managers (who are acting at one or two removes for beneficiaries) to over-diversify is neither helpful to the beneficiaries nor to the prospect of developing an interest in corporate governance. Coupled with heavy trading, it is costly and incompetent. The cost of trades shaves off the beneficiaries' capital; Lowenstein estimates that in 1987 $25 billion was spent in trading stocks, an amount equivalent to one-sixth of corporate profits and 40 per cent of all dividends paid out that year. What they trade is largely an unknown quantity, since they lack the resources to study the underlying companies in depth.

Lowenstein had not changed his tune in 2004; writing in *Barron's* on 11 October he pointed out that ten well-regarded value funds had handsomely beaten the market between 1999 and 2003 with average annual returns of 10–80% against the S&P 500—0.57%. This group held their shares for an average of five years; the average holding period of a domestic equity fund is apparently ten months. To run a value fund means holding one's nerve during parts of the cycle which others appear to be doing better.

Index funds

Even a big fund will only hold a small proportion of the equity of any given firm. This would suggest non-intervention on the 'free rider' principle—a fund would bear the cost and hassle and the benefits would go to others. But there is another way of looking at it. An index fund is locked in—the investor cannot sell even when bad things are happening to a company. It can therefore be correct to say 'if you cannot sell, you must care'. In other words institutions cannot just turn a blind eye but should take action.

Index funds started about twenty years ago and were the first investment product of the 'basket' variety. Many are based on the S&P 500—the 'plain vanilla' index (which comprises 400 industrials, 40 utilities, 20 transportation companies, and 40 financial institutions; 474 of the shares are listed in the NYSE). This index is capitalization weighted.

There are many indices. They vary from the NASDAQ composite containing 4,000+ companies (though it is unclear whether any funds attempt to track it) to the WILSHIRE 5000 total market index which includes 6,500+ companies. Some funds do track it, but they tend to be expensive. At the other end of the spectrum there are funds that track the thirty companies that comprise the Dow Jones Industrial Average.

The growth of index funds is dramatic. The Columbia Project research shows that $342 billion of assets were so managed in May 1991 (up 25.8% from December 1990) by the top fifty-three money managers: the top fifteen managers manage about $300 billion out of the total $342 billion, and nearly $100 billion was in the hands of the biggest, Wells Fargo Nikko Investment Advisers.

The annual survey of assets linked directly to all the Standard & Poor indices (S&P) showed that at the end of 2003 there had been a 36% rise over the twelve-month period to $1.2 trillion. Of this $1.1 trillion was based on the S&P 500. In 1983 the figure had been $44 billion.

Actively managed heavily diversified portfolio

Much the same considerations apply as the index funds, except that fund managers have the option of selling if they feel the company's performance warrants it. Even so, whilst they remain shareholders they will come under increasing pressure to vote; and if they fall within the scope of the ERISA law they must do so.

If funds continue to diversify, as they now do, beyond the range of both knowledge and resources, they are unlikely to have enough of either to play a part in corporate governance even if they wished to do so. In fact they are content not to bother as their eyes are firmly set on the criteria by which they are judged. They are not judged on their effectiveness in corporate governance matters—a different world from the league tables of performance which overhang them like the sword of Damocles. No wonder so many funds simply replicate in their portfolios the firms that constitute a particular index, in the proportion in which the index is itself calculated: the managers do it in self-defence. They know that otherwise three-quarters of them will in any year underperform the index.

A target fund

The difference between a concentrated portfolio and a target fund is one of intention. In the former the investment is made because of a company's perceived potential and present competence. In the latter present performance is deemed to be below potential and the objective is to get management in place better qualified to produce results. RAG Monks's Lens fund was an example of this as is the Hermes Lens Fund in the UK.

A *concentrated portfolio*

There is available to the institutional investor, within the law, a totally different strategy—concentration, that is, buying more of fewer stocks and holding them. The ultimate example of this kind of fund is Warren Buffett's Berkshire Hathaway Corporation. The principles behind it are, first, not to invest in a company until you thoroughly understand it—including its strategy; to have a big enough holding for it to matter to you, and to them; and to maintain good contact with the company to ensure the board's stewardship is up to the mark—think long and trade little. The size of the holding must vary with the size of the company and the size of the fund, so the number of different shares in the portfolio will depend on both. Lowenstein (1991) calls concentration 'Patience and Selectivity'. Concentration incidentally does not mean putting all one's eggs in one basket. Twenty to forty stocks would be enough (in the views of some) for all but the biggest funds, where the resultant holding would constitute too large a chunk of the equity of all but the biggest companies (see Lowenstein supra p268).

Clearly a portfolio of this kind is much more likely to lead to closer relations between shareholders and companies and it usually does. Such funds, over time, often seem to do well.

Shareholder *activity*

The above analysis shows how differing policies produce different pressures and opportunities. The shareholders' role has always been a 'longstop' one—there was never any need for them to intervene whilst present performance and future prospects were satisfactory. Boards resent encroachment—for instance, the 1992 revision of the SEC rules to make communication easier between shareholders who are not bent on acquiring control.

The modest changes were notable for the vigour with which the conflicting arguments were pressed. 'Leave us alone and keep off our backs,' said management, 'or you will inhibit our risk taking—and what do you know about our business anyway; you're just market gamblers.' 'We own you,' respond the shareholders, 'and as good Americans we believe in accountability. If you aren't accountable to us, where else is there? We don't want to run your business but we have a right to feel that the stewardship of our assets is in good hands.' This indeed is the crux of the US dilemma—a dislike of concentrations of power (in this case in the hands of the institutions), versus a respect for effective accountability. The conflict is nicely poised.

One of the problems with shareholders' activism is that, like the old English legal adage 'He who comes to Equity must come with clean hands', those of some institutions do not. Federal Reserve Board Governor Susan Schmidt Bies, speaking in February 2004 at the Economic Club of Memphis, Tennessee, weighed in on a whole series of issues from inadequate disclosure to 'directed brokerage', 'soft dollars', 'market timing', and inadequate internal management. In short, the corporate governance of some mutual funds is itself suspect.

But progress is on the way: on 31 August 2004 mutual funds reported for the first time on how they had used their proxy votes; what that shows is a wide variety of activity. Indeed the propensity to vote was inverse to the size of net assets (see Table 5.2).

Some public pension funds were the most proactive of all the US institutional groups. Some had no taste for it, others feared political interference, because the businesses they might wish to reproach may well have the ears of their political masters as contributors to campaign funds. 'Mr Governor, we have been generous contributors to your campaign funds—get your pension fund off my back.' In any case, the Columbia project research showed that in 1990 the public pension funds controlled only 8.3% of equities. Most private pension funds—which have as we have seen a legal obligation to vote—have parallel fears, of upsetting suppliers or customers, or even simply because of an unspoken non-aggression pact: 'You don't vote against my company and I won't vote against yours.'

It is commonly argued that money managers are totally preoccupied with their place in the league tables, measuring their performance against that of competitors. This is true, but we should not draw the inference from it that dismissal waits round the corner. In 1989, 32 out of 427 were terminated with an average of 7.6 years' service (cf. 1987, 8.7 years). The fact is that fund managers often build up good personal relationships with those who hire them, and will be given the benefit of the doubt for a long time ('he's going

Table 5.2. Size and voting records of institutions

	Size of fund (US$m.)	Voting score (%)
Fidelity	513	25
American Funds	393	50
Vanguard	355	75
Franklin Templeton	100	45
Janus	72	71
Oppenheimer	56	70
American Century	55	100

through a bad patch'). This is so, although there is now a powerful new consultancy profession whose members help trustees pick fund managers—another manifestation of the pervasive tendency to diffuse responsibility in the face of possible litigation. In short, fund managers are not prevented by fear of dismissal from taking an interest in corporate governance. They simply do not feel they are paid to do it; are not measured by their success in it; and lack the skill and resources they would need to do it properly. Vote they must if they are managing funds covered by the ERISA legislation and the trustees order it, and they must follow whatever guidelines they are given. But that does not make them care. 'They vote woodenly,' as one commentator said of a big index fund manager.

Money managers and even banks' trustee departments also come under pressure. They can find themselves with a conflict of interest. The Investor Responsibility Research Center knows how widely attempts at persuasion occur. The answer often suggested is for voting to be confidential, but this is widely opposed by some business groups precisely because it is likely to be effective. Proxy solicitors oppose it as it weakens their position; and there are certain technical problems.

Apart from the strenuous efforts of a handful of public sector pension funds and the work of some representative organizations, there are few signs of shareholder activism. On rare occasions a public-spirited private shareholder (with sufficient means) enters the lists. A notable example a decade ago was Robert Monks, who founded Institutional Shareholder Services in Washington DC after a successful career in industry and the Administration. Among his more spectacular forays was a tilt at the board of Sears, a company whose results had been mediocre for some time. He failed to win a seat on the board, but his attempt hassled the company into defensive actions of a questionable nature and certainly drew the attention of the investing community to the alleged shortcomings of the board. It may have been pure coincidence, but the company made some radical structural changes not very long afterwards.

As we noted above, focus funds present a more direct challenge; there seems little doubt that US management is angry at the hint of greater shareholder activism and perhaps a little frightened, judging by the vigour of its reaction. They would argue that the temporary holders of share certificates bought as mere counters for trading purposes are not and cannot be true owners in any real sense of the word. But this argument would not apply to any shareholders or group of shareholders who deliberately set out to implement the alternative strategy—concentration rather than diversity, holding rather than selling, meaningful stakes rather than penny numbers, knowledge and loyalty rather than ignorance and unconcern. With such a policy which emphasizes 'voice' as a useful alternative to 'exit' goes a natural desire to reduce the legal constraints which now impede it, particularly as joint action by shareholders may on rare occasions be desirable. There are indeed already straws in the wind. Some big funds do intend to concentrate their portfolios. And 'concentrated' funds have been established as a vehicle for a number of investors (private or institutional) to get together so that the sums they put into any one company require attention and interest by all the parties.

The changes in the law and NYSE rules that followed Enron have increased the potential oversight role of the shareholder:

- They will approve equity compensation plans.
- They will review more closely the voting history and procedures of registered investment companies through which they won shares.

The changes are more profound than this however. It may well be that there will be more attempts to make board nominations by access to their companies' proxy statements and, if necessary, to make proposals to change the companies' by-laws to facilitate this, if supported by a qualifying proportion of outstanding shares. The SEC has indicated that it may change the proxy rules to provide such shareholder access. How far this will go remains to be seen. Many resent the managerial abuses (and sometimes crimes) that resulted in a wave of scandals, but others are concerned that there should be a sense of proportion. Most of American management is able and honest and needs no new shackles. The debate has a long way to run. In essence it is about the balance between enterprise and accountability. Shortage of the former leads to stagnation. Shortage of the latter leads to incompetence or fraud or both.

The Stock Market

The New York Stock Exchange ('The Big Board') is the dominant institution; NASDAQ is also important but it tends to cater for smaller, newer high-tech companies—some of which graduate to the NYSE each year (in 2002, 36 did so).

There were 2,746 companies listed in the NYSE in August 2004, of which 59 had been added during the previous twelve months. Of this total 451 were non-US companies; 351 were quoted in ADR form. At August 2004 the market capitalization of domestic companies quoted on the NYSE was $11.5 trillion (compared with NASDAQ $2.7 trillion, Tokyo $3.2 trillion, and London $2.4 trillion). In the year 2000 it processed 300,000 orders a day. The daily value of trades for 2003 was $38.5 billion. In the year to 31 August 2004 there were 73 domestic IPOs (initial public offerings) which raised $30.9 billion.

This bunch of statistics from recent years is intended merely to give a sense of scale to the operation of the greatest capital market in the world. Furthermore US investors in 2001 held about $1,550 billion dollars of non-US equities, up from a mere $60 billion in 1987 (source: Federal Reserve Board Flow of Funds). As noted above, the NYSE trades extensively in non-US companies. At 31 August 2004 their market cap stood at $5.9 billion. IPOs raised $5.8 billion. The NYSE states that if the foreign equities was a stand-alone market it would be bigger than any outside the USA.

As noted earlier, Lowenstein estimates that as far back as 1987 the total cost of commissions and other trading expenses exceeded $25 billion—more than one-sixth of corporate earnings that year. Unfortunately high turnover does not guarantee that liquidity will be maintained in times of financial disruption. Less than 1% of the total float was traded on Black Monday (19 October 1987), that is, $21 billion, but the Dow fell over 500 points.

No analyst or stockbroker ever made a cent in the short term by advising clients to 'hold' even if that was the best advice (in the long term their honesty might well produce rewards). Action is the name of the game, with every morsel of information used to titillate clients' palates. The US trading machine is greased by soft dollars, that is, a rebate on commissions paid to a fund manager by the broker in the form of services of various kinds. The subject is shrouded in secrecy and the fund managers' employers often do not know, or shut their eyes; published guesses are that the soft dollar business is worth $1 billion per annum and involves a third of all institutional brokerage business. The practice encourages churning, but those who benefit of course defend it, and it is not illegal. The SEC published a release indicating permissible limits and investment managers who do it or intend to do it must make disclosure.

The tidal wave of governance reform has not spared the NYSE itself. Speaking on 23 September 2004 the CEO John Thain spotlighted these changes:

- The board is much smaller (about 11 as against 27) and is now independent, barring the CEO.
- The role of the chairman has been separated from that of the CEO.
- The regulatory function is being separated from that of ordinary business.
- The creation of a board of executives, which meets in the same day as the main board, but separately.

There was a very public and unedifying row about the terms on which Richard Grasso, the previous CEO, departed.

Hedge funds

I used to regard hedge funds as a sort of glorified and 'scientific' betting shop with sophisticated techniques and an armoury of jargon with no relationship whatsoever to the companies whose shares they were buying or selling (or indeed with the commodities in which they were trading). Like all gambling institutions those who run them benefit most. Investors in them are interested in 'absolute returns', not the state of the market and certainly not in any of the underlying securities being dealt in. The degree of sophistication of these funds is often as formidable as their jargon is impenetrable, but even having Nobel Laureates among the advisers is no guarantee of success as the case of Long-Term Capital Management demonstrated. Hedge funds are significant, indirectly, to governance issues, simply because 'shorting' in the market will tend to depress the share price and thus send a signal to the board. They may not wish to heed the signal, but that is another matter. As these funds grow and a greater proportion of shares floats around in various forms (and is often borrowed) one does begin to wonder about the point at which the fundamental principles of accountability may be vitiated.

Private equity firms

The *Wall Street Journal* of 10–12 September 2004 led on page M1 with the headline 'For sale again and again and...'. It cited the case of the Simmons bedding company, which has changed, hands six times since October 1986.

The emergency of private equity firms has intensified a process that was always in evidence to some extent as companies grew and investors wanted a share of the action. For those who engineer these deals it is a lucrative process; for the principals there is the prospect of profitable exit in due course. Their relevance to corporate governance is the dividing line between quoted and unquoted companies. The regime governing the latter is less demanding. There may be cases where a board is attracted by this prospect, but it is unlikely to be the prime determinant of a decision to 'go private'.

There is however an associated problem about conflict of interest if the management of a company that is being bought by a private equity firm intends to continue to run it; it has an incentive to ensure that the terms of the purchase are not too demanding. The existing shareholders on the other hand want the highest price possible.

There are some fears that the sheer success of the movement may lead to excess. In the words of the article quoted, a venture bubble may be starting. Bubbles are a concomitant of free markets, but they hurt when they burst. In

Acquisition Monthly of November 2004 the writer said (in the UK) that these funds were 'over financed, over competitive and over here'. The top nine already had £160 billion under management.

Takeovers

As we have seen, control of a US company can pass by replacing enough of the board through the proxy process, but the more usual route is by acquiring a majority of the votes through a tender offer.

There is no equivalent to the UK's Takeover Panel to police the process, though the SEC imposes certain requirements and constraints; for example, the secret accumulation of stakes is regulated by Section 13(d)(1) of the Exchange Act, which requires beneficial owners to make a Schedule 13D filing with the SEC within ten days of crossing the 5% threshold, and give full details of their identity and intentions. Changes of more than 1% thereafter or of intentions must be promptly notified; but bigger stakes can legally be accumulated during the so-called '10-day window'. In the Norlin case (1984), a 37% stake had been accumulated before the notification date. Since then the introduction of poison pills has made it difficult to accumulate a large stake in the open market.

Contested bids, or as Americans call them, 'hostile takeovers', first became common in the 1960s. They were, and are, an invitation to shareholders to accept an offer, whether or not the board recommended it. At first they were welcomed as an instrument for sharpening or replacing poor management, and their increasing numbers put corporate America on notice that management could not disregard shareholders' interests (for instance, by building up cash mountains whilst being mean with dividends). Naturally management did its best to persuade shareholders to refuse an offer, blandishing them with stock splits, raised dividends, and optimistic news. The tender offer was for control, not necessarily for total ownership. There used to be no US requirement that such an offer must extend to all the shareholders. Viewed in that light they were a step forward from proxy contests, which do not necessarily imply any shares changing hands.

Incidentally, unequal treatment for shareholders took various forms. It might mean paying a lower price to the minority shareholders after control had changed, or depressing the stock price by cutting the dividend or by other means. It could mean paying a premium to a predator for the stake he had accumulated (greenmail), or it could mean freezing the predator out by paying a premium for everyone else's shares (the Lollipop defence used in 1985 by UNOCAL against T. Boone Pickens). Fairness, it appears, is at a discount, but less than in those days. The SEC now requires an offer to be made to all shareholders, but not for all the shares.

The final step in the developing takeover saga came in the mid-1970s after Morgan Stanley decided to break with what had been accepted practice and act for a 'hostile' bidder. This marks an important turning-point. The focus was no longer a correction to a defective system of corporate governance—it was to do with empire-building: the skill of the management of the target company became an irrelevance (though it might affect the price). (A study by Herman and Lowenstein showed that there was a change about 1980. After then, broadly speaking—though there remain many exceptions—the target companies were as well managed (and sometimes better) than the bidders.) The dual nature of the market, which meant that there was generally a premium for control over the normal trading price, meant also that shareholders' attention was focused on the premium and scarcely on the quality of the management they were abandoning by tendering their shares (or for that matter on the bidder's management). That premium is remarkably constant—34% in 2001, 33% in 2002, 29% in 2003, and 25% in the first half of 2004—taking the bid price against the market price the previous day.

Many professional fund managers find the premium irresistible; indeed they feel legally obliged to accept a tender offer. It is as if a 'For sale' notice hangs over most of corporate America.

With finance available mergers have multiplied—there were 5,914 completed deals in 2003 worth $447,767,000,000.

Some years ago beleaguered corporate management cast around for ways of defending itself, and the ingenious legal profession produced some brilliant answers. In essence they were all based on a single principle. A company would set in place an arrangement which in normal times would lie dormant. Only a tender offer would activate it. Then, once the alarm bells rang, management could set the machinery in motion to change, grant extra shares, and so forth, the result of which would be to make it virtually impossible for the bidder to succeed. These were the so-called 'poison pills'. An alternative strategy was 'Crown Jewels', that is, to give a third party an option to buy a prime asset to stop the bidder getting it. Yet another was a 'supermajority' provision, for example, a requirement that there be a 75% majority to remove a board of directors. These devices were often challenged in the state courts (which might not necessarily produce consistent judgements), but generally they seem to have survived, at least in certain forms. And in most cases management introduced them without consulting the shareholders. 'Supermajority' provisions (which have in any case proved a less effective tactic) have to be approved by the shareholders.

Opinion is still divided on whether the shareholders have benefited. Two things seem to be true. On the one hand, entrenching management means that if there is a takeover bid the board can usually exact a bigger premium (from an opening price that would probably have been higher but for the protective mechanism). On the other hand, if no takeover bid is in the offing, shareholders fare worse if management is deeply entrenched. It must be remembered that two-tier offers were permitted and that any resultant non-accepting minority might be mercilessly squeezed at a later date: the principle of equal treatment for shareholders was and is notably absent. Poison pills have rarely if ever been swallowed—it is not their purpose, which is delay—but they have been effective in preventing hostile two-tier offers, which have all but disappeared. Companies with poison pills tend to fetch better prices than those without, because they strengthen management's bargaining position and bidders cannot go direct to shareholders over management's heads. However, they may deter bidders from attacking a company where management is incompetent. They are based on the principle that it is right for management to nanny shareholders and under-state the agency costs implicit in management's personal interests. Companies did not have to consult their shareholders before putting a poison pill in place, but shareholder activism has often targeted such arrangements and many have now been dismantled.

In a smart mixture of metaphors many companies have now 'dismantled their poison pills'—18 in 2002, 29 in 2003. They have now been renamed—more elegantly—as 'shareholders' rights plans', but new ones fell to a ten-year low in 2003—just 99. It looks as if 2004 will see a similar number of plans being dismantled as the previous year. Whether this will increase M&A activity remains to be seen.

After poison pills has come legislation. There have been some recent instances of normally leaden-footed state legislatures galvanized into instant action to protect some beloved industrial enterprise at the behest of the unlikely combination of its management and its labour unions. (The protective legislation for Armstrong World Industries and Norton are cases in point.) Indeed, some state legislation has been so overprotective that many enterprises, in Pennsylvania for instance, exercised their right to opt out, perhaps through fear that it might affect their share price adversely.

The Pennsylvania Statute is one of the most extreme and enshrines in law an 'other constituencies' clause: that is, directors are empowered to take into account constituencies other than shareholders when they make decisions—especially relevant in a takeover bid. The directors are exempted from suit from any interested party. The statute also contains a 'disgorging' provision which makes a failed bidder who sells his shares at a profit within eighteen months give it to the target company. Moreover, shareholders who acquire more than 20% of the shares are disenfranchised unless 'disinterested' share-holders have first approved their purchase (of more than 20%).

During the 1980s imaginative methods of financing takeover bids prolifer-ated, of which the most prominent was the issuing of bonds graded as being below investment level (junk bonds). Very often these were used as part of the arrangements by which existing shareholders were replaced by manage-ment in some combination with those who financed them (management buy-outs/leveraged buy-outs). LBOs are not new in the USA and were known in the old days as 'bootstrapping'. What was new was their number, size, and sophistication.

The LBO movement started quite quietly and was conservatively managed. Kohlberg Kravis and Roberts (KKR) were one of the leading firms organizing them. The principles on which they operated were to avoid cyclical indus-tries, ensure margins were adequate, and maintain careful supervision. From the point of view of corporate governance, the resulting structure could be compared either with a holding company or an active supervisory board whose meetings had substance. Operating management of the new entity (itself well motivated by its substantial equity stake) was generally given a free hand, but KKR (and other firms) stood in the background keeping a fatherly eye on the success of the new enterprise. Because of the conservatism of the original choice of targets many early LBOs were wildly successful. Companies which had been taken private were refloated a few years later at a vast profit. At the time of writing (2004) KKR announced a record distribution to its shareholders.

One of the main points of divergence between the interests of shareholders and CEOs is the quality of growth. Shareholders want long-term increases in income and value and may be prepared to make short-term sacrifices to achieve it, provided it is soundly based. That is, however, a slow grinding business, often beyond the span of office of a CEO. His temptation is to try to take the short cut—growth by diversification, aided by some accounting rules that often created an illusion of growth where little or none existed. With growth the CEO's status (and rewards) could be enhanced rapidly; acquisition is quicker than organic growth. However, the idea that manage-ment skills were always transferable across industries proved not to be true and led to the markets tending to price down conglomerates on the convoy principle, that is, a disparate group moves at the pace of the slowest main business in it.

By the 1980s, therefore, some of the unwieldy conglomerates assembled in the 1970s were looking vulnerable and duly became targets of 'bust up' LBOs (55% of completed LBOs in 1988). Tears need not be shed; what investment

banks had cobbled together in unholy conglomeration, LBOs might legitim-
ately rend asunder. Some of the early break-up artists made fortunes.

All these well-publicized successes attracted more players into the game
and competition became fiercer. Money was pumped in until at one time
there was enough to buy 10% of quoted companies. The prices rose to
amazing levels, so the financial burdens on the new entities became heavier.
Less attention was paid to the cyclical nature of business so that cash flows
and profits could very easily become insufficient to service the debt. And
supervision became laxer. The results of these excesses are well known and
with us still—restructuring and bankruptcies for businesses, bad debts for
bankers, junk bonds for investors living up to their name. Such movements
come in waves and many waves finally break on the rocky shore of Chapter
11—like Worldcom and Global Crossing.

The threat posed by the takeover market is more widespread than first
appears and is not confined to companies for which bids have actually been
made. Many have sought to render themselves unattractive by 'restructuring'
and were aided and abetted in this by investment bankers. One said in my
hearing at a public seminar in 1986, 'Restructure or our 26-year-olds will get
you.' Restructuring or recapitalization meant borrowing vast sums (which
were paid to shareholders), often at the same time retiring equity. The present
shareholders had a windfall, but the company was often so weakened that it
could not sustain a downturn in business. Academics who had preached the
virtues of leveraging as a new faith found gearing a dangerous god. Sad to say,
the effects of such policies have not yet worked themselves out.

It is unnecessary to explore the financial excesses of the 1980s and late
1990s in detail, fascinating though they are. Lowenstein, writing in 1988, was
among the commentators who felt that whatever virtue there may have been
at one time in using the market to secure management changes had long
since been outweighed by the cost and damage inflicted on US industry by
those who exploited apparent imperfections in the market to make massive
short-term gains. Displacing poor management is one thing; replacing good
management at great cost with a group that is no better, in a structure which
has less industrial logic, is quite another.

Commentary

When times are good and industry is flourishing, no one takes an interest in
corporate governance, however ominous the signs or flawed the hero in
charge. As Margaret Blair puts it, 'In good times, with markets growing,
capital cheap, and competition limited, almost any governance system can

seem to work well. The test comes when markets are flat or shrinking, capital costs are high, and competition is tough' (Blair 1991: 13). This test is here now. That is why there is so much interest in the subject.

There is no system of corporate governance in the world that is perfect. Companies, like people, are born, grow, and die. In the economic sphere what needs to be emphasized is the capacity for renewal and the avoidance of waste, in an ever more competitive environment. How does that of the USA shape up, in regard to the two universal criteria?

Dynamism

Management, however individual or collective, must be able to drive the business forward without undue bureaucratic interference, or fear of litigation, or fear of displacement. This is the first and crucial principle for an entrepreneurial free market economy in a competitive world. This is or should be the management's right and its charter.

The first potential source of infringement of this charter is government. No one doubts, however, that it is the government's task (whether at Federal or state level) to hold the balance between the competing interests in the economy—producers and consumers, employers and employees, providers and users of capital. Fifteen years ago there were very few complaints from the CEOs' side that government or state law as manifested by bureaucratic interference was considered an undue or unfair handicap, even though many governmental requirements impose costs (e.g. in respect of the environment). SOX and the subsequent rule changes have changed this perception, though few would say unfairly.

The ground is less certain in regard to litigation. In the USA the law is seen as a unifying force, a way of ensuring equality for all the heterogeneous elements in society. At one time the business judgement rule provided directors with a nearly impregnable defence against lawsuits alleging they had made a poor decision. In the case of *Smith* v. *Van Gorkom* a considerable dent was made because the Court ruled that the process by which the decision had been reached was inadequate. Over the last few years cases have moved further down this track. The rule still lives, dented it is true. Perhaps the feeling that litigation lurks in the wings is pervasive; it might be worth a behavioural study. Section 102(b)(7) of the Delaware General Corporation Law, which permits corporations to include in their charter a provision eliminating personal liability of a director for a breach of a fiduciary duty (except for breaches of the duty of loyalty or good faith) also put into corporations' hands a powerful weapon to protect its directors from lawsuits. And, if it can be obtained in the market, there is always directors' and officers' insurance, expensive as it is.

There are indeed some signs that the old common law concepts of loyalty and good faith may be getting a new lease of life. They were very much to the fore in a well-publicized lawsuit concerning the Disney Corporation and the compensation paid to Michael Ovitz on his dismissal. The London *Financial Times* made the most of it with a headline on 11 October 2004, 'Pension Funds test Disney on Governance', 'How Disney Crossed Delaware' on 21 October, and 'Directors Face a Disney Doomsday' on 25 October. The case made other headlines—including shareholder activism and proposals for some new independent candidates for the board.

There was much talk about outside directors being inhibited from accepting office because the threat of litigation outweighed any potential reward, though it was impossible to measure the effects. My own judgement is that it is an element to be considered, but not yet a matter for deep concern. If it became really difficult to find good candidates it would be truly serious because sound boards are the keystone of the structure.

As regards displacement, US CEOs do not in general look more vulnerable than their counterparts elsewhere. There is a great deal of discussion on the effects of the fear of takeover, and it is difficult to determine to what degree it exists, and what its effects are. To those who deny the existence of what they cannot measure, it is insignificant. How much fear of takeover matters depends on many variables, such as the vulnerability of the company, the personality of the CEO and his age, and the stockholding position. Certainly Americans' traditional robustness—about picking themselves up and starting again—would suggest that fear of displacement would not generally loom large, were it not for the vigour of their defence against bids, often far in excess of what might profit their shareholders, not just in the short or medium term but on any reasonable time scale.

We are dealing here with a psychological issue, in which the subjects may not themselves realize how deeply their thinking has been affected. A robust CEO who prides himself on his macho view of life may assert vehemently that market pressures mean nothing to him; he invests what he and his board feel essential for the long-term well-being of the company. And he may be wrong simply because subconsciously he has set his sights too low, in unknowing recognition of what his instinct tells him the market will stand. The important point to make is that the market, which in some ways acts as a spur, in others acts as a shackle, because of the complexity of managerial motivations. And managers whose firms 'go private' seem to relish the diminution of risk.

Business may be an economic activity, but man is not just an economic animal. He looks to his job for other satisfactions—the pride of construction, the warmth of camaraderie, and the excitement of mental stimulation. It is a source of power and influence and a means of recognition. These multiple satisfactions account for people working long hours after they have accumulated more riches than they could spend in a dozen extravagant lifetimes. They are the cause of CEOs defending their territory and achievements so fiercely, often in the face of economic logic. These are the reasons why the fear of takeover is so damaging—it absorbs the nervous energy that would otherwise go into the proper task of driving the business forward.

What are we to make of the economic consequences of takeovers? It is easy to accumulate a mass of literature on US takeovers and takeover defences and funding, some set out as blueprints, others as factual accounts, and others as drama like Bruck's *The Predators' Ball*. The language is colourful: 'poison pills', 'junk bonds', 'White Knights' and 'Black Knights'; and many of the principal players larger than life, dealing in billions. Some are disgraced; many bask in luxury. Is the USA the richer? The creation of real wealth can only come from investment and production, but the transfer of wealth is justified if in fact a better use of resources ensues. Hard evidence on whether 2+2 sum out to 10, 5, 4, 3, or less, is hard to come by. But there is no doubt that in the opinion of many US commentators (Eisenberg 1989 is one example of many) a large number of good businesses have been destroyed and many others emasculated.

It is part of the function of the market in the USA to reallocate resources to those who will make best use of them—over a reasonable time scale. The time scales of decision between investor and industry are totally different. An investor may decide to switch from a chemical company into textiles and achieve the change in a single telephone call. Company management, hemmed in by its present plant, people, and commitments, may take a decade to change direction radically. A system which places so much emphasis on shareholders' *immediate* values may be at a competitive disadvantage with others which take a longer-term view. There is a great entrepreneurial spirit and it is free, but not quite as free as it thinks it is.

Accountability

Some writers refer to 'The Imperial CEO', meaning that he is the master of his world. He is the hero who charges into battle, and, later after winning his struggles, rides off, rich and content into the sunset. Not for him the dulling and irresolute rumination of a committee. That atypical spasm in the 1980s when the more collegiate systems of Germany and Japan seemed to give them

competitive advantage has long since disappeared; their relatively poor showing in the 1990s seemed to confirm to Americans that their way was best.

The American recipe was not to ape the longer time scales those systems
facilitated, but to move smartly in the opposite direction under the banner of
'shareholder value'. This was interpreted to mean 'shareholders' immediate
value' and led to the tyranny of quarterly earnings, in which juicy options
plus a desire at least to match analysts' expectations led to the figures often
being massaged in ever more sophisticated ways. Officialdom stood by. The
processes of governance atrophied as boards met for too short a time and the
individual members had no opportunity, or leadership, or inclination, to
become more deeply involved. External auditors served the management who
often awarded them lucrative consultancy contracts, instead of serving the
shareholders.

As a general principle, the greater executives' freedom of action, the greater
the need for accountability. The two go hand in hand. The concept of
accountability in this context derives to some extent from its counterpart
in the political sphere, where it is the main prophylactic against tyranny.
A strong board and vigilant shareholders may be crucial in stopping a
dynamic and powerful CEO from running amok. In business, accountability
is essential as a means of maintaining standards of competence. The way in
which it is exercised is of secondary importance.

The general feeling in the USA among thoughtful commentators has for
many years been that US management is often not accountable enough. The
board does not often work properly, and shareholders seldom work at all:
management may fear the market but its tendency will be to entrench itself in
the ways described earlier and reward itself well enough to reduce the
financial consequences of displacement.

We can appreciate the gloomy summary at the beginning of Jacob 1991:

Lack of communication prevents investors from understanding management's long-
term goals and objectives. Shareholders trade stocks so often and hold such broadly
diversified portfolios that they cannot possibly keep up with the business activities of
the companies they own. Because most US investors are detached from the businesses they fund, they rely on outward manifestations of what is really going on
within the company; namely, quarterly earnings and other accounting measures of
performance. These numbers only measure the past; they do not explain the future.
When they are dissatisfied with corporate performance shareholders sell stock,
rather than trying to discern the causes of poor performance and using their
collective voice to communicate their concerns to management.

Companies exacerbate the problem by stacking their boards with directors
handpicked by top management and insulating themselves from the oversight

traditionally provided by shareholders and lenders. In recent years companies have consistently disenfranchised their owners; they want access to capital with no strings attached. But a lack of trust makes investors hesitant to fund projects with no visible results for extended periods of time.

Jacob's gloom turned out to be justified by the 1998–2001 collapse of high flying companies like Enron, Wordcom, Adelphia, Global Crossing, Tyco, and many others. In an address to the Commercial Club of Chicago, Illinois, in November 2002, Martin Lipton described the measures that will lead to a 'Tectonic shift in power away from the CEO to the board, board committees and Shareholders'. Many of them have been described in the discussions on board and shareholders. Lipton stressed the practical consequences, like allowing enough time for the board and its committees, especially the audit committee to attend to business thoroughly.

There is always a danger of making the mistake that because the quality of the people individually is high, the quality of the board as an *entity* necessarily follows suit. It does not. Many a company has foundered despite having good talent aboard. The dynamics of the board are largely in the hands of the CEO, who can make or mar it. In my conversations with many able ones I was struck by the way they seemed to fall into two camps: those who were very powerful and admitted it, and those who were very powerful and did not—though I cannot say with certainty which group used its board better! If some boards work better than others it is because the CEO wills it. The new reforms are designed to ensure he does.

The audit, compensation, and nomination committees, have as unspoken objectives the task of improving the board's dynamics, of giving the outside directors a real role, of deepening the flow of information, and of improving collegiality among the independent directors. The potential importance of the nomination committee is sometimes underestimated by those who do not understand the far-reaching consequences of the CEO's grip of patronage. The acid test of the balance of any board is its capacity to stand up to the CEO when really necessary. Of how many US boards is this actually true today? This capacity does not imply constant friction but the degree of reciprocal respect between CEO and director necessary for real accountability.

The second part of the problem concerns the accountability of the board to shareholders. In the USA, as elsewhere, weak CEOs and weak boards allow companies to drift and decline. In cases where shareholdings are widely dispersed the Berle and Means analysis (1932) is still valid—no one has the interest and few the knowledge to intervene. Now when shareholdings are becoming more concentrated the analysis no longer holds—there are many signs of action. In looking at the vast panorama of US companies and the regiments of institutional shareholders, it is clear that at the moment action is confined to few of the latter in relation to relatively few of the former. But the situation is changing.

Future Developments

At the end of the final chapter there is list of items that can be regarded as 'unfinished business'. There is some overlap with the following, as some themes are of international significance. Most of those below, however, are USA-specific:

1. Starting at the top, most companies resist separating the role of Chief Executive from that of chairman.
2. It remains to be seen how the SOX requirement for one of the members of the audit committee to be a financial expert actually works out in practice, both in regard to the standard required and to its effect on other members of the committee.
3. The rules governing the election of directors will continue to attract attention—especially staggered boards, plural voting, and the impossibility of recording a negative vote as well as abstentions.
4. The debate on transparency has focused on boards and market. The Enron case—and others—show that transparency between management and board may also be of paramount importance, and arguably comes first.
5. The recent emphasis on accountability was overdue. There will need to be a careful eye on the balance between that and drive. If board members see themselves primarily as monitors there might as well be a two-tier system. The success of unitary boards depends on a sensible balance being maintained. There could easily be too much process and not enough decisions.
6. Stopping fraud is important and the post-SOX world should make life tougher for the fraudsters. But 'the bomber will always get through'. Improving internal controls is proving expensive and doubtless it is generally a sound investment and there is a cost limit beyond which it is a mistake to go. When it comes to the transfer of funds the security of IT systems is paramount but one does not need a platoon of Marines to guard a cash box.
7. Despite the minimalists, Corporate Social Responsibility is a concept that will have increasing ramifications; but there is no point in being CSR-perfect, and bankrupt.
8. Shareholder activism is growing. We can expect it to become better focused and sharper, though not necessarily more public.

9. Accounting and audit will gradually become international, though this will be difficult for the USA to absorb given the fundamental difference in approach.

10. Possibly as a reaction to scandals, companies' ethics programmes are attracting more attention and many have specific officers assigned to them with a duty to report to the board. Most US companies have some kind of whistle-blowing procedures (86%). There is of course a distinction between compliance (which means obeying the law and regulations) and morality, which means behaving ethically in all circumstances. The company is now required by the SEC to adopt a code of ethics some elements of which are basic, like avoiding conflicts of interest, confidentiality, and compliance. Many executives are practising members of one of the world's great religions; do they all behave ethically all the time? If not, will a company code make the difference? An ounce of conspicuously ethical leadership is worth a ton of precepts and codes of ethics; and how does that sit with greed?

11. The governance rating game has begun, with ISS and S&P to the fore, as well as the Corporate Library. I counted nearly 100 items, some of which are common to all. It will be interesting to see how ratings develop—the weightings in particular, and how at the end of the day they cope with the behavioural unquantifiables which all on boards know well. The more that people believe that good performances and good governance go hand in hand, the greater the tendency will be to try to put numbers to the latter as well as the former.

12. Beyond SOX and all the governance reforms, most of which were arguably overdue, there lurks the danger of believing we can use structural solutions to solve behavioural problems. Total conformity to all the new requirements will not *of itself* produce results. It is how people behave that matters most—displaying the ancient virtues of candour, trust, and integrity. Without these, plus sheer competence, 'people', and leadership skills, we are doomed to disappointment. (Enron and Worldcom are examples.) J. A. Summerfield made this case with great eloquence in the *Harvard Business Review*, 1 September 2002 (ISSN Number 0017–8012). We have to see structure and process—even ethics statements—for what they are, road markings and signposts. Someone still has to pick the route and drive the car.

Annex 5: *Audit Committee Requirements*

NYSE Requirements	NASDAQ Requirements
Audit Committee Charter The audit committee charter must specify the committee's purpose, which must include (i) assisting board oversight of the integrity of the company's financial statements, the company's compliance with legal and regulatory requirements, the independent auditor's qualifications and independence, and the performance of the company's internal audit function and independent auditors and (ii) preparing an audit committee report that SEC rules require be included in the company's annual proxy statement. The charter must also detail the duties and responsibilities of the audit committee, including: • appointing, retaining, compensating, evaluating and terminating the company's independent auditors (this includes resolving disagreements between management and the independent auditor);	*Audit Committee Charter* The audit committee charter must now specify all of the duties and responsibilities of the audit committee under the Act, including: • Appointing, retaining, compensating, evaluating and terminating the company's independent auditors (this includes resolving disagreements between management and the independent auditor); • Establishing procedures for the receipt, retention and treatment of complaints from company employees on accounting, internal accounting controls or auditing matters, as well as for the confidential, anonymous submissions by company employees of concerns regarding questionable accounting or auditing matters; • Having the authority to engage independent counsel and other advisors as it determines necessary to carry out its duties; and

Continued

Audit Committee Requirements

NYSE Requirements	NASDAQ Requirements
• establishing procedures for the receipt, retention, and treatment of complaints from company employees on accounting, internal accounting controls, or auditing matters, as well as for the confidential, anonymous submissions by company employees of, concerns regarding questionable accounting or auditing matters; • having the authority to engage independent counsel and other advisors as it determines necessary to carry out its duties; and • receiving appropriate funds, as determined by the audit committee, from the company for payment of compensation to the outside legal, accounting or other advisor employed by the audit committee. *Note: The foregoing charter requirements correspond to the requirements of Exchange Act Rule 10A-3.* • at least annually: (i) obtaining and reviewing a report by the independent auditor describing the independent auditor's internal quality control procedures; (ii) reviewing any material issues raised by the auditor's most recent internal quality control review of themselves; and (iii) assessing the auditor's independence; • discussing the annual audited financial statement and quarterly financial statements with man-	• Receiving appropriate funds, as determined by the audit committee, from the company for payment of compensation to the outside legal, accounting or other advisors employed by the audit committee. *Note: The foregoing charter requirements correspond to the requirements of Exchange Act Rule 10A-3.* In addition, each issuer must certify that it has adopted a formal written audit committee charter and that the audit committee has reviewed and reassessed the adequacy of the charter on an annual basis.

agement and the independent auditor,

- discussing earnings press releases, as well as financial information and earnings guidance that is given to analysts and rating agencies;
- discussing policies with respect to risk assessment and risk management;
- meeting separately, from time to time, with management, with the internal auditors and with the independent auditors;
- reviewing with the independent auditor any audit problems or difficulties and management's response to such issues;
- setting clear hiring policies for employees or former employees of the independent auditors;
- reporting regularly to the board of directors; and
- evaluating the audit committee on an annual basis. The Company's website must include the charter of the audit committee and its annual report must state that the charter is available on its website and is available in print to any shareholder that requests it.

6

The United Kingdom

'O wad some power the giftie gie us to see oursels as ithers see us.'
(Robert Burns)

General Background

In the UK as elsewhere, corporate governance is set in the framework of its political and social history and attitudes. Here are some of the factors that have affected its development or colour its present-day execution.

Insularity/separateness

The narrow stretch of water that separates the UK from mainland Europe has enabled the country to be free of foreign invasion for nearly a thousand years. The gradual, but not always painless evolution of forms of government has created a confidence in its institutions which to this very day can be accompanied by suspicion about the institutions of others which have not stood the test of time for so long a period. In the background there is a history of gradual change; this is part of the price to pay for avoiding revolution, but it has meant change coming tardily. The recent spasm of interest in corporate governance, for instance, was precipitated by scandals; the underlying dangers were already well familiar.

Tolerance

The British Isles include several nationalities. There is a difference between being British (a broad concept) and the narrow concept of being English, Scottish, Welsh, or Irish, as the UK's sports arrangements demonstrate. The crucial point is that the two concepts coexist. The unseen benefit of this duality has been a residual tolerance and open-mindedness, especially since the seventeenth century, towards the different nationalities within the UK and towards immigrants from other countries' cultures, which has shown itself in an ability to accept and assimilate minorities as part of Britain who in their turn have added much to the country's cultural and commercial life. Huguenots, Jews, Muslims, West Indians, South Asians, and others have successively arrived and joined in. They have been able to preserve a certain sense of separate identity whilst feeling themselves British. From such people (uninhibited by the more enervating influences of the British aristocratic value system) have often come ideas and energy, thrust and entrepreneurial desire. The commercial strength of the UK has drawn advantage from the willingness of both majority and minority alike to accept this duality. Many of these communities came with a great reverence and respect for learning—which they imparted to their children. The success that this so often brings ought to excite emulation, but more often it causes envy. Absorption is facilitated by an honest and effective legal system—even though the UK does not share the USA's tendency to use 'due process' at the drop of a hat. So we find even today that 'rules' can have in practical terms the force of law without recourse to the courts being necessary most of the time (see below the Combined Code and the Takeover Panel's rules for instance). That this should be so often amazes others.

Trade and industry

Being an island with a limited domestic economy pushed Britain into overseas trade from earliest times, and the development of a merchant marine (with a navy to protect it, from Henry VIII's time onwards) meant that traders' horizons were broad; the world was their oyster. Many who lacked land at home ventured abroad in search of fortune if not fame, and this was socially acceptable too—indeed, admired, especially as the empire developed so that the traders could confer on people who in their opinion needed both the joys of Anglicanism and honest administration. Despite all the faults, the benefits conferred were far from negligible. The breadth of perspective of the old empire lives on in 'British' companies today. The successors of those who ran the East India Company, planted rubber in Malaysia, built railways in the Argentine, constructed Sydney Harbour bridge, are the new and committed in great multinational companies. Britain has for centuries looked outwards across the world and does so still and its horizons have never been limited to Europe, however important it is—hence the reluctance in recent years to pursue policies that might inhibit its facing two ways. Two of the world's great companies, Shell and Unilever, are binational (UK and the Netherlands, as it happens). Very many 'British' companies now do more business abroad than at home and they operate promotion policies that depend mostly on merit and little on nationality. Foreign companies which operate from the UK are welcome, and if they deserve admiration receive it.

At home the aristocratic settlement of 1066 survived and does so to this day to some degree—think of the monarchy, peerage, and honours system. As elsewhere, land was the basis of wealth, social influence, and political power, and trade was ancillary to it. It took the first Industrial Revolution of the nineteenth century to create a separate source of significant wealth. The growth of the Empire and the opportunities it offered for non-commercial careers plus the growing aversion to the physical effects of the Industrial Revolution (stimulated by the Church) produced an unusual effect. Being 'in trade' was regarded as socially inferior. Among the works which helpfully shed further light on industrial development and attitudes over the last 140 years are those by Wiener (1981) and Barnett (1986). The British establishment's approach to the question of industrial strategy was rooted in a Victorian mercantile conception of a myriad firms competing in a market place-industry. It was still often referred to as 'trade': 'the coal trade; 'the steel trade'. The establishment—politicians, civil servants, hired economists—had not yet grasped the twentieth-century concept, pioneered by the great American and German corporations, of the massive technology-led operation that conquers its own market almost on the analogy of a great military offensive (Barnett 1986: 275).

It does seem however that, not before time, the kind of respect and esteem so obvious elsewhere for commerce and industry is not as rare in the UK as it was. The enterprise culture has become bi-partisan. The interest in corporate governance is much broader than it might have been a generation ago.

Employees and unions

The anti-industrial bias of the ruling class/aristocracy was mirrored for many years by the Luddite or anti-capitalist attitude of trade unionists, many of whom were at best indifferent to the success of the enterprise which employed them. They felt alienated from it—not at all surprising given the past attitudes of so many owners and managers, and the fact that they did not greatly participate in its prosperity. This hostility or indifference sprang from the concentration of most nineteenth-century owners and managers on technology and production and their neglect of people. The UK has changed radically since 1979, to be sure: management has improved and so have attitudes generally. The unions have changed constructively both in

approach and structure. The practices in the best UK plants now demonstrate that the indigenous workforce is second to none if well led, trained,
and motivated. Japanese companies operating in the UK often find that the
plants they run are as efficient as those at home or even better. Even if the law
sometimes protects employees after a takeover or merger, people are often
dealt with like chattels, regarded as 'structural imperfections' in microeco-
nomics, and sometimes called 'livewire' in the computer world. Their right
to be informed—even about matters which affect their vital interests—is not
enshrined in UK law but the EEC now covers this aspect in Directive 2002/
14/EC. This applies to all enterprises that either employ 20 or 50 people (each
country can choose). It is significant that when the Bullock Report (1977)
advocated two-tier boards on the German model with employee representation on the upper tier, the idea was not supported by the unions, who feared
it might inhibit their collective bargaining.

Making money; making things

It is not an accident that the UK is a leading provider of financial services and
its manufacturing industry has been in decline for many years. Providing the
mechanisms for gathering savings for investment and providing the goods
and services society needs both render a valuable service to society. In the
UK, however, it has long been more acceptable socially to make money rather
than things. Being 'something in the City', or in a profession, or the public
service, would pass muster, so that is what the younger sons of the nobility
(kept off the land by the rules of primogeniture) and the aspiring
middle class generally did if they were going to enter commercial life. Their
natural habitat was the partners' desk, the bank, or the stockbroker's office,
rather than the management mess or boardroom of manufacturing companies. On the other hand British society has always been and still is
pragmatic. If people did choose industry and made an overwhelming success
of it, most doors would open to them—including the House of Lords.
Hugely successful retailers earn and get respect and honour to go with
their riches, but 'petits commerçants' are not to be found in *Who's Who*
any more than they are likely to become members of the Jockey Club in
Newmarket or Paris.

The decline of UK manufacturing has accelerated in recent years under
competitive pressure from low-wage/high-technical skills economies—and it
is not alone in this. Survival lies in inventiveness and sophistication, not
cheap labour; it also requires investment and a venture capital industry as
effective as that of the UK's competitors. The new industries are different
creatures from those that bore the burden of nineteenth-century moralizing.

One of the results of the drive for better corporate governance has been to enfold the financial as well as the commercial and industrial sectors. Furthermore with the Financial Services Authority now in the saddle, the investment institutions they supervise are under its beady eye in regard to the composition of boards and committees.

The adversarial approach and accountability

The working of many UK institutions reflects a preference for the adversarial approach. We see this pattern in Parliament, industry, the law, and sport. The UK distrusts cooperation, combinations, and cartels because it fears they will act primarily to their own advantage. Charles II's coterie of advisers—Clifford, Arlington, Buckingham, Ashley, Lauderdale—caused a word to be added to the language, and it was a word of opprobrium: CABAL. The rituals of destructive collective bargaining are matched by the adversarial nature of the customer/supplier relationship. It is a great relief for the UK that some of the worst excesses of both are diminishing. The UK is a sporting nation and the adversarial approach is generally conducted in that spirit; it is not generally so aggressive that it degenerates into warfare.

Behind the adversarial style lies a principle in the constitution for which one monarch was humbled by his barons and, four centuries later, another was executed and a third deposed. The principle was *accountability*, at least to the extent that the standards of the age suggested. It is not perfect even today, given the increasing control by the executive of the House of Commons, but it is palpable and ministers ignore it at their peril. Ministers themselves over the centuries have found themselves accountable to the ever-broadening electorate. It is one of the more curious features of the UK's arrangements that accountability, which has been so great a consideration in the political sphere, has counted for so little in the economic. This is a subject worthy of deep study, for it may be to blame for many of the UK's problems. The development of corporate governance this last decade has been aimed at redressing this imbalance.

Accountability should not be confused with publicity. The media understandably have a preference for a good story built around individual people. Tales about personalities sell more papers than paragraphs about products. They find their subjects generally willing, not to say eager, to cooperate. A few shrinking violets apart, the UK may be divided into two groups: those who enjoy publicity and admit it and those who enjoy it and pretend otherwise. The emphasis on individual responsibility which such publicity implies might be admirable were accountability real. As, generally speaking, it is not, the mixture of power and publicity often observably leads to problems.

The media can exploit the fall of their heroes as effectively as they facilitated their rise.

Enterprise

The negative attitude towards 'trade' has perhaps softened with information technology. It would seem moreover that there is another dimension—a growing understanding of the importance of enterprise. There is no word in English which quite conveys the flavour of 'entrepreneur', so in the best UK tradition the term has been adopted and incorporated. What is more its full significance is appreciated. As I write I have before me GEM—the Global Entrepreneurship Monitor 2003 providing UK and regional reports. Corporate governance attempts to institutionalize best practice, but entrepreneurship is about encouraging a state of mind which is constantly on the alert for opportunities to make money—a far distant call from the belief that the only way to live an honourable and constructive life was to choose a career at a 'fair' salary and thus avoid the need to grub about. Both attitudes are essential in a well-balanced modern society, but it is refreshing to observe that it is now widely understood across the political spectrum that the prosperity of the nation depends on getting that balance right. The importance of enterprise is being recognized too in the corporate governance debate. This started with the focus on accountability and very properly so given the scandals. But it has become recognized that this must not eclipse the importance of enterprise on which progress depends.

Gambling

Gambling is a particular form of enterprise. 'If you do not speculate you cannot accumulate' is an old adage. All enterprise is a risk, a gamble. As an element it is vital, and often fun; as a way of life, it is short-term and negative. Getty when asked whether he gambled replied, 'In business I take risks, having measured them; in your sense, if I wanted to gamble I'd buy a casino.' (Investors in hedge funds, please note!)

Gambling enjoys rather a special place in the UK. Merit is on the whole rather suspect because meritocracies are for the meritorious and most people are neither able nor energetic enough to qualify. Luck on the other hand is impartial, in that all can aspire to the fortune it bestows, whatever one's capacity or station. Fewer envious eyes are cast on Lottery winners than on the keepers of 24-hours-a-day convenience stores who accumulate wealth by toil and application. Gambling, whether on the races or the tables or in stocks, has always therefore been acceptable. Indeed, gamblers in shares are said to be positively virtuous by adding liquidity to the market: how much liquidity is optimal and how gamblers help in a crisis has never quite been explained. Even the terminology is confusing: many a bookmaker calls bets 'investment'. Many of the derivative instruments have their origin in risk management and are generally used for this purpose, but the risk they are hedging may itself be of the nature of either an investment (or trade) or a gamble. The borderline can be blurred. Many fund managers treat their investments as bets: they do not take much of an interest in corporate governance. A 'punter's' view of a horse is vastly different from that of a bloodstock agency: it is no coincidence that people are often said to 'take a punt' in shares. Perhaps it is the same the world over. In the UK it is as well to remember what an honoured place gambling has amongst its activities.

As a typical example of the UK's attitude we need look no further than the section on takeovers. The UK's system is so constructed as to ensure that any bid made without the target board's agreement is bound to lack crucial information—it is, in other words, a gamble. It is no surprise that hedge funds have taken such a hold this last decade; they are the apotheosis of gambling and far removed from traditional long-term investment on a 'long only' basis in the new jargon.

The role of government in corporate governance and the role of the law

When we consider the direct role of government in corporate governance we see it has been minimal. It has been the British tradition since the Conquest to let trade and industry get on with it within the law—and indeed to create a legal system that facilitated their doing so. Successful commerce has better potential for taxes. The system as designed in the mid-nineteenth century (based on the 1855 Companies Act) seemed to work quite well and most faults could be ascribed to the fraud or incompetence of individuals. There never was any guarantee that all businesses would prosper. There needed to be clear evidence of systemic malfunction before any action was taken. When there was a series of scandals in the late 1980s there grew a general sense that something had to be done. Even then, the government was content to leave it to a non-public body—the Cadbury committee—to do the hard work. The furthest it wished to go was to provide the (able) secretariat. It was a relief to them when the Report and Code found general favour. They could then smile sweetly from the touchlines.

There are many reasons for such an approach. Having read their Machiavelli, they knew that changes were bound to upset someone. Moreover it was not clear that what was called for was a legal response; even now it would be difficult to enforce at law some of the requirements of the Combined Code.

Legal process does not mix well with the normal conduct of business. Very sensibly they accepted the 'comply or explain' principle mandated by Cadbury and repeated in the Combined Code. It is then up to those whose interests are adversely affected to take appropriate action.

All societies have to decide the extent to which individual freedom must be curtailed in the general interest. The fundamental British attitude is that freedom is the natural state which should be staunchly guarded against proposed derogations by governments or others even in hours of the nation's mortal peril. The burden of proof lies on those who would propose restrictions—like abolishing or limiting the right to silence in a criminal trial. The Rule of Law is taken for granted, although the British Isles are the home of two quite different legal systems. The English (for in this one must exclude the Scots) feel a great sense of pride in the Common Law. Its gradual and pragmatic 'discovery' by the judiciary is in direct contrast to the systems based on codes like Roman, Dutch, or French law. The same contrast can be observed in regard to the constitution. The encroachment of statute law on both has narrowed the gap, but even so there is a distinct preference for organic development rather than tidy revelation which to this day affects the UK approach. The law once enacted generally commands respect: the UK may not always welcome EC legislation as effusively as its partners and may argue both the merits and details more thoroughly, but when it does accept it, it implements properly what it enacts. Confidence in the legal system has never, however, been matched by affection for lawyers and people want wherever possible to keep out of court. The laws of maintenance and champerty whose ancient names reflect their antiquity have only recently been modified to allow conditional fees, originally prohibited to restrain the legal profession from inciting the litigious poor and the litigious middle class who would have had to pay heavily for 'their day in court'. (We shall encounter the debate about the role of the law at various points, for instance, in considering the Takeover Panel.)

Laws and 'Soft' Law

Background

As in most economies there are three types of limited liability company operating in the UK: those quoted on a stock exchange, large unquoted companies, and small companies. Quoted companies are covered in this section. Towards the end of the chapter there is a separate section covering unquoted companies both large and small. Before we examine current law it is helpful to consider its historical origins as they affect attitudes to this very day.

There were from early times joint stock companies where ownership and management were separate from the start. The Muscovy Company founded in the sixteenth century is one of the first examples. Some businesses were incorporated under Statute or Royal Charter. In the nineteenth century, major enterprises like the railway companies needed to attract capital from a wide range of subscribers, and were financed by public subscription from the beginning. They had formal boards of directors, composed mainly of the 'Great and Good', which were quite separate from management. The directors of such enterprises may have held some shares but were not the sole or even controlling proprietors; and most of them had no management function.

Apart from a relatively small number of big enterprises such as these, incorporated under Charter or Act of Parliament, businesses in Britain up to the middle of the nineteenth century were run by sole traders or partnerships (often a family); their common characteristic was unlimited liability, which although not an absolute bar, was a considerable disincentive to expansion. The Act of 1844 was the first attempt to make incorporation easy, but as it did not introduce the principle of limited liability the residual risks remained too great. The principle of limited liability came with the Acts of 1855 and 1862. The directors were usually managers and owners as well; the 'board', if it met at all, was a perfunctory and formal affair—and it stayed that way even when in the effluxion of time some of the shares found their way into other hands. Only at a later stage, when the business grew, did formality creep in and the concept of a board become a reality.

Such businesses often stayed private for a long while, and either died or were absorbed. Of the successful a relative few were floated later; even so, they retained most of the characteristics of the family business with few if any outsiders on the board. Many of them, if truth be told, made the transition without changing habits, in the mistaken belief that it was they, the proprietors, who were conferring a favour on those who subscribed for some shares in their business, an error which occasionally persists.

The way in which people think about companies in the UK reflects this double ancestry and accounts for the continuing debate about boards and the role of directors. There is a world of difference between a committee of owner-managers in a private company and a board of a great public company on which no one owns more than a few shares, but the fundamental structure of both is identical. In law a company can organize the kind of board it believes it needs if it needs one at all; its shareholders can dissent if they wish.

The law

It is not surprising if the UK system is erratic since the legal framework which defines the governance of companies in the Companies Acts is extraordinarily sketchy. Defenders of the Act praise its 'flexibility'. It is open to doubt whether flexibility is double-talk for 'fudge'. 'Flexibility' implies a choice of means towards a given end; 'fudge' means obscuring or not facing the real issue. The intention of the Act is that management should be accountable to the directors and the directors to shareholders. In many cases it is clear beyond doubt that the intention is not met. Indeed it might be said that corporate governance in the United Kingdom exists despite the Companies Act, not because of it.

The legislators, realizing the Act's deficiencies, have had their legs under the table for some time, and various pronouncements and consultations have taken place. It would be premature to guess what will be in the primary legislation and what in regulations—and what will be left to 'soft' law. What is beyond doubt is that there has been a better and more thorough debate than for seventy years and some credit should go to the corporate governance movement which has sought it. It is to be hoped that at the end we will not wish to use that overworked Latin quotation 'The mountains are in labour—and out pops a silly little dormouse' ('Parturiunt montes, nascetur—ridiculus mus').

Transparency is a key element in accountability and the reforms have stressed its importance and increased the obligations on the board. This has increased the burden on NEDs (non-executive directors), as have their duties on board committees and their role in respect of internal controls. A conscientious NED today has a demanding job in any company—and it is worse if it is a supervised entity and he or she has to deal with the supervisors too. It will be no surprise to see their remuneration rise sharply. They must have adequate time to devote to an ever more time-consuming job. The point where their independence may be threatened will depend on their characters and their other sources of income.

The present UK law is contained in the latest of a series of Companies Acts, which seek to balance the interests of those concerned, for instance, would-be subscribers, shareholders, and creditors. The legislation has been under review for some time and there have been numerous consultative papers on various aspects. At the time of writing, 2004, a definitive text is awaited—and then it will have to go through all the parliamentary stages. It seems unlikely that this process will be complete before 2006 or 2007, though some changes may be introduced before then by statutory instrument. It is understood that a statutory operating and financial review (OFR) may become mandatory as a result of regulations to be laid before Parliament during 2004.

The 1948 Act was regarded at the time as a milestone in updating and modernizing previous laws; the 1985 Act is the current version, which must be read with the Statutory Instruments which supplement it, including Table A (which deals with aspects of management). It provides for various kinds of company including companies limited by guarantee and unlimited companies. These are not significant in the economy and are outside the scope of this book. All the rest are joint stock companies as defined in Section 683, with limited liability. Such companies are divided into two types, 'Limited' and 'Public Limited', and the Act provides that their names shall end with Ltd or PLC respectively. Contrary to what is sometimes believed, being a PLC does not mean that the company's shares are publicly quoted on a stock exchange. It does mean that the company has capital above a certain size (£50,000) (sect. i. 18)), and that it may, if it acts in accordance with the law, issue shares to the public, a thing which a Ltd company is expressly forbidden to do. There is, however, no restriction on the size of a Ltd company. Some Ltd companies and some unquoted PLCs are big: we shall examine some issues that arise from this later. It is, however, quoted PLCs that are the subject of this chapter. At the end of 2003 there were 2,123 on the London Stock Exchange and AIM together. Ninety-seven companies accounted for 79.9% of the total market capitalization; 147 had market caps of less than £2 million. The Act only provides for one kind of formal structure; there is no choice. Many other Acts bear on the way companies are run, for instance the Insolvency Act 1986 which, *inter alia,* defines the point at which it is unlawful for a director to continue trading. (And in effect removes from someone who does so the protection of limited liability, as well as imposing other penalties.)

All British limited liability companies, regardless of size, are registered at Companies House, a governmental agency. Basic information is available free of charge on the Companies House website.

'Soft' law

A bare knowledge of the relevant Acts is insufficient for understanding the regime under which UK companies operate. The Acts must be read alongside a series of rules and regulations which affect various aspects of business. Some are close to being laws, others are definitely not, yet command as much respect as if they were. At best, this way of proceeding secures flexibility and avoids the need for primary legislation at every turn. At worst such sanctions as there are seem inadequate to secure compliance. It rests on the shareholders to enforce them. If they do not, codes will not do the trick. In short, there needs to be an enforcement mechanism, 'private' if possible, public if necessary.

The main 'soft' laws are as follows:

(A) The Combined Code. This is the key document on the governance of fully listed UK companies and incorporates the conclusions of many reports including Cadbury, Hampel, Greenbury, Turnbull, Smith, and Higgs.

Its development illustrates the point made in the introduction about the UK's preference for gradualness, and the dislike of legislation. It was issued by the Financial Reporting Council (FRC) in 2003. References to it in this chapter are listed as CCCG/ n (n being the clause). The main principles are at Annex I.

(B) The Rules Governing Flotation and Continuing Obligations of Quoted Companies. These used to be administered by the Stock Exchange, but the powers have now been transferred to the Listing Authority Arm of the Financial Services Authority (FSA) which has replaced the 1998 Code annexed to the Listing Rules and made the necessary rule changes. The CCCG will apply for reporting years beginning on or after 1 November 2003.

(C) The Takeover Panel's Code. This is considered below in the section on takeovers.

(D) The Accounting and Auditing Rules and Conventions.

These change so often that I have not attempted to capture them all. But boards and audit committees will have to pay special attention to the changes that will flow from the internationalizing of accounting standards during the next years. The deadline for adopting them is 2005, and this means in practice getting accounts into the right shape during 2004.

The CCCG goes beyond rule setting and gives advice on how to comply especially on matters relating to Internal Control (following the Turnbull Report) and on audit committees (following the Smith report). UK companies with quotations on the New York Stock Exchange find that the Sarbanes-Oxley Act has an extra-territorial effect—more compliance to worry about!

Enforcement

The *Financial News* of 12–18 January 2004 reported that according to surveys by the Association of British Insurers (ABI) and Pensions Investment Research Consultants (PIRC), company compliance with the CCCG had improved sharply. The ABI say that 55% of the FTSE companies comply fully (2001: 40%). PIRC reported that in 1999 only one-tenth of companies in the FTSE asserted they complied fully but by 2003 this had risen to nearly 60%

(PIRC using their own standards said the figure should have been one-third). Even so, progress has been significant; remuneration seems to be a main stumbling block. Enforcement of the CCCG is based on the principle 'comply or explain' and it is up to the shareholders to decide whether the explanation is acceptable, and if not what to do about it—or about a situation where a company has done neither. Such monitoring takes time and effort so shareholders may well decide to act only where a breach is serious *and* a company is performing badly. It is possible, however, that by incorporating the CCCG in the listing rules, the FSA will police it more stringently, demanding compliance or a 'satisfactory' explanation. In the eyes of some critics, this could lead to 'box ticking'—formal compliance which falls short of delivering the desired result. In principle the FSA can now fine companies—and the directors as well—as a sanction for blatant failure to explain. It remains to be seen whether this degree of prescription, which is alien to the British approach, does in fact take hold and whether the FSA will spring into action.

The CCCG is relatively short and is based on principles. Each principle is supported by 'Code Provisions' and these do amount to detailed rules, compliance with which is a box-ticker's paradise. The main provisions of the CCCG are considered below in the appropriate places.

Reporting remuneration is now covered by 'the Directors Report Regulations 2002' and is therefore not covered by the CCCG.

The 'comply or explain' way of enforcement is not universally admired. In October 2004, the EU internal markets commissioner, Fritz Bolkestein said, 'We think the days are passed unfortunately for self-regulation in this area... the dangers involved are simply too great. We cannot afford to have other cases like Parmalat and Ahold.' He was speaking in the context of EU legislation to force companies to have independent directors on their audit committees. But the latest consultative document accepts it.

Sources of Finance

The sources of companies' finance are relevant to issues of governance because—to use the old English proverb—'He who pays the piper calls the tune.' Put another way, those who provide the finance have the possibility of wielding power or influence depending on the terms on which funds are provided and the willingness of providers to see what tunes they want played. We will deal later with the shareholders' rights and powers, but we should look first at the banks as they remain such an important element in financing industry to this very day.

The interesting feature about UK banks is that they have never seen themselves as having a governance role whether or not a company had access to the capital markets. In this regard their views differ greatly from countries where the banks played a much larger part in the development of industry (and it developed later). Even in times of difficulty banks are chary of getting too close, lest they find themselves 'shadow directors' within the meaning of the Insolvency Act 1986.

It follows from the nature of companies' and banks' views of one another that UK banks do not take equity stakes to cement the relationship with a customer or to secure influence. Historically the acquisition of such stakes has often been accidental; that is, they have been taken in lieu of debt as part of a restructuring. The general UK stance is that such interdependence is potentially dangerous. The banks consider equity stakes a poor use of funds and unnecessary for a relationship with clients: besides, there could be a conflict of interest between their role as lender and their role as shareholder. Moreover, if a bank has too much of its balance sheet in company shares it may be vulnerable if their value declines.

The banks' attitude towards governance is logical if we accept the premiss that their role is to provide short-term trade finance and that it is up to the markets to provide long-term equity. In reality life is more complex. The main instrument is the overdraft, which has to be repaid on demand. It is generally, but not always, secured, usually by a floating charge over the company's assets. This kind of finance is the one most used by small and medium businesses. Their preference for it rests on its simplicity and flexibility, and the fact that they do not have to surrender any equity. From the banks' point of view it simplifies lending decisions and is a perfect instrument in a 'stand-off'. In reality overdrafts are often rolled forward and become in practice part of a company's core capital; and in recent years there has been much greater use of term loans. None of these instruments, nor for that matter bonds, entitle the lender to interfere in governance matters unless there is a specific clause in the contract conferring such powers.

It can be argued that this arrangement leaves a gap, a sort of power vacuum, in which one of the parties with much to lose is powerless to affect events. This is not necessarily so, since banks can impose conditions on renewing facilities, but they seldom do so. Even so they can find themselves in the awkward position of being the arbiters of a company's survival. The crisis can be sharp and sudden and is all the more difficult for the banks to handle because of the underlying nature of the relationship.

In the UK there is no comprehensive system for collecting data about a borrower's total indebtedness, or a central bureau such as Centrale des

Risques to which a lender can refer. It is evident from many cases where a company has collapsed that most of the lenders did not possess the full facts; severe competition had doubtless impelled them to lend without asking the right questions, however injudicious this may appear with hindsight. With banks lining up to lend, companies could refuse to borrow from the inquisitive.

Just as competitive pressures can make banks lower their guard, so they can encourage companies to hit them as hard as possible by squeezing the last ounce from every transaction. Treasury departments become turned into profit centres; relationships become secondary to securing the keenest terms. It became common for a company to have a multiplicity of bankers and for relationships virtually to disappear except perhaps with a leading bank. Companies in trouble have often found it very difficult to deal with such a situation and difficult to hold facilities in place whilst problems were being settled or variations agreed. Companies ignore the banks' need to make profits too, overlooking the fact that forcing a marginal existence upon them was not costless. Complaints about a lack of loyalty when a bank financed a bidder (and some did) seem singularly ill placed from those who gave neither loyalty or headroom. If the value set upon a relationship is low, one cannot expect too much from it in an hour of need. Where loyalty had not been earned, companies get the relationship they deserve. Companies which maintain a key relationship even at a price have observably found they had bought a bargain.

There are no doubt varying views within the UK banking system about the role of the main banks. At a debate on 27 March 1992, Wyatt of the Midland Bank spoke in the following terms:

Short-term unplanned liquidity requirements and working capital are clearly where we should be offering services. We should not be used for long-term lending, while being happy that refinancing for long-term lending requirements in the market place can be carried out by corporate treasurers who can borrow as cheaply or more cheaply than a bank. However, relationship bankers should be given a more than equal chance at capital markets business. If banks are in a long-term enduring relationship of mutual trust then capital markets business is an area in which most relationship banks will want to be active.

The Stock Exchange

The London stock market has been active since the sixteenth century albeit in the early days on a limited number of stocks. By 1697 the authorities found it active enough to want to regulate it 'to restrain the number of ill practices of brokers and stock jobbers'. From those days to the present, with various vicissitudes, the market has continued to flourish. The Industrial Revolution hastened developments. Even for smaller enterprises the limitations of partnerships were exposed. Secondly, the bigger ones, like railways, needed to cast the net for capital more widely. In due course there were new Acts of Parliament governing joint stock companies. The stock market grew in size and importance both in its primary function (of raising capital) and its secondary role, of trading shares already issued.

The market capitalization of domestic quoted companies in trillions of dollars at 31 January 2004 was:

New York Stock Exchange	11.6
NASDAQ	2.9
Tokyo	3.0
London	2.5
Euronext	2.1
Deutsche Borse	1.1

Some idea of the size of share trading in London in 2003 comes from the London Stock Exchange, which reports a turnover of £1,877 billion in UK and £1,759 billion in international equities. There were 2,311 domestic and 381 international companies listed. The year saw 194 new domestic and 7 new international companies listed. The statistics published by the Federation of European Securities Exchanges in January 2004 quote the market capitalization of domestic equities (in euro millions) as 1,972,559, compared with Deutsche Bourse at 865,866 and Euronext at 1,680,242.

The Alternative Investment Market (AIM) saw a flurry of activity in the third quarter of 2004—91 companies were listed.

Thus the function of intermediating between savers and industry is shared by banks (and similar institutions) and the stock market in the UK as elsewhere; broadly speaking, the bigger companies get, the more likely it is that they will want and be able to tap the capital markets direct and also to see their shares quoted.

Although the UK has a relatively large number of quoted companies, many of them are quite small and in any case they only constitute a fraction of the total number of companies trading (most of which are private and unquoted). As in other countries the choice of when to take a company public rests with its shareholders, some of whom are likely to be directors with significant holdings. They contemplate flotation as a means of

- Improving the capital structure (by replacing debt by equity or by improving the debt/equity ratio).
- Realizing part of their investment to diversify.

- Dealing with succession problems.
- Dealing with taxation problems.
- Enhancing their status.
- Making take-over bids easier as they can use 'paper' as well as cash.

For many years those who sought flotation had little to concern them except the costs of the transaction. They had to conform with the regulations of whatever stock exchange(s) they chose and to the Companies Act, but they did not have to worry about officious non-executive directors (since there was no pressure to appoint them, and if any were chosen they were likely to be old friends or great names or both). The attitude of many proprietors was that the public were exceedingly fortunate to be able to participate and they themselves fully intended to carry on as before. The public were free to buy their shares or not; if they purchased they must be deemed to accept the package as it was, because of and not despite the company's leadership. Many directors have told me over the years that much the same argument was used to defend the issue of non-voting shares; namely, purchasers should understand what they were getting and not complain that it should be something else.

Who Holds Shares and How

Private shareholders

(These data are taken from Proshare's 2003 yearbook quoting official sources—page numbers in parentheses. This is a mine of useful information on many aspects.)

By the end of 2002 there were about 11 million private shareholders in the UK. This number has fluctuated over the years. In 1979 when the first employee schemes had been introduced there were only about 3 million. Denationalizations took this to 11 million by 1990, and further up to 15 million after the demutualization of building societies. Since then weak stock markets and the dot.com. debacle have led to a decline (pp. 3–7).

By the end of 2001 private share holders only held 14.8% of quoted equities compared with

Pension funds	16.1%
Insurance companies	20%
Overseas holders (including institutions)	31.9%
Investment trusts, other financial institutions, banks	14.2%

This decline is dramatic. As recently as 1957 the personal sector owned nearly 70% of quoted equities; this had fallen to about 20% by 1989. The position is reflected in stock-market activity. By 2000 it accounted for only

8.25% of total customer business (1987: 21.6%); 54% of portfolios were less than £10,000, 18% were more than £50,000 (p. 33). Predictably 74% of private shareholders come from the wealthier socio-economic groups (A, B, and C1). In fact it is group C1 that shows the sharpest growth—from 29% in 1993 to 37% in 2002.

C2 and DE holders had dwindled to 26% (from 38% in 1993) (p. 30). Nearly a quarter of all shareholders live in the greater London area. (p. 29).

To set the present position into context, the personal sector held £2,428 billion of financial assets by the end of 2002, but only £382 billion was in shares and of these £137 billion were quoted UK shares (and £117 billion in unquoted shares) (pp. 13–14).

UK shares are held in registered form. The registrar is not obliged to record the name(s) of the beneficial owners and in practice most shares are held in nominee accounts ('street names') as a matter of administrative convenience. In such cases the beneficial owner does not receive any communication from the company unless he requests it, and this may be costly. Companies have the right under section 212 of the Companies Act 1985 to seek to know who the beneficial owners are and to withhold dividends if they are not told (a sanction which is only effective if the company is paying dividends!). Shareholders can instruct the company to do this so they can know who owns it. The DTI has produced a model 212 notice.

In recent years CREST has been set up to act as the central securities depository for the UK market. Shares are held electronically rather than in paper form. Private holders can use it via a sponsor (generally a stockbroker), and it will forward the company's materials to them.

American depositary receipts

American depositary receipts (ADRs) are a convenient way for Americans to own shares in foreign companies including some UK companies. In essence they are receipts for shares and are tradable instruments. The share certificates themselves are held by an American bank which issues the ADRs, then collects dividends and distributes them to ADR holders after converting them into dollars. The ADR holders have some shareholder rights, but BP was able to stop them filing a resolution.

Directors and Boards

We can now turn to corporate governance in its various facets, accepting as a starting point the definition in the Cadbury report that it is the system by which companies are directed and controlled. We shall consider in turn:

- the formal legal position in relation to directors;
- different classes of director;
- board structure and composition;
- the appointment and dismissal of directors;
- the chairman;
- the Chief Executive Officer;
- the company secretary;
- committees of the board.

Directors: the position in law

The legal structure rests on very simple principles. The owners (shareholders) appoint agents (directors) to run the business, and the directors report annually on their stewardship. The directors can delegate their powers but cannot abandon them. In practice in PLCs there is therefore a two-link chain of accountability, management to directors, and directors to shareholders. The Companies Act 1985 (section 282) requires all companies registered after 1 November 1929 to have at least two directors. There is no distinction between classes of directors, for instance, between 'executive' and 'non-executive', only obscure references to a 'chairman' and little mention of a 'board'. Any duties laid on directors, for instance, to prepare annual accounts (section 227) and laying and delivering annual accounts (section 241), are laid on them all, and they are all guilty of an offence (section 243) if section 241 is not complied with. On this extremely narrow legal base, which Table A does little to widen, is the whole edifice of UK corporate governance constructed. The various parts of superstructure as we know it—boards, board committees, chairmen, non-executive directors—are pragmatic adaptations. In law none is essential; to this day even the biggest company could legally be run by two directors, like the Consulate of the Roman Republic.

Directors owe a company (in common law) a duty of loyalty and a duty to put its interests before their own: they must act in good faith. They are expected to bring to their duties skill and care, but the precise nature of the obligation this imposes is far from clear even now. The Penrose report into Equitable Life, for instance, said that the standard of skill required there included deep knowledge of actuarial matters. The implications of this are far reaching.

The general requirements of the common law are, so to speak, the armour directors must wear when they undertake the office. The series of Reports and Codes ending with the CCCG do now provide for better structure, process, and standards. The Companies Act and other pieces of legislation lay specific duties on them—as do other pieces of regulatory bodies like the Stock Exchange and

Takeover Panel. For what directors should actually do (as directors) we have to look elsewhere. 'Guidance for Bank Directors' (GBD), published by the World Bank, contains a useful summary, most of which is applicable generally.

Different classes of director

Language often contains important clues about attitudes and sometimes about misconceptions. The popular term for an 'outside' director in the UK is a 'non-executive director' (NED). The use of the negative implies that not having executive powers is special. In law the reverse is true. In many ways the US term 'outside' or 'non-management' director is preferable. The Companies Acts do not require directors to be managers; they require directors to see that the business is properly managed, which is quite a different matter. In law there is indeed only one class of director and all are equal—or, at least, nearly equal. Any qualifying adjective is descriptive but not in law definitional. A 'finance director' or 'marketing director' is simply a director who has responsibility for specific executive functions. Strict logic would render the term 'non-executive director' superfluous. In law it is the norm. This may sound like an exercise in semantics, but it conveys an important reality—that being a director imposes a quite different set of responsibilities from those which attend any specific executive function, a fact which is not always appreciated by directors who are also executive 'barons' with responsibility for sections of an enterprise.

Nowadays there are two classes of NED, and the focus is on those who are independent of management. There are various definitions of what constitutes independence, the most important of which—attitude—is subjective and unmeasurable. It is generally held that independence is threatened by familiarity, so staying on a board too long jeopardizes it, as does any kind of other relationship with the company or its leading lights, including having been a senior executive. NEDs who are not classified as independent may yet be of service to the board, but are not qualified to sit on the audit and remuneration committees.

Only in recent years has it become generally recognized that being a director requires a set of skills and a range of knowledge that even the ablest manager may not possess and that therefore at the very least some special training, in whatever form, should be available. The CCCG (69–75) covers the appointment of new directors from various angles—a checklist for them, and an induction checklist. But it is still assumed that a director's skills are a natural development of those of a manager and that this includes how to behave on the board. This is not necessarily true, and many a good manager has failed to shine there. Perhaps the Guidance on evaluating the performance of the board (CCCG 77–9) will lead to an improvement in interpersonal skills on the board—so necessary if able individuals are to be welded into an effective team.

Research for the Higgs review conducted in July 2002 revealed that there were 3,908 NEDs in UK listed companies and 80% of these held only one NED post; the average age for a director of a company in the FTSE was 59. PIRC reported in January 2004 that they had been able to identify only six NEDs in FTSE companies aged less than 40—and one of these was the chairman's son. Another survey showed (*Financial Times*, 1 August 2002) that Parliamentarians held 819 directorships (640 Lords, 179 Commons)—though these included unquoted companies. As for women, 2003 saw them hold more than 100 FTSE directorships for the first time. According to a study of 94 companies, mostly from the FTSE 250 by PriceWaterhouseCoopers in 2001, a NEDs average age was 58 and the average time in their present post was six years. There tended to be more NEDs in financial companies (median 8 against 5).

The appointment and dismissal of directors

In practice all directors are appointed by the board and elected by the shareholders (who also have the power to remove them by ordinary resolution—and they can convene an EGM to do it). Shareholder nominations are rare for quoted companies (except perhaps when companies are in deep trouble), though quite common for small companies where a supplier of venture capital may wish to nominate a director or two.

In the case of executives appointed as directors the dominant voice is that of the CEO, whose subordinates by definition the others are. By the same token it is he who will in practice have the prime responsibility for removing them if they prove unsatisfactory and sometimes, power being what it is, if they are exceptionally good and a threat to him. The CEO himself can be removed by the board; strangely enough this happens more often when the board is dominated by executives than when it is dominated by non-executive directors. There have been occasions recently where the shareholders have intervened directly to unseat a CEO and change a board by exerting pressure (with the stated or implied threat of a vote); there are on the other hand many examples of board coups. It is the UK style for these things to be managed rather noisily; not for the UK the quiet tap on the shoulder and the discreet shunt sideways that typifies the Japanese system. Of course there is nothing the media enjoy more than a public fracas, especially if some of those concerned are already public figures. The media therefore had a field day at the General Meeting of Euro Tunnel in 2004, where some shareholders staged a revolt against the company's top management and removed two of them, replacing them with their own nominees. Such a move is rare.

Non-executive directors are a different matter. In the old days the search tended to put status and compatibility before relevance and acuity; the candidates often preceded the specification; like the Queen in *Alice in Wonderland*, the verdict preceded the evidence. The pioneering work of PRO-NED in the 1980s did much to bring better order. The CCCG (A4) requires a 'formal, rigorous and transparent procedure' and then in a series of Code provisions lays the responsibility on a Nominations Committee. This does not preclude its members considering successively people known to them personally or to advisers and friends. The TPRG/3I 2002 survey shows that 28% of appointments were made as a result of personal contacts. The use of professional search firms has increased. The committee's work is summarized on pp. 67–8 of the CCCG and it has to be described in the annual report (CCCG: A4.6).

The CCCG covers in detail the re-election of NEDs stressing the need for defined terms and setting the normal duration as two three-year terms. If an NED stays longer than nine years he must be re-elected annually and his status as an independent may be at risk.

The dismissal of non-executive directors is an important and neglected subject. It is not mentioned in the CCCG. The shareholders have the power to do so, but company Memoranda and Articles sometimes give the board this power too (the EMAP case some years ago for instance). Unless the articles do so permit a board cannot dismiss a director (though it can strip him of executive powers if he has any), though I notice an increasing tendency to introduce such a provision. On this crucial fact rests the shareholders' main power and directors' independence. Of course, if they wish him to resign they can make his life uncomfortable, but they have no right to force him out—even after a takeover. In practice the unwanted generally go, often with a *douceur*. And sometimes the shareholders' interests are badly served by their leaving. The chairman is chosen by his fellow directors and they can equally cause him to stand down; but in practice cases are rare of a chairman being removed against his will and yet remaining as director.

Where a group of board members—or an individual—is actually or effectively the controlling shareholder, no other director has any security of tenure; all are there at the will of the shareholders. This was true of Robert Maxwell's directors on Maxwell Communications Corporation and Mirror Group Newspapers which finally collapsed in 1991, and remains true of many a smaller PLC where the family retains control. What this boils down to is that in such companies, rather as in private companies, the board is basically an advisory committee to those who exercise power. This also applies to the outside directors on the board of a wholly owned subsidiary. Such appointments may be extremely useful to the company and are to be welcomed; many a company of this sort will acknowledge the debt it owes to directors whose experience and wisdom have proved invaluable. They can only act as monitors to the extent that those with power permit it. They themselves may have influence, but they have no power. Those who control the business are in effect accountable to no one but themselves (unless they constitute the board of a quoted company; in which case they are answerable to its shareholders). The presence of outside directors should mislead no one that they have power, even though the CCCG has strengthened their position by its support for the committee structure and reporting requirements. The practical problem is that even if the institutions invest in such companies they may be too small for them to take the actions necessary to enforce the code effectively—short of gross scandal.

Resignation on grounds of fundamental disagreement is a non-executive director's ultimate weapon and it appears to be most useful as a deterrent or if it is feared it may make a big bang. A quiet retreat 'to concentrate on other interests' has generally not helped to protect shareholders' interests: arguably it would have served the company better had the resigned stayed on, however uncomfortable, to continue the struggle. Few directors have resigned noisily, partly because of potential damage to the company, which is the last thing they want, partly because of an understandable lack of relish for a fight. Few resignations signify. If there is only one director, no one notices. If there are more than one, and one resigns, it seldom makes a stir. Resignation is a weapon of dubious value; any virtue it may have is associated with publicity and, if there are several directors, with joint action. The existence of the Senior Independent Director and of a separate chairman should help to make non-executives more effective in action—and action is undoubtedly better than resignation. It would be idle to pretend that life will always be easy for them. The removal of a chairman, for instance, still poses problems.

The old regime in which a director might be appointed for his name and little else has gone. Anyone reading the CCCG will note the much greater degree of professionalism now expected at every stage, from the nomination and appointment process right through to stringent and regular appraisals. Furthermore the range of duties has in practice been greatly extended, largely because of the growing importance of the Audit Committee (the Smith Guidance CCCG 43–58) and the Turnbull guidance on internal controls (CCCG pp. 27–41).

At least NEDs are better paid than they were. The TPRG/3I 2002 survey found that the average remuneration of an NED reflected the size of the company (by turnover). The biggest paid £43,500; companies with a turnover between £31 m. and £100 m. paid £25,000. In both cases the payments included payment for board committees. The more the NEDs do the more they should be paid; at what point does independence become threatened?

Furthermore the Equitable case has shown that D&O cover may be insufficient to save a director from ruin, so discussions are taking place to see whether their liability can be capped without creating a moral hazard.

Board structure and composition

Structure

Boards are not mentioned in the Companies Act where it might be expected, but in odd places like schedule 6 as amended (whether a connected exposure is sufficiently material to be reportable) but nowadays practioners look to the Combined Code rather than the Companies Act for guidance on the work of the board.

The UK never developed a formal two-board system. There was a separation of function of a sort on the boards (or courts) of chartered companies and many of the early joint stock companies. Few if any of the board had executive functions (and the same was true until quite recently of some of our joint stock banks), so it acted in effect as a supervisory board. The chief general manager (whatever his title) gathered round himself the group that managed the business and this in due course became an executive committee or management board. This informal kind of two-tier system persists within the UK to this day in many companies, but few have wanted to formalize it. The idea of a formal supervisory board became anathema because it might facilitate employee representation as was recommended in the Bullock Report (1975) and ever since the issue of employee representation on boards has been dead; neither employees nor unions wanted it then and few would advocate it today. It has not been part of the Labour government's programme.

We shall return to this issue later. With the UK system in its present form many companies have an executive committee, which is similar to a management board in a two-tier system. There is however an overlap of membership—the CEO, the COO if there is one, together with some functional directors like the finance and personnel directors. If there are more executives than this on the board, there is always a danger that the executive committee will act as a caucus before board meetings. The more executive directors there are, the more difficult it may become for them do other than 'toe the party line' at board meetings. This makes it more difficult for the non-executives to get at the heart of the matter since so much of the real discussion will have been pre-empted. The effect of the CCCG will be to reduce this possibility if only because directors' duties have now become more explicit and they will not suffer being bypassed. There is however a new possibility in regard to institutions supervised by the FSA. Their regime is becoming so intrusive that there is a danger of its being de facto a supervisory board—a danger that may increase with staff numbers and experience there. A further complexity is the overlap between board and audit committee which we consider below. There is indeed a tension between using committees to expedite the board's business and the danger that in doing so the board's role will be pre-empted. It is up to committee chairmen and the chairman of the board to see this does not happen. It would certainly help if all the independent directors were financially literate up to a reasonable standard; it is part of basic competence.

Composition

There has been a constant shift in the composition of UK boards towards a greater proportion of non-executive directors (NEDs). As far back as 1973, the Watkinson report for the Confederation of British Industry (CBI) commended their use. The effect of the Codes of best practice over the last decade has been to make non-executive directors mandatory in quoted companies—CCCG Principle A3: 'The board should include a balance of executive and non-executive directors (and in particular independent non-executive directors) such that no individual or small group of individuals can dominate the board's decision taking.'

The 2003 Annual PIRC Review shows what a great change there has been over the past decade. Only one company in the FTSE 100 had no NEDs (W. M. Morrison). In 76% NEDs constituted a majority, with an average of 6.7 for companies in the FTSE 100. Even mid-cap companies had a majority of NEDs in 51% of those who responded to the survey.

All these statistics must of course be interpreted in the light of the sample of companies from which they were drawn. Even so a fairly clear picture is emerging. The Audit Committee Institute (ACI) reported in its September 2004 quarterly issue that returns from the FTSE 100 companies showed that there were twelve directors on average; half were independent NEDs; and that the board met nine times in the year. The audit committee had an average of four members and met four times in the year. The remuneration committee had four members and met five times in the year. The nomination committee had five members and met three times in the year.

Independent directors under the CCCG (A.3.1) have to be identified in the Annual Report. Although the conditions are quite stringent, some commentators are even more severe, notably PIRC, who take a tougher line on two of the elements that might weaken independence—previous service as an executive, and length of service as a NED. (This has to be taken into account when using their tables.) The fact remains that on any reasonable definition the proportion of independent NEDs on UK companies of any size has greatly increased and is increasing. This is just as well, as the CCCG requires audit committees to be composed entirely of independent NEDs, one of whom has recent and relevant financial experience (CCCG C3.1). Independent NEDs also form the remuneration committee (CCCG B2.1) and should constitute a majority of the nomination committee (CCCG A41).

The UK system imposes severe strains on all participants, but particularly on the non-executive directors, whose range of responsibilities has been extended, latterly by their role in relation to risk and controls following the Turnbull report. On the other hand their position has in some ways improved. In days gone by a non-executive director might often feel alone, fearful of raising what seems an obvious point or checking a basic assumption which executives treated like the laws of the Medes and Persians. Nowadays the better balance between executive and non-executive directors, the division of the top role, and the identification of a senior independent director (SID) mean that they should not feel isolated. Moreover the chairman is expected to hold meetings with the NEDs without executives being present (CCCG.1.3), and the SID without the chairman being present.

Even with this improved structure, it is not a job for the bashful or timid and requires courage; and yet he or she is part of a team so that firmness must never degenerate into abrasiveness. Non-executive directors must position themselves correctly knowing which issues to consider and which to ignore; not for them the crystalline delineation of authority that goes with the formal powers of a supervisory board. They must have a clear concept of their role combining as it does both a strategic and a monitoring element. Their value to the company lies in part in considering difficult issues with sympathetic objectivity, seeing them in the broad context of the company as a whole, and questioning the critical assumptions on which proposals are based. If they become unnerved they may find their critical faculty dulled.

Even if an NED satisfies himself he has done all that a reasonable person could do, and has displayed all the requisite virtues of loyalty and integrity, he may still be at the mercy of dishonest executives whose actions are difficult to penetrate if the conspiracy is well enough organized even to deceive the auditors. Furthermore some recent cases have illustrated their vulnerability to lawsuit if things go wrong, despite D&O insurance. We consider litigation separately below.

It is observable that a board's dynamics are as important as its structure. Structure is the handmaiden of dynamics, not vice versa; the rules rely on the board operating effectively as an entity. This is difficult even for its members to ascertain, let alone outsiders: three people who have attended the same meeting often have a totally different perception of how effective its process was. Some chairmen who regard themselves as models of unassuming collegiality are regarded by colleagues as unreconstructed autocrats. These considerations are of greater importance in companies on whose boards there is a dominant personality, often by virtue of the shares he controls. What matters is that the board should consider and take decisions in an informed way on what counts; that the executive should be competent enough to drive the business forward; and that the board should be strong enough to say 'No' when it feels it must. This is the acid test. It may sound negative but it is based on an important principle, that of reciprocal respect. If a CEO and the board do not respect each other the system will not work as it should.

Because dynamics are so difficult to judge, we do have to rely on structure to give us some guide about whether they are likely to be satisfactory, but it is only a guide. If pay goes wild it suggests the board isn't working well whatever its structure may look like. Boards of all shapes, composition, and size have been known to work—or not. But if they fail the acid test—the saying 'No' test—they are not really boards at all but advisory committees.

The 2004 survey carried out by IRS—Independent Remuneration Solutions—in conjunction with the 3I independent directors' programme, states that there is additional pressure on NEDs and the chairman but this leads to better use of their time—better information before meetings, more contacts with the institutions, and more informal meetings at which the NEDs can speak their minds more freely.

The size of the board

Anyone who is used to committee work knows that the bigger the committee the more difficult it becomes for each person to contribute. Size is inhibiting and time runs short. A cynic might suspect that this used to inspire company chairmen to overpopulate their boardrooms.

The data in the following paragraphs come from the 2003 Corporate Governance Annual review published by PIRC.

The average size of boards fell slightly from 8.6 to 8.5 directors during the year. Companies in the FTSE 100 index had 11.4 and small-cap companies 7.3. The largest board in the sample was HSBC with 21, but 7 companies had 4 directors or fewer. There is an iron law which states that the larger a board or committee the more certain it is that the real business will be done by a caucus or subcommittee. The CCCG says that boards should not be so big as to be unwieldy. I think that boards of more than, say, 15 should be viewed with suspicion.

Frequency of board meetings

Of UK boards 72% meet monthly or more—or at least nine times a year (Top Pay Research group/3I Survey 2004). There are many variations; 89% meet separately to discuss the budget or strategy. (Some have two-day strategy meetings in some comfortable retreat; and peregrinations to less comfortable seats of distant operations.) Only 6% meet quarterly or less, but it is surprising to find among them the boards of some quite substantial businesses. Meetings of the board committees tend to cluster round main board meetings for convenience. The total number of days a director must commit varies a little with the size of the company—18 for the smallest, 28 for the biggest.

The chairman

One of the disadvantages of the 'CEO' title is that it implies the summit of power and almost by definition makes the chairman's role 'non-executive'. Part-time he may be—and usually is—but he still retains some executive authority in relation to the board and perhaps more besides. The aggregation of power which occurs when the roles are combined, as is still usual in the USA and France, is seen as potentially dangerous; it benefits the company to have better checks and balances. Besides, the jobs are too much for one pair of hands. If the concentration of power exists without such checks it is only too easy for the unscrupulous to be corrupted by it. There are circumstances in which it is sensible to combine the roles—especially in the short term—but if the board decides to do so it must carry the shareholders with it by a suitable explanation in the Annual Report and nowadays there will usually have been informal discussions with major shareholders beforehand. Increasing pressure from the Cadbury report onwards has resulted in most major companies splitting the role of CEO from that of chairman. In the PIRC sample it was 90%; a company which still combines the roles has to justify itself, but some do not (14% of the rather few non-compliers).

It is worth adding that although general sentiment is against the dual role in the UK, supporting the CCCG, some other countries remain to be convinced. There is some research on whether it adds value but the outcome is indecisive.

The chairman's position in the UK is indeed a strange one. In law there is no such post as chairman of the company but he is mentioned in sched. 6, para. 3 (Companies Act 1985 amended 1989) as a person elected by the company's directors to chair their meetings. There is no requirement in law to have a board, so it follows there can be no requirement to have a chairman of the board, let alone a chairman of the company.

That statement of the formal position is about as far away as it is possible to get from reality. Almost every company in the land has a chairman. In practice, of course, directors tend to meet in committee—that is the board—and they choose someone to chair it. From this has sprung the notion that the chairman of the board is something more. The role of the chairman varies greatly, depending on the size, complexity, and nature of the business, the division of duties with the CEO, and the amount of time devoted to the job. There is no set pattern in the UK. Most chairmen are part-time, giving perhaps a day a week to the company or even less: others are full-time, or nearly so. Circumstances alter cases: if there is a crisis, like a takeover bid, even a part-time chairman will find himself in overtime. When the survey was conducted for the Higgs review in July 2002 there were 1,689 chairmen posts in UK-listed companies. The average age of a FTSE company chairman was then 62. Almost 40% were 65 or more. Their post takes time—between 54 and 60 days a year for companies with a turnover of >£100 million—going down to 33 days for the smallest.

As this is so the CCCG (in A.4) sets it out as a supporting principle that appointees to the board, especially the chairman, should have enough time for the job. In this, had they but known it, they were echoing part of the advice given to the Bank of England in 1697 on appointments to the Court, all of which still reads freshly: 'Men of opportunity that have time and leisure from the crowd of other Affairs; for if a person cannot give his Attendance he will be but useless to you . . .'.

Over-commitment still attracts adverse press comment and the *London Evening Standard* ran an article on 19 March 2004 under the headline 'Britain's empty chairs crisis'.

There has been a debate on whether a CEO should be allowed to become the chairman of a company in which he has been CEO— prohibited under CCCG A2.2. unless there are sound reasons. It is in fact general practice in Japan but the circumstances there are different.

The division of duties with the CEO will reflect their respective capacities and inclinations. A chairman will often handle some or most external relations and be so to speak the public face of the company. But this is not clear cut, and the cake is observably cut in various ways. So much depends on personalities. Even when a powerful CEO is the person most in demand the chairman may find himself with a substantial ambassadorial role. The chairman may have a crucial contribution to make in setting the tone for the business externally and internally; his example is of the greatest importance. There is one responsibility every chairman has and it is of vital importance— the running of the board.

It is impossible to overemphasize the chairman's role in regard to the board (see CCCG A2). It is his task to get the size, balance, and composition of the board right (with his board colleagues' help, of course). He is responsible for the agenda—nothing important missed, nothing trivial included. He must insist on appropriate and timely information (which emphatically does not mean swamping directors with wheelbarrows of computer printouts of peripheral value). And he must conduct the meeting in such a way as to ensure he gets the best from those present. In many of these things he will be working closely with the CEO, but one thing is absolutely personal: he must display at all points the utmost integrity. He sets the tone. Any chairman can 'fix' the composition of the board or the agenda or the information or the meeting. It is no wonder that two boards with identical structures may be quite different in their effectiveness. It is the possibility of such extreme variation that underlines the importance of the role of the non-executive directors—and as we shall see later, requires the active vigilance of the shareholders. With such a range of responsibilities the chairman has considerable influence and some power—as can be seen when he steps down and a successor takes over.

We find that almost every company report contains a chairman's statement, sometimes as if he or she personally had something to say that was in some way different and separate. Shareholders welcome a succinct report on policy, progress, and prospects, and it does not matter who puts a name to it, as long as it is clear they are writing on behalf of their co-directors, who ought at least to have a chance to clear it. It may hurt their vanity to say so, but chairmen have no authority in law save what they derive from the support of their colleagues.

A word of warning for those studying UK companies. Over the years a combination of roles at the top plus the adulation of the media has tended to induce a condition of overconfidence in the 'hero' which has led to his downfall.

Corporate Governance and Chairmanship by Sir Adrian Cadbury (2002) contains an admirable account of every aspect of a chairman's job.

The Chief Executive Officer

We shall use the title CEO for the person with the top executive authority, though the title varies and they may be called the 'chief executive', the 'managing director', or the 'chief operating officer'. In fact, 'CEO' is an importation from America and has presidential overtones: 'managing director' used to be the common term in the UK, and is in some ways a better designation but it is now seldom used. As noted earlier we are used to thinking in terms of individual accountability and for directors to have among them a dominant individual, clearly identifiable as the leader—and not just a *primus inter pares*. The UK prefers individual leadership, with personal responsibility, risks, and rewards. Annual reports often look like a

CEO's scrapbook; I counted thirteen photographs of the CEO in one! The media thrive on this cult of the individual; on which they can build drama and romance; CEOs enjoy the limelight and are sometimes corrupted by it, gradually getting to believe the hyperbole of their public relations department. The overdramatization of their rise and fall seems to represent the industrial interpretation of 'A crowded hour of glorious life is worth an age without a name'. But it does not seem in the long run to benefit the business, whatever excitement it may temporarily produce The CEO's tenure is increasingly fragile—about 3½ years. A Booz Allen Hamilton survey for 2003 suggested that 6.3% of CEOs lost their jobs that year. The separation of their role from that of the chairman may indeed have made them more vulnerable.

A 2004 report by The Work Foundation (by Nick Isles) states that 86% of the CEOs in the FTSE 250 are UK citizens and 60% of them have been with the company at least eight years.

The company secretary

Under the 1985 Companies Act (section 283) every company public and private must have a company secretary. Except in companies where there is a sole director, one of the directors may also act as company secretary. In the case of public, but not private companies, section 286 lays down certain requirements about their qualifications, e.g. legal or accounting. There are in law no specified tasks they must undertake but they are one of the named individuals who can authenticate documents for the company. It is common for them to have the responsibility of ensuring the company's official returns are made on time, for maintaining the statutory records, for minuting board meetings, and for dealing with many of the administrative arrangements appertaining to the board.

In recent years their duties have broadened as corporate governance has developed. CCCG A5, for instance, says:

Under the direction of the chairman, the company secretary's responsibilities include ensuring good information flows within the board and its committees and between senior management and non-executive directors, as well as facilitating induction and assisting with professional development as required. The company secretary should be responsible for advising the board through the chairman on all governance matters.

Committees of the board

Committees of the board are used for various purposes, the main one being to assist the dispatch of business by considering it in more detail than would be convenient for the whole board. Some are established ad hoc to consider a particular problem or issue, perhaps a conflict of interest; others may derive from issues which flow naturally from a company's operations, for example, an environment committee in a mining company. The classic and now universal example of this kind of committee is the audit committee, which is considered in detail below.

The second purpose is to increase objectivity either because of inherent conflicts of interest such as executive remuneration, or else to discipline personal preferences as in the exercise of patronage.

In all instances they serve an additional purpose, to involve the non-executive directors by familiarizing them in detail with some important aspect of the governance of the company. Membership of a remuneration committee, for instance, implies considering both performance and succession. Greater involvement is important. It gives the non-executives a chance to work together and the confidence to intervene when they should and the knowledge about when not to. Let us look at the most important committees.

Audit committees

Audit committees have come a long way since they first came to prominence in the USA in the late 1970s as a riposte to some cases of financial abuse. (The New York Stock Exchange made them a listing condition in 1978 and stipulated that they should be composed of outside directors, thereby changing the shape of American boards—at least for the minority of companies that did not already have outside directors). In the UK they are now a prime organ of governance, manned as they are by independent NEDs (at least three, or two for smaller companies), one of whom should have 'recent and relevant financial experience' (Smith Guidance 2.3).

CCCG devotes a whole section to them (C.3) and their range of duties should be read with the Smith guidance (ibid. 43–58). Their formal functions have always included monitoring the integrity of the financial statements, considering the scope of the external audit, the appointment or replacement of external auditors, the internal audit system, and liaising with the internal auditors. Although the guidance makes it clear that the system of internal controls is a matter for the whole board, C.3.2 places on the audit committee the responsibility for reviewing them and for monitoring the effectiveness of the internal audit function. Another committee under Douglas Flint was set up in 2004 to review the Turnbull guidance and it is commissioned to provide revised guidance to apply for accounting periods after 1 January 2006.

In reality the dividing line between the board as a whole and the audit committee in these matters tends to blur, especially as audit committees have the right to invite executives to attend and would normally do so—particularly the finance director. It is normal practice for the audit committee to see the external auditors without management being present—and likewise the head of internal audit. One of the greatest services the audit committee renders is the improvement in the relationship with internal and external auditors, who often have a 'dotted line' to the chairman of the committee.

Chairmen of audit committees have to be on their guard against encroaching on board matters. There are many kinds of risk, and some fall within the remit of the audit committee, but business risk is a matter for the board (see below).[1] In many companies the committee meets only a day or two before the board (as a matter of convenience, if directors have far to travel) and the board can find itself regurgitating matters most of its members have already considered.

The committee also has to keep an eye on the auditors carrying out non-audit work—a sensitive subject because of the increasing fear that too much of it could prejudice their independence.

The CCCG deals with the generality of UK companies. There are additional considerations in respect of the financial sector supervised by the Financial Services Authority (FSA), which has a special interest in the work of the audit committee and does not hesitate to call in its members. Being the chairman of such a committee is no light task and their extra remuneration recognizes this.

The committee's task is complicated by the stream of 'improvements' in accounting and auditing. December 2003 saw the publication of no fewer than thirteen improved standards. The committee will have the auditors to hold its hand (and one of its members, at least, will be financially qualified), but even so it is a lot to absorb on the run up to the adoption of IFRS in 2005. Some of the changes will have a material effect on the results.

Does the increase in the power and scope of the audit committee especially in supervised companies mean that the UK is imperceptibly moving towards a two-tier system? I believe the answer to that is still 'no', because no one wants it; but it needs watching.

Whistle-blowing The committee's duties include ensuring the whistle-blowing function works.

This is a hugely delicate subject as it runs counter to the traditional British dislike of 'sneaking' or 'grassing', and is in any case quite difficult to organize effectively. CCCG (C.3.4) sets out the general principles. The Institute of Chartered Accountants in England and Wales offered guidance to audit committees in March 2004 in 'whistle-blowing arrangements'. The fact

---

[1] I define business risk as one in which an activity can produce either a profit or a loss. Operational risks are potentially only loss producing.

remains that the problem is psychological. Potential whistle-blowers have to feel their allegiance to the company is far greater than 'loyalty' to colleagues. And there aren't many medals in it. A charity called 'Public Concern at Work' is there to help, but even so it is an intractable problem.

Remuneration committees

The Companies Act says nothing about remuneration. There has been increasing interest in the subject over the last decade, but to keep it in perspective, it is narrowly focused on the executive directors, especially the CEO. However large the remuneration of other employees it does not seem to have attracted the attentions of shareholders, media, or regulators. When it does 'hit the headlines' it causes a stir. A visitor from Mars studying the UK's newspapers might be forgiven for believing that the only newsworthy aspects of a company were the personality and pay of its Chief Executive. From the media's viewpoint this is understandable. They have stumbled upon a real dilemma—the tension between greed, envy, justifiable reward, and the social fabric. Public interest was first aroused by leaps in the pay of executive directors after denationalization. It now extends to cases where increases are not matched by increases in profits, or where they just seem unduly lush. This is not an exact science. Additionally there tends to be concern when compensation payments for loss of office seem to be out of proportion to the poor performance that led to the premature ending of the contract of employment.

The original idea of remuneration committees was to stop executive directors fixing their own remuneration. It was assumed that by putting the decisions into the hands of the NEDs, objectivity would produce moderation. This is still the prevailing doctrine. Under the CCCG the committee must consist entirely of independent NEDs who should apply the principle (B.1), 'Levels of remuneration should be sufficient to attract, retain and motivate directors of the quality required to run the company successfully... but not more than necessary.' Quite so, but as usual, the devil is in the detail, and remuneration committees have a difficult task when confronted by the apparently indispensable. Notions of moderation are few and far between; greed has become institutionalized, and it can be defended by reference to the professions where at the top rewards are great, by selecting comparators judiciously and by veiled threats.

Some people detect a seismic change—priority being given to the operators at the expense of the shareholders. If this is indeed the case, it covers only a narrow band of operators.

The forces of upward pressure are for the most part more vigorous than those for containment: consultants are widely used but they are not loved if they recommend parsimony; there is an inbuilt ratcheting effect because review dates vary; and maintaining both internal and external relativities is never easy and usually results in the choice of the more favourable indicator. Meanwhile, there is external pressure to relate remuneration to performance—and that is not easy either. Section B of the CCCG is full of sage advice about process but the fact remains there is no such thing as a 'right' level of remuneration; judgements may be 'informed' but they are nevertheless judgements, and they are unlikely to please everyone especially in hard times. The fashionable tendency is to shy away from discretionary payments, but many managers feel that rigidity serves them poorly—as when trading conditions are bad and bonus schemes do not kick in—yet an able executive has been able by outstanding skill and effort to serve the company exceptionally well.

Over the years companies have been required to publish more and more in the Annual Report about remuneration. Remuneration comes in many shapes and forms—basic salary, short-term bonus, long-term incentive plans, share options, pensions, and it is difficult for a 'lay' shareholder to calculate what a CEO has and is entitled to receive. One of the aims of any remuneration package is to motivate; some are now so complex that even the executives concerned are not totally clear about what they will produce. There are those who criticize the requirement to publish individual remuneration, arguing that it institutionalizes 'me-too-ism', and that it would serve the shareholders' interests better were disclosure arranged by groups (which the company would define), which would produce a clearer picture of how remuneration had changed over time in relation to profits. Disclosure is currently governed by the Directors' Remuneration Report Regulations 2002 (DRRR). This mandates *inter alia*:

- Quoted companies must publish a detailed report on directors' pay as part of their annual reporting cycle. This report must be approved by the board.
- A graph of the company's total shareholder returns over five years against a comparator group must be published in the remuneration committee report.
- Names of any consultants to the committee must be disclosed along with the cost of any other services they provide to the company.
- This vote is advisory but even so it gives the shareholders a chance to let off steam and a company will take it seriously.

PriceWaterhouseCoopers have helpfully produced a checklist for the Remuneration Committee Report which draws on both DRRR and the CCCG. 'Transparency' has become an overworked metaphor when what is meant is 'openness' and 'disclosure' is the order of the day. The ICGN recommendations regard it as fundamental. As 'packages' are often so complex what emerges is more comprehensive than a telephone directory. PWC feel it can be useful to the company to cover the ground in a way that would focus on how reward policies support corporate strategy and also on the total reward picture as well as the individual components:

- Description of policy
  Reward objectives and link with corporate strategy
  Principles underpinning setting of reward
  Role of each element of reward in supporting strategy
- Disclosure of reward for 2004
  Salary and justification for changes
  Target and maximum bonus opportunity
  Long-term incentive grant sizes and value
  Significant benefit provisions and expatriate allowances
  Total reward showing long term v. short term and fixed v. variable
  Potential reward under different performance scenarios.
- Disclosure of and justification for short- and long-term performance measures
  Scales, targets, and measures
  Demonstration of link with corporate strategy
  Impact on probability of payout
- Description of reward realized in 2003
  Salary
  Bonus received and explanation of performance v. targets
  Long-term incentives vesting including description of performance v.targets
  Benefit contributions
  Comparison of total remuneration received and company performance
- Accumulated reward and related transactions
  Accrued shareholding
  Total options holdings
  Outstanding but unvested performance share plan grants
  Accrued pension entitlements

PWC's thesis is that such a report would be useful as the basis for a structured proactive shareholder relationship programme. CCCG B2.4 requires shareholder approval for all new long-term incentive schemes (LTIPs), in accordance with the provisions of the listing rules. Shareholders are indeed already becoming more active in monitoring remuneration. In May 2003 GlaxoSmithKline's management was defeated on a vote on the remuneration report and in June two NEDs retired from the board including the chairman of the remuneration committee. The case is instructive in many ways, not least in the awkward situation that arises when a major international company operates in the USA where salary levels are far higher.

The PIRC survey shows that the average total cash emoluments of a FTSE executive director was over £800,000 in 2002 (up 7.7% on the previous year). The relative figures for mid-cap companies are £430,000 (7.4%) and for small-cap companies £260,000 (6.9%). To these numbers must be added gains from options and LTIPs. These had dropped substantially in 2002 reflecting the weak stock market but even so they were worth £200,000+ for FTSE companies, about £90,000 for mid-cap companies and around £35,000 for small-cap companies. PIRC produced a snapshot of non-executive directors' remuneration in the ten biggest UK companies (by market capitalization) (PIRC alert, 20 August 2004.)

Further evidence from the 2004 IRS survey shows that NEDs in the biggest companies received £35,000–55,000 per annum plus £10,000–20,000 for being a committee chairman—and £5,000–10,000 for being a committee member. Rates rose by 15%+ in many cases. Except in the smallest companies 35–45% of NEDs held shares. The CCCG rules out the award of share options to NEDs (B1.3).

There is evidence of much greater shareholder interest both in the structure and quantum of remuneration, and sometimes plain disagreement as in the case of the remuneration of the CEO of GlaxoSmithKline, for instance, or

Table 6.1. Directors' remuneration (£000s)

Company	Basic fee	SID fee	Committee chair fee			Committee membership fee		
			Audit	Rem.	Nom.	Audit	Rem.	Nom.
BP	65	85	15	15	15			
HSBC	35		15	15		10	10	
Vodafone	80	124	10	10	10			
GSK	60		30	20	20			
RBC	44[a]							
Astra Zeneca	49[a]	74						
Shell	50		5	5	5			
Barclays	75							
HBOS	40[a]	53						
Lloyds TSB	63[ab]							

Note: GSK's fees assumes that the proposed changes to the fee structure are enacted. £20,000 of fees at Barclays must be deferred in shares. Twenty-five per cent of the fees to be paid at GSK will be deferred into shares. Figures as at the date of the last report and accounts.

[a] Amounts include fees for committee membership. Individual committee fees are not disclosed.

[b] Represents average fees paid to non-executives over the year.

Standard Life. And the Confederation of British Industries (CBI) have weighed in with their recommendations on Golden Parachutes (2003).

Nomination committees

Patronage is an enjoyable and satisfying pastime, but the Combined Code has tried to put it to rest by declaring that 'There should be a formal rigorous and transparent procedure for the appointment of new directors to the board' (A.4). The chairman (or CEO) would be less than human if he did not prefer to be surrounded by like-minded and congenial spirits, rather than by those with an angular personality, however clever. The chairman/CEO inevitably has great influence on the choice of colleagues and this can result in the appointment of sycophants or buddies: my impression is that as the spotlight on non-executive directors has brightened, the selection process has improved. Now that companies have to describe the background of NEDs in the annual report the world can at least share the chairman's wisdom in his exercise of patronage. A nominating committee is really designed to do two things: to improve the selection process by introducing method and object-ivity and to give the chairman a conscience when he picks buddies. In the best-run companies specification precedes search and choice; this is what CCCG requires. In many cases the reverse often used to happen. At the very least a nominating committee brings an element of discipline into the process, starting with the preparation of a job description. Smaller com-panies may hesitate to have one because of the workload but even they should work out the ideal specification before plunging into the market. The service that agencies can render makes the exercise of patronage not only respectable but also effective – in the sense that candidates have to evince other qualities besides ingratiating themselves with the chairman.

The committee's duties extend further, to considering succession plan-ning, supervising letters of appointment, and making sure candidates have enough time to do the job.

Board appraisal

The CCCG demands (A6) that 'the board should undertake a formal and vigorous annual evaluation of its own performance and that of its committees and individual directors'—and then say in the Annual Report how the evalu-ation has been conducted. It then goes on to give guidance (pp. 77–9). This is designed to be demanding, so it is no surprise to find the authors of the IRS survey record that they know of twenty-two consulting and other firms who are offering board performance audits—at £12,000–80,000. Their comment is that it looks like a new consulting honeypot. At present there is no unanimity on whether advisers or consultants would be a benefit or just an expense, though as far as I can see no one feels able to suggest that appraisal is out of place; after all, in most firms there are appraisal processes for everyone else. Whether appraisal should be done annually is sometimes doubted. It would seem that the appraisal of the chairman is the most delicate matter to arrange. It will be instructive to monitor progress on this requirement of the CCCG, as its thoroughness and formality breaks new ground. It could turn out to be highly significant. On the other hand, one of the enduring problems in companies is that of 'reciprocal mediocrity', where the board and management are both rather weak. Assessing each other will not be the answer; the shareholders have an important residual responsibility in such cases.

Dynasties

Many private companies have remained not only in family control but also under family direction for two or three generations. It would be interesting to have some hard facts on this, but the general impression is that the old saying 'Clogs to clogs in three generations' is still not far wide of the mark. The most promising members of the family may prefer another career; or the line does not produce the requisite talent. Being succeeded by one's offspring gratifies an understandable human desire to defy mortality, but appears only too often to hasten the mortality of the business.

Some families succeed in maintaining their central role long after the company has floated and their shareholdings have dwindled or been diluted; it is surprising to learn that they sometimes hold less than 5%. It seems to be more widely recognized than it was that succession should be governed more by competence than by heredity. Institutional shareholders are now increasingly opposed to the practice and perhaps for that reason boards seem increasingly reluctant to allow CEOs/chairmen to hand over the reins to an offspring or relation unless he is really qualified for the post. Some of course are, and when this is so turn out to be among the very best because of their exceptional dedication to the enterprise. The succession at Great Universal Stores and Associated British Foods in the 1970s produced two successors worthy of their fathers, and although there were protests against the succession at Next at the time (2001), performance has stilled the critics. Time will tell how well the Murdoch dynasty works out.

Even so, Sir Lewis Robertson, doctor to many ailing companies, warned his audience in 1983 to beware:

Management imbalance comes in many forms. One of these is the area of family and family deference; a true entrepreneur can build up a remarkable business, to the advantage of investors' staff and customers, but it can be disastrous if his (or his family's) influence continues too long. On more than one occasion I have seen a very good company brought close to disaster by this... Beware of families; press for the professionalization of family businesses, be they small or large.

Reporting to the Shareholders

Under UK law the directors are obliged to provide information to the shareholders in the annual report and accounts, but there is no shareholders' committee as there is in some other countries. Their statutory obligations are limited, but the CCCG main principle on financial reporting is brief: 'The board should present a balanced and understandable assessment of the company's position and prospects.' There should in other words be a high degree of transparency, without which there cannot be effective accountability.

Figures are not enough, for they are at best a snapshot, an approximation of past facts. The often held view that numerical data enshrine the truth and words are equivocal is the reverse of reality. Many numbers have perforce to be based on subjective judgements: for instance, provisions for bad debts, incomplete contracts, and the value of stock and real estate. Furthermore, all the numbers, even if accurate, do not necessarily add up to the whole story. The numbers themselves have to be calculated and presented in accordance with the conventions the accounting profession has adopted. A fundamental change is taking place as quoted companies switch from UK GAAP to IFRS in the course of 2004/5. All the new standards—and there are many of them— will apply from 1 January 2005 but some may be staggered between 2005 and 2007 depending on whether the entities opt to use fair value accounting and whether they are listed. The Companies Act 1985 (International Accounting Standards and Other Accounting Amendments) Regulation came into force on 12 November 2004 and was effective from 1 January 2005 (SI 2004/2947). It is not necessary to recite all the provisions here, many of which are highly technical but not the less important on that account. Boards and especially audit committees were busy in 2004 making sure the company was geared up to cope with the changes and fully understood all the implications. Many decided to ease the pain of transfer by preparing 'dummy' accounts in the new mode for the present year. The major accounting firms helpfully supply detailed accounts of the changes.

The Financial Reporting Council and Accounting Standards Board are revising reporting standards, and the Financial Reporting Review Panel now monitors companies whose accounts fall below accepted reporting standards. At the end of the day, whatever standards are adopted, it will be the primary responsibility of directors to see they are followed. The auditor's role is secondary, despite the propensity to sue them on the 'long pocket' principle when something goes wrong.

As to *what* should be said, here for convenience is the list from the CCCG:

- A statement on how the board operates, including a high-level statement on which types of decision are taken by the board and which are to be delegated to management (A1.1).
- The names of the chairman, deputy chairman, CEO, SID, and the chairmen and members of the nomination, remuneration, and audit committees— plus an attendance record for each (A1.2).
- Identification by the board in the annual report of each NED it considers independent (A3.1).
- Changes to a chairman's significant commitments (A4.3).
- A description (in a separate section) of the work of the nomination committee (A4.6).
- A statement about the evaluation of the directors', committees', and board's performance (A6.1).
- The director's explanation of their responsibility for preparing the accounts (C1.1).
- A statement by the auditors about their reporting responsibilities (C1.1).
- The 'Going concern' assumption (C1.2) which repeats the Cadbury requirement that 'The directors should report that the business is a going concern with supporting assumptions and qualifications where necessary'.
- A report on internal controls (C2.1).
- If there is no internal audit function, an explanation of why this is so (C3.5).
- Any differences between the audit committee and board on recommendations about the appointment or dismissal of auditors (C3.6).
- An explanation of how auditors' objectivity and independence is safeguarded if they supply non-audit services.
- The steps the board has taken to ensure that members of the board and in particular the NEDs develop an understanding of the views of major shareholders about the company (D1.2).
- A description of the work of the remuneration committee as required by the Directors' Remuneration Reporting Regulations.

The Operating and Financial Review (OFR)

Towards the end of 2004 the Department of Trade and Industry announced that quoted companies will be required to issue an Operating and Financial Review for financial years starting on or after 1 April 2005. The following checklist is based on the UK Accounting Standards Board's (ASB) exposure draft (OFR RED1) issued on 30 November. The main principles are:

1. The OFR shall set out an analysis of the business through the eyes of the directors.
2. The OFR shall focus on matters that are relevant to directors.
3. The OFR shall have a forward-looking orientation, identifying those trends and factors relevant to the investors' assessment of the current and future performance of the business and the progress being made towards the achievement of its long-term business objectives.
4. The OFR shall complement as well as supplement the financial statements, in order to enhance the overall corporate disclosure.
5. The OFR shall be comprehensive and understandable.
6. The OFR shall be balanced and neutral, dealing even-handedly with both good and bad aspects
7. The OFR shall be comparable over time

The Disclosure framework is as follows (extracted):

2.1 The OFR shall provide information to assist directors to assess the strategies and the potential for these to succeed—

   a the nature, objectives, and strategies of the business

   b the development and performance of the business both in the period under review and in the future

   c the resources risks and uncertainties and relationships that may affect long term value

   d position of the business (capital structure, treasury, policies, objectives, liquidity) for the period under review and in the future.

2.2 This means covering where necessary: market and competitive environment, technological change, customers, suppliers etc, employees, environmental matters, social and community issues, receipts from and returns to shareholders.

3 The nature, objectives and strategies of the business:

3.1 The OFR shall include a description of the business and the external environment, as context for the directors' discussion and analysis of performance and financial position

3.2 The OFR shall discuss the objectives of the business to generate or preserve value over the longer term

3.3 The OFR shall set out the directors' strategies for achieving the objectives of the business

3.4 The OFR shall include key performance indicators, financial and non-financial, used by the directors to assess progress towards their objectives.

3.5 Directors should consider what else should be included

4   Current and future development and performance

4.1 The OFR shall describe the significant features of the development and performance of the business for the period etc.

4.2 The OFR shall analyse the main trends and factors that directors consider likely to impact future prospects

5   Resources
The OFR shall include a description of the resources available and howthey are managed

6   Risks and uncertainties
The OFR shall describe the principal risks and uncertainty with a commentary on the directors' approach to them

7   Relationships

7.1 The OFR shall include information about significant relationships with stakeholders other than investors which may influence the performance of the business or its value

7.2 If necessary the OFR shall describe receipts from and returns to shareholders (distributions, capital raising, share repurchases)

8   Financial position

8.1 The OFR shall contain an analysis of the financial position

8.2 The OFR shall contain a discussion of the capital structure of the business

8.3 The OFR shall set out the treasury's policies and objectives

9   Cash flows
The OFR shall discuss the cash inflows and outflows along with the ability to generate cash to meet known or probable cash requirements and to fund growth.

10 Liquidity
The OFR shall discuss liquidity current and prospective. Where relevant this shall cover the level of borrowings, borrowing requirements and maturity profile of borrowings and undrawn committed borrowing facilities.

There follows an elaboration of the presentation of Key Performance Indicators (KPIs) and finally a Compliance statement about the OFR meeting the ASB reporting standards—and if not why not!

The OFR should be seen against pre-existing pressure on company boards to provide ever more numerical data. This springs from the natural desire of investors and analysts to produce what can easily be compared. Charts and league tables can be constructed from numbers (however suspect) more easily than words (however reliable). The plain fact is that qualitative data require judgement and that judgement requires both skill and experience—hence the urge to provide data which reduces the importance of both. The same problem surfaced in the USA as a search for series of data which would cover the aspects of the accounts now omitted (e.g. quality and market share). It remains to be seen how the OFR requirements will be met in practice; some of the requirements get close to the borderline of commercial confidentiality which it would suit neither management nor shareholders to breach.

How it should be said

There is widespread agreement that it serves the interest of both shareholders and company for there to be regular communication between them; numerous bodies have warmly commended it for years and it is now enshrined in the CCCG. It is realized that this leaves the small shareholders who have no access to company management at a relative disadvantage, but it is argued that this is less important than the benefits good communication brings both to the market and to the company by making them better informed. The conventional UK position is that investor relations activities are useful for company, market, and investors and should be encouraged, and that problems about price-sensitive information are containable. It is impossible anyway to set a dividing line between all information that is price sensitive and all that is not. There is nothing illegal in having price-sensitive information as long as one does not trade on it until it is generally available; an investor may always consent to become an 'insider'; that is, to accept information on the understanding he or she will not trade. The Institutional Shareholders' Committee (ISC) wrote long ago that those who criticize UK practice as a fudge should be required to produce a formula that confers greater advantage on all the parties. That said, the degree of delicacy various parties feel about giving, receiving, and using price-sensitive information varies greatly even today.

There is now some information on what actually occurs. Professor Claire Marston's European Investor Relations Project 2002 for Heriot Watt University elicited 186 responses from the top 500 European companies, and of the 186, 61 were British. The following figures reflect European practice but as a third are UK companies they may be regarded as indicative for the UK.

What the study shows is that investor relations have been a growth industry this past decade: 57% of the respondents now rated investor relations as important in their country compared with 2.2% a decade ago. As to their own companies 72% now rated them important as against 12% a decade ago. This is now reflected by 92.7% of companies in the sample having an investor relations department or section established on average about seven years ago with an average of nearly four full-time staff—but widespread use is also made of external consultants (either investor relations or financial public relations by about 70% of the respondent companies). At senior levels 119 CEOs and 145 Finance Directors (CFOs) spent more than 5% of their time on investor relations. The project gives details of the subjects covered and of the range of contacts between companies and investors.

From a governance viewpoint one of the most interesting aspects is the relationship between a company and the sell-side analysts who invariably issue forecasts of earnings. Companies always face a dilemma if these are grossly inaccurate. Should they remain silent and let the particular analyst look foolish when the figures appear? (Meanwhile, those who put faith in his judgement will have been misled.) Or should they in one way or another tip him off (and in doing so inevitably give him by inference price-sensitive information)? The Marston Survey in 1993 (UK companies only) showed that the companies were evenly divided: 49.11% did offer comments on the accuracy of analysts' predictions; 53.43 % gave some guidance regarding the size and direction of the error in the forecast (Marston 1993: tables 6.6 and 6.12). Because of the European dimension the 2003 report is not strictly comparable, but it is revealing nevertheless. In fact 17.3% of the respondents asserted that there were no laws or regulations to inhibit their commenting.

Question 4.5 gets to the heart of the matter—'What action does your company take when it receives a draft analyst's report for comment or when an analyst telephones to discuss a draft report?' *No one* fails to provide feedback: 60.8% offer comments on the accuracy of the analysts' predictions in general; 35.5% offer comments on the accuracy of the analysts profits forecasts; and 30.6% offer comments on the size and direction of the error in the profits forecast.

It is not quite the free-for-all these figures suggest since most respondents reported they prohibited or restricted contacts with analysts during certain parts of the year, generally on the run-up to announcements about results. And most companies do either restrict the range of people to whom their personnel outside the investor relations unit may speak or offer them guidelines.

Professor Marston's 2004 study presents empirical evidence of the way in which the top 500 UK companies engage in investor relations meetings. It shows that such meetings of all types are an important part of the financial and business communications package offered by companies to their institutional investors and analysts. The demand for one-to-one meetings has increased since 1991 despite the opportunities for automation provided by the Internet. That said, the most important activity, the one-to-one meeting (or other contact), is not amenable to observation.

What all this seems to mean is that analysts are in a privileged position with price-sensitive information before it is generally available. On the other hand the public should be able to assume that their forecasts are reasonably accurate much of the time. Even so, the jury is out on the question of whether all these Investor Relations meetings do really improve market efficiency by reducing information asymmetry.

The rating agencies have access to privileged non-public information. It is beyond the scope of this book to comment on the use made of it.

The role of institutional shareholders is considered below. Suffice it to say here that contacts between them and companies have been a feature of the landscape for many years; they are not one-way traffic. An institution may express its views about the company, its leaders, and its policies in no uncertain terms; but both parties generally prefer a private demarche to a public fracas. Generally speaking, the bigger the holding the more senior the people involved. As to insider trading, it is not the purpose of these meetings to elicit price sensitive information and it would not be acted upon if any emerged.

Shareholders' Rights and Activism

One of the advantages of a joint stock company and the concept of limited liability is that a person may venture his savings in an enterprise without putting at risk a penny more than he has staked, and without either a duty or a right to manage the enterprise. The bundle of rights with which the shareholder is left include

- A share of money distributed by way of dividend.
- A share of any surplus if the enterprise is wound up.
- A vote on matters specified in the Act, including the election of those to whom its stewardship is entrusted—the directors; the vote can be cast by mail and a proxy may be appointed.
- A right to put a resolution on the Order paper for an Annual General Meeting if he has the support of 5% of the votes, or of 100 shareholders who have on average paid more than £100 for their shareholdings; it must not be longer than 1,000 words and must be lodged six weeks before the AGM (sect. 376). Ordinary resolutions do not bind. Extraordinary ones do.
- A right to speak at an AGM.
- A right to see the report and accounts.
- A supply of information as laid down by the Companies Act and supplemented by the Stock Exchange's rules at listing and now the CCCG.
- The right to subscribe when new capital is sought unless pre-emption rights have been disapplied beforehand.
- The right to dispose freely of stock at the best price. This is in reality the most precious of all and it is one that is notably absent in unquoted companies.

- A right to elect and remove the auditors.
- A right to call an EGM.

Most rights are proportionate to the capital owned—a vote per share, not a vote per shareholder. This proportionality leads to a differentiation between shareholders which is based on the reality of power, not on status. A shareholder with ten votes is entitled to the same status as one with a million; but a platoon was never equal to a regiment, except in fairy stories. In Orwellian language, all shareholders are equal but some are more equal than others. The AGM provides an oddity—here on a show of hands it is 'one person one vote', however many shares they may hold. If a poll is demanded the system reverts to 'one vote per share'.

Private shareholders

We saw from the Proshare figures quoted earlier that private shareholders in 2003 owned less than 15% of UK equity shares. Their relative power may be limited but it is not negligible. They have as much right at an annual general meeting to hold the floor as the representative of Omnium Gatherum Insurance plc, and if they have the wit (and courage) to ask the right questions with the media present may cause quite a stir (though the media only cover an AGM as a rule if they expect a story). They have the Report and Accounts and newspaper comments; they may have their broker's advice. Most lack the power or knowledge to delve into the figures or peer behind the mask. Their only sight of company management is at the AGM itself—and this would often tell them quite a lot were they to take the trouble to attend, but few do. If the company is big, rich, and forward looking, it may make a presentation in different localities, but this is rare.

These obstacles are on the whole treated by private shareholders as insuperable. If they lose confidence in the company they either sell or hold on and wait for better days. There is nowhere for them to turn for help if they feel that what is wrong is the board; they can vote against the directors of course, but feel as they do as if they were shaking a pepper-pot on to desert sand. Who notices? Who cares? All this was seen and analysed seventy years ago by the American professors Berle and Means, who understood the implications of shareholdings being dispersed and fragmented. It meant accountability by the board to the shareholders was effectively dead (Berle and Means 1932).

Some private shareholders may well feel that the market treats them poorly and indeed it does cost them more per share to trade than bigger dealers because of diseconomies of scale. Viewed properly in terms of the cost of making a long-term investment the difference is marginal. There are few classes of asset one can buy or sell more economically. They would not expect to have the knowledge or clout of a major institution. It is to be hoped that they do not resent the power of the institutions or the use they now seem willing to make of it. They may well welcome the institutions having sensible and close relations with companies. If they keep an eye on them it will be a general benefit. Some will sadly abuse their position and the insider trading laws do not seem adequate to trap those who do. Even so they should rejoice that the Berle-Means analysis is being invalidated.

The private shareholders could write in to the company more often; few companies ignore sensible enquiries, and they may produce an effect. My experience is that such communications are seldom ignored, if not satisfactorily answered. I once queried the age of a director who looked antique in the Report. I was given the response 'I can assure you he is young in heart'. They could ask more penetrating questions at AGM about the conduct of the company's business, not just on extraneous matters like the environment or the rights of the indigenous population in countries where they operate. Their influence is therefore marginal. It would be difficult and expensive to organize concerted action. It is seldom done, but it could be.

Institutional shareholders

Institutional investors are not a homogeneous class. They vary greatly in size from a pension fund with perhaps a few million pounds to a major insurance company managing forty billions. Pension funds, insurance companies, unit and investment trust managers serve different purposes, have different obligations, and are under different pressures. They can discharge their obligations in various ways, choosing to manage funds in-house, or employing external managers. The one thing they all have in common is that the managers are investing someone else's money, which imposes on them and those who employ them standards a private individual can choose to ignore if he is acting for himself. The institutions do not put all their funds into the UK equity market by any means. Their asset allocation decisions may propel some proportion to property, or bonds, or into other equity markets abroad. With capital flows now unrestricted they still need to be able to match their obligations in the currency in which they have to be paid.

The UK's tax arrangements favour collective savings so many people save in this way rather than individually—besides it is a way of getting financial advice. The proportion of equity shares in the hands of those who administer them now predominates. There have been periods when inflation was nonexistent or low and funds could largely meet their obligations by investing in fixed interest securities; inflationary pressures made fund managers seek better, if riskier, returns. With the exception of a short period in the Great

Depression equities have been a better investment. Taking a long view, 1899–2001, the real return with all income reinvested on £100 invested in 1899 would have produced £19,671 against £291 for gilts. Without reinvesting income the comparative figures are £195 and £1! (Proshare, p. 46.)

As noted earlier, by 2001 20% of UK equities were held by insurance companies, 16.1% by pension funds, and about 15% by other financial institutions (Proshare, p. 5). Foreign holdings were about 32% (these figures were virtually unchanged for 2002—National Statistics Online). Institutional shareholders then accounted for fractionally under half of UK equities with a combined value of £571 billion.

The four main groups of institutions that constitute the Institutional Share-holders' Committee (ISC) are the Association of British Insurers (ABI), the Association of Investment Trust Companies (AITC), the National Association of Pension Funds (NAPF), and the Investment Management Association (IMA). The ISC's focus changes over time. In 1992 for example it was much concerned about the disclosure of information about research and development costs in the belief that this gives a good indication of the depth of commitment. In those days the term 'corporate social responsibility' had barely been coined—now it is all the rage.

It used not to be the case that institutions needed to seek to play an active part in the corporate governance of the companies in their portfolio. Many, especially the smaller ones, had neither the time nor the resources to do so. If they did not like what they had bought they sold—known in the USA as the 'Wall Street walk'. Or they hung on, hoping that something would turn up—such as a takeover bid. Nowadays many hold their shares in 'indexed' funds and if they do they cannot sell. If they cannot sell, they must care. And as indexed funds are cheaper to run, there should be resources available to do the job.

The Bank of England in the 1970s saw numerous cases where the boards seemed too weak to require a satisfactory standard of executive management. Takeover bids were often the wrong answer. The shareholders could take action if they had a mind to. That is why the Bank made a valiant attempt to rally the institutions and inspire them to action, since control lay with them. It was thus that the ISC was born. In its early days it did occasionally achieve results through its 'case committees' (specially convened to deal with the problems presented by a particular company), but it proved better at hand-ling general policy issues like pre-emption rights.

Even today with stronger and better balanced boards, there are still occasions when it is appropriate for shareholders to take action. It may be the product of reciprocal mediocrity—weak managers appointing weak NEDs and vice versa, a condition mentioned earlier—or it may be strong leaders bent on a course that investors fear or dislike. That is the point at which shareholders may wish to use the rights they have always possessed even from the first Companies Act. It is not often, but it is crucial.

Even if an institution is happy to accept the thesis that there is a point at which their interests would be best served by some form of intervention, there are obstacles in their path. Acting alone they may lack firepower. This highlights the 'free rider' issue; why should one institution carry all the costs when 95% or more of the benefits go to others? Besides some are driven by internal conflicts of interest, for instance where they are both fund managers and merchant bankers. In addition they may be reluctant to share their thoughts and research with competitors, and finally they may lack the confidence to act and also hate hassle and publicity. All the attempts so far to persuade them to get together in their own interests have been unsuccessful, though there have been isolated cases of concerted action as well as 'band wagons'—where one institution takes a lead and others follow.

The degree of monitoring (with the ultimate possibility of intervention) reflects the way an institution approaches investment. If it is a short-term holder, in and out of a share to take short-term profits, and focused on short-term market considerations, it is less likely to consider issues of corporate governance unless it becomes a serious market factor. All shares are *in principle* held for the short term (even if in the event some part of some holdings remains in the portfolio for years). This is what many do, despite what they say.

The ISC's 2002 policy document does not recognize such distinctions. It requires members, apparently irrespective of size or investment strategy:

1. To set out their policy on how they will discharge their responsibilities. These are defined and they cover policies for requiring compliance; for meetings with investor companies; for solving conflicts of interest; for strategy on intervention; for further action; and for voting.
2. To monitor the performance of, and establish where necessary a regular dialogue with investor companies. Board and committee structure get special mention as does the adequacy of the NEDs in providing oversight. And the institutions themselves are bidden to record their connection with companies including meetings, and votes—with reasons.
3. To intervene when necessary if they have concerns about the company's strategy; operational performance; acquisition/disposal strategy; adequacy of the NEDs internal controls; succession planning; failure to comply with the CCCG; remuneration; CSR.
4. To evaluate the impact of their activism—and the various stages of 'escalation' are listed all the way from additional meetings with managers to express concerns to requisitioning an EGM, possibly to change the board.
5. To report back to clients/beneficial owners.

During the last decade informed professional commentators have become more influential—PIRC come to mind as leaders in providing advice on voting on items on the agenda for the AGM which they regard as undeserving of support. It is of course open to shareholders to assess the advice, but at the very least their attention will have been clearly drawn to the issues. Corporate governance has become an industry with massive academic resources on both sides of the Atlantic studying every conceivable aspect, and this has been reflected in the more active stance taken by some institutions. A special report in the *Financial Times* on 5 April 2004 was headed 'Shareholders ready to flex their muscles'. They certainly weren't a decade ago.

The CCCG avoids the subject, contenting itself with beefing up communications (D.1) and bringing the NEDs into them, especially the SID. It advises institutional shareholders to apply the ISC's principles. The emphasis is increasing on two-way communications between company and major shareholders. As between a company and its owners jaw-jaw is certainly better than war-war, but there are times when a conflict is inevitable and there have been some prominent ones of late, like the Carlton Communications affair (2003). Michael Green was forced to stand down. Some felt that this was a proper way for the shareholders to flex their muscles. Others like Sir Brian Pitman, the Senior Independent Director at Carlton, felt that investors had crossed the line between constructive engagement and micro-management. Such a division of opinion is likely to be common and is healthy enough as long as the battleground is well judged.

Voting sounds simple enough, but most private shareholders do not do so routinely judging by the numbers of votes cast. If their shares are held in nominee accounts they never see the papers. They can get them if they insist but it is a hassle, and few would vote anyway. So in practice few get hold of the papers in time to vote.

Exhortations notwithstanding, the institutions do not seem to regard voting as part of their duties on routine matters. The average turnout for a FTSE company is just over 50%. But this number included Shell in 2002/3 at 12.8%, Boots at 26.6%, and BAT at 32.7%. Bigger figures are seen when someone holds a large block of shares which accounted, for instance, for 44% of the votes cast at Schroders (out of 73.9%), while the Rothermere family voted their 63.1% holding at the Daily Mail (out of 87.9%). It appears that overseas shareholders seldom vote. One of the reasons for requiring routine voting is to make sure the machinery works in a timely fashion. Sadly votes 'go missing' sometimes, as Unilever reported, and this is not unique.

At least the existence of a problem is recognized, as the activities of the shareholders' voting working group confirm. Paul Myners' committee is the latest in a line set up to tackle the impediments to voting UK shares.

The possibilities of electronic voting have yet to be realized. The report makes it clear that a solution involves many parties and lists a series of recommendations covering the beneficial owners, issuers, registrars, investment managers, custodians, investment consultants, and the trade associations. The recommendations end by suggesting that the FSA will need to amend the listing rules to make it a requirement for the full results of polls to be disclosed and for quoted companies to publish their annual reporting documents on the Internet as soon as they have been published. It remains to be seen whether the recommendations will be accepted and if so how long it will take to implement them.

The ISC's principles are more comprehensive and forward looking than any earlier guidance. Nevertheless, the practical problems remain. To monitor properly is costly and demands skilled people. It also implies a readiness to incur costs and face hassle. There is no ready mechanism for concerted action. Sometimes one of the proactive funds like Hermes starts the ball rolling and then it is an easy matter for others to climb aboard and offer their support. But until the question of concerted action is settled the 'free rider' problem will deter many institutions except in dire cases. And as for cases where governance falls short but the share price is rising—why, most institutions will think they have better things to do. Sadly, it is just this kind of case where judicious action early on would prevent avoidable decline later.

In the last year or two there have been several high-profile cases of intervention by the institutional investors. Three that come to mind are the top management structure and appointments at Carlton (2003), the problems at Shell (2004), and the succession to the chairmanship of Sainsbury in which Sir Ian Prosser felt it politic not to proceed (2004). Some commentators have expressed reservations about activism, and it is indeed a matter of judgement in every case. My own view is that the forces of inertia are so great that active and positive intervention is always going to be rare and is more likely to be justified than not.

The mention of Hermes reflects a point made in the first chapter—the emergence of a new kind of investor who deliberately targets companies which are considered to have greater potential than their present management is capable of realizing. They tend to buy significant stakes. This gives them leverage and in terms of reward makes the exercise worthwhile despite the 'free rider' issue. Hermes manages the pension funds of BT and the Post Office and is therefore a major player. It has built up a formidable monitoring team (45 at the time of their 2003 conference) regarding this as a worthwhile investment. Their Focus Funds provide a shareholder engagement asset class to twenty-nine clients from eight countries—with £1.5 billion under management. Among the firms with whom Hermes Focus Asset management Limited (HFAM) have had successful engagements are Smith and Nephew, Mirror Group/Trinity Mirror, and Tomkins.

At the time of writing Hermes are considering a new way of tackling two special types of situation:

1. There are occasional circumstances where shareholders might find their interests best served by collaborating with a company's banks. These are when a company is in trouble and its very existence depends on facilities being maintained and new money brought in. Such cases are bound to be rare as the circumstances that give rise to them imply a sense of such urgency that it is difficult to assemble all the interested parties quickly enough. (This would imply extending the scope of the Bank of England's 'London Approach' which is designed to keep all a company's banks in play whilst the future of the company is assessed.)

2. Where the board of a company wants to take it private, and the directors on that account have a conflict of interest. (They want to keep the price down if they are staying aboard, whilst the shareholders want a fair price.)

In both cases some kind of voluntary ad hoc association of interested shareholders may be proposed and guidance is offered on the way action would be conducted.

Corporate Governance: Commentators and Ratings Systems

There has never been a shortage of press comment on companies in both generalist and specialist journals and periodicals. Even if it is honest and objective, it is not always right or accurate, for if it were the public could make a fortune by routinely following its advice. In days gone by, the comment would concentrate on products, profits, and personalities. Interest in corporate governance is an entirely new development of the last decade. In the UK, PIRC was one of the early suppliers of such advice but now it is no longer alone. Their 2003 paper on Glaxosmithkline is exclusively on governance issues. Apart from revealing that it is in the pharmaceutical sector, nothing is said about products. Its fifteen pages are devoted entirely to examining who the directors are, whether they are independent, whether they have enough time to do the job properly, and how they are paid, with a detailed commentary on all the aspects of remuneration. There are similar operations in the USA and elsewhere.

Reading a company report carefully, analysing, and evaluating it take time, and some of the rating agencies whose business had hitherto focused on the financial dimension conceived the idea of making life easier for investors by rating governance as a separate service. Their problem is that formal compliance with a set of governance standards is indicative but not conclusive; whether there are rating agencies or not, the quality dimension is hard to assess for it takes us into the realm of the behavioural sciences. Structure and process are at best proxies for dynamics, but the view seems to be gaining ground that they are useful, which is why 'well-governed companies'—in the sense of being code compliant—appear to command a premium in the market. This being so the rating agencies have a contribution to make and Moody's and S&P among others are already involved.

Trustees

Like the lay magistracy, trustees are a typical Common Law device—sensible, acceptable, effective, and cheap. In both cases, for hundreds of years responsible people were charged with dealing with the familiar in a context which came within their range of knowledge. Both institutions have endured, although the world in which they were called upon to act has become ever more complex and technical. The comparison is not exact since by and large magistrates have a uniform task (with some specialists, e.g. in respect of juvenile offenders) while the scope of a trust may vary immensely from a small house or legacy with a single beneficiary, to a monster pension fund with a myriad pensioners.

The importance of the role of pension fund trustees is underlined by the realization that, although their objects are fixed, they are not guaranteed years of plenty with which to meet them. Indeed, whilst this book was being written pension funds themselves were being changed in very many companies from 'Defined Benefit' to 'Defined Contribution' with many important consequences. The trustees must grapple with the volatility that flows from minimum funding and pension accounting, underfunding, and scheme changes and closures. There are many stories of funds requiring topping up by their companies. Some life companies have to grapple with changing expectations and the agony of disappointing them. In the context of corporate governance the trustees are important because they are in effect the owners of so much of UK industry. They have strategic investment decisions for which most are likely to need training, like asset allocation, diversification, policy on takeover bids, and the replacement of fund managers. They are expected to handle the assets as a prudent man would his own. But 'prudence' in today's world surely calls for skills and knowledge of a different order from the days when trustees dealt with the familiar and straightforward. It is not to be expected of trustees that they should become versed in detail but they need to be able to evaluate alternative policies and the skill with which they are being implemented. One of the areas that has now become important is the corporate governance of the companies in which their managers have chosen to invest. Trustees are expected to state their policy and report on how it has been executed—and this covers communications with companies and their managers' voting records.

Whether this means that over time a new profession of trustee should emerge, properly trained and remunerated, is an interesting point: after all, it is not thought wrong to pay the Public Trustee for his trained services. Stockbrokers are paid for their services and so are fund managers. Those who appoint trustees, and trustees themselves in their own best interests, may seek proper training and remuneration. This was the view of the 2001 review of institutional investment by Paul Myners for HM Treasury (p. 21). It not only endorsed the need for training and pay but also stressed that the level of skill and care required is that of a person *familiar with the issues concerned* (his italics). As things stood, 67% of pension fund trustees had no professional qualifications in finance or investment; more than 50% had fewer than three days training; and 44% had attended no courses since their first year.

Like their counterparts on boards, the non-executive directors, trustees of pension funds (or for that matter of other collective savings schemes) must be independent, that is to say, not subject to interests which conflict with those of the beneficiaries as a class. However they are chosen—and the selection process ought to take into account the nature of the duties to be performed and the candidates' skills and character, and not to be distorted by other considerations—they must be clear when they enter office whose interests they serve and what duties they have accepted. In a celebrated judgement in April 1984, Megarry J. told the National Union of Mineworkers that its trustees must put the interests of the pension fund's beneficiaries before union policy. It was not for them to make 'moral gestures': they had a duty to obtain expert advice and to act on it prudently. Mere prudence is not enough.

The paradox is whether this singleness of purpose in favour of the beneficiaries extends to the company itself. The trustees of a company pension fund must ensure that it can meet its obligations when they fall due (for which they will receive actuarial advice). If, however, a manager of the company is, as so often, a trustee of its pension fund, he has another aim. He wishes to maximize the value of the pension fund so as to minimize the firm's contribution ('pension holidays'), and to minimize its obligation to put in more money if the fund needs topping up. If the fund is in surplus he would like to take this back into the company to swell its profits. In the last few years, he is likely to have had the opposite problem—how to make good a shortfall in the fund without ruining the company itself.

This duality of objective has important consequences for corporate governance. The pressures a trustee and company director exerts on his fund managers are related far less to the pension fund's beneficiaries than to the pension fund as a 'profit centre' or source of liabilities. All directors want their own shareholders to exhibit loyalty based on long-term perspectives. To the extent that they put pressure on their own pension fund managers for short-term results they stand in danger of pushing them in another direction. There is in fact an unresolved question about who 'owns' a pension fund—and until this is settled the trustee/company director is bound to have a difficult role. Some critics believe that all trustees should be 'independent' of the company—or at least, a majority should.

It is often claimed that one of the factors that drives fund managers into excessive concern with the short term is performance measurement. Consultants have an important part to play, for it is they who often guide trustees into their choice of managers, and they do so largely on the basis of limited product differentiation that the league tables quantify. American research, however, suggests that once a manager is appointed—and provided he sticks to whatever strategy he has 'sold'—he is unlikely to be quickly displaced if he takes trouble to court the trustees and establish a strong relationship with them. Of course, if he performs disastrously for long enough he will be sacked, but a good salesman who sticks to his guns will often find trustees making excuses to continue backing him. Besides, knowledgeable trustees realize there is often 'performance drag'—new managers tend initially to underperform. There is pressure periodically for fund managers to be given longer mandates on the argument that this will protect them from having to take short-term decisions.

Performance measurers are increasingly influential, often attending reviews between trustees and investment managers and counselling trustees on selection—that is, both sacking and replacement. Some commentators consider the measurers' influence has been on balance malign, a criticism which measurers have been anxious to refute, by advocating *inter alia* longer-term contracts for managers.

Performance measurement has been blamed for 'short-termism' in that it drives fund managers into frenetic action which in turn destroys any possibility of long-term thinking. It makes them look on their shares as gaming chips, not part-ownership of real companies performing a useful service. This is an exaggeration. Most intelligent trustees tend to want to think in terms of a cycle despite the difficulty of deciding when a cycle starts and ends, and they want to give managers a fair chance. Measurement is inevitable. It may be abused or used foolishly; or as an excuse for consultants to earn themselves a fee. But gunning for performance measurement is aiming at the wrong target. The right inference is once again the skill, knowledge, and training of trustees. This is a book that has scarcely been opened; it should be. And the pressures on them are so great that many commentators now consider they should be paid for their pains.

At the end of all this there is a new dimension—the accountability of the trustees themselves to their beneficiaries and that includes their policy on issues of corporate governance and the way in which they were executed.

Some commentators consider trustees to have outlived their usefulness— at least to pension funds in the modern complicated world—but if they are to be replaced there will need to be people with roughly the same functions. Their disappearance does not seem to be planned.

Annual General Meetings

There is no escaping the fact that individual shareholders have far less of a chance to meet a company's management than do the institutions. The main opportunity they have to see the directors is at the Annual General Meeting (AGM). Although there is no legal obligation on all the board to attend, the CCCG requires them to do so (D2.3). UK companies are run by an elected oligarchy, that is, the board; an Athenian type of democracy would be totally impracticable. 'Democracy' is limited to the prescribed rights of the electorate (i.e. the shareholders) to choose or dismiss the oligarchs. Additionally, the directors may convene general meetings which all shareholders may attend: if a tenth of the shareholders require it in due form, the directors must convene such a meeting (Companies Act 1985, section 368 ff.). And a company must call an AGM (section 366) on pain of fines for it and its directors; if it does not the court may call one. The CCCG requires companies to send shareholders the notice of the AGM and related papers at least twenty working days beforehand (D2.4).

Having thus assured shareholders of a day's democracy, the Companies Act gives it substance by requiring the directors to lay the accounts before the AGM with the auditors' report (section 24.1). The shareholder does not have to attend in person but is entitled to appoint someone else as proxy or lodge a proxy vote (section 37.2).

In normal circumstances an AGM is poorly attended. Penetrating questions are seldom put. Institutional shareholders prefer to ask quietly on another occasion rather than give an appearance of public confrontation: besides, if they have fastened on to an interesting point they may not wish to reveal it to their 'competitors'. Private shareholders are as likely to be concerned with peripheral social issues or with their own experience as customers.

A PIRC survey released in November 1999 stated that for the top 350 companies proxy voting levels had risen by 4.8% from the previous year to 50.3%. Turnout for the all-share index was 48.9%. Votes at extraordinary general meetings (EGMs) tend to be higher.

There is no required quorum at law at an AGM, though the company's articles will prescribe one (generally two or three in person or by proxy). No profession of proxy solicitor has emerged. Even when a contentious issue arises and both parties are trying feverishly to marshal support, it is rare for half the shares to be voted. And the voting mechanisms often creak, with votes going astray or arriving late (one of the reasons for the institutions to vote routinely is to make sure the mechanics of voting actually work).

Shareholders rarely exercise their right to make the company circulate a resolution and accompanying statement of up to 1,000 words, even though it only needs 5% of the vote or a hundred members with £100 each of paid-up capital to do it (section 3.76).

At first blush AGMs appear a waste of time as so few attend. Even when a company's management has not covered itself with glory a public démarche is rare (but may be effective if carefully mounted). Companies do not on the whole seek to evade responsibility by arranging the AGM for an awkward time on an inconvenient date in an inaccessible place: some go to the opposite extreme and offer refreshments to restore the weary. Despite all this, many chairmen I have questioned are far more sensitive to the potential problems of an AGM than their shareholders might imagine; it concentrates their minds far more than might be supposed. It also now involves other directors. CCCG (D2.3) requires the chairman to arrange for the chairmen of the audit, remuneration, and nomination committees to be available to answer questions. The auditors, who are appointed by the shareholders and who report to them, are present, but they have no right to speak unless the chairman invites them to do so, even though a shareholder may direct a question to them.

It is the privilege of the UK's kind of democracy for voters to abstain, however much doing so weakens the system. CCCG offers sage advice (D.2): 'The board should use the AGM to communicate with investors and encourage their participation.' It is not as if all UK companies perform so well there is nothing to answer for; nor is it the case that messages delivered in private even by major institutions always produce results. Some well-directed judicious questions, adequately reported in the press, could well have a salutary effect. Even if chairmen do not fear losing control of an AGM, they respect penetrating and apposite questions and views. And it is to be hoped that someone is monitoring the effect of D2 of the CCCG which requires the board to 'Use the AGM to communicate with investors and to encourage their participation'.

The Company Law Review looked at the possibility of dispensing with AGMs—and a company can do so if all its members agree—an impossible condition. In the end the conclusion seems to have been that with all their faults and weaknesses it is better to retain them especially to protect minority shareholders. (See *Corporate Governance*, 11/1 (January 2003), article by R. Stratling.)

Stakeholders and Corporate Social Responsibility

The 'other constituencies' debate

In one important respect the law does not need to be changed: namely, the bodies to which the board is accountable. In the 'other constituencies' debate, it is argued that management has a great many interests to consider other than the shareholders, such as employees, customers, suppliers, bankers, and the community. Of course it does; it cannot hope to succeed unless it takes all these interests properly into account. At the end of the day, however, it has to be able to service its debt and attract new capital when it needs it. If it fails in this it will lose control—or the company itself will fail. In today's world the demand for capital is likely to rise (and its price with it if supply does not expand). Shareholders may come at the end of the queue for dividends (and for distribution if the company ceases to trade), but they are the anchormen. If the board's accountability to them is lessened it will be altogether weakened: the distinction between 'taking into account' and 'being responsible to' is fundamental. That said a statutory statement of directors' duties would require stakeholders' interests to be taken into account

Corporate social responsibility (CSR) remains high on the agenda, with over 75% of FTSE 350 companies publishing environmental and health and safety policies. To select two at random from very different spheres, RTZ have for years been strong on their environmental concerns, and Marks & Spencer on their social work, one aspect of which is dealt with in their Marks and Start scheme (2004). Fewer companies publish social responsibility and ethics policies, but some have established special committees of the board to look at CSR issues generally or at particular aspects like safety, the environment, or child labour.

Some companies are generous with their shareholders' funds. The *Investors' Chronicle* reported (12 November 2004, p. 24) that GSK gave charities 5.34% of pre-tax profits, ITV 6.92%, Reuters 5.1% , Rexam 5.02%, and Northern Rock 4.99%.

Managerial attitudes have changed over the years according to some research by Poole, Mansfield & Mendes quoted in the *Journal of General Management* 28/4 (Summer 2003); note especially how suppliers have climbed up the ladder (Table 6.2).

Table 6.2 Survey of private sector board members. Question: Which interests should management promote within the organization?

	Yes, I definitely think so. . . . . No, I definitely do not think so				
	1	2	3	4	5
Owners or shareholders					
1980	62.6	26.2	8.4	1.9	0.9
1990	55.8	32.0	9.6	1.0	1.5
2000	29.9	61.9	8.2	0	0
Managers					
1980	22.7	36.1	28.1	9.0	3.3
1990	20.8	38.6	28.4	10.2	2.0
2000	16.0	72.3	7.8	3.5	0.4
Other employee groups					
1980	22.0	33.0	31.6	9.1	4.3
1990	17.9	43.9	29.6	6.6	2.0
2000	18.1	65.9	12.5	3.0	0.4
Consumers					
1980	42.2	26.0	22.3	5.7	3.8
1990	43.7	36.0	14.2	4.1	2.0
2000	35.3	52.2	11.2	0.9	0.4
Suppliers					
1980	8.9	12.4	30.6	29.7	17.7
1990	9.3	18.1	36.3	25.9	10.4
2000	10.4	57.1	23.8	8.2	0.4
Public at large					
1980	20.0	20.0	26.7	20.4	12.9
1990	16.3	24.0	41.3	11.2	7.1
2000	11.2	41.4	36.2	7.8	3.4
Environmental groups					
2000	8.2	40.9	39.2	9.9	1.7

Note: Total sample (1980, n = 236; 1990, n = 302; 2000, n = 236). Figures in percentages.

Mergers and Takeovers

UK companies live in a turbulent world. In the year ending 31 December 2003 there were no fewer than 11,214 deals worldwide in which European companies were involved at least one end of the transaction. The value of these deals summed to $615,251 million.

A comparison of the FTSE of 1984 with 2004 shows that only 23 of the originals remained (*Independent*, 23 December 2003). Some have shrunk and dropped out of the top 100, some have failed altogether, and some have been absorbed. Mergers and takeovers have been frequent. (The term 'takeover' tends to be reserved for cases in which a company seeks to acquire another against the will of its board.) Some would-be 'friendly' mergers turn into takeovers because the 'target' company's board does not wish to proceed: some 'hostile' bids end in negotiated terms, so the distinctions are not necessarily clear-cut. 'Takeovers' began in the 1950s, gathered pace in the 1960s, and took off in the 1980s. According to *Acquisitions Monthly* of January 2004, 3,573 deals were struck in 2003 in which UK companies were involved. (Some of the other parties were foreign and some unquoted; 2,501 were arranged without a financial adviser.) In the twenty-year period 1969–88 takeovers accounted on average for 1.6% of the replacement cost and 2% of the market value of the UK capital stock per annum. The peak years were 1972 and 1988, at around 4% of the market value of the capital stock.

The desire to acquire another company may spring from various motives:

- Increased size affords better protection from takeover.
- It may produce needed diversification in mature industries.
- It may be the most efficient way to break into new markets or obtain new lines.
- It may massage the CEO's ego (status and even honours).
- Sheer opportunism, riding on the back of helpful accounting conventions especially where the target appears to be sitting on underutilized assets which can be profitably sold off. This kind of asset stripping was common in the 1960s and is not dead.

One of the most important of the board's functions is to agree a policy on organic growth versus acquisitions and, if acquisitions are made, to control the process, so that too high a price is not paid. This is a world in which advisers get much more from completed deals than aborted ones. Their interests are patently not identical with those of their clients. A string of cases in the USA in the 1980s highlighted the director's responsibilities and was one of the stimuli towards better governance.

Some bids are still made as a means of installing superior management. We noted earlier that this is an expensive and illogical way to sort out governance deficiencies.

The other aspect of takeovers which lies at the heart of governance is the fair treatment of shareholders. The pioneering buccaneers of the 1950s and early 1960s caused a reaction that led in 1967 to the establishment of the Takeover Panel (TOP) and the drafting of its code. In its first twelve months to March 1969 it handled 575 cases. The Report for 2002/3 shows that it handled 108 cases, of which 85 had involved a change of control. The Panel in that year heard only one appeal from a decision by the executive and none came before the Appeal Committee.

The Panel is a non-statutory body which commands the support both of industry and the financial world. It is managed by a director (seconded for a limited period from one of the financial houses), who is supported by a small professional staff (one of whom is usually seconded from the Bank of England). The Panel itself is drawn from leading members of the financial, professional, and industrial worlds. The chairman is usually a prominent lawyer.

The TOP is both legislator and court. Being non-statutory it can change the code rapidly if needs be. It hears cases and makes decisions. The courts have been reluctant to interfere with the substance of the TOP's decision, so appeals to them are rare (though of course there is always judicial review). The TOP has its own appeal procedure. Cases are heard by three members of the Panel who did not hear it at first instance; they are chaired by a lawyer. It is still a matter for conjecture whether the TOP will be able to continue on its present basis if the EC's Takeover Directive ever becomes law: the idea that such an important body can work effectively (as it clearly does) without a formal statutory framework is odd to non-British eyes especially as it has no formal powers to enforce its rulings. Its rulings are, however, almost always observed, because the power of those who support the Panel cannot be ignored: the Stock Exchange might, for instance, suspend the listing of a company which flouted the Panel. One or two securities firms in the 1980s became so full of themselves that they felt they could treat the TOP with scant respect—for instance, by exploiting what they saw as gaps in the rules—but their reputation was, to say the least, not enhanced as a consequence.

The TOP Code has had an important effect on the process of takeovers. It has now become a substantial document of seventeen sections, thirty-eight rules, plus appendices. The General Principles, however, are quite short and are stated here for convenience:

1. All shareholders of the same class of an offeree company must be treated similarly by an offeror.

2. During the course of an offer, or when an offer is in contemplation, neither an offeror, nor the offeree company, nor any of their respective advisers may furnish information to some shareholders which is not made available to all shareholders. This principle does not apply to the furnishing of information in confidence by the offeree company to a bona fide potential offeror or vice versa.

3. An offeror should only announce an offer after the most careful and responsible consideration. Such an announcement should be made only when the offeror has every reason to believe that it can and will continue to be able to implement the offer: responsibility in this connection also rests on the financial adviser to the offeror.

4. Shareholders must be given sufficient information and advice to enable them to reach a properly informed decision and must have sufficient time to do so. No relevant information should be withheld from them.

5. Any document or advertisement addressed to shareholders containing information or advice from an offeror or the board of the offeree company or their respective advisers must, as is the case with a prospectus, be prepared with the highest standards of care and accuracy.

6. All parties to an offer must use every endeavour to prevent the creation of a false market in the securities of an offeror or the offeree company. Parties involved in offers must take care that statements are not made which may mislead Shareholders or the market.

7. At no time after a bona fide offer has been communicated to the board of the offeree company, or after the board of the offeree company has reason to believe that a bona fide offer might be imminent, may any action be taken by the board of the offeree company in relation to the affairs of the company, without the approval of the shareholders in general meeting, which could effectively result in any bona fide offer being frustrated or in the shareholders being denied an opportunity to decide on its merits.

8. Rights of control must be exercised in good faith and the oppression of a minority is wholly unacceptable.

9. Directors of an offeror and the offeree company must always, in advising their shareholders, act only in their capacity as directors and not have regard to their personal or family shareholdings or to their personal relationships with the companies. The shareholders' interests taken as a whole, together with those of employees and creditors, should be considered when the directors are giving advice to shareholders. Directors of the offeree company should give careful consideration before they enter into any commitment with an offeror (or anyone else) which would restrict their freedom to advise their shareholders in the future. Such commitments may give rise to conflicts of interest or result in a breach of the directors' fiduciary duties.

10. Where control of a company is acquired by a person, or persons acting in concert, a general offer to all other shareholders is normally required; a similar obligation may arise if control is consolidated. Where an acquisition is contemplated as a result of which a person may incur such an obligation, he must,

before making the acquisition, ensure that he can and will continue to be able to implement such an offer.

The underlying themes are those of openness, timeliness, and even-handedness. Openness means revealing the accumulation of stakes (in accordance with the Substantial Acquisition Rules), plus the rules about 'concert parties' (i.e. where various parties act together in secret concert). In less picturesque language its rules promote fair dealing and limit conspiracies. As a more general point, it is interesting to note how standards have changed. The Companies Act 1948 contained no provisions about disclosing interests in shares. The 1985 Act devotes the whole of Part VI to the subject, sections 198–220. The obligation to disclose ownership has become more stringent. At the time of the 1985 Act a 'notifiable percentage' was 5%. This has been reduced to 3%.

Timeliness means conducting the bid according to a timetable, thus saving the bidders the cost of keeping finance in place indefinitely, and the target company the uncertainty of an extended battle. Anyone who has received an unwanted bid will attest to the amount of management time and nervous energy it consumes. On the other hand, there are those who feel it wrong that businesses which it has taken generations to build should be dispatched with indecent haste. If a bid fails, however, the bidder may not normally bid again for a year.

Even-handedness means, first, that it is the shareholder, not management, who decide the outcome of the bid: management may not put a wall around them to stop a purchaser (e.g. by using poison pills), or frustrate the bid in other ways (e.g. by an arrangement where a company arranges to sell one or more of its prime assets to a third party on the basis that the deal will only be completed if an unwanted bidder tries to take the company over—(the 'Crown Jewels defence').

Second, it means fairness among shareholders. Offers must be made for all the shares on equal terms and the price must not be lower than the bidder has paid before or after he made the bid. Furthermore, if someone acquires more than 29.9% of the shares, control is deemed to pass and he must bid, in cash, for the rest. If, however, the purchaser is foreign it may get away with unequal treatment. (Bosch bought the Worcester Group for £71.8 million, but gave management shareholders (38.4%) different terms from the others.)

Although the Code is now detailed, the Introduction to the General Principles makes it clear that what is intended is not a legalistic search for loopholes but an approach which is consonant with the Code's general spirit: 'It is impracticable to devise rules in sufficient detail to cover all circumstances which can arise in offers. Accordingly, persons engaged in offers should be aware that the spirit as well as the precise wording of the General Principles and the ensuing Rules must be observed.' In fact, clever merchant banks have often searched for cracks in the brickwork into which to insert a knife—a legalistic approach not in keeping with the spirit of a system that does its best not to be legalistic. Big money is at stake, enough to dull the sensibilities of the unscrupulous.

Whether or not the threat of takeover is a spur or harmful to managerial performance is considered below under the title 'marketophobia'.

Public To Private

Writing twelve years ago it was essential to mention leveraged buy-outs (MBOs) and buy-ins (MBIs). Many were based on the proposition that if management owns a big enough stake the agency costs (in economists' parlance) are reduced; performance will improve with motivation. It ought to have been clear that motivation needed to be accompanied by competence: if that were not so, no family business would ever fail as long as the directors remained fully motivated—but as we all know, many do collapse. The failure of so many MBOs and MBIs told us that reducing accountability and 'improving' motivation were not enough in themselves; the general principles of good corporate governance apply as much to MBOs and MBIs as in other companies, and investors ignore this factor at their peril. This is all the more important because there are so many cases of successful MBOs and MBIs scurrying back to the market and getting a new quotation, thereby presumably to some extent reopening the issue of agency costs and reopening the question of conformance with governance standards.

Since those days the Public To Private market (PTP) (where a company abandons its quotation) has expanded rapidly, but many of the same caveats apply. It is often in the minds of directors who take their companies down that route that one day they may return to the market. What they are doing is seeking an interval whilst they line their pockets before returning once again to a proper governance regime. Some do so because they feel vulnerable at the discount to value that often occurs with small cap companies. Others prefer less public (and maybe less stringent) accountability. This is a profitable game for them, but there are signs that shareholders are disenchanted. They are right to believe that the directors have conflicts of interest. In the UK the number of deals fell from 53 in 1999 to 35 in 2003, but in Europe the total had grown to 96 from 73 in 2002 (source: Dealogic, quoted on p. 39 of *Financial News*, 26 January 2004). There were cases in which a move towards a PTP brought in other bidders. Finally Hermes was considering an initiative to rally the shareholders in such cases to safeguard their interests, as noted above.

Of course any attempt to modify the UK's system and process will excite the opposition of those who make their living by it. The City of London is superbly professional and brilliant at selling its services. Those who made fortunes from the creation of conglomerates some years ago are now making second fortunes from dismembering them. They score when a company goes private and when it floats again. Employees from chairman to canteen hand have to accept that others can settle their livelihoods and prospects, changing at will the implicit contracts on which they entered employment. Meanwhile it is the shareholders who foot the bill—or the public in terms of higher prices.

Litigation

There was a time many years ago when it was rare for directors to be sued. Even so there were enough awkward cases in the 1980s like Guinness (1986) to cause directors to realize that there could be abnormal circumstances when they might need legal or other professional advice; this subject was addressed in the Cadbury report (para. 4A8) and is now covered in CCCG (A5.2). This gives directors a right to get the independent professional advice they need at the company's expense as long as it is in furtherance of their duties. At the time of writing (2004) the Queen's Moat House case is *sub judice* and so is Equitable Life, in which the sums claimed are ruinous—way beyond any D&O cover.

The 'deep pocket' principle has long been a feature of English law; the courts allowed plaintiffs to sue employers, for instance for damage inflicted by their employees even though they were acting against express instructions. The same kind of thought (the directors are not rich enough to be worth powder and shot) has led to there being an increased tendency to sue auditors, especially after a company has failed unexpectedly shortly after its accounts have been passed, though the well-known judgement by the House of Lords in the Caparo case restricted the right of suit by defining narrowly the persons to whom auditors owed a duty of care. The DTI is now consulting about 'proportional' damages and limits on auditors' liability. It may well look at directors' liability too. There is widespread concern that UK NEDs are saddled with unlimited liability and inadequate D&O cover. The risks they run are out of all proportion to the rewards they receive. Some kind of limitation is sought, but at the same time it is well understood that they should not be given a charter to be grossly negligent with impunity.

In short, litigation has not yet played an important part in corporate governance in the UK—even in or after takeovers. The Takeover Panel should get much credit for this.

The Insolvency Act 1986 has made directors more wary of their role in troubled companies lest they trade wrongfully and so open themselves both to a suit for damages and the prospect of disqualification.

Internal Controls

Probably the most significant governance development in the last five years has been on the policy and practice of internal controls. They form a link between governance (as defined) and management since they involve not just members of the board but managers at any level.

'The CCCG has a 24-page section on Guidance on Internal Control (The Turnbull Guidance). The purpose of the guidance is twofold. It is to ensure that managers throughout the organization understand the risks they are running and take the necessary steps to evaluate them and then deal with them by avoiding them, controlling them or insuring against them—or a combination of all three. Some risks simply have to be accepted, but the point is that managers should factor the methodical consideration of risk into their way of working. It should be 'embedded'—not an optional or added extra. At board level different risks are considered in different ways. Business risk—where the company stands to make a profit or incur a loss—is a matter for the board though it may delegate. Operational risks are those which only carry the possibility of loss. Many companies process these through the audit committee whose function it is to make sure the risks are faced and dealt with appropriately. It will generally have the internal auditors to guide it, whose programme of work will be based on an assessment of the incidence and impact of risks so that they can allocate resources most effectively. The internal auditors will report to the committee on material outstanding matters where managers have not taken the necessary action to reach a satisfactory standard. The second purpose is to reassure shareholders and this is given effect by the requirement for the board to report annually on how it has implemented Principle D2 of the CCCG—'The board should maintain a sound system of internal control to safeguard shareholders' investment and the company's assets.' The guidance is intended to produce flexibility in the way that companies work and report, but it covers two pages for maintaining a sound system of internal control (CCCG, pp. 32–3) a further two on reviewing the effectiveness of internal control (pp. 34–6), and a page on the board's statement on internal control (pp. 36–7).

It has been suggested that the Turnbull guidance is one of the most significant developments in corporate governance over the last decades. It may well be that all it does is codify what the best managed companies were already doing, and the only extra burden on them is to describe their practices. In other cases it may lead to beneficial changes. The strengthening of the internal audit function may sometimes be a highly desirable step forward. Without this happening (or there being an extension of the external auditors' duties) it is difficult to see how directors will be able to sign off on 'the effectiveness of their system of internal control' as required by the CCCG (C2.1). Note that this is for the board, not the chairman, as in France or the CEO/CFO, as in the USA under Sarbanes-Oxley.

Unquoted Companies

General

Most unquoted companies are SMEs (small and medium enterprises) which are defined in various ways. The DTI uses the number of employees—medium firms have 50–249, small firms 10–49. Smaller than this and they are defined as micro. In its tenth report on finance for small firms, in April 2003, the Bank of England comments (p. 6) on the dearth of accurate statistics on formation and closures. There are roughly 2.7 million such firms and around 45,000 bankruptcies and liquidations more or less balanced by the number of new firms set up. Their importance to the economy is suggested by the fact that 42% of the country's employees work for them and they produce 44% of its turnover.

The same report comments on the profusion of advice available to SMEs in various parts of the country and the lack of coordination. Quoted Companies Alliance, formerly CISCO (1999), addresses issues affecting smaller quoted companies but I could find no specific reference to corporate governance of unquoted companies. The Department of Trade and Industry is keenly interested in SMEs and in January 2004 published 'A Government Action Plan for Small Business', but governance does not figure in it. Indeed the subject may seem totally irrelevant to the directors of SMEs that may be short of finance and struggling to gain a foothold in the market for their products or services. They will feel that in their sphere the old British approach still holds sway—directors should be left to get on with their job with as little interference as possible as long as they stay within the law. No one will have as sound a motivation as they—who have most to lose. If proprietors understand sound governance they will apply it; there is never any guarantee they will not fail whether they do or do not. In fact governance matters to SMEs as much as to big companies—perhaps more, since they have fewer resources to tide them over when mistakes are made—but the very title is guaranteed to make the subject sound remote. It would sound less so were it called direction and control—its core purpose.

In 1995 the Institute of Accountants in England and Wales did a diagnosis of the failure of owner-managed businesses. Most were small and young, but some had over a hundred employees and one at least was over a hundred years old. In some cases there was an element of bad luck but in many it was a failure of governance, even though that word does not appear in the text. Good governance after all addresses such points as capital structure, financial management, planning, marketing and succession—all elements that rank high amid the causes of failure. In its concluding paragraph the report says 'Owner-managers are often single-minded and very independent...but many did not have the range of management skills necessary to grow the business successfully nor are they inclined to take remedial advice.'

In the 2004 paper mentioned above the Department of Trade and Industry put the spotlight on enterprise: 'It is the dynamism of individual entrepreneurs that drives small businesses but government, through its actions, can do much to stimulate enterprise, support small business and overcome barriers to growth'(1.4). After this it elaborates on what needs to be done and what the government's role will be.

The elevation of enterprise to a higher status is a welcome change from the era in which profits and private enterprise were despised. But enterprise to be successful must encompass good governance. We can think of successful businesses having a box into which are packed both dynamic enterprise and sound governance. One might conclude (with apologies to Einstein) that the formula $E = CG_2$—where enterprise is E and CG is corporate governance—is an elegant way of illustrating the relationship.

The law

There are few differences in law as between quoted and unquoted companies, whether they are PLCs or Ltd, though the takeover code only applies to PLCs or Ltd companies where there is a market in their shares. The government has addressed the question of whether it can make life easier for small unquoted companies, but until there is a Bill and it goes through Parliament it is impossible to say for certain what the changes will be. It seems likely that they will move in the direction of simplification. The published policy paper deals for instance with the requirement to hold an AGM and it suggests simplifying the procedures for resolutions. It also tackles the awkward question of shareholder disputes, which can so easily wreck a small business.

The time has come to look more closely at the governance of the rest, if only because they are such an important part of the economy today and potentially its great firms tomorrow.

Perhaps the best way of approaching the subject is to apply the classic analysis of enterprise and accountability (including transparency).

Enterprise

The founders of small businesses have identified market opportunities which they believe they can exploit and thus secure returns above the cost of capital. Although there is no 'agency problem' if they own all the shares, they are not always proficient as the analysis of failure shows. This is often due to shortage of essential skills, like accounting, or shortage of capital. There is, moreover, insufficient structure to monitor and plan. The pressures to do crowd out the time to think. With all the principals up to their necks in activity they can easily lose sight of their objectives. In the opening chapter I recognized how difficult it might feel for those running smaller businesses to haul themselves away from the pressing burdens of the day to look in a considered way at the future.

No one is in a position to tell these businesses what to do; they need to be convinced that it is in their own interests. It would be pleasant to think that this point was always part and parcel of the support they receive from whatever source; I have not encountered evidence that this is so. What they often need is advice—and discipline in the way they set about their entrepreneurial activities. An experienced adviser is often invaluable to such companies. He does not have to be an NED—indeed he may become associated with the company when formality of any kind is minimal and talking of a 'board' dignifies an informal gathering with a title it does not deserve. At the very least he can improve process and this may in time lead to a board developing with a real role. It does not matter that he has influence but not power. In many small companies poor process—governance by any other name—was often a contributory factor to failure.

In Christine Mallin's book *Corporate Governance* (2004: 55) she suggests a chain of development from family assembly, through family council, and later advisory board, to eventually a board of directors including NEDs. She quotes Cadbury (2000) in defining the three requisites for growth—recruiting the best people, developing a culture of trust and transparency, and creating logical and efficient organizational structures.

Accountability

If the founders hold all the shares and are running the business, accountability is a meaningless concept, as by definition they would be accountable to themselves—though if there are equal partners they may be accountable to each other—a sort of lateral accountability. In the true sense accountability starts when there are shareholders who are not on the board—either members of the family or complete outsiders, including venture capitalists. This implies at the very least that they will receive the accounts—not always the case with elderly members of the family who may have inherited their shares.

Minority shareholders in unquoted companies can be very vulnerable; the executives can by one means or another purloin for themselves an undue share of the profits, and it is difficult to get redress in the UK courts short of such dire circumstances that they will uphold a claim that the minority is being oppressed. Unless there is a shareholders' agreement in place (as there would be with a venture capital infusion) the minority shareholders cannot even escape on reasonable terms. There is indeed no pressure that can be brought to bear on such companies to improve their governance and the banks are reluctant to get involved in such matters.

So far I have been writing in the context of the myriad of SMEs (small and medium enterprises), and especially about the smaller ones. But a large and increasing number of bigger companies are unquoted—some, indeed, who have deliberately delisted to escape the public eye and avoid the CCCG. If they are relying on venture capital their sponsors may insist on their following some of the CCCG requirements.

The corporate governance movement rode on the back of big company scandals because the 'fall-out' was significant. When an SME perishes the damage done is limited. The same cannot always be said of big unquoted companies, most noticeably perhaps when they are concentrated in a single location and their demise gravely impairs local employment. It is perhaps for such reasons that the Germans, as we have seen, prescribe a specific structure for companies with 500 employees or more. There could be other measures of size like turnover, but the point is that size suggests disciplines for the public good. This is an area that merits further thought.

This is not as revolutionary as it sounds, bearing in mind that in the financial sector the FSA already supervises companies that lie outside the scope of the CCCG—for instance a wholly owned subsidiary of a foreign entity. They do so whether or not its demise would have knock-on effects within the financial system. In doing so they are silently accepting the principle that it is not just the shareholders who matter. Arguably the same is true of big unquoted companies outside the financial sector.

An Evaluation of the UK System

Externalities

Systems of corporate governance are not the only thing that matters when we assess a country's relative performance. They are one factor among many. Sometimes externalities have proved important. In that regard the UK has no excuses as it possesses:

- defined boundaries;
- effective government;
- the rule of law (without having a surfeit of lawyers);
- great tolerance, and liberal attitudes towards trade;
- many well-trained/educated people;
- remarkably little chauvinism in regard to the nationality of companies;
- no consistent financial disadvantage from the relative cost of money. (A paper produced for the National Economic Development Office in 1990 (CF(90)3) stated: 'A comparison of real bank borrowing costs in the UK and Germany revealed little difference for the period 1979-87; however the nominal cost of debt (which has direct implications for companies' cash flows) shows UK industry to have been at a considerable disadvantage relative to its competitors in the 1970s; nominal borrowing rates have been both high and more volatile in this period.')

There is, however, one aspect which may have been a disadvantage—societal attitudes. All the other societies examined in this book accord commerce and industry an honoured place. That is not to assert that materialism is or should be all-conquering or that money is or should be the only target in life and measurement of value. It is simply that everyone enjoys the products and services that industry and commerce provide, and that it is hypocritical to pretend that supplying them is inestimable: it is fair to scorn what is useless or superfluous, but absurd to extend this to what one uses and enjoys. And it betrays the mentality of a bygone age to pretend that somehow these things can be produced by Untermenschen, whose lives and contributions can be regarded by any element in society, whatever their self-esteem, with disdain. The surplus wealth their efforts provide fund all the laudable objectives the high-principled (correctly) wish to pursue, from care for the aged to support for struggling artists. This wealth can only be won by being successful against international competition. Those who compete are like the country's champions of old, worthy of esteem and support. In time every society will get, more or less, the commerce and industry it deserves. All starts with esteem, for without it nothing else will be made available. Nor must esteem be reserved wholly for success, for if it is, failure even with heroic efforts will earn neglect and opprobrium. The industrialists' apparent disdain of educationalists ('ivory tower... those who can do, those who can't teach'), is matched by reciprocal feelings: 'You have the intelligence to seek a career in the civil service or professions; you do not have to go into industry.' If these trite caricatures did not have so much truth in them they would be pitiable.

Since the advent of New Labour these attitudes appear to have softened, and enterprise is being accorded the respect it deserves—not before time. It is to be hoped that it signifies a widespread and sincere change to the value system, to elevate commerce and industry and all those who are employed in them to the same level of public esteem in which they are held in all the other countries studied. Perhaps we are coming to the end of a long road which started when influential sections of society began to feel that many of the malaises of their day could be attributed to industry, so those who dirtied their hands with production had somehow slipped socially. Such attitudes must be relegated to the sidelines of history; even now the UK's improving productivity does not match that of the USA.

The heart of corporate governance

Introduction

We saw in previous chapters that there are two basic principles of corporate governance which apply at all times and in all places. They do not deny the importance either of power or patronage, but require them to be exercised within a framework of accountability. These two principles can be briefly restated:

1. That management must be able to drive the enterprise forward free from undue constraint caused by government interference, fear of litigation, or fear of displacement.
2. That this freedom—to use managerial power and patronage—must be exercised within a framework of effective accountability. Nominal accountability is not enough. Accountability implies transparency.

To evaluate the UK system of corporate governance requires us to consider carefully whether or to what extent these principles are followed or breached. The account of the system given above has already touched on some of the issues.

The freedom of executive management

Government. The UK does not have to face some of the worst manifestations of interference by ministers or civil servants: management does not have to seek permission for most things, nor does it need to bribe its way forward.

In most sectors, UK regulation of commerce and industry is far more comprehensive than it was—not least because of Brussels. Much is based on the assumption that the modern world has become so complex that citizens, however careful, cannot adequately protect themselves from the dangers of the goods and services they procure. The doctrine of *caveat emptor* is not quite dead, but it is in intensive care. What UK management has to contend with are periodical convulsions by the government of the day, which is galvanized into action and then produces a monumental piece of legislation like the Financial Services and Markets Act 2000, which imposes great costs in its pursuit of imagined safety.

Fear of litigation or prosecution. The directors of UK companies are seldom sued and on the whole do not fear litigation. This is partly because there are few causes of action which apply and partly because the machinery is not available (e.g. there are no derivative suits and class actions as there are in the USA, and no contingency fees either). Of course, if directors break the law they may face penalties—for instance, if they are guilty of trading wrongfully within the meaning of the Insolvency Act 1986. People will even accept appointment to the boards of troubled companies, provided they feel they know the facts and that the financial support is adequate to keep them on the right side of the law. There are signs that this relaxed regime may be severely disturbed in the 'blame' culture. So far the cloud is 'no bigger than a man's hand'. But it looks bigger since the Penrose report (2004) into Equitable Life, which has put a spotlight on the risks.

The risk of prosecution has certainly grown under various statutes, not forgetting breaches of the listing rules, market abuse, and insider trading—though it must be said that successful prosecutions for the last named are astonishingly few, given the opportunities that exist.

Fear of displacement. No one is wholly secure in their job; in any case total security can lead to complacency. In governance terms the question is whether excessive insecurity reduces efficiency. If a competent manager is displaced after a merger the market will soon absorb him, though not necessarily at his former level of remuneration. In any case the effects of displacement are now usually mitigated by compensation (to a degree that some find over-generous). Do managers in countries where there are fewer takeovers show themselves more or less competent as a result? It is difficult to judge but the most ruthless of all countries in this respect—the USA—also produces good results in terms of productivity, and it is difficult to accuse it of the dreaded 'short-termism' which is part of 'marketophobia'.

'*Marketophobia*'. The question is whether the fear of the market inhibits management from making the decisions it considers to be in the longer-term interests of the company. In principle better communications with shareholders should ease matters. They will understand that there are different time horizons in different industries. What has changed in the last decade is the greater effort by management to put its case across and a greater disposition by shareholders to listen—a benign development, but managers have to be careful not to destroy their credibility by excessive optimism which later proves unjustified. Life is more difficult for managers of small-cap companies outside the 'go-go' industries. The market for their shares is often thin and they trade at a discount. So, even if the company is well managed, shareholders may be tempted to accept a bid premium on the current price instead of waiting for the market to catch up with the clearly improving results. This has happened to me twice.

The UK has all the ingredients conducive to takeover activities—diffuse shareholdings, and a process designed to facilitate deals. None of the artificial defences like 'poison pills' or 'crown jewels' is available. There are safeguards against monopolies or overconcentration now in the hands of the Office of Fair Trading (OFT) and the Competition Appeal Tribunal (CAT) (set up by the Enterprise Act 2002 and busy carving a name for itself).

In these circumstances managers know that poor performance will expose them to a takeover especially if the company is asset rich. To that extent the possibility of such an event acts as a spur. Managers do not wish to exchange the forbearance of their existing shareholders to the pressures of new ones—especially as they themselves will probably lose their jobs. In theory, management should never be allowed to underperform for long. The board ought to see to that; and if it fails to do so the shareholders should address the problem. The role of the market only becomes possible for this kind of takeover because both board and shareholders have failed. The market does have this role as a sort of long-stop, although it only provides a fraction of the funds companies employ. This type of takeover rides on the back of supine shareholders. In these more bracing times, the kind of stimulus administered by Hermes and other focus funds should reduce this kind of opportunity.

It is, however, now apparent that the existence of a bid premium does not depend on the target company being badly managed. An innoculation of good corporate governance does not necessarily keep takeovers at bay. There are always two pricing systems at work on a stock exchange, one for parcels of shares, one for control, and control always carries a premium. (For fuller discussion of this, see Charkham 1989.) However good a management may be, a bidder prepared to offer a premium is bound to have some appeal to shareholders—how much depends on the size of the premium divided by the sense of loyalty shareholders feel, less their fears about the market. There is one area which receives little attention and is perhaps worthy of more—the vulnerability of well-run small-cap companies whose shares are relatively illiquid. In such cases the share price is likely to languish to the point when a bidder cannot help getting a bargain. The board of the target company feels helpless. Although they may have every confidence in the company's future they are powerless to resist an offer at say 20% above the present market price. From the point of view of the economy as a whole such bids may prove destructive in the long run, since the new merged enterprise may prove worse than its previous component parts. The value of mergers has often been discussed, but the weak point in examining them is that it is usually impossible to conjecture how the parties would have fared had they not been joined together. The City often sells mergers on promises of the benefits of synergies. It is high time that some dispassionate research was undertaken into the extent to which such hopes have been realized. Asking an investment banker about the virtues of mergers is like asking a butcher whether to eat meat.

The vulnerability of companies to takeover because of the bid premium has been mentioned along with the spur to better performance that is implied. The difficult question concerns the negative effects of fear. It is impossible to measure the effects of the prospect of being taken over. It may produce economies; head offices in the UK are noticeably less opulent than they were and now tend to be small and sparsely manned. What about investment? Most CEOs will assert that their investment programmes are unaffected by fear of takeover. And yet no CEO ignores his share price. Are these points compatible? My doubts are reinforced by the apparently greater robustness of attitudes in private companies which do not have to worry about a public share price: directors who have 'gone private' tell me of their relief at being able to concentrate on the longer term without fear of a hostile bid. Much can be done by directors making sure their shareholders understand the company, but even so they are nervous about their share price. It is difficult to escape the conclusion that the emphasis the market naturally places on 'shareholders' immediate values' is likely to lead to management opting for shorter-term payback wherever possible. Managers have to wrestle with a world in which there is neither sentiment nor loyalty because an institutional fund manager cannot properly allow himself such latitude—he must decide on economic grounds what is in the best interests of his beneficiaries, whatever view he takes of the parties. Quite probably he will already hold the purchaser's shares as well. In strict logic he ought to hold on if a bid contains a premium which looks as if it will evaporate, only if he cannot do better by investing the proceeds elsewhere (or perhaps by buying back in if the bid fails and the price drops); and in many cases he would do well to sell the shares of both bidder and target, especially if the price is full.

It may be argued that UK industry is at a continuing competitive disadvantage against countries in which market pressures are not so severe, for instance because concentrated share ownership and networked systems of accountability work mean that managements have less to fear from the market: they therefore tend to have more latitude for investments which take longer to pay off.

Merger activity is however substantial in other countries too. *Acquisitions Monthly* recorded in January 2004 that in the previous year there had been 1,447 cases in which French companies had been involved and 1876 with German involvement. The same paper records a figure of 7,570 for USA companies.

Consideration of the merger scene brings home to us once again that although it is the law that is the starting point and economics are important, we are in fact in the realm of the behavioural sciences much of the time in governance matters. We met this when considering the structure of the board and its committees—the dynamics matter most of all. It is true of the takeover world; what matters here is the impact of the takeover jungle. There is a solid basis of concern about being bid for. It is not surprising that bids are feared and fought. It is not just a matter of money or compensation. Society wants its enterprises to be run by people who are motivated and dedicated, not just economic machines that suck what they can from an enterprise and leave it happily for a golden hello. Strong motivation is consistent with a fear of being displaced, of having to abandon the spiritual investment of many years, not because of one of the normal calamities to which business may be prey, but for a convulsive response of the stock market to a rich raider, prompted by a financial industry that makes vast fortunes from buying and selling what others have so painstakingly built up. For them the deal's the thing and little else matters.

Because it is so important, it is worth repeating that it is impossible to measure the effect of fear on the individual members of company boards, for this would take us into deep psychological waters. As noted above, CEOs often assert vigorously that they carry on regardless, doing what is best for the company, ignoring the share market. And yet . . . may it just be that they are now so conditioned by its continuing pressures that they factor them into their subconscious without even knowing it? May the standards they set themselves be lower than they would otherwise be? Is not fear a poor motivator, distracting and destructive? The physical systems of mankind equip us to respond to danger in one of two ways: to stand and fight or run like hell—not, however civilized we may think ourselves, to ignore the threat and get on with planning for our children's futures.

Adam Smith still casts a long shadow. In the final chapter of Book 1 of the *Wealth of Nations* he wrote, 'On the contrary it [the rate of profit] is naturally low in rich and high in poor countries, and it is always highest in the countries which are going fastest to ruin.'

Accountability

General

'Accountability' has an unpleasant and threatening ring to it; no one really rejoices in being accountable. Its importance however is twofold, both prophylactic and curative. If the system of accountability works well high standards will tend to be set; if management consistently fails to maintain them, accountability leads to remedial action.

It would be idle to pretend that any amendment to the system or change to the law could of itself guarantee brilliance, originality, or sheer competence. Nor does it guarantee success or freedom from failure or effective group dynamics, but some reforms obviously help more than others. The accountability of management to the board as a whole is by common consent the bedrock of the system. The reforms of the last decade have aimed at better structure, process, and standards to make the outturn less erratic. Even so, personalities still matter. The dominant will not suddenly become docile, and the weak will not suddenly become strong, so it remains to be seen how successful the reforms will be.

The role of shareholders

Historically the weakest link in the UK system of corporate governance was that between board and shareholders. Most shareholders did not see their interests, or those on whose behalf they hold shares, being best served by their taking any interest in or playing any part in corporate governance. Accountability is like a telephone conversation: it requires both parties to listen, and if one party has taken its phone off the hook it cannot take place at all. In days gone by many UK institutions switched off their phones and relied on market operations, even though the counter-party was usually an institution like themselves.

The system is built on the assumption that shareholders will monitor the performance of the companies in which they invest, not in the sense of vetting every move or double-guessing management, but by being concerned about the handful of strategic issues a company faces every decade and above all about the continued competence of its leadership. At long last this assumption is beginning to look justified, as well it might since there are no other viable alternatives.

Envoi

Rewriting this book after an interval of twelve years brought home to me how much things had changed. The main reforms that seemed so desirable then have largely been put in place, or are being tackled. The law itself is the laggard and it remains to be seen what will eventually emerge. New patterns of behaviour—particularly by shareholders—are emerging which are on the whole desirable.

All this reform is affecting shareholders, who according to the London *Financial Times* (11 October 2004, p. 2 of weekly review of the investment industry) are 'complaining of information overload as companies struggle to prove their corporate governance credentials'. Some regret that interest is being deflected from strategy to formal compliance: 'It doesn't matter if the deck chairs on the Titanic are imperfectly arranged.'

An even more important point to emerge is the belated appreciation that even a megaton of governance is no substitute for invention, entrepreneurial skill, originality, and sheer managerial competence and integrity. We need good governance, certainly, and the movement towards it was overdue. This means turning our backs on the old days of indiscipline and adopting a discriminating approach to substance and priorities so that everyone plays their part and does well the things that really need to be done. The idea of having directors whose independence brings a fresh spirit to the board in both its entrepreneurial and monitoring functions is a sound one—if it is not pushed too far. NEDs cannot know as much as the executives, and it is to be hoped that the courts will recognize this fact and not expect too much of them. It has often been suggested that the burdens they now bear merit payment at levels which are bound to sap independence. What is more, society should not expect too much; they are not Sherlock Holmes or Socrates. They may be duped or mistaken.

The evidence is that even good governance does not prevent fraud. There is no substitute for integrity and competence.

Finally, there is a moral dimension. It has surfaced in the stakeholder angle and in corporate social responsibility. There is something we might call the fabric of society and it is elastic. But greed may, in the end, tear it, whatever fashions and fancy names are used to justify it. We return to the formulation of the purpose of the company—'to provide profitably and ethically the goods and services society wants'.

Annex 6: *The Combined Code of Corporate Governance 2003*

Main Principles

1. Every company should be headed by an effective board, which is collectively responsible for the success of the company.
2. There should be a clear division of responsibilities at the head of the company between the running of the board and the executive responsibility for the running of the company's business. No one individual should have unfettered powers of decision.
3. The board should include a balance of executive and non-executive directors (and in particular independent non-executive directors) such that no individual or small group of individuals can dominate the board's decision taking.
4. There should be a formal, rigorous and transparent procedure for the appointment of new directors to the board.
5. The board should be supplied in a timely manner with information in a form and of a quality appropriate to enable it to discharge its duties. All directors should receive induction on joining the board and should regularly update their skills and knowledge.
6. The board should undertake a formal and rigorous annual evaluation of its own performance and that of its committees and individual directors.
7. All directors, should be submitted for re-election at regular intervals, subject to continuing satisfactory performance. The board should ensure planned and progressive refreshing of the board.
8. Levels of remuneration shall be sufficient to attract, retain and motivate directors of the quality required to run the company successfully, but a company should avoid paying more than is necessary for the purpose. A significant proportion of executive directors' remuneration should be structured so as to link rewards for corporate and individual performance.
9. There should be a formal and transparent procedure for developing policy on executive remuneration and for fixing the remuneration packages of individual directors. No director should be involved in deciding his or her remuneration.
10. The board should present a balanced and understandable assessment of the company's position and prospects.
11. The board shall maintain a sound system of internal control to safeguard shareholders' investment and the company's assets.
12. The board should establish formal and transparent arrangements for considering how they should apply the financial reporting and internal control principles and for maintaining an appropriate relationship with the company's auditors.
13. There should be a dialogue with shareholders based on the mutual understanding of objectives. The board as a whole has responsibilities for ensuring that a satisfactory dialogue with shareholders takes place.

14. The board should use the AGM to communicate with investors and to encourage their participation.
15. Institutional shareholders should enter into a dialogue with the company board on the mutual understanding of objectives.
16. When evaluating the company's governance arrangements, particularly those relating to board structure and composition, institutional shareholders should give due weight to all relevant factors drawn to their attention.
17. Institutional shareholders have a responsibility to make considered use of their votes.

7

Unfinished Business

Introduction

In the opening chapter we examined the basic principles that underlie good corporate governance everywhere—enterprise, transparency, and accountability. It is not surprising to find many similarities between countries; indeed on close examination many of the differences are more apparent than real. Is it significant that some countries prefer the clarity of law, whilst others use a non-statutory regime alongside the law which depends on a 'comply or explain' approach? This transfers enforcement from the state to private enterprise in the form of those most affected. Does it work better? The European Commission's proposed use of this approach is indeed a milestone. So far it would seem that nations choose methods that fit most easily with their culture. To amend Alexander Pope very slightly:

> For forms of Governance let fools contest
> Whate'er is best administered is best.

The wave of corporate governance reforms that has swept across much of the world resulted from a perception that many companies' difficulties were attributable at least in part to poor governance. The market seems to believe them effective, even though there are some misgivings about their complexity and attention to detail. In many countries it would seem to me that there should now be a pause so that the effects of the reforms can be coolly evaluated.

The USA has long known that there is competition between governance regimes. That is why so many companies chose Delaware. There is little evidence of companies switching their country of incorporation primarily to gain such a benefit although it may sometimes be a consideration.

The dividing line between quoted and unquoted companies means that the governance obligations on the former are far greater than those on the latter. Does this weigh with managements which seek to take quoted companies private? Do such managements act in their own interests or those of their shareholders? To believe these to be identical is like believing Hans Christian Andersen's tales.

To say that there should be a pause for reflection whilst existing reforms work through does not mean failing to tackle some important issues left unresolved. These will now be considered.

The Rule of Law

The conduct of business is of course subject to market forces and market mechanisms. Many of the relationships will be covered by the laws of contract or partnership. The state may introduce laws with criminal sanctions to cover certain activities like safety at work and protection of the environment. The creation of limited liability companies requires special laws, and these are often supplemented by regulations in one form or another as well as 'voluntary' codes in some countries designed, as we have seen, to supplement existing laws. It is one thing to set out the rights of each of the parties, but quite another to have a judicial system in which they can be enforced rapidly, fairly, and honestly. The parties need to be confident about the integrity of the legal system—the rule of law.

The strengthening of the rule of law in any country is one of the best investments it could make for the quality of life and economic progress. That means paying judges at levels that make bribery resistible, plus swingeing penalties against those who try to corrupt or intimidate them; it also means keeping judges free from intimidation from whatever quarter, including the state itself.

Just as there are benefits from the rule of law, so there are penalties of many kinds if it does not obtain. In the governance sphere these include deterring investment especially from abroad. Private investors may decide to risk their money in countries where the rule of law is at best partial, but institutions which are investing clients funds have to answer for it if they take such a risk. Corporate governance statements and codes have emerged in countries where the rule of law is incomplete; in such cases they are at best a pious expression of hope and should be treated as such.

Accounting and Auditing

Any visitor from outer space would be entitled to assume that accounts anywhere in the world were governed by the same conventions and meant the same thing. They would not suspect that the Tower of Babel affected the language of accounting as well as words. Many experts have for years been trying to find an accounting Esperanto—a common language. Great steps have been made as many accounts in the previous chapters demonstrate, not least the introduction of International Accounting Standards (IAS), but much remains to be done to achieve uniformity. This is not as simple as it sounds, however, because:

1. Accounts serve many purposes. US accounts, for instance, are primarily there to serve the stock market. UK accounts were designed to serve everyone. This is why to this day the UK requires a company that wishes to avail itself of limited liability, however small it may be, to file accounts with a government agency. An unquoted US company is under no obligation to file accounts.
2. In some countries the main purpose of the accounts is for the tax authorities.
3. Some systems are rule-based, others principle-based. Reconciling these approaches is no easy matter yet it is essential.
4. As has been noted earlier the figures in accounts are all a matter of judgement, however precise they may appear. For accounts to mean the same the judgements that underlie them must be as similar as possible. The German attitude towards reserving, for instance, is far more conservative than others. The French view of the volatility that might be caused by the implementation of IAS39 to their banks' balance sheets is another example. Can differing objectives be reconciled? To the layman it is absurd that they should not be.

The independence of auditors

This subject has received increasing attention and restrictions have been imposed in some countries on the amount of non-audit work an audit firm may conduct as it may impair their independence.

In most jurisdictions auditors are technically appointed by shareholders and are answerable to them. I know of no case where shareholders dismissed the auditors. In reality they answer to management. Understandably they do not wish to lose the audit and will not be popular with their own firm if they do. Does this impair their independence and, if so, how can it be restored? It is vital that it should be. They must feel free to stand upon their principles even if it means qualifying the accounts—which currently they seldom do, partly for fear of suit. Does this point towards the compulsory rotation of audit firms every five to seven years, not just audit partners? Greater independence lies that way.

Transparency

This is an overworked metaphor, and all-embracing rather than precise. It sounds like a giant plate glass window through which everyone can see and know everything about a company. Disclosure is a better term—information should not be withheld from those entitled to it. There are several contexts.

The usual one is between company and shareholders, but the recent cases of Enron and Equitable suggest that transparency between management and board is even more vital. In neither instance was the board's attention drawn to the crucial importance of some of the information. It was as if the helmsman on the *Titanic* knew of the iceberg but concealed its importance or minimized the threat it posed.

Another dimension is disclosure by management to employees. Some countries, like Germany, are better than others; some companies are better than others. Some countries have laws or regulations on the subject, like the EC's Works Council Directive. But there is no common general policy for informing and involving a company's employees. It has become so common-place for companies to be bought and sold without the employees having any say in the matter that it is no longer regarded as odd. They are protected to some extent by TUPE (Transfer of Undertakings Protection of Employment Regulations 1981) but is that the proper limit of their rights?

'Transparency' as between the board/management of a company and the market is governed in many countries by extensive formal reporting require-ments covering variously shareholders, markets, the media, intermediaries, and governments. The range of topics has broadened and now sometimes extends to non-financial reporting on social, environmental, and governance matters. 'Investor relations' have become an industry, analysis a pseudo-science. Rating agencies can hold the future of a troubled company in the palm of their hands; they have great power—are they adequately accountable for its use?

The response to an alleged shortage of information has been to produce a flood of it—company reports of literally hundreds of pages and accounts of such Babylonian complexity that accountants need hours of application and the highest powers of penetration to understand their true meaning. Before us lies the task of combining integrity, clarity, and immediacy and telling the world what it needs to know about the material matters that bear upon a company's position and its future.

The Oppression of Minorities

Buying shares is a voluntary act and purchasers should know what they are doing and the risks they run—which may be anything from competitive pressures to fluctuations in currency or political upheaval. We have already touched on those inherent in the absence of the rule of law. These risks include 'abuse' in the takeover market in some jurisdictions. In others they stem from a separation of ownership from control—as in Italian and other pyramidic structures where a large edifice can be run by a person or group with a tiny shareholding. As we have seen many companies in some countries, like France and Germany, are controlled by a dominant shareholder—with perhaps no more than 15–25% of the equity.

Many investors buy shares in such companies with their eyes wide open. They may even welcome such control on the grounds that management has the greater incentive to succeed. And in quoted companies they can usually sell easily enough in the market if they need the cash or they become disenchanted with their investment. I say 'usually' because there is often a very thin market in small-cap companies and a big sale may move it sharply unless handled adroitly. This factor too should have been taken into account at the time of purchase, and it often leads to a discount in the share price (which incidentally makes small-cap companies all the more vulnerable to takeover).

Purchasing a minority stake always involves risk. It appears, however, that in some jurisdictions it has been decided that the risk should be reduced in the public interest. This is at its most obvious in the handling of minority rights in a takeover. At one time it was common practice for a purchaser to buy enough shares to get control (often at a premium price) and leave the rest stranded, as it were. In some jurisdictions, notably the UK, this is now unacceptable. All shareholders must receive the same offer. The moral argument is one about fairness—even though there is precious little about fairness in the financial markets generally. The economic argument is that fairness reduces risk and therefore the cost of capital.

Minority shareholders—and that is nearly all of them—can be abused by management overpaying itself. The most egregious cases are now attracting attention, and not before time. The remedies are there—but shareholder activity needs organizing to be effective. More serious are depredations in countries where the rule of law is fractured. The ostentatious lives abroad of some who have purloined the assets of 'their' companies bear witness to their predatory success. The unfinished business here is to find effective ways of internationally attaching such ill-gotten gains and restoring them to their rightful owners. As it is, in some jurisdictions miscreants only turn to corporate governance when they realize it may yield more than they can steal.

This book has only touched lightly on unquoted companies, but they do in fact present a far more serious problem for minority shareholders since there is no escape through the market. Even in countries with sound legal systems they tend to be poorly protected. They will often be people who have inherited shares in a company run by a family. The active members may be honourable and fair but they are just as likely to feel a rather weak sense of obligation. Some regrettably so milk the business that there is little or nothing left for the non-active shareholders; and they may do it by means that would be of interest to the Revenue, like charging personal expenses to the company whilst making sure that the invoices did not reveal the fact.

The vulnerable minority shareholders will probably not know what is going on; even though they may be suspicious, they will be powerless to prevent abuses. They would not wish to bear the cost of expensive lawsuits that might ruin everyone including the company itself. Investments made by professionals in private companies nowadays generally cover 'exit' arrangements, but in thousands of companies there are none. What is needed is a low-cost way of ensuring that minority shareholders in unquoted companies can get at the facts and can get relief at low cost through the courts. There might for instance be a Small Companies Tribunal, which could command the use of investigating accountants, dedicated to solving this problem. This is an area to which governments might with advantage turn their minds. I have seen enough to know that the present position is, in many countries, thoroughly unsatisfactory.

Shareholder Activism in Quoted Companies

Perhaps a better title for this subject would be 'shareholder passivity', since this would represent reality nearly all the time.

The original structure of the company as promulgated in the UK's 1855 Act has proved brilliantly successful much of the time. It did facilitate the aggregation of savings by limiting potential losses to the investment itself; it did produce potential immortality in the company (unlike partnerships); and it did provide for the concentration of management power necessary for complex long-term businesses. It assumed that managers would see it in their own interests to make a success of the business since their incomes and reputations would depend on it; even if there were 'agency' problems these would be subsumed by the greater need to achieve a degree of prosperity from which everyone would benefit. Just in case things went wrong—by incompetence or venality—the shareholders had the power to sack the directors; and they had audited accounts by which they could judge whether such treatment was warranted. Most of the time, if a company was faring reasonably well the shareholders would leave well alone. They had neither mandate nor opportunity to try to micro-manage it anyway.

What the Act did not foresee was that the fragmentation of shareholdings would make inaction logical—even when action might have been desirable. Small shareholders would feel that they should not go to the trouble (and cost) of promoting actions which would benefit more than 99% of other people. Most of them would not even vote, costless though this was. The state of affairs was well described seventy years ago by Berle and Means (1932). This remains the case today in some countries as the previous chapters showed.

The scene has changed as more shares are held by the 'institutions' and fewer directly by the public. Better information, especially on subjects like directors' remuneration and compensation for loss of office, has goaded some institutions into action. In some countries private shareholders have joined organizations that will advise and act for them, thus reducing the cost of action to individuals and producing enough votes to be significant. Even so, the truth is that for institutions and private individuals alike there is no wish to interfere from one year to the next. If the share price is rising most shareholders feel that whatever formal shortcomings there are in corporate governance, they should concentrate on companies with poor performances or excessive greed. The motto is rather 'conform or perform', than 'conform or explain'!

Shareholders need always to be vigilant to sense dangers even when current figures seem satisfactory. They will conclude that most of the time the best course of action is to leave well alone. The one thing they should always do is to vote—to support sound boards, send signals when warranted, and from a practical aspect to make sure the voting process actually works. I have seen cases where it did not do so because of elementary administrative failure.

The shareholders should have the power to effect change (but often don't) when the circumstances warrant it, but to do this effectively they need to organize. This is important unfinished business—for the market to find solutions to ways of mobilizing shareholders to act effectively to defend their interests, having identified where these interests were being impaired either by a board's incompetence or by its conflicts of interest. There are straws in the wind like the activities of 'focus' funds. Bandwagons need drivers and arguably conductors.

There is also a fair amount of unfinished business in relation to institutional shareholders—their accountability for what they do or do not do, for instance, in relation to corporate governance. The basic principles of disclosure, for instance, which institutional investors require of companies ought as a minimum apply to them as fiduciary investors.

To some extent, in supervised institutions like banks, the supervisors are showing an increasing tendency to intervene when faced with what they consider to be an inadequate board. Their objective is to safeguard depositors and the financial system, not nurture the shareholders. But the shareholders benefit too. We do not however suggest for a moment that such supervision be extended outside the financial sector.

A final piece of unfinished business is the need to simplify and hasten all cross-border processes from settlement to company reports and accounts to voting at meetings. The free flow of capital is one of the great advances of recent years but the attendant processes often lag behind.

The Governance of Banks

The mention of banking supervision takes us directly into an important area—the governance of banks. This book is about quoted companies—hence all the information about stock markets and takeovers—but in every country in the world they constitute only a tiny fraction of those engaged in commerce and industry. All the rest look first to the banking system if they need funds that the founders cannot provide. It follows that the governance of banks themselves is a matter or vital importance for two reasons. The first and greater is that their good governance will stop funds going astray (what has been described as the leaky hosepipe effect). This is particularly important where the banks have had infusions of foreign capital, perhaps from an international organization, and there is a great temptation on some of its staff to spirit away enough to go and enjoy the *dolce vita* in foreign climes. But even honest directors and managers may be unskilled and waste money. (Fools as well as knaves can be dangerous!) This leads to the second reason. A well-governed bank will be able to assess better the quality of governance in the companies that approach it for loans.

The Basel Committee on Banking Supervision recognized the importance of this subject as far back as 1999 and is expected to return to it in 2005. The World Bank held a conference on it in London in May 2004 and published 'Guidance for the Directors of Banks' (produced by the author) to set out in uncomplicated language what bank directors should have in mind when approaching their task. There is doubtless a superfluity of skilled bankers in some developed countries, but this is not true elsewhere. Countries understandably want their own people to be heavily involved and indeed to run their banks. This means special training—not necessarily an attractive proposition for people who have made their way on other walks of life and have the stature to serve on bank boards, but not the specific skills.

The unfinished business here is for the banking supervisors in each country to set high standards of skills for anyone aspiring to be a bank director and for the appropriate institutions in each case (universities, business schools, professional bodies) to fill the gap. This gap-filling may need a more prestigious title than 'training' to preserve the *amour propre* of the distinguished people who nevertheless need it—perhaps something like 'refresher courses in banking expertise'. The World Bank guidance is a reasonable starting point.

Whistle-blowing

Anyone who has worked in a large organization will know that however good its systems of control and its governance are, that will not be total proof against those who are intent on defrauding it. People who would be horrified at the thought of stealing in their private lives simply regard the company's property as articles to be purloined, and this can be anything from a few pieces of stationery to the abuse of expense accounts. Somehow there seems to be a double moral standard. At its worst it may involve wholesale corruption, into which new recruits to the company can be inducted by a combination of threats and promises.

Industries vary greatly of course. If one is building ships it is difficult to steal one (though bits can be filched). Not so with beds, as I know to my cost—and certainly not so in financial services where well-run businesses operate a pincer movement—elaborate preventative procedures, like the 'four eye' principle, and sophisticated compliance and internal audit regimes. Nick Leeson of Barings taught the world an expensive lesson.

Conspiracy is especially difficult to stop—a corrupt buyer passing phoney invoices from a supplier would be a simple example. A complex one was the huge scam by ISS that broke Ferranti.

Against this background the boards and management of many companies have sought to mobilize their honest employees in the struggle against crime within the company by inviting them to come forward to identify it. This is 'whistle-blowing'. A necessary first step is to preserve the anonymity of the whistle-blower by providing secure and private access to authority. The Institute of Chartered Accountants in England and Wales has produced a booklet offering guidance. A new organization called 'Public Concern at Work' has been set up to help companies provide appropriate systems.

The tendency is to think of this subject in mechanistic, legalistic, structural, or procedural terms. 'Safe harbours', for instance, are provided to ensure that the source of information remains secret. Is this the right approach? Perhaps we should start by considering the behavioural aspects. The clue to this comes from cases where whistles have been blown and it has emerged that the blower had a personal grudge against the 'culprit'—a scorned secretary perhaps, disappointed that the boss's advances led nowhere except bed—or someone who considers that he or she was unfairly passed over for promotion.

The point is that in many countries socializing with one's fellow employees is one of the most agreeable aspects of employment. To put the welfare of the company first seems a remote idea. (The bosses can look after themselves. Who are the shareholders anyway? What does it matter?) In some countries it runs back to childhood mores—in the UK 'sneaking' or 'grassing' (depending on one's background) is seen as shameful. Does virtue have its own rewards? People who have blown whistles successfully are seldom loved and may find their careers damaged.

It might well take an event or series of events so serious as to undermine the organization to make a normal decent person say 'I must put an end to this'. If Leeson's immediate colleagues had known what he was doing would they have stayed silent? Yet in Chapter 5 I quoted the example of an internal auditor who did blow the whistle, only to be put down. I have not encountered any trustworthy assessment of present arrangements and was surprised to read in KPMG's Audit Committee Institute's 1994 report that at a straw poll 80% of delegates thought their procedures effective or very effective—how does one measure the unknown, cases where people knew but stayed silent? Perhaps it is unrealistic to expect much from whistle-blowing except in dire circumstances or when someone has a grudge to settle. But, given that we cannot, alas, always depend on ethical behaviour, is there an alternative policy?

When it comes to money laundering there are now penalties for not informing the authorities if one becomes aware of apparent offences. Could this principle be extended to cover cases of material or serious fraud or theft or other felonious acts, such as attempted rape? It might work, but we have reservations; there are too many resonances with Hitler's and Stalin's informers for comfort.

This is an example of unfinished business for which we cannot see any satisfactory conclusion, except a regime within the company that engenders trust, sound systems of control, constant vigilance, a nose for trouble, and a sense of the intolerable.

Corporate Social Responsibility

Some will feel that this is the biggest issue of all. It is a debate with years behind it and years to run. Compared with this, the Hundred Years War was but a preliminary skirmish.

The state is the main and obvious engine of social policies in any country—all the way from education to health and the protection of the environment, though observably its policies and the length of its reach vary greatly. Alongside the state hundreds of other organizations are at work—religious houses among them. There are innumerable charities and charitable foundations with a myriad of good causes. And there are countless individual people subscribing to some of these or simply acting alone. The people who create a beautiful garden, endow it, and leave it to the nation believe they are conferring a social benefit upon it. Some of the most ruthless commercial pirates down the ages have made benefactions to the undoubted benefit of future generations who little knew how tainted was the inheritance. They would not have cared anyway; it is astonishing how quickly money loses a tainted smell and if put to beneficent use becomes positively fragrant! We start with this recital of the obvious because it forms the backcloth to the drama of the moral duty of companies.

The spectrum of views about the role of companies runs from the Right— 'The company is an economic instrument. Its purpose is profit' to the Left— 'The company is a social instrument with an economic role; profit is necessary but not sufficient'. Earlier we proposed a synthesis, which runs across the spectrum: 'The purpose of the company is to produce ethically and profitably the goods and services people want'. Even the right-wingers could not openly jibe at the word 'ethically', as it would mean saying either 'Leave the ethics to others' or, worse, 'Be unethical if that increases profits'. The mis-selling of financial instruments to pensioners is a case in point.

Those who espouse an extreme right-wing view at least have a clear and uncomplicated vision. It is of a commercial life without morality or ethics governed only by law. As for their customers, 'caveat emptor' is restored to rude health; the lawyers can lick their lips. Inside the company relationships will be brutally competitive; anything goes. Mammon is God; its worshippers struggle—no holds barred—for the front row in this temple. There is no limit to their demands. Greed is his high priest. The company's report may include some paragraphs about social responsibility as a form of camouflage.

To be fair we need to look at the other end of the spectrum, with an oily morality seeping through all the operations. The board becomes so concerned about its social responsibilities that its energies are diverted from its prime commercial purposes. The decoration of the local village hall takes priority over the packaging of its best-selling lines. Its training programmes are well meant but ill directed. Its results constantly disappoint the market— even though its chairman and CEO are prominent in their trade organizations, even at a national level. Indeed, they may be respected spokesmen, whose faces are prominent on television. They do not necessarily gain plaudits for rewarding themselves moderately—and this is especially true if the worm turns and long-suffering shareholders exert enough pressure to get one of them ousted. It then turns out that the soft company has a hard centre.

These would be caricatures were they not taken from life.

Even those with 'hard' views will concede that the company must obey the law. It should pay its taxes, not evade them. It should follow the environmental standards that government establishes. It should obey health and safety regulations. It should honour its contracts—including those with its staff. All these things lie in the area where morality has legal sanctions attached to it. The proponents of such views argue that the only way to ensure fair competition is for governments to legislate on what really matters and enforce the law. Noxious emissions, for instance, are no respecters of state or national boundaries. A strictly enforced international convention is needed to stop competitive advantage going to those who choose to ignore decent standards.

Of course most boards in practice are somewhere between the two. They have little difficulty in being ethical and at the same time caring about profits.

As we remarked in an earlier chapter, corporate social responsibility (CSR) is a portmanteau into which are stuffed many items. The first group could be classified as decent behaviour towards those who have a relationship with the company—and that includes employees and suppliers. The 'stakeholder' thesis argues that their 'rights' constitute a prior claim on the company—before that of shareholders. In terms of their legal rights which can be enforced in courts of law this is true. But how far should management go when these legal rights have been satisfied? It isn't an academic question in countries where there is no law (for instance, on child labour) or where the law is not enforced (for instance, the cases of thousands of suppliers who are mercilessly squeezed despite their contracts by powerful customers who dare them to sue). If a company cannot honour these rights it has no business to be trading. If it does not look after its stakeholders its long-term future will be clouded—and 'look after' does not mean just honouring strict legal obligations.

As we edge forward from this series of propositions which look self-evident, we find ourselves with others that are not. How far should a company go in its people policies? A regime dedicated to help people make the most of their lives suggests well-articulated and integrated schemes of succession planning, career development, and training. Many small companies lack the will and resources to go down this road. If they need skills, they find it more cost effective to buy in the market than to train. But if everyone behaved like that, where would the skills be found? The German answer, as we have seen, is for the state to fund immense training programmes—and for their best companies deliberately to train more people than they need as a contribution to the common good (incidentally fulfilling the German law that companies should have regard to the common weal). In highly entrepreneurial cultures like that of the USA the state can rely on people to acquire the necessary skills, even at a considerable cost in terms of effort and stress, regarding them as a passport to job satisfaction, material benefits, influence, power, and prestige. It is only too easy to forget how much individuals can achieve for themselves given the willpower, the energy, and an attitude of mind that despises being spoon-fed.

There are many examples of companies taking especial care of their employees in many ways—including housing. Some date back to times when such policies were regarded as extraordinary, because they went way beyond enlightened self-interest. This was an early manifestation of CSR though the term itself was coined a century later.

We now move to the centre of the battlefield. Most boards probably feel themselves to be so positioned and are ready to consider the company's obligations that lie outside its strict legal liability and its direct relationships. This means that they are ready to consider what the company's polices should be to deal with CSR and stakeholders. The subjects listed above will be on many agendas, but not all judging by what one sees. In practical terms they have to consider what the company can afford, bearing the shareholders in mind. As we have seen in the five countries, attitudes towards them vary, all the way from 'the tyranny of quarterly earnings' to the concept of 'shareholders last—if at all'. Pressures are slowly changing if only because dividends matter more to institutions who need them to honour their obligations to pensioners and savers. Another paradox is that mean companies will generally include employees and pensioners who would resent meanness in other companies.

So the struggle is set to continue—but at least it now starts with the acceptance that profits are not only essential for economic reasons but also the basis by which social responsibility, however defined, can be satisfied.

Some of the more obvious elements are directly related to its operations. The example quoted earlier was the adoption by mining companies of a programme to restore the countryside that their extractive work had necessarily damaged. It may be argued that this is not CSR at all but simply part of the price of the licence to operate. Just so, but what if the programme extends to health and education for local communities not directly employed by the company? Is the moral boundary crossed when the company does more than it needs to? Would the right wing decry this?

Further beyond that lies the whole range of actions that a company takes that have no bearing on its operations at all. They may be social (like building a community centre) or educational (like the establishment of bursaries) or purely charitable (to this worthy cause or that). The benefit to the company (if any) is reputational in the broadest sense. Its image may be improved. Viewed in this light it is a form of long-term advertising. We have seen no data on whether any part of it makes a commercial difference. Such activities have to be disclosed in the UK, but that does not answer the question.

The people who really benefit from such generosity are not the shareholders for the most part (unless one believes that the actions undertaken really do enhance the image of the company to such an extent that it becomes more profitable) but the directors whose personal prestige is enhanced thereby. In many countries it produces recognition of one sort or another—in the UK through the honours system. When CSR is promoted one should bear in mind that giving away other people's money is easy!

But the idea of the company in society should not be glibly dismissed as irrelevant. It would be a great start if all its senior members led by example in their attitude to the law and their treatment of all their fellow employees. But we have left the most important till last—the firm's customers. It should be considered simply good business not to cheat or delude or exploit them, but we look around and see common examples of all these. In the long run such policies are generally self-defeating but it can be a very long run indeed—consider some of the bad practices in the world of financial services such as mis-selling. The blame for these starts in the boardroom. It reeks of bad governance. It's not an adequate response to say 'This is a market matter—the market will make miscreants pay'. By then many will have suffered loss or even ruin.

Finally, and most controversially, there is executive remuneration. Even if remuneration committees are unbelievably generous, is there not a case for regarding ever-expanding differentials as socially irresponsible? As we have seen, there are countries where this is undoubtedly the case. Social responsibility is a moral issue; its prime ingredients are personal integrity and concern for others. And in its broadest sense that surely includes the social fabric.

Independent Directors

One of the greatest changes over the last decade has been the growing importance of directors who are not only without executive duties in the company (and are therefore 'non-executive', or 'non-management', or 'outside') but also 'independent'. With its supervisory function separated from management through its two-tier structure Germany approaches this debate from a different angle. In the other countries studied, and in many others around the world, the question of what constitutes 'independence' has assumed greater importance as more and graver duties have been heaped on those who fall into this category.

We have already seen how in the UK not all commentators accept the definition in the Combined Code—in most cases seeking something more stringent.

There are definitions in many Codes, reports, or laws such as Viénot (France), Combined Code (UK), Minon (Spain), Tabakplatz (Netherlands) Mertzanis (Greece), BXS/CBF (Belgium), Dey/Saucier (Canada), Norby (Denmark), Sarbanes-Oxley (USA). This is not an exhaustive list. Most cover some of the points I have listed below—but not the patronage issue which is, in practice, of vital importance. At least one code asserts that independence is threatened by holding shares—a proposition some would argue is wrong.

It should not be impossible to produce a definition that was internationally acceptable. What ought its dimensions be? 'Independence,' one is told, 'is an attitude of mind.' Just so, but most of humanity is not made of granite, and is susceptible to charm, flattery, bullying, or self-doubt in various circumstances; modesty requires one to accept the possibility of being wrong.

What can certainly be asserted is that one's sense of independence is *less* likely to be weakened if

- One is imbued with a sense of loyalty to the company, not to a particular person to whom one feels indebted for being appointed. This is the main reason why nomination committees are so vital. In other words, personal patronage weakens independence.
- One does not have to feel alone in one's doubts. That is why committees of independent directors (audit or remuneration) are especially valuable. So are meetings of the independent directors with no executives present.
- One carries no company baggage—as one does if one has been an executive in recent years. Such people may have a useful role as 'non-executives' but not as independents.
- One is not under any kind of personal obligation to the chairman or Chief Executive. Being the mother-in-law of either is obvious enough, but there are many personal relationships which could affect the matter, all the way from the local golf club to having been comrades in arms. This is a matter for self-examination. Could we lay our hand on our heart and say 'If I felt it was in the company's interests, I would gainsay him'?

To this list is added something more dubious—length of service on the board. Some say 'six years is enough!' Many have seen people who have served a decade or more whose independence was beyond doubt—indeed they have generally been there longer than either chairman or CEO. This illustrates a general point—the need for judgement in the application of formulae. It is tempting to try to eliminate it as it makes a box-ticker's job easier. But that temptation should be resisted and as long as there is adequate disclosure, it can be.

This is not only unfinished but also unfinishable business since the interplay of personalities is beyond rules. But if the issues of patronage and connections are tackled strenuously in all countries, perhaps enough progress will be made to produce a satisfactory standard even if perfection is unattainable.

Envoi

Corporate governance must not become a religion or cult, complete with high priests and competing sects, nor must it become a honey-pot for consultants. When the last principle has been pronounced, when the last code promulgated, when the last sanction has been sanctified, it will be seen for what it is—the proposition that the business of the world will be better run if:

- the men and women who drive it forward enjoy power without abusing it, and are competent to exercise it;
- they act with integrity and do not just pontificate about the morals they have no intention of following if they do not suit this quarter's results;
- they describe clearly, succinctly, promptly, and honestly how matters stand;
- they have the wit and skill to balance the economic imperatives of the company with the need to tend the fabric of society;
- accountability is real, and produces the appropriate responses from directors and shareholders.

The head of a small German public company quoted there and on NASDAQ put a manager's view succinctly: 'You have to live corporate governance otherwise it is worthless pieces of paper.'

Annex 7: *The Role of International Organizations*

This book has described the corporate governance arrangements in only five countries—chosen because their economies are significant and there are interesting differences between them. There are many variations in the systems of other countries around the world, and each is worth studying in its own right. Indeed there are publications reporting on a wide range of countries setting out their main features sometimes in tabular form.

Meanwhile all the great international organizations have gradually reacted to the importance of the subject and tried to tackle it, each in its own way. We referred above to the Basel Committee on Banking Supervision setting out some guidance.

There are also some private sector initiatives including the Commonwealth and the ICGN.

The International Corporate Governance Network (ICGN)

ICGN is what its name suggests—a global network of about 300 members representing institutional and private investors from thirty countries. It is funded by them and not by official sources. It is dedicated to the promotion of good governance and fair treatment of equity investors around the world. Its main function is to bring practitioners of various kinds together, and to do this it holds conferences from time to time at various places. It sees itself as one element in the international exchange of information and experience as a means of improving policy and practice. The ICGN for example formulated a response to the EEC's 2004 consultative document—see below.

The World Bank Group and the Organization for Economic Cooperation and Development

These organizations together with the United Nations realized that sound corporate governance had its part to play 'in attracting and enhancing in flows of productive capital'—which requires a 'transparent stable and predictable investment climate' (from the document signed by 75 heads of state from the developed and developing worlds at Monterey, Mexico). Private sector flows of funds to developing markets rose from US$69 billion in 1990 to about US$300 billion a decade later. The currency crisis of 1997–8 (from Thai baht to US hedge funds) was like a douche of cold water. It became obvious that standards of accounting and auditing mattered, as did conflicts of interest, related party transactions, weak boards, and oppressed minorities—in short, governance.

With the strong support of UK Chancellor Gordon Brown, the World Bank Group and OECD concentrated on corporate governance reform. The OECD principles have become a standard work.

OECD periodically refines its principles of governance (the last time in 2003). Their function is to act as a benchmark for governments; they are general and non-prescriptive, they are intended to assist countries in raising standards. Mats Isaakson of the OECD in an article on 6 December 2004 described the investment process as mobilizing capital, allocating it among alternative ends and monitoring its use when invested. He saw the corporate governance framework influencing the outcome at each stage by specifying the distribution of rights and responsibilities among the participants to the corporation. Accordingly the principles cover (*inter alia*):

- policy making and enforcement;
- the shareholders' and stakeholders' role;
- conflicts of interest and self-dealing;
- executive and director remuneration;
- the integrity of the financial markets;
- transparency and effective enforcement;
- the control of abuses between related companies—the full text is on the OECD website www.oecd.org/daf/corporate/principles but I have included them below as a matter of convenience.

Under a memorandum of understanding signed by the OECD and World Bank, a Global Corporate Governance Forum was established and a series of regional round tables was organized. The Forum also formed a private sector advising group (PSAG) so as to marshall international experience. Round tables were designed to bring together all the relevant interests in a particular country—Brazil and Russia were among the first and others followed in Asia, Latin America, and South Eastern Europe.

The G7 through its Financial Stability Forum agreed twelve standards and codes of which three related to the private sector—accounting and auditing, insolvency, and corporate governance. Other groups had also been busy—like the Commonwealth, which developed its own Principles of Good Business Practice following pioneering work in South Africa. Quietly behind the scenes, progress is being made—in training for instance (and in some cases in which the IFC is involved, the loan of a director).

It has not always been easy. I was engaged in the round tables in Russia. In view of the rapacity of some of the 'oligarchy' and the defects of the legal system, the idea of corporate governance being the subject of conferences excited hollow laughter in some quarters. Russia is distinguished by the brilliance of many of its people, but eighty years of centralized government meant that there was no tradition of normal entrepreneurial activity to fall back upon. As a consequence it had—and has—many of the characteristics of a frontier society (with some resemblance to the USA of the 1880s) in which anything goes. But as a subject governance is taken seriously and it was encouraging in 2004 to hear problems freely and openly discussed. When the shortcomings of the accountancy profession in Russia are discussed, one needs to remember that to this very day Delaware Law does not impose on *unquoted* US companies registered there any obligation to produce audited accounts and the strenuous efforts by the Russian government to improve the situation are much to be admired.

The European Economic Community

The European Community (EC) was an early starter and approached the subject from the perspective of uniformity which they considered would facilitate commerce. At the time it only had six members but even so it found the going tough. The Vth Directive aimed to standardize company structure on the German two-tier model, but even a compromise to permit the single-tier structure did not save it. The idea of a single model which companies in any member country might adopt as an alternative to their own—the European Company Statute (ECS)—seems to have faded away.

It is more than a matter of harmonizing formal laws, for it goes to the heart of national norms and attitudes. The problems with a takeover directive exemplify the practical difficulties. The UK's system, which is not based on formal laws, works perfectly well there, but other countries feel they need a statutory basis for a takeover regime to be effective and that that would fit their approach better. It does not mean that anyone is necessarily 'right' but it makes standardizing difficult.

As noted earlier International Accounting Standard No. 39 provides a clear example of how one country's perception of its national interests may run to the general view of many others.

Just to give some indication of the range and scope of Brussel's labours I have included the list currently posted on the web (December 2004) and this list is not comprehensive (including the transparency directive which is due to be adopted in 2004). Business may well ask itself about the cost benefits of conformity and uniformity. It would be odd if the states of Europe which are not formally united were to be more centralized than the USA itself. That said, international commerce does need common standards, and where they do not yet exist—as in accounting and auditing—problems do arise.

Directives

- Directive 2004/25/EC of 21 April 2004 on takeover bids
- Directive 2003/58/EC of 15 July 2003 amending Council Directive 68/151/EEC, as regards disclosure requirements in respect of certain types of companies
- Directive 2001/86/EC of 8 October 2001 supplementing the Statute for a European company with regard to the involvement of employees

- Twelfth Council Company Law Directive 89/667/EEC of 21 December 1989 on single-member private limited-liability companies
- Eleventh Council Directive 89/666/EEC of 21 December 1989 concerning disclosure requirements in respect of branches opened in a Member State by certain types of company governed by the law of another state
- Eighth Council Directive 84/253/EEC of 10 April 1984 based on Article 54 (3) (g) of the Treaty on the approval of persons responsible for carrying out the statutory audits of accounting documents.
- Seventh Council Directive 83/349/EEC of 13 June 1983 based on the Article 54(3)(g) of the Treaty on consolidated accounts
- Sixth Council Directive 82/891/EEC of 17 December 1982 based on Article 54(3)(g) of the Treaty, concerning the division of public limited liability companies
- Fourth Council Directive 78/660/EEC of 25 July 1978 based on Article 54 (3)(g) of the Treaty on the annual accounts of certain types of companies
- Third Council Directive 78/855/EEC of 9 October 1978 based on article 54 (3) (g) of the Treaty concerning mergers of public limited liability companies
- Second Council Directive 77/91/EEC of 13 December 1976 on coordination of safeguards which, for the protection of the interests of members and others, are required by Member States of companies within the meaning of the second paragraph of Article 58 of the Treaty, in respect of the formation of public limited liability companies and the maintenance and alternation of their capital, with a view of making such safeguards equivalent
- First Council Directive 68/151/EEC of 9 March 1968 on coordination of safeguards which, for the protection of the interests of members and others, are required by Member States of companies within the meaning of the second paragraph of Article 58 of the Treaty, with a view to making such safeguards equivalent throughout the Community

Regulations

- The European Company Statute
- Press Release (8 October 2004)

Recommendations

- Recommendations by the Company Law Slim Working Group on the simplification of the first and second Company Law Directives

Communications—Proposals

- Proposal for a Directive on cross-border mergers of companies with share capital (18 November 2003)

- Communication from the Commission to the Council and the European Parliament Modernizing Company Law and Enhancing Corporate Governance in the European community—A Plan to Move Forward
- Communication pursuant to the second subparagraph of Article 251 (2) of the EC Treaty concerning the Common position of the Council on the adoption of a European Parliament and Council Directive on companylaw concerning takeover bids, European Commission, 26 July 2000.

The EEC Consultative Document 2004

The Internal Market Directorate General issued a consultation document 'Fostering an Appropriate Regime for Shareholders' Rights' [MARKT/16.09.2004] in preparation for a Directive. Its twin aims are to protect shareholders and enhance competitiveness. The main issues on which contributions are sought are:

- Scope; should unlisted companies be covered too?
- Voting rights, especially those of the ultimate owners—covering cross-border investment.
- Better information flows for general meetings and participation in them.
- Better information about the results of general meetings

The document also has a section of draft recommendations. They are so relevant to much of the content of this book that I include it in full, noting with interest the acceptance of the 'comply or explain' approach.

Section I

Scope and Definitions

1. *Scope*

    1.1 Member States are invited to take the steps necessary to introduce at national level, either through a 'comply or explain' approach or through legislation and with the instruments best suited to their legal environment, a set of provisions concerning the role of non-executive or supervisory directors and the committees of the (supervisory) board to be used by listed companies.

    They should however duly consider the specificities of the collective investment undertakings of the corporate type under the scope of Directive85/611/EEC of the Council, as amended by Directives 2001/107/EEC and 2001/108/EEC of the European Parliament and the Council. Member States should also consider the specificities of collective investment undertakings of the corporate type which are not subject to these directives and which sole purpose is the investment of money raised from investors in a diversified range of assets and which do not seek to take legal or management control over any of the issuers of its underlying investments.

1.2 When Member States decide to use the 'comply or explain' approach, whereby companies are required to explain their practices by reference to a set of designated best practice recommendations, companies should be required to specify annually the recommendations with which they have not complied (and, in the case of recommendations whose requirements are of a continuing nature, for what part of the accounting period such non-compliance occurred), and explain in a substantial and specific manner the extent of—and the reasons for—any material non-compliance.

1.3 In their consideration of the principles set out in this Recommendation, Member States should take into account in particular, the following:

1.3.1. The functions and characteristics assigned by Member States to any of the committees created within the (supervisory) board and advocated in this Recommendation should duly take into account the rights and duties of relevant corporate bodies as defined under national law.

1.3.2 Member States should be able to replace, in whole or in part, the creation within the (supervisory) board of any of the committees with the characteristics advocated in this Recommendation, by the use of other structures—external to the (supervisory) board—or procedures, which could be either mandatory for companies under national law or best practice recommended at national level through a 'comply or explain approach', and considered to be functionally equivalent and equally effective.

1.4 With respect to listed companies incorporated in one of the Member States, the set of provisions to be introduced by Member States should cover at least those listed companies which are incorporated within their territory.

With respect to listed companies not incorporated in one of the Member States, the set of provisions to be introduced by Member States should cover at least those listed companies which have their primary listing on a regulated market established in their territory.

2. *Definitions for the purposes of this Recommendation*

2.1 'Listed Companies' means companies whose securities are admitted to trading on a regulated market within the meaning of Directive 2004/39/EEC of the European Parliament and of the Council in one or more Member States.

2.2 'Director' means any member of the administrative, managerial or super-visory bodies of a company.

2.3 'Executive Director' means any member of the administrative body (unitary board) who is engaged in the daily management of the com-pany.

2.4 'Non-executive Director' means any member of the administrative body (unitary board) of a company other than an executive director.

2.5 'Managing Director' means any member of the managerial body (dual board) of a company.

2.6 'Supervisory director' means any member of the supervisory body (dual board) of a company.

Section II

PRESENCE AND ROLE OF NON-EXECUTIVE OR SUPERVISORY DIRECTORS IN (SUPERVISORY) BOARDS

3. *Presence of non-executive or supervisory directors*

    3.1 The administrative, managerial and supervisory bodies should include in total an appropriate balance of executive/managing and non-executive/supervisory directors such that no individual or small group of individuals can dominate decision making of these bodies.

    3.2 The present or past executive responsibilities of the (supervisory) board's chairman should not stand in the way of his ability to exercise objective oversight. In a unitary board, one of the possible ways to ensure this is that the roles of chairman and chief executive are separate; in unitary and dual boards, one option may be that the chief executive does not immediately become the chairman of the (supervisory) board. In cases where a company chooses to combine the roles of chairman and chief executive, this should be accompanied with information on any safeguards put in place.

4. *Number of independent directors*

    A number of independent non-executive or supervisory directors should be elected to the (supervisory) board of companies sufficient to ensure that any material conflict of interest involving directors will be properly dealt with.

5. *Organisation in board committees*

    Boards should be organised in such a way that a sufficient number of independent non-executive or supervisory directors play an effective role in key areas where the potential for conflict of interest is particularly high. To this end, but subject to Point 7, nomination, remuneration and audit committees should be created within the (supervisory) board, where the latter is playing a role in the areas of nomination, remuneration and audit under national law, taking into account Annex 1.

6. *Role of the committees towards the (supervisory) board*

   6.1 The nomination, remuneration and audit committees should make recommendations aimed at preparing the decisions to be taken by the (supervisory) board itself. The primary purpose of the committees should be to increase the efficiency of the (supervisory) board's work by making sure that decisions are based on due consideration, and to help organise its work with a view to ensuring that the decisions it takes are free from material conflicts of interest. The creation of the committees in principle is not intended to remove the matters considered from the purview of the (supervisory) board itself, which remains fully responsible for the decisions taken in its field of competence.

   6.2 The terms of reference of any committee created should be drawn up by the (supervisory) board. When permissible under national law, any delegation of decision-making power would have to be explicitly declared, properly described and made public in a fully transparent way.

7. *Flexibility in setting up the committees*

   7.1 Companies should make sure that the functions assigned to the nomination, remuneration and audit committees are carried out. However, companies may group the functions as they see fit and create less than three committees. In such a situation, companies should give a clear explanation both of the reasons why they have chosen an alternative approach and how the approach chosen meets the objective set for the three separate committees.

   7.2 In companies where the (supervisory) board is small, the functions assigned to the three committees may be performed by the (supervisory) board as a whole, provided that it meets the composition requirements advocated for the committees and that adequate information is provided in this respect. In such a situation, the national provisions relating to board committees (in particular with respect to their role, operation, and transparency) should apply, where relevant, to the (supervisory) board as a whole.

8. *Evaluation of the (supervisory) board*

   Every year, the (supervisory) board should carry out an evaluation of its performance. This should encompass an assessment of its membership, organisation and operation as a group; include an evaluation of the competence and effectiveness of each board member and of the board committees; and consider how well the board has performed against any performance objectives which have been set.

9. *Transparency and communication*

9.1 The (supervisory) board should make public at least once a year (as part of the information disclosed by the company annually on its corporate governance structures and practices) adequate information about its internal organisation and the procedures applicable to its activities, including an indication of the extent to which the self-evaluation performed by the (supervisory) board has led to any material change.

9.2 The (supervisory) board should ensure that shareholders are properly informed on the affairs of the company, its strategic approach, and on how risks and conflicts of interest are managed. The roles of directors regarding communication and engagement with shareholders should be clearly designated.

Section III

PROFILE OF NON-EXECUTIVE OR SUPERVISORY DIRECTORS

10. *Appointment and removal*

Non-executive or supervisory directors should be appointed for specified terms subject to individual re-election, at maximum intervals to be determined at national level with a view to allowing both the necessary development of experience and sufficiently frequent reconfirmation of their position. It should also be possible to remove them, but their removal should not be easier than for an executive or managing director.

11. *Qualifications*

11.1 In order to maintain the presence of a balanced set of qualifications, the (supervisory) board should determine its desired composition in relation to the company's structure and activities, and evaluate it periodically. The (supervisory) board should ensure that it is composed of members who, as a whole, have the required diversity of knowledge, judgement and experience to properly complete their tasks.

11.2 With respect to the audit committee, where recent and relevant experience of finance and accounting for listed companies appropriate to the company's activities should be present, it should comprise individuals that collectively provide this from their individual backgrounds and experience.

11.3 All new directors should be offered a tailored induction programme on joining the (supervisory) board, which covers to the extent necessary the company's organisation and activities and his responsibilities as a director. The (supervisory) board should conduct an annual review to identify areas where directors need to update their skills and knowledge.

11.4 When the appointment of a director is proposed, disclosure should be made of his particular competences which are relevant to him serving on the (supervisory) board. To allow markets and the public assess whether these competences remain appropriate over time, the (supervisory) board should disclose every year a profile of the board's composition and information on the particular competences of individual directors which are relevant to their serving on the (supervisory) board.

12. *Commitment*

12.1 Each director should devote to his duties the necessary time and attention, and should undertake to limit the number of his other professional commitments (in particular any directorships held in other companies) to such an extent that the proper performance of his duties is assured.

12.2 When the appointment of a director is proposed, his other significant professional commitments should be disclosed. The board should be informed of subsequent changes. Every year, the board should collect data on such commitments, and make the information available in its annual report.

13. *Independence*

13.1 A director should be considered to be independent when he is free from any business, family or other relationship—with the company, its controlling shareholder or the management of either—that creates a conflict of interest such as to jeopardise exercise of his judgement.

13.2 A number of criteria for assessment of the independence of directors should be adopted at national level, taking into account the guidance provided in Annex II, which identifies a number of situations reflecting the relationships or circumstances usually recognised as potentially leading to the presence of material conflict of interest. The determination of what constitutes independence is fundamentally an issue for the (supervisory) board itself to determine. The (supervisory) board may indeed consider that, although a particular director meets all of the criteria retained at national level for assessment of independence of directors, he cannot be held to be independent owing to the specific circumstances of the person or the company, and the converse also applies.

13.3 Proper information should be disclosed on the conclusions reached by the (supervisory) board in its determination of whether a particular director should be regarded as independent.

13.3.1 When the appointment of a non-executive or supervisory director is proposed, the company should disclose whether it considers him to be independent; when one or several of the criteria retained at national level for assessment of independence of directors is not met, the company should disclose its reasons for nevertheless considering this director to be independent. Companies should also disclose annually which directors they consider to be independent;

13.3.2 When one or several of the criteria retained at national level for assessment of independence of directors has not been met throughout the year, the company should disclose its reasons for considering this director to be independent. To ensure the accuracy of the information provided on the independence of directors, the company should require the independent directors to revalidate their independence periodically.

The OECD Principles of Corporate Governance

I. *Ensuring the Basis for an Effective Corporate Governance Framework*
The corporate governance framework should promote transparent and efficient markets, be consistent with rule of law and clearly articulate the division of responsibilities among different supervisory, regulatory and enforcement authorities.

A. The corporate governance framework should be developed with a view to its impact on overall economic performance, market integrity and the incentives it creates for market participants and the promotion of transparent an efficient markets.

B. The legal and regulatory requirements that affect corporate governance practices in a jurisdiction should be consistent with rule of law, transparent and enforceable.

C. The division of responsibilities among different authorities in a jurisdiction should be clearly articulated and ensure that the public interest is served.

D. Supervisory, regulatory and enforcement authorities should have the authority, integrity and resources to fulfil their duties in a professional and objective manner. Moreover, their rulings should be timely, transparent and fully explained.

II. *The Rights of Shareholders and Key Ownership Functions*
The corporate governance framework should protect and facilitate the exercise of shareholders' rights.

A. Basic shareholder rights should include the right to: 1) secure methods of ownership registration; 2) convey or transfer shares; 3) obtain relevant and material information on the corporation on a timely and regular basis; 4) participate and vote in general shareholder meetings; 5) elect and remove members of the board; and 6) share in the profits of the corporation.

B. Shareholders should have the right to participate in, and to be sufficiently informed on, decisions concerning fundamental corporate changes such as: 1) amendments to the statutes, or articles of incorporation or similar governing documents of the company; 2) the authorisation of additional shares; and 3) extraordinary transactions, including the transfer of all or substantially all assets, that in effect result in the sale of the company.

C. Shareholders should have the opportunity to participate effectively and vote in general shareholder meetings and should be informed of the rules, including voting procedures, that govern general shareholder meetings:

  1. Shareholders should be furnished with sufficient and timely information concerning the date, location and agenda of general meetings, as well as full and timely information regarding the issues to be decided at the meeting.

  2. Shareholders should have the opportunity to ask questions of the board, including questions relating to the annual external audit, to place items on the agenda of general meetings, and to propose resolutions, subject to reasonable limitations.

  3. Effective shareholder participation in key corporate governance decisions, such as the nomination and election of board members, should be facilitated. Shareholders should be able to make their views known on the remuneration policy for board members and key executives. The equity component of compensation schemes for board members and employees should be subject to shareholder approval.

  4. Shareholders should be able to vote in person or in absentia, and equal effect should be given to votes whether cast in person or in absentia.

D. Capital structures and arrangements that enable certain shareholders to obtain a degree of control disproportionate to their equity ownership should be disclosed.

E. Markets corporate control should be allowed to function in an efficient and transparent manner.

  1. The rules and procedures governing the acquisition of corporate control in the capital markets, and extraordinary transactions such as mergers, and sales of substantial portions of corporate assets, should be clearly articulated and disclosed so that investors understand their rights and recourse. Transactions should occur at transparent prices and under fair conditions that protect the rights of all shareholders according to their class.

  2. Anti-take-over devices should not be used to shield management and the board from accountability.

F. The exercise of ownership rights by all shareholders, including institutional investors, should be facilitated.

    1. Institutional investors acting in a fiduciary capacity should disclose their overall corporate governance and voting policies with respect to their investments, including the procedures that they have in place for deciding on the use of their voting rights.

    2. Institutional investors acting in a fiduciary capacity should disclose how they manage material conflicts of interest that may affect the exercise of key ownership rights regarding their investments.

G. Shareholders, including institutional shareholders, should be allowed to consult with each other on issues concerning their basic shareholder rights as defined in the Principles, subject to exceptions to prevent abuse.

III. The Equitable Treatment of Shareholders

The corporate governance framework should ensure the equitable treatment of all shareholders, including minority and foreign shareholders. All shareholders should have the opportunity to obtain effective redress for violation of their rights.

A. All shareholders of the same series of a class should be treated equally.

    1. Within any series of a class, all shares should carry the same rights. All investors should be able to obtain information about the rights attached to all series and classes of shares before they purchase. Any changes in voting rights should be subject to approval by those classes of shares which are negatively affected.

    2. Minority shareholders should be protected from abusive actions by, or in the interest of, controlling shareholders acting either directly or indirectly, and should have effective means of redress.

    3. Votes should be cast by custodians or nominees in a manner agreed upon with the beneficial owner of the shares.

    4. Impediments to cross border voting should be eliminated.

    5. Processes and procedures for general shareholder meetings should allow for equitable treatment of all shareholders. Company procedures should not make it unduly difficult or expensive to cast votes.

B. Insider trading and abusive self-dealing should be prohibited.

C. Members of the board and key executives should be required to disclose to the board whether they, directly, indirectly or on behalf of third parties, have a material interest in any transaction or matter directly affecting the corporation.

IV. The Role of Stakeholders in Corporate Governance

The corporate governance framework should recognise the rights of stakeholders established by law or through mutual agreements and encourage active co-operation between corporations and stakeholders in creating wealth, jobs, and the sustainability of financial sound enterprises.

A. The rights of stakeholders that are established by law or through mutual agreements are to be respected.

B. Where stakeholder interests are protected by law, stakeholders should have the opportunity to obtain effective redress for violation of their rights.

C. Performance-enhancing mechanisms for employee participation should be permitted to develop.

D. Where stakeholders participate in the corporate governance process, they should have access to relevant, sufficient and reliable information on a timely and regular basis.

E. Stakeholders, including individual employees and their representative bodies, should be able to freely communicate their concerns about illegal or unethical practices to the board and their rights should not be compromised for doing this.

F. The corporate governance framework should be complemented by an effective, efficient insolvency framework and by effective enforcement of creditor rights.

VI. *The Responsibilities of the Board*

The corporate governance framework should ensure the strategic guidance of the company, the effective monitoring of management by the board, and the board's accountability to the company and the shareholders.

A. Board members should act on a fully informed basis, in good faith, with due diligence and care, and in the best interest of the company and the shareholders.

B. Where board decisions may affect different shareholder groups differently, the board should treat all shareholders fairly.

C. The board should apply high ethical standards. It should take into account the interests of stakeholders.

D. The board should fulfil certain key functions, including:

1. Reviewing and guiding corporate strategy, major plans of action, risk policy, annual budgets and business plans; setting performance objectives; monitoring implementation and corporate performance; and overseeing major capital expenditures, acquisitions and divestitures.

2. Monitoring the effectiveness of the company's governance practices and making changes as needed.

3. Selecting, compensating, monitoring and, when necessary, replacing key executives and overseeing succession planning.

4. Aligning key executive and board remuneration with the longer term interest of the company and its shareholders.

5. Ensuring a formal and transparent board nomination and election process.

6. Monitoring and managing potential conflicts of interest of management, board members and shareholders, including misuse of corporate assets and abuse in related party transactions.

7. Ensuring the integrity of the corporation's accounting and financial reporting systems, including the independent audit, and that appropriate systems of control are in place, in particular, systems for risk management, financial and operational control, and compliance with the law and relevant standards.

8. Overseeing the process of disclosure and communications.

E. The Board should be able to exercise objective independent judgement on corporate affairs.

1. Boards should consider assigning a sufficient number of non-executive board members capable of exercising independent judgement to tasks where there is a potential for conflict of interest. Examples of such key responsibilities are ensuring the integrity of financial and non-financial reporting, the review of related party transactions, nominations of board members and key executives, and board remuneration.

2. When committees of the board are established, their mandate, composition and working procedures should be well defined and disclosed by the board.

3. Board members should be able to commit themselves effectively to their responsibilities.

F. In order to fulfil their responsibilities, board members should have access to accurate, relevant and timely information.

References
and Further Reading

ABEGGLEN, JAMES C., and STALK, GEORGE, jun. (1985). *Kaisha: The Japanese Corporation* (Basic Books: Hobart, Ind.).

ALLEN, W. T. (1992), 'Defining the Role of Outside Directors in an Age of Global Competition', *Directors' Monthly* (Nov.), 16/11. 1–6.

AOKI, MASAHIKO (1990), 'Toward an Economic Model of the Japanese Firm', *Journal of Economic Literature*, 28:(Mar.)1–27 .

AUERBACH, A. J. (1988), *Mergers and Acquisitions, 1988* (University of Chicago Press: Chicago).

—— (ed.) (1988), *Corporate Takeovers: Causes and Consequences* (National Bureau of Economic Research: University of Chicago Press: Chicago).

BACON, JEREMY (1979), *Corporate Directorship Practices: The Audit Committee* (Conference Board Report 766; The Conference Board: New York).

—— and BROWN, JAMES K. (1977), *The Board of Directors: Perspectives and Practices in Nine Countries* (Conference Board, Report 728: New York).

—— and——Date (1975) *Corporate Directorship Practices: Role, Selection and Legal Status of the Board* (Conference Board, Report 646: New York).

Bank of England Quarterly Bulletin (May 1988) (issued by Economics Division).

BARCA, FABRIZIO, and BECHT, MARCO (eds.) (2001), *The Control of Corporate Europe* (Oxford University Press).

BARNETT, CORELLI (1986), *The Audit of War* (Macmillan: London).

BAUMS, THEODOR (1992), 'Takeovers vs Institutions in Corporate Governance in Germany' (Oxford Law Colloquium).

BERLE, A. A., and MEANS, G. C. (1932), *The Modern Corporation and Private Property* (rev. edn. 1967).

BIERSACH, JEFFREY W. (IRRC) (1990), 'Voting by Institutional Investors on Corporate Governance Issues in the 1990 Proxy Season' (Investor Responsibility Research Center) (Oct.).

BLACK, BERNARD S. (1990), 'Shareholder Passivity Re-examined', *Michigan Law Review* (Dec.).

—— (1992), 'Agents Watching Agents', *UCLA Law Review*, 39.

—— (forthcoming), *The Value of Institutional Investor Monitoring: The Empirical Evidence*.

BLAIR, MARGARET M. (1991), 'Who's in Charge Here? How Changes in Corporate Finance Shape Corporate Governance', *Brookings Review* (Fall).

BOOTLE, ROGER (2003), *Money for Nothing* (Nicholas Brealey Publishing: London).

BREALEY, RICHARD A., and MYERS, STEWART C. (1991), *Principles of Corporate Finance*, 4th edn. (McGraw-Hill: New York).

BRITTAN, SAMUEL (1995), *Capitalism with a Human Face* (Edward Elgar: London).

BRUCK, CONNIE (1988), *The Predators' Ball* (Simon & Schuster: New York).

BURROUGH, BRYAN, and HEYLAR, JOHN (1990), *Barbarians at the Gate: the Fall of J. R. J. Nabisco* (Harper & Row: New York).

BUSHKIN, ARTHUR A. (President, Telemation Associates Inc.) (n.d.), *Breaking the Language Barrier: How to do Business with the Japanese* (Telemation Associates: Washington, DC).

BUXBAUM, RICHARD M. (1991), *Institutional Owners and Corporate Managers: A Comparative Perspective* (Working paper series; School of Law, Center for Study of Law & Society, California).

CADBURY, SIR ADRIAN (2000), *Family Firms and their Governance* (Egon Zehnder International: London).

—— (2002), *Corporate Governance and Chairmanship* (Oxford University Press).

—— (1990), *The Company Chairman* (FitzWilliam Publishing: Cambridge).

The Cadbury Committee Report: Financial Aspects of Corporate Governance (1992) (Burgess Science Press: UK).

CARLSSON, R. H. (2001), *Ownership and Value Creation* (John Wiley: London).

CARMOY, HERVÉ DE (1990), *Global Banking Strategy* (Blackwell North America: Blackwood, NJ).

CARY, W. L. (1974), 'Federalism and Corporate Law: Reflections upon Delaware', *Yale Law Journal*, 83.

Central Statistical Office (1989), Share Register Survey.

CHARKHAM, J. P. (1989), 'Corporate Governance and the Market for Control of Companies' (Bank of England Panel Paper, 25; Mar. 1989).

—— and SIMPSON, ANNE (1999), *Fair Shares* (Oxford University Press).

CHEFFENS, BRIAN R. (1997), *Company Law: Theory Structure and Operation* (Clarendon Press: Oxford).

CLARK, RODNEY (1979), *The Japanese Company* (Charles E. Tuttle: Tokyo).

COFFEE, JOHN C., jun. (1991), 'Liquidity versus Control: The Institutional Investor as Corporate Monitor', *Columbia Law Review*, 91/6 (Oct.).

Competitiveness Policy Council (1993), Reports of the Sub-Councils; Report of the Sub-Council on Corporate Governances and Competitiveness Policy Council.

COLLIER, P. A. (1992), *Audit Committees in Large UK Companies* (Research Board of ICAEW: London).

CORBETT, JENNY (1987), 'International Perspectives on Financing: Evidence from Japan', *Oxford Review of Economic Policy*, 3/4.

CRYSTAL, GRAEF S. (1991), *In Search of Excess: The Overcompensation of American Executives* (W. W. Norton & Co.: New York).

Center for International Private Enterprise (2003), *In Search of Good Directors* (Washington, DC).

DAVIS, EVAN, and KAY, JOHN (1990), 'Corporate Governance, Takeovers and the Role of the Non-executive Director', *Business Strategy Review* (Autumn 1990).

DAVIS, STEPHEN M. (IRCC) (1989), 'Shareholder Rights Abroad: A Handbook for the Global Investor' (Investor Responsibility Research Center: Washington, DC).

DIXON, NORMAN F. (1988), *Our Own Worst Enemy* (Futura: London).

DORE, RONALD (1988), *Flexible Rigidities: Industrial Policy and Structural Adjustment in the Japanese Economy, 1970–80* (Athlone Press: London).

—— (2000), *Stock Market Capitalism* (Oxford University Press).

DRUCKER, PETER F. (1968), *The Practice of Management* (William Heinemann: London).

Department of Trade and Industry (2003), *Transtec plc Investigation under section 432(2) of the Companies Act 1985* (TSO).

Deutsche Bundesbank (n.d.), 'The New Principles I and Ia Concerning the Capital of Banks' (Special Series (2*a*).

ECCLES, ROBERT, HERZ, ROBERT, KEEGAN, MARY, and PHILLIPS, DAVID (2001), *The Value Reporting Revolution* (John Wiley & Sons Inc.: London).

EDWARDS, JEREMY, and NIBLER, MARCUS (2000), 'Corporate Governance: Banks versus Ownership Concentration in Germany', *Economic Policy* (October).

EISENBERG, M. A. (1989), 'The Structure of Corporation Law', *Columbia Law Review* (Nov.), 89/7.

EPSTEIN, EDWARD JAY (1986), *Who Owns the Corporation? Management vs Shareholders* (Priority Press Publications: New York).

ETZIONI, AMITAI (1988), *The Moral Dimension: Towards New Economics* (The Free Press: New York).

Federal Securities Law Reports, 1117 (20 Mar. 1985), pt. ii, 'Responsibilities of Corporate Officers & Directors under Federal Securities Laws' (Commerce Clearing House: Chicago).

FLEISCHER, ARTHUR, jun., HAZARD, GEOFFREY C., jun; and KLIPPER, MICHAEL Z. (1988), *Board Games: The Changing Shape of Corporate Power* (Little, Brown & Co.: Boston).

FRANKS, J., and MAYER, C. (1990), 'European Capital Markets and Corporate Control', *Economic Policy* (Winter).

——, and —— (1994), *Ownership and Control of German Companies* (ESRC).

FRIEDMANN, W. (1984), 'Business Finance in the United Kingdom and Germany', *Bank of England Quarterly Bulletin*, 368–75 (Sept).

FUKUDO, HARUKO (1992), 'A New World Order and Japan' (Speech to American Chamber of Commerce in London, 21 May).

'The Future Development of Auditing: A Paper to Promote Public Debate' (1992) (a paper by the Auditing Practices Board; 16 Nov.).

GALBRAITH, J. K. (1967), *The New Industrial State*.

—— (1975), *The Great Crash, 1929* (Penguin Books: Harmondsworth).

GARRATT, BOB (2003), *The Fish Rots from the Head* (Profile Books: London).

GIARDINA, JAMES A., and TILGHMAN, THOMAS S. (1988), *Organization and Compensation of Boards of Directors* (Arthur Young: New York).

GIBSON, R. J., and ROE, M. J. (1992), 'Understanding the Japanese Keiretsu; Overlaps between Corporate Governance and Industrial Organization' (Stamford Law School Working Paper, Aug.) (Stamford, Calif.).

GOOLD, MICHAEL, CAMPBELL, NIGEL, and KASE, KIMEO (1990), 'The Role of the Centre in Managing Large Diversified Companies in Japan) (Manchester Business School) (Sept.).

GOYDER, GEORGE (1987), *The Just Enterprise* (André Deutsch: London).

GRAHAM, B., and DODD, D. L. (1934), *Security Analysis* (McGraw-Hill: New York).

HALBERSTAM, DAVID (1986), *The Reckoning* (William Morrow & Co.: New York).

HEARD, JAMES E., and SHERMAN, HOWARD D. (1987), *Conflicts of Interest in the Proxy Voting System* (Investor Responsibility Research Center: Washington, DC).

HERZEL, LEO, and SHEPRO, RICHARD (1990), *Bidders and Targets: Mergers and Acquisitions in the US* (Basil Blackwell: Cambridge, Mass.).

HOLLINGTON, ROGER (1994), *Minority Shareholders' Rights* (Sweet & Maxwell: London).

HOUSTON, WILLIAM, and LEWIS, NIGEL (1992), *The Independent Director: Handbook and Guide to Corporate Governance* (Butterworth-Heinemann: Oxford).

HUTTON, WILL (1990), 'Takeover Legacy has Touched us all at Great Cost', *Financial Times* (3 Sept.).

Industrial Groupings in Japan, 1982/83 (1982) (Dodwell Marketing Consultants: Tokyo; Sept.).

INSEE (n.d.), *Rapport sur les comptes de la nation.*

Institute of Chartered Accountants of Scotland (1988), *Making Corporate Reports Valuable* (Kogan Page: London).

Investor's Chronicle (1992), 'Management Buy-out' (Survey; 3 Apr.).

IPPOLITO, RICHARD A. (1986), *Pensions, Economics and Public Policy* (Pension Research Council of the Wharton School, University of Pennsylvania).

ISAKSSON, MATS, and SKOG, R. (eds.) (2004), *The Future of Corporate Governance* (OECD).

IRRC (1990), *Writing Proxy Voting Guidelines (Feb.)* (*Investor Responsibility Research Center: Washington, DC*).

JACOBS, MICHAEL T. (1990), 'Corporate Boards and Competitiveness' (A paper presented to the Conference on Fiduciary Responsibilities of Institutional Investors, New York University, June).

—— (1991), *Short-Term America: The Causes and Cures of our Business Myopia* (Harvard Business School Press: Boston, Mass.).

—— (1993), *Break the Wall Street Rule* (Addison Wesley: Reading, Mass.)

JENKINSON, T., and LJUNGQVIST, A. (1997), 'Hostile Status and the Role of Banks in German Corporate Governance' (mimeo).

JOHNSTON, ALEXANDER (1980), 'The Panel and Code' in authors ? *The City Take-over Code* (Oxford University Press).

JOHNSTON, KRISTA M. (IRRC) (1990), 'How Institutions Voted on Social Policy Shareholder Resolutions in the 1990 Proxy Season' (Investor Responsibility Research Center: Washington, DC) (Sept.).

KAKU, RYUZABURO (1991), Speech to Caux Round Table, Caux, Switzerland on 20 Aug. 1991 (Mr Kaku is the Chairman of Canon Inc.).

KEELEY, MICHAEL C. (n.d.), 'Deposit Insurance, Risk, and Market Power in Banking' (Mr Keeley is Vice-President, Cornerstone Research, 1000 El Camino Real, Menlo Park, CA 94025, USA).

KUROKAWA, M. (1988), Chairman of Nomura Securities, Inc., Speech.

KYNASTON, DAVID (1990), 'The City and Industry, 1880–1990: An Uneasy Relationship' (paper to the LSE Business History Unit, 15 Oct.).

Korn/Ferry International (2003, 2004), *World Study on Corporate Governance* (Los Angeles).

—— *International Survey, 1990.*

LAMY, RENÉ (1992), 'Narration Authentique d'une OPA'.

LEARMOUNT, SIMON (2002), *Corporate Governance: What can be Learnt from Japan* (Oxford University Press).

LINDEN-TRAVERS, KEN (1990), *Non-Executive Directors: A Guide to Their Role, Responsibilities and Appointment* (Director Books: Cambridge).

LIPTON, MARTIN (1992), 'Takeover Bids and United States Corporate Governance' (speech given to the Oxford Law Colloquium).

—— and ROSENBLUM, STEVEN A. (1991), 'A New System of Corporate Governance: The Quinquennial Election of Directors', *University of Chicago Law Review,* 58/1 (Winter).

London Stock Exchange (1992), *A History of the London Stock Exchange.*

LONGSTRETH, BEVIS (1991), *Modern Investment Management and the Prudent Man Rule* (Oxford University Press: New York).

—— and KANE, NANCY (1992), 'Executive Compensation: A Current Issue of Corporate Governance' (paper given to University of California, San Diego, Nineteenth Annual Convention of Securities Regulation Institute, 22 Jan.).

LORSCH, JAY, W., with McIVER, ELIZABETH (1989), *Pawns and Potentates: The Reality of America's Corporate Boards* (Harvard Business School Press: Boston, Mass.).

—— with—— (1993), *Corporate Governance and Investment Time Horizons* (Harvard Business School Press: Boston, Mass.).

LOWENSTEIN, Louis(1988), *What's Wrong with Wall St.: Short-Term Gain and the Absentee Shareholder,* (Addison-Wesley: Reading, Mass.).

—— (1991), *Sense and Nonsense in Corporate Finance* (Addison-Wesley: Reading, Mass.).

—— (1991a), 'The Changing Role of the Stockmarket in the United States', *Rutgers Law Review* (Spring), 43/3.

MACE, MYLES L. (1971), *Directors: Myth and Reality* (Harvard Business School Classics, Harvard Business School Press: Boston).

MAIN, B. G. M., and JOHNSTON, J. (1992), 'The Remuneration Committee as an Instrument of Corporate Governance' (University of Edinburgh).

MALLINS, CHRISTINE (2004), *Corporate Governance* (Oxford University Press).

MARSH, PAUL (London Business School) (1990), *Short-Termism on Trial* (Institutional Fund Managers Association, London).

MARSTON, C. (1993), *Investor Relations Project* (University of Northumbria at Newcastle: Newcastle Business School, and University of Glasgow: Glasgow Business School, Dept. of Accounting and Finance).

McLAGAN, PATRICIA, and KREMBS, PETER (1988), *On-the-Level: Performance Communication that Works* (McLagan International: Minnesota).

MEYER, BROWN, and PLATT (1991), 'American Depositary Receipts', *Cross-Border Newsletter* (25 Sept.).

MILLSTEIN, IRA M., and MaCAVOY, PAUL M. (2003), *The Recurrent Crises in Corporate Governance* (Palgrave Macmillan: London).

MONKS, ROBERT A. G. (1998), *The Emperor's Nightingale* (Capstone: London).

—— (1991), *Power and Accountability* (Harper Collins: USA).

—— and MINNOW, NELL (1996), *Watching the Watchers* (Blackwell: Cambridge, Mass.)

Monopot Kommission (1973–83). Summaries of the first five *Biennial Reports* (Nomos Verlagsgesellschaft: Baden-Baden).

MORGAN, E. V. and A. D. (1990), *The Stockmarket and Mergers in the UK* (The David Hume Institute: Edinburgh).

MULBERT, PETER O. (1998), *Large Shareholder Activism in Corporate Governance* (Trier).

NASH, JOHN M., and LAJOUX, ALEXANDRA R. (1988). *A Corporate Director's Guide to Responsibility and Liability under Current State Law and Federal Securities Laws* (rev. edn.) (Publications Inc.: Washington, DC).

National Academy of Engineering (1992), *Time Horizons and Technology Investments* (National Academy Press: Washington, DC).

NEUBERGER, DORIS, and NEUMANN, MANFRED (1991), 'Banking and Antitrust: Limiting Industrial Ownership by Banks?', *Journal of Institutional and Theoretical Economics,* 147.

Nippon Steel Corporation (1984), *Nippon: The Land and its People* (Nippon Steel Corporation: Japan).

O'BARR, WILLIAM M., and CONLEY, JOHN M. (1992), *Fortune and Folly: The Wealth and Power of Institutional Investing* (Business One Irwin: Homewood, Ill.).

O'SULLIVAN, INSEAD (2003), 'The Political Economy of Comparative Corporate Governance', *Review of International Political Economy* (February).

OHMAE, KENICHI (1987), *Beyond National Borders: Reflections on Japan and the World* (Dow Jones-Irwin: Homewood, Ill.).

On Trust (1992), Report of the NCVO/Charity Commission Working Party on Trustee Training, Chair: Winifred Tumin (NCVO Publications).

Paribas Conjoncture, [André Lévy-Lang], *Japan: Waiting for Confidence.* (Compagnie Financière de Paribas, Paris.)

PARTNOY, FRANK (2003), *Infectious Greed* (Profile Books: London).

PEMBERTON, LOUIS W. (1989), *The Enigma of Japanese Power* (Bear Stearns & Co.; Fortune Book Excerpt, 8 May 1989).

PE-International Survey, Summer 1991.

PENROSE, LORD (2004), *Report of the Equitable Life Enquiry* (HMSO: London).

PORTER, MICHAEL (1992), *Capital Choices* (report to Council of Competitiveness).

PRO NED 1990 Survey.

PUGH, PETER (1991), *A Clear and Simple Vision* (Cambridge Business Publishing).

Price Waterhouse, *Doing Business in France* (London).

ROBERTSON, Sir L. (1993), Speech to the National Association of Pension Funds (25 Feb.).

ROCK, EDWARD B. (1991), 'The Logic and (Uncertain) Significance of Institutional Shareholder Activism', *Georgetown Law Journal*, 79/3(Feb): 399–590 .

ROE, MARK (1991), *Political Elements in the Creation of a Mutual Fund Industry.*

—— (1994), *Strong Managers, Weak Owners* (Princeton University Press).

SAMETZ, ARNOLD W., in collaboration with BICKSTER, JAMES L. (1991), *Institutional Investing: The Challenges and Responsibilities of the Twenty-first Century* (Business One Irwin: Homewood, Ill.).

SCHRAGER, RONALD E. (1986), *Corporate Conflicts: Proxy Fights in the 1980s* (Investor Responsibility Research Center: Washington, DC).

Seiroren (1992), *Eiri Kigyo no shushoku no shonin ni kan-suru nenji hokokusho.*

Shearson Lehman Hutton Securities, 'The Secret Restructuring of European Financial Services'.?

Sherman & Sterling LLP (2004), *Corporate Governance Practices of the 100 Largest US Public Companies.*

SHLEIFER, A., and SUMMERS, L. H. (1988), *Corporate Takeovers: Causes and Consequences* (University of Chicago Press).

SINGH, AJIT (1992), 'Regulation of Mergers'.

SMITH, ADAM (1986), *The Wealth of Nations*, I–III (Penguin Classics: Harmondsworth).

SMITH, TERRY (1992), *Accounting for Growth* (Business Books: London).

SODERQUIST, LARRY D., and SOMMER, A. A. (1990), *Understanding Corporation Law* (Practising Law Institute: New York).

TAKEUCHI, HIROTAKA (1991), 'The Japanese System of Corporate Governance: Will Stakeholders Remain Silent?' (prepared for UK/Japan 2,000 Group 8th annual conference, Brocket Hall, 6–9 March 1992; Hitotsubashi University, Dec.).

TRICKER, R. I. (1984), *Corporate Governance* (Corporate Policy Group, Oxford; Gower Publishing: Aldershot).

Toyo Keizai Shinposha (1991), *Toyo keizai tokei geppo*.

—— (1992), *Kigyo keiretsu soran*.

WAGNER W. H., and LAU, S. C. (1971), 'The Effect of Diversification on Risks', *Financial Analysts' Journal*, 27 (Nov.–Dec.), 48–53.

WALTER, INGO, and SMITH, ROY C. (1990), *Investment Banking in Europe* (Blackwell: Oxford).

WASSERSTEIN, BRUCE (1998), *Big Deal: The Battle for Control of American Leading Corporations* (Warner: New York).

WHITING, ROBERT (1990), *You Gotta Have Wa'* (Vintage Books: Random House, New York).

WIENER, MARTIN (1981), *English Culture and the Decline of the Industrial Spirit, 1850–1980* (CUP).

WOLFEREN, KAREN VAN (1990), *The Enigma of Japanese Power* (Macmillan: London).

WRIGHT, RICHARD W., and PAULI, GUNTER A. (1987), *The Second Wave: Japan's Global Assault on Financial Services* (Waterlow Publishers: London).

YAMAMOTO, ISAO (1992), 'Corporate Governance in Japan' (paper given at Namura Equity Seminar).

YATES, IVAN (1992), *Innovation, Investment and Survival of the UK Economy* (Royal Academy of Engineering: London).

YOSHINO, M. Y. (1968), *Japan's Managerial System: Tradition and Innovation*.

INDEX